CW01218419

Rabbis and Classical Rhetoric

Sophistic Education and Oratory in the Talmud and Midrash

Training in rhetoric – the art of persuasion – formed the basis of education in the Roman Empire. The classical intellectual world centered on the debate between philosophers, who boasted knowledge of objective reality, and sophists, who could debate both sides of any issue and who attracted large audiences and paying students. The roles of the Talmudic rabbis as public orators, teachers, and jurists parallel those of Roman rhetors. Rabbinic literature adopted and adapted various aspects of the classical rhetorical tradition, as is demonstrated in the Talmudic penchant for arguing both sides of hypothetical cases, the midrashic hermeneutical methods, and the structure of synagogue sermons. At the same time, the rabbis also resisted the extreme epistemological relativism of the sophists, as is evident in their restraint on theoretical argumentation, their depiction of rabbinic and divine court procedure, and their commitment to the biblical prophetic tradition. Richard Hidary demonstrates how the rabbis succeeded in navigating a novel path between Platonic truth and rhetorical relativism.

Richard Hidary received a PhD from New York University and is Associate Professor of Judaic Studies at Yeshiva University where he teaches courses in Second Temple Jewish history, Dead Sea Scrolls, and rabbinic literature in its cultural context. He is the author of *Dispute for the Sake of Heaven: Legal Pluralism in the Talmud* (2010) and his articles appear in *AJS Review, Conversations, Dead Sea Discoveries, Diné Israel, Encyclopaedia Judaica, Encyclopedia of the Bible and Its Reception, The Jewish Review of Books, Jewish Studies, an Internet Journal,* and *Okimta*. He has been a fellow at Cardozo Law School's Center for Jewish Law and Contemporary Civilization, an affiliate scholar at the Tikvah Center and a Starr fellow at Harvard University's Center for Jewish Studies.

Rabbis and Classical Rhetoric

Sophistic Education and Oratory in the Talmud and Midrash

Richard Hidary
Yeshiva University

CAMBRIDGE
UNIVERSITY PRESS

CAMBRIDGE
UNIVERSITY PRESS

University Printing House, Cambridge CB2 8BS, United Kingdom

One Liberty Plaza, 20th Floor, New York, NY 10006, USA

477 Williamstown Road, Port Melbourne, VIC 3207, Australia

314-321, 3rd Floor, Plot 3, Splendor Forum, Jasola District Centre, New Delhi - 110025, India

79 Anson Road, #06-04/06, Singapore 079906

Cambridge University Press is part of the University of Cambridge.

It furthers the University's mission by disseminating knowledge in the pursuit of education, learning and research at the highest international levels of excellence.

www.cambridge.org
Information on this title: www.cambridge.org/9781316628355
DOI: 10.1017/9781316822722

© Richard Hidary 2018

This publication is in copyright. Subject to statutory exception and to the provisions of relevant collective licensing agreements, no reproduction of any part may take place without the written permission of Cambridge University Press.

First published 2018
First paperback edition 2020

A catalogue record for this publication is available from the British Library

Library of Congress Cataloging in Publication data
NAMES: Hidary, Richard, author.
TITLE: Rabbis and classical rhetoric : sophistic education and oratory in the Talmud and Midrash / Richard Hidary.
DESCRIPTION: First edition. | New York : Cambridge University Press, [2017] | Includes bibliographical references and index.
IDENTIFIERS: LCCN 2017023745 | ISBN 9781107177406 (hardback)
SUBJECTS: LCSH: Rabbinical literature–History and criticism. | Rhetoric, Ancient. | Reasoning.
CLASSIFICATION: LCC BM496.6 .H53 2017 | DDC 296.1/208808–dc23 LC record available at https://lccn.loc.gov/2017023745

ISBN 978-1-107-17740-6 Hardback
ISBN 978-1-316-62835-5 Paperback

Cambridge University Press has no responsibility for the persistence or accuracy of URLs for external or third-party internet websites referred to in this publication, and does not guarantee that any content on such websites is, or will remain, accurate or appropriate.

To my parents,

David and Aimée Hidary

Contents

Preface and Acknowledgments *page ix*
Translations and Abbreviations *xi*

Introduction 1
The Second Sophistic 2
Schools of Rhetoric: From Gaza to the Galilee and from Antioch to Elusa 6
Rabbinic Attitudes to Greek Language and Wisdom 10
Previous Scholarship and Methodology 15
Philosophy and Rhetoric, Truth and Language 23
On Rhetorical Arrangement 35
Outline of the Book 39

1 **Rabbis as Orators: The Setting and Structure of Rabbinic Homilies** 41
The Setting of Rabbinic Declamation: The Sabbath Sermon 43
The Structure of Rabbinic Declamation: The Proem Form 48
The Yelamdenu Form 57
The Passover Haggadah 68
Conclusion 73

2 **Rabbis as Instructors: Rhetorical Arrangement and Reasoning in the Yerushalmi** 78
The Setting of Rabbinic Instruction 78
Rabban Gamaliel's Nonconformity 84
Source-Critical Analysis 86
Rhetorical Analysis 95
Conclusion 104

3 **The Agonistic Bavli: Greco-Roman Rhetoric in Sasanian Persia** 106
Greco-Roman Rhetoric in Sasanian Persia 108

Must a Father Feed His Daughter? 114
Reading Four Portions in Second Adar 122
Leaven Owned on Passover 124
Further Examples 127

4 **Progymnasmata and Controversiae in Rabbinic Literature** 131
Progymnasmata 133
Controversiae and Hypotheticals 150
Controversiae and the *Ta Shema* Form 163
Rabbinic Paideia 170

5 **Talmudic Topoi: Rhetoric and the Hermeneutical Methods of Midrash** 174
Midrashic Hermeneutics as Rhetorical Topoi 175
Midrashic Hermeneutics as Anti-Sectarian Polemics 183
The Skeptical Pushback 190
Qal va-ḥomer 196
Gezerah Shavah 207
Conclusion 212

6 **The Role of Lawyers in Roman and Rabbinic Courts** 216
Adversarial and Inquisitorial Courts 217
The Roman Court System 221
The Rabbinic Court System 222
Conclusion 238

7 **Why Are There Lawyers in Heaven?** 240
Heavenly Advocates in the Bible and Second Temple Literature 242
Heavenly Advocates in Rabbinic Literature 247
Plato's Heavenly Court 262

Conclusion: Rabbinic versus Christian Approaches to Rhetoric 264
The Rabbis and Classical Rhetoric 266
Christianity and Classical Rhetoric 268
Forty-Nine Ways: On Truth and Interpretation 277

Bibliography 288

Index of Sources 319

Index of Names and Subjects 329

Preface and Acknowledgments

The idea for this book began during my dissertation research while I was analyzing a section of Talmud Yerushalmi that follows the structure of a typical five paragraph essay of an introduction, three proofs, and a conclusion. I traced the origins of this form back to Aristotle's *On Rhetoric*. Fascinated by the connection between rabbinic literature and classical rhetoric, I found more and more examples of classical rhetorical arrangement and reasoning in rabbinic literature and came to appreciate how pervasively Talmudic dialectics flourished within a broader intellectual culture that educated its students to argue both sides of every question – *disputare in utramque partem*.

In many ways, the themes of this book develop those in my first book, *Dispute for the Sake of Heaven: Legal Pluralism in the Talmud.* That project focused on how legal controversies in the Talmud translated into pluralism of halakhic practice. This work analyzes the educational and oratorical settings that developed those controversies in the first place and the philosophical and religious worldview that promoted dispute of opposing opinions. I've always been intrigued at how equally intelligent people can make compelling cases for opposing positions and how that impacts our comprehension of truth, interpretation, and the possibility for mutual understanding. Although the Talmud is an authoritative compendium of religious law and lore, it does not demand acceptance of a monistic authoritarian dogma but rather involves one's critical sensibilities to make reasoned arguments, derive proofs, compare traditions, reject some opinions, reinterpret others and leave the debate open for a new generation to continue adding further insight. While I wrote this as a strictly historical academic work, I nevertheless hope that the rabbinic paradigm of multiple divine truths can serve as a model for contemporary communities to help us avoid falling into extremes of relativism or absolutism and inspire us to appreciate diversity while also holding fast to our convictions.

I would like to express my deep gratitude to Michal Bar-Asher Siegal, Christine Hayes, Keith Povey, Hakham Isaac Sassoon, and Shayna Zamkanei, each of whom reviewed the entire manuscript of this book and provided detailed and extremely helpful comments. I am especially indebted to Lew Bateman for his early enthusiasm for this project and for shepherding it during the years of its development. I would like also to thank many others whose insights and assistance along the way have been invaluable, including: Ronald Benun, Yaakov Elman, Steven Fine, Alexander Haberman, Robert Penella, Rabbi Moshe Shamah, Ralph Sutton, Meira Wolkenfeld, Miriam Zami, my students at Yeshiva University, and the participants at the various AJS, RSA, SBL, and other conference sessions at which I presented this material while writing was in progress.

I dedicate this book to my parents who have always encouraged and supported me in my intellectual pursuits and professional goals. Through their wisdom and example, they have taught me the value of being simultaneously tolerant and discerning of different people's viewpoints. Their commitment to family, community, honesty, and integrity are my guideposts and I feel truly blessed to be their son. Together with my wife Esther, I hope to pass on these values to my own children, David, Ronnie, Aimée, and Zachary.

Translations and Abbreviations

Translations of biblical verses follow the *New Jewish Publication Society Tanakh* (NJPS).

References to rabbinic texts follow the editions included in *Bar Ilan's Judaic Library* Version 22 (Monsey, N.Y.: Torah Educational Software, 2014). Quotations of rabbinic texts derive from critical editions and manuscripts as noted for each citation. Unless otherwise noted, all translations of rabbinic texts are my own. The following abbreviations are used followed by the tractate name:

M. = Mishnah
T. = Tosefta
Y. = Talmud Yerushalmi
B. = Talmud Bavli

Introduction

> Aristotle trained young men ... that they might be able to uphold either side of the question in copious and elegant language. He also taught the Topics . . . a kind of sign or indication of the arguments from which a whole speech can be formed on either side of the question.[1]
>
> R. Yose from Mamleh, R. Yehoshua of Sikhnin in the name of R. Levi: Children during the time of David, even before they tasted sin, knew how to interpret the Torah [by adducing] forty-nine [arguments that something is] impure and forty-nine [arguments that the same thing is] pure.[2]
>
> Said R. Yoḥanan: One who does not know how to derive that a reptile is pure and impure in one hundred ways, may not investigate [testimony] in merit [of the defendant].[3]

Rhetoric, the art of public persuasive speaking, formed the basis of education throughout the Roman Empire for anyone privileged enough to continue his[4] studies past childhood.[5] Professional orators performed in theaters for public entertainment and were venerated like today's

1 Cicero, *Orator*, trans. H. M. Hubbell (Cambridge: Harvard University Press, 1952), xiv.46. See also Quintilian, *Institutes of Oratory: or, Education of an Orator in Twelve Books*, trans. John Selby Watson (London: George Bell & Sons, 1892), 12.2.25 cited on p. 233.

2 Pesikta de-Rav Kahana, *Parah 'adumah, pis. 4:2*, to Num 19:2 (ed. Mandelbaum, 1:56). See also Lev Rabbah 26:2.

3 Y. Sanhedrin 4:1, 22a. The number one hundred here may simply be a rounding up of the forty-nine plus forty-nine interpretations mentioned in parallel sources; see Qorban ha-`Edah to this Yerushalmi passage, s.v. "*me'ah pe`amim.*" See further analysis of this source on pp. 198, 233–36, and 278–80; and see parallels cited and analyzed elsewhere: pp. 277–84 on Pesikta Rabbati 21; p. 191 on Y. Pesaḥim 6:1, 33a; p. 233 on B. Sanhedrin 17a; and pp. 280–4 on B. Eruvin 13b, which makes reference to both 48 and 150 for the number of ways students could purify the impure.

4 I will be using masculine pronouns throughout this book considering that both rhetorical and rabbinic advanced education was available almost exclusively to boys; see p. 131 n. 2.

5 See Teresa Morgan, *Literate Education in the Hellenistic and Roman Worlds* (Cambridge: Cambridge University Press, 1998), 190–239.

rock stars. A skilled lawyer could make all the difference in deciding a jury's verdict. Political, religious, and military leaders alike relied on rhetorical skill to inspire, motivate, and influence their followers. The rabbinic authors of the midrash and the Talmud lived, studied, and taught within this culture. Whether or not they attended nearby schools of rhetoric in Palestine and its environs, and whether or not they ever read Aristotle, Cicero, or Quintilian, the rabbis[6] certainly witnessed legal orations in courts and epideictic orations in ceremonial public gatherings. A rhetorical culture suffused the atmosphere in which the rabbis lived and breathed in the Greek East.

This interaction prompts us to ask several questions: What happens when the biblical presentation of prophetic truth comes into contact with human reason and endless argumentation? How deeply did classical rhetoric impact rabbinic literature and thought? How did the rabbis view professional orators and the use of rhetoric? How does the rabbis' attitude compare with that of the ancient schools of philosophy and that of Christianity? How does the role of the rabbis as public orators, teachers, judges, and legislators compare with the similar set activities undertaken by professional rhetors? This book seeks to answer these questions by analyzing relevant texts and genres from both legal and homiletic parts of the Talmud and midrash.

The epigraphs at the beginning of the chapter, which compare the value of arguing both sides of an issue in both classical and rabbinic thought, present just one indication of the depth of the interrelationship between these two worldviews. For the classicist, the Talmud provides a good case history for how rhetoric resonated in a particular minority community in the Greek East. Reciprocally, the study of classical rhetoric in the Talmud reveals a new appreciation and understanding of essential aspects of rabbinic activity.

THE SECOND SOPHISTIC

The rabbis of the first centuries CE flourished in an era that late antique writers already called the Second Sophistic. In order to understand the role that oratory and the art of persuasion played during this period of renaissance, we must begin with the first blossoming of sophistic activity centuries earlier. The first stages of classical Greek rhetoric developed hand in hand with the birth of democracy in ancient Greece. From the

[6] The term rabbis throughout this book refers to the sages of the Mishnah, Talmud, and midrash who flourished from the first to seventh centuries CE. See further p. 8.

fifth century BCE onwards, legislative power in the Athenian government lay with the Assembly of adult citizens, some 25,000 men.[7] Several thousand Athenians would attend regular meetings where political speakers – rhetors[8] – would seek to persuade the crowd towards one policy or another. Courts also consisted of hundreds of jurors who decided both the law and facts of the case; the litigants or their representatives had limited time to convince the mass of jurors with formal speeches before the dies were cast.[9] In this environment, the ability to speak effectively could not only bring prestige, power, and influence to the presenter, but could also sway a verdict between life and death.

It was for this reason that those who could afford secondary education sought out rhetorical training from sophists – itinerant teachers who would charge great sums with the promise of producing future politicians and lawyers. These sophists would instruct students to argue for both sides of any controversy. One rhetorical work from ancient Greece called *Dissoi Logoi* (two arguments), for instance, provides dozens of examples proving that good and bad are subjective since they differ dramatically from one culture and context to the next.[10] The sophistic curriculum was designed to teach students wisdom and virtue as well as the ability to think critically and communicate clearly.[11] This training prepared the student for the three types of speeches delineated by Aristotle: judicial orations to convince a jury concerning what happened in the past, deliberative orations to persuade an assembly to vote on a policy or law that would affect the future, and epideictic speeches in praise or blame of a person or figure, or to honor special occasions.[12]

[7] Robin Lane Fox, *The Classical World: An Epic History from Homer to Hadrian* (New York: Basic Books, 2006), 88.

[8] On the ancient usage of this term, see Jeffrey Arthurs, "The Term Rhetor in Fifth- and Fourth-Century B.C.E. Greek Texts," *Rhetoric Society Quarterly* 23, no. 3/4 (1994): 1–10.

[9] George A. Kennedy, *A New History of Classical Rhetoric* (Princeton: Princeton University Press, 1994), 15–16.

[10] Thomas Robinson, *Contrasting Arguments: An Edition of the Dissoi Logoi* (Salem, NH: Ayer, 1979); and Edward Schiappa, "Dissoi Logoi," in *Classical Rhetorics and Rhetoricians: Critical Studies and Sources*, ed. Michelle Ballif and Michael Moran (Westport, CT: Praeger Publishers, 2005), 146–8.

[11] See, *Dissoi Logoi*, chapter 6; and William Grimaldi, "How Do We Get from Corax-Tisias to Plato-Aristotle in Greek Rhetorical Theory?," in *Theory, Text, Context: Issues in Greek Rhetoric and Oratory*, ed. Christopher Johnstone (Albany: State University of New York Press, 1996), 19–44.

[12] Aristotle, *On Rhetoric: A Theory of Civil Discourse*, trans. George A. Kennedy (New York: Oxford University Press, 2007), I.3; and Cicero, *On Invention*, trans. H. M. Hubbell (Cambridge: Harvard University Press, 1949), I.7.

Albeit with some variations in emphasis and application, the use and importance of rhetoric continued into the Hellenistic period and throughout the Roman Republic.

With the rise of the Roman Empire, local governors replaced juries as court decisors and this more autocratic government meant less practical need for the art of rhetoric.[13] Nevertheless, this change did not significantly diminish the status of the sophists – even if their job description was now somewhat modified. On the contrary, rhetoric dominated Greco-Roman education for all of the classical period and beyond. As Graham Anderson writes: "Throughout the Imperial period rhetoric itself enjoyed a paramount prestige and those who stood at the top of the rhetoricians' profession could expect a paramount influence over the education and literature they themselves did so much to condition."[14] Teachers declaimed not only for their students but also performed before larger public audiences and could thereby achieve great stardom.[15] The first two and a half centuries CE therefore became known as the Second Sophistic, a term coined c. 235 CE by Philostratus in his *Lives of the Sophists* to refer to the great renaissance in the Roman East of Greek culture, especially rhetoric. Military and political disruptions diminished this activity somewhat during the third century, but rhetoric once again flourished in the fourth century and continued into the fifth and sixth centuries in the form of Christian sermons.[16]

During the Second Sophistic, orators still played a significant if slightly diminished role as lawyers in jury courts,[17] arguing cases before government officials, traveling as envoys to represent communities and getting involved in politics. However, rhetorical skill became much more focused on epideictic speeches: presenting encomium, offering funeral orations, entertaining audiences in theaters, engaging in philosophical debates, and teaching pupils in rhetorical schools.

The Second Sophistic upheld the pride of classical Greek culture against the power of Roman political domination. As Timothy

[13] Elaine Fantham, "The Contexts and Occasions of Roman Public Rhetoric," in *Roman Eloquence: Rhetoric in Society and Literature*, ed. William Dominik (New York: Routledge, 1997): 112.

[14] Graham Anderson, *The Second Sophistic: A Cultural Phenomenon in the Roman Empire* (New York: Routledge, 1993), 240.

[15] See William Reader, *The Severed Hand and the Upright Corpse: The Declamations of Marcus Antonius Polemo* (Atlanta: Scholars Press, 1996), 26–8.

[16] Kennedy, *New History*, 230.

[17] See Marcus Annaeus Seneca, *Declamations*, trans. M. Winterbottom (Cambridge: Harvard University Press, 1974), I.ix and p. 221–22 on the continued prominence of lawyers in Roman courts.

Whitmarsh explains: "Oratory was not just a gentle pastime of the rich: it was one of the primary means that Greek culture of the period, constrained as it was by Roman rule, had to explore issues of identity, society, family and power."[18] While the ancient sophists were the radical thinkers of their time, those of the Second Sophistic upheld tradition and "encouraged belief in inherited values of religion and morality."[19] These orators from the Greek East imitated and revived the Attic grammar, vocabulary, and style in order to connect themselves with the classical age from centuries back.

In these respects, the Second Sophistic bears affinities with its contemporary rabbinic movement. The rabbis also pushed to uphold their own distinctive Jewish identity and pride in the face of Roman dominance and they too studied and taught inherited religious traditions from antiquity. Amram Tropper analyzes the similarities between Mishnah Avot and works such as Philostratus' *Lives of the Sophists*, and goes on to note parallels between the movements that each work embodies: "Just as the members of the Second Sophistic considered the study of rhetoric and Greek literary classics to be a worthwhile activity in and of itself, Avot presents Torah study not as a pragmatic skill needed for the definition of halakhic obligations but as an elevated religious experience."[20] In other words, in order to uphold their own identity and pride in the face of Roman political power and Greek cultural dominance, the rabbis adopted the strategies and values of the Second Sophistic itself and adapted them to their own needs. In particular, as this book will demonstrate, the Talmudic sages also – like the Greek

[18] Timothy Whitmarsh, *The Second Sophistic* (Oxford: Oxford University Press, 2005), 1. There is some scholarly debate over the extent to which the Second Sophistic was associated with opposition to the Roman Empire and a fundamental antagonism between Greek and Roman culture. Christopher Jones, "Multiple Identities in the Age of the Second Sophistic," in *Paideia: The World of the Second Sophistic*, ed. Barbara Borg (Berlin: Walter de Gruyter, 2004): 13–21, argues for a more complex overlapping set of allegiances. This very range of views towards Rome is neatly summarized in the rabbinic discussion recorded at B. Shabbat 33b, indicating that the modern scholarly debate may simply reflect various ancient points of view. For our purposes, it suffices to point out that the Second Sophistic spread a message of pride in classical Greek culture – independent of its attitude towards Rome.

[19] George A. Kennedy, *Classical Rhetoric and Its Christian and Secular Traditions from Ancient to Modern Times* (Chapel Hill: University of North Carolina Press, 1999), 48.

[20] Amram Tropper, *Wisdom, Politics, and Historiography: Tractate Avot in the Context of the Graeco-Roman Near East* (Oxford: Oxford University Press, 2004), 148. See also Elias Bickerman, "La chaine de la tradition Pharisienne," *Revue Biblique* 59 (1952): 44–54; and Hayim Lapin, *Rabbis as Romans: The Rabbinic Movement in Palestine, 100–400 C.E.* (New York: Oxford University Press, 2012), 92–5.

orators – studied, codified, and lectured about their own past traditions and in a similar way used this as a strategy for upholding their culture and values.

SCHOOLS OF RHETORIC: FROM GAZA TO THE GALILEE AND FROM ANTIOCH TO ELUSA

Before delving into the range and extent of overlap between classical rhetoric and rabbinic literature, let us map out the geography of the rhetorical schools with an eye towards their proximity to centers of rabbinic activity. My claim is not that the rabbis attended these schools but rather that their proximity serves as a gauge of the possibility and likelihood of their interaction. Rhetorical training began in antiquity in the study circles[21] of the sophists and continued in schools of rhetoric for many centuries thereafter. While the leading school of rhetoric resided in Athens, smaller schools dotted the Roman Empire and included important centers of study in and near Palestine that flourished during the Talmudic period (50–400 CE).[22] There are some indications of rhetorical instruction in Jerusalem during the Herodian period.[23] Fourth-century letters mention the names of sophists who were active in various cities in Palestine – one of whom even held a chair.[24] Caesarea, the Roman capital of Palestine and an important center of rabbinic activity, was a deeply Hellenized city that was known to have "compensated sophists lavishly."[25] Further south, in the Negev, Elusa maintained a school and an official teacher of rhetoric.[26] Gaza boasted a prominent school of rhetoric that flourished under Procopius and Choricius in the late fifth and sixth centuries but had its roots in the early fourth

21 See p. 79 n. 11.

22 Kennedy, *Classical Rhetoric*, 149, writes: "Rhetorical schools were common in the Hellenized cities of the East" in the first century CE. Yosef Geiger, "No'amim Yevanim be-Ereṣ Yisrael," *Cathedra* 66 (1992): 47–56, especially n. 3, further documents the activity of the Second Sophistic in Palestine.

23 See Martin Hengel, *The Pre-Christian Paul* (London: SCM Press, 1991), 54–61; and Andrew Pitts, "Hellenistic Schools in Jerusalem and Paul's Rhetorical Education," in *Paul's World*, ed. Stanley Porter (Leiden: Brill, 2008): 19–50.

24 Raffaella Cribiore, *The School of Libanius in Late Antique Antioch* (Princeton: Princeton University Press, 2007), 76–7.

25 Ibid., 76; and see Lee Levine, *Caesarea Under Roman Rule* (Leiden: Brill, 1975); Saul Lieberman, *The Talmud of Caesarea* (New York: The Jewish Theological Seminary, 1968); and Lea Roth, "Cappadocia," *Encyclopaedia Judaica* (2007).

26 Cribiore, *The School of Libanius*, 76; Hagith Sivan, *Palestine in Late Antiquity* (Oxford: Oxford University Press, 2008), 80; and Michael Avi-Yonah and Shimon Gibson, "Elusa," *Encyclopaedia Judaica* (2007).

century.[27] While there is no evidence of any rabbis ever attending the school of Gaza, it was very likely to have had direct or indirect influence through students (perhaps some Jews) who studied there and then travelled throughout Palestine speaking in public or arguing in courts.[28]

Famous centers of education also flourished just north of Palestine. There were teachers of rhetoric at Cappadocia, a city with a large Jewish population that maintained regular contact with Palestinian rabbis.[29] Berytus hosted perhaps the most prominent law school in the Roman Empire.[30] In Antioch, Libanius headed one of the most important rhetorical schools in the fourth century.[31] He was not only a prolific writer and Antioch's official rhetor, but also the most famous rhetor of his time. Significantly, Libanius was a friend of the Jewish patriarch, perhaps Rabban Gamaliel V, with whom he corresponded. In fact, as a letter from Libanius to the patriarch written in 393 CE informs us, the son of the patriarch went to Antioch to study with Libanius, having already had rhetorical training from a previous teacher.[32] It so happens that this student ran away from the school, but Libanius encouraged the patriarch not to be angry with the boy. That a member of the foremost rabbinic

[27] See ibid, 77; George A. Kennedy, *Greek Rhetoric under Christian Emperors* (Princeton: Princeton University Press, 1983), 169–77; and Fotios Litsas, "Choricius of Gaza: An Approach to His Work" (PhD diss., University of Chicago, 1980), 2–5. See also p. 274 on Zacharias Scholasticus.

[28] The rabbis certainly maintained contact with Gaza. For example, the Bavli discusses whether one may bathe in the water of Gerar, a city likely to have been south of Gaza (B. Shabbat 109a). Rabbis also discuss how fat the birds in Gaza are (B. Shabbat 145b), they mention a leprous house there (B. Sanhedrin 71a), and they refer to the bazaar and marketplace of the city (B. Aboda Zara 11b). More significantly, R. Isaac bar Naḥman, a third-century sage, was sent to Gaza to serve as a sage and a judge, which indicates that there was also a sizable Jewish community in Gaza during late antiquity. Thus, there were Jews and rabbis who lived in and visited Gaza and who could possibly have participated in its school.

[29] Cribiore, *The School of Libanius*, 69–71.

[30] Warwick Ball, *Rome in the East: The Transformation of an Empire* (London: Routledge, 2000), 173–4. On the presence of Jews in Berytus see Linda Hall, *Roman Berytus: Beirut in Late Antiquity* (London: Routledge, 2004), 185–6.

[31] Cribiore, *The School of Libanius*; and Kennedy, *New History*, 428–51.

[32] See Menachem Stern, *Greek and Latin Authors on Jews and Judaism* (Jerusalem: The Israel Academy of Sciences and Humanities, 1980), 580–99; Wayne Meeks and Robert Wilken, *Jews and Christians in Antioch in the First Four Centuries of the Common Era* (Missoula: Scholars Press, 1978), 62; Burton Visotzky, "Midrash, Christian Exegesis, and Hellenistic Hermeneutics," in *Current Trends in the Study of Midrash*, ed. Carol Bakhos (Leiden: Brill, 2006): 120–1; and Moshe Schwabe, "The Letters of Libanius to the Patriarch of Palestine," [Hebrew] *Tarbiz* 1, no. 2 (1930): 85–110. Cribiore, *The School of Libanius*, 76 and 321, raises doubts that this letter is addressed to the Patriarch; see, however, Stern, ibid., 596, and also p. 104.

family formally studied rhetoric opens the possibility that other Jews and even rabbis did so as well.

The geography and time period in which these rhetorical schools flourished coincided with the era of the Talmudic sages. These rabbis consisted of two groups: the Tannaim and the Amoraim. The Tannaim (plural of Tanna, literally reciter) lived in Judea and the Galilee (50–220 CE) and composed the Mishnah, Tosefta, and tannaitic midrashim. The Amoraim (plural of Amora, literally speaker) in the Galilee (220–400 CE) generated the Yerushalmi (Palestinian Talmud) and the amoraic midrashim. The amoraic midrashim further divide into two: earlier works such as Genesis Rabbah and Leviticus Rabbah, redacted in the early fifth century CE at around the same time as the Yerushalmi; and later works such as Exodus Rabbah, Numbers Rabbah, Deuteronomy Rabbah and Tanḥuma, which also consist of amoraic material but were redacted in the Palestinian yeshivot that were active into the ninth century. Finally, the teachings of the Amoraim in Babylonia formed the basis of the Bavli (Babylonian Talmud), whose redaction likely continued into the seventh century.[33] All of these works went through many stages of redaction by anonymous editors who lived long after the named sages and whose voices sometimes loom large over their source material.[34] Through careful source-critical analysis, one can often dig down to recover the various layers that undergird the final product and we will pay special attention to these redactional issues throughout this book.[35] Nevertheless, because the culture of rhetoric was so widespread throughout the Roman and Persian Empires[36] and lasted throughout all of late antiquity and beyond, the exact date of a given text matters less when performing comparative rhetorical analyses.[37]

[33] Yaakov Elman, "The Babylonian Talmud in Its Historical Context," in *Printing the Talmud: From Bomberg to Schottenstein*, ed. Sharon Lieberman Mintz and Gabriel Goldstein (New York: Yeshiva University Museum, 2005): 19, opts for a date, "no later than c. 542." David Weiss Halivni, *The Formation of the Babylonian Talmud*, trans. Jeffrey Rubenstein (Oxford: Oxford University Press, 2013), 26, dates the latest layer of the Bavli to "about the middle of eighth century CE." Charlotte Fonrobert and Martin Jaffee, eds., *The Cambridge Companion to the Talmud and Rabbinic Literature* (Cambridge: Cambridge University Press, 2007), xvi, provide a date of 620 CE.

[34] See further at H. L. Strack and G. Stemberger, *Introduction to the Talmud and Midrash*, trans. Marcus Bockmuehl (Minneapolis: Fortress Press, 1992); and p. 83.

[35] For this methodology see the seminal studies by Shamma Friedman, "Pereq ha-isha rabbah ba-Bavli, be-ṣeruf mavo kelali `al derekh ḥeker ha-sugya," in *Mehkarim u-mekorot*, ed. H. Z. Dimitrovsky (New York: Jewish Theological Seminary, 1977): 275–442; and Halivni, *Formation*.

[36] See pp. 108–114.

[37] Although the history of rhetoric covers many centuries and dozens of writers and handbooks, certain fundamental principles and tools remained fairly constant. The

Clearly, there were large swaths of time and space in which rabbis and rhetors had opportunities to interact. Starting with Alexander the Great's conquest of the East, Hellenism penetrated deeply into every corner of life in Palestine, and rhetoric was a significant part of this cultural movement.[38] Evidence shows that at least some Jews received rhetorical training during the late Second Temple period and later on as well.[39] Philo and Josephus employed rhetoric in their writings.[40] The use

rhetorical model of the Attic orators and of Aristotle persisted as the basis for Roman rhetoric in Latin as well as for the Second Sophistic and its renaissance in the fourth century, even if some local variations occur in various periods and geographies. See Edward Corbett and Robert Connors, *Classical Rhetoric for the Modern Student* (New York: Oxford University Press, 1999), 493; and Kennedy, *Greek Rhetoric under Christian Emperors*, 52–103. This makes it difficult to pinpoint a single author as particularly influential during the rabbinic period. While Libanius may be closest to the rabbis in time and space, and may even have corresponded with the patriarch (see p. 9), no rhetorical treatise by Libanius is extant. The progymnasmata of Libanius and his student Aphthonius discuss various elements of declamation but do not mention the arrangement of elements in a full speech, even though Libanius clearly utilized such arrangement in his own orations. That the rhetorical model described by Aristotle, Cicero and Quintilian continued to thrive in later centuries in the East is evident from various later Greek handbooks that summarize their system. See Kennedy, *New History*, 208–29; and Mervin R. Dilts and George A. Kennedy, *Two Greek Rhetorical Treatises from the Roman Empire: Introduction, Text and Translation of the Arts of Rhetoric Attributed to Anonymous Segeurianus and to Apsines of Gadara* (Leiden: Brill, 1997). Most significant in this regard is *On Invention* attributed to Hermogenes but probably written in the third or fourth century; see Kennedy, *Invention and Method*, xvi. I have, therefore, utilized all of the classical authors whose aggregate teachings best approximates the common rhetorical culture of late antiquity.

38 A few representative titles from the vast literature on this topic are: Elias Bickerman, *The Jews in the Greek Age* (Cambridge: Harvard University Press, 1988); Martin Hengel, *Judaism and Hellenism: Studies in Their Encounter in Palestine during the Early Hellenistic Period* (Minneapolis: Fortress Press, 1991); Lee Levine, *Judaism and Hellenism in Antiquity: Conflict or Confluence?* (Peabody: Hendrickson Publishers, 1999); Louis Feldman, *Judaism and Hellenism Reconsidered* (Leiden: Brill, 2006); John Collins, *Jewish Cult and Hellenistic Culture: Essays on the Jewish Encounter with Hellenism* (Leiden: Brill, 2005); and Steven Fine, *Art and Judaism in the Greco-Roman World: Toward a New Jewish Archaeology* (Cambridge: Cambridge University Press, 2010).

39 Jews participated and even excelled in this training. Caecilius of Calacte, who is identified as Jewish, was an important rhetorician in Rome during the reign of Augustus; see W. Rhys Roberts, "Caecilius of Calacte," *American Journal of Philology* 18, no. 3 (1897): 302. Closer to the end of the Talmudic period, the Byzantine encyclopedia *Suda* (Z 169) mentions the sophist Zosimus "of Gaza or Ascalon" who lived "in the time of the emperor Anastasius." See Kennedy, *Greek Rhetoric under Christian Emperors*, 169–77; and Malcolm Heath, "Theon and the History of the Progymnasmata," *Greek, Roman and Byzantine Studies* 43, no. 2 (2002/3): 150 n. 57.

40 See Thomas Conley, "Philo's Rhetoric: Argumentation and Style," in *Aufstieg und Niedergang der römischen Welt II, 21/1*, ed. H. Temporini and W. Haase (Berlin and New York: De Gruyter, 1984): 343–71; Stanley Porter, ed. *Handbook of Classical*

of rhetoric in the New Testament similarly indicates widespread presence of rhetoric in Palestine during the first century CE.[41] This historical backdrop sets the stage for the subject of this book, which focuses on the rhetoric of the rabbis from the first to the seventh centuries CE.

It is certainly possible that Jewish students of rhetoric shared their training with the rabbis or even became rabbis themselves. However, even barring rabbinic formal training in rhetoric, rabbis certainly came into regular contact with professional oration in law courts, theaters, and public spaces throughout Palestine where lawyers and traveling sophists were active. Rhetoric permeated the Hellenistic culture in which the rabbis were entrenched and so they could hardly have remained insulated from it. We should therefore expect parallels to rhetorical thought and style throughout rabbinic literature. What remains to be seen is what resulted from these manifold and complex interactions. What were the attitudes of the rabbis towards the world of the sophists, and to what extent did rabbinic sermons, lectures, and argumentation reflect classical rhetorical modes?

RABBINIC ATTITUDES TO GREEK LANGUAGE AND WISDOM

The attitude of the rabbis towards classical rhetoric closely relates to their attitude towards Greek language. Rabbinic literature includes thousands of Greek words, and it is clear that the rabbis knew Greek well enough to make Greek puns.[42] They appreciated the beauty of

Rhetoric in the Hellenistic Period 330 B.C.–A.D. 400 (Leiden: Brill, 1997), 695–713 and 737–54; Steve Mason, ed. *Flavius Josephus: Translation and Commentary, Volume 9: Life of Josephus* (Leiden: Brill, 2001), xxxvi–xli; and Denis Saddington, "A Note on the Rhetoric of Four Speeches in Josephus," *Journal of Jewish Studies* 58, no. 2 (2007): 228–35, who concludes: "It is apparent that Josephus could deploy the full range of rhetorical technique as sophisticatedly as the Greek and Latin writers of his time."

41 Paul's letters exhibit elements of classical arrangement and other techniques of rhetorical reasoning. See Kennedy, *Classical Rhetoric*, 149–51; and Mark Nanos, ed. *The Galatians Debate: Contemporary Issues in Rhetorical and Historical Interpretation* (Peabody, MA: Hendrickson, 2002), chapters 1–11. Other books of the New Testament similarly "employ some features of classical rhetoric" for the benefit of their Greek audience, "many of whom were familiar with public address in Greek or had been educated in Greek schools" (Kennedy, *Classical Rhetoric*, 143). See also Kennedy, *A New History of Classical Rhetoric* (Princeton: Princeton University Press, 1994), 258–9; and more extensively at James Kinneavy, *Greek Rhetorical Origins of Christian Faith* (New York: Oxford University Press, 1987), 57–100. See further pp. 268–77.

42 Samuel Krauss, *Griechische und lateinische Lehnwoerter im Talmud, Midrasch und Targum* (Berlin: S. Calvary, 1899); Saul Lieberman, *Greek in Jewish Palestine* (New York: The Jewish Theological Seminary, 1942); Daniel Sperber, *A Dictionary of Greek*

Greek for poetry[43] and at least one rabbi permitted his daughters to learn Greek in order to give them an air of sophistication.[44] Some rabbis even permitted writing a Sefer Torah in Greek[45] and grounded this ruling in a midrashic interpretation of a verse:

> Bar Qappara taught, "'God enlarge Japheth, and let him dwell in the tents of Shem' (Gen 9:27). They will speak the language of Japheth in the tents of Shem."[46]

Japheth, whose son is Yavan (Gen 10:2), represents the Greeks while Shem is the ancestor of the Israelites. The midrash uses Genesis 9:27 to predict and approve using Greek for translating and enhancing the understanding of Torah. Greek, according to these sources, stands out as a glorious, beautiful,[47] and even sacred language second only to Hebrew.

At the same time, the Mishnah also mentions a ban against teaching one's son Greek that was enacted as a result of the Kitos War (115–117 CE), perhaps as an anti-Hellenistic reaction to the antisemitism felt by diasporic Jewry.[48] When asked whether one may teach his son Greek, R. Yehoshua responds that it is permitted only at a time that is neither day nor night since one must devote all of one's time to Torah study.[49] The Yerushalmi rejects this view since one may and even must devote time to teaching his son a trade, even though that also interferes with Torah study. Rather, the Yerushalmi explains that teaching Greek

and Latin Terms in Rabbinic Literature (Ramat-Gan: Bar-Ilan University Press, 1984); Daniel Sperber, *Greek in Talmudic Palestine* (Ramat Gan: Bar-Ilan University Press, 2012); and Henry Fischel, "Greek and Latin Languages, Rabbinical Knowledge of," *Encyclopaedia Judaica* (2007); and A. Wasserstein, "Greek Language and Philosophy in the Early Rabbinic Academies," in *Jewish Education and Learning*, ed. G. Abramson and T. Parfitt (Switzerland: Harwood Academic Publishers, 1994): 221–32.

43 Y. Megilah 1:9, 71b; and Esther Rabbah 4:12.

44 Y. Soṭah 9:15, 24c.

45 M. Megilah 1:8; B. Megilah 9b.

46 Y. Megilah 1:9, 71b, and see parallels at B. Megilah 9b and Gen Rabbah 36:8.

47 See formulation at B. Megilah 9b.

48 M. Soṭah 9:14 following MS Kaufman that reads, "Kitos," probably referring to the Roman general Lusius Quietus. MS Parma and printed editions read, "Titus." See further at Moulie Vidas, "Greek Wisdom in Babylonia," in *Envisioning Judaism: Studies in Honor of Peter Schäfer on the Occasion of His Seventieth Birthday*, ed. Ra`anan Boustan et al. (Tübingen: Mohr Siebeck, 2013): 287 n. 3.

49 T. Abodah Zara 1:20; Y. Soṭah 9:15, 24c; Y. Pe'ah 1:1, 15c, and parallel at B. Menaḥot 99b. The question in the Tosefta actually asks about Greek books: "ספר יווני" in MS Vienna and printed editions, and "יווני ספר" in MS Erfurt. The above paraphrase of R. Yehoshua's words follows the Yerushalmi, which mentions simply Greek. See also Marc Hirshman, *Torah for the Entire World* [Hebrew](Tel Aviv: Hakibbutz Hameuchad, 1999), 134–40 and 145–6.

is nevertheless prohibited because of traitors, presumably to prevent them from being able to communicate with government officials.

The Bavli elaborates on these traditions with its own version of the link between the ban, a war, and traitors:[50]

> When the Hasmonean kings besieged each other, Hyrcanus was outside and Aristobulus was inside.[51] Every day [those inside] would lower coins in a basket and would raise up [animals for the] daily offerings. There was an elder there who knew Greek wisdom (חכמת יוונית). He spoke against [the people inside] to them [the people outside] with Greek wisdom[52] and told them, "As long as they are involved in [Temple] service, they will not be delivered into your hands." That day,[53] they [the people inside] lowered coins in a basket and they raised up a pig. When the pig reached halfway up the wall, he dug in his nails and shrieked[54] and the Land of Israel quaked for four hundred parsangs. At that time, they said, "Cursed is one who raises pigs and cursed is one who teaches[55] his son Greek wisdom."[56]
> Is this true? Did not Rabbi[57] say, "Why would one speak Syriac in the Land of Israel? Either speak Hebrew or Greek." ...
> Greek language is different from Greek wisdom.[58]
> And is Greek wisdom prohibited? Did not Rav Yehudah say in the name of Samuel in the name of Rabban Shimon ben

[50] B. Soṭah 49b, following MS Munich 95 unless otherwise indicated. See parallels at B. Baba Qama 82b–83a; B. Menaḥot 64b; and Y. Berakhot 4:1, 7b. The Bavli manuscript analysis throughout this book is based on The Sol and Evelyn Henkind Talmud Text Databank of The Saul Lieberman Institute of Talmudic Research of JTSA (www .lieberman-institute.com); The Friedberg Project for Talmud Bavli Variants (www .genizah.org); and Yaakov Sussmann, *Thesaurus of Talmudic Manuscripts* [Hebrew] (Jerusalem: Yad Izhak Ben-Zvi, 2012). For other works of rabbinic literature, I have consulted the texts at Maagarim of the Historical Dictionary Project of the Academy of the Hebrew Language (http://maagarim.hebrew-academy.org.il/).

[51] MS Oxford – Bodl. heb. d. 20 (2675) reads, "Hyrcanus was inside and Aristobulus was outside," but it is corrected in the margin. All other MSS and printed editions read as above, agreeing with the description at Josephus, *Antiquities of the Jews*, 14.25–28.

[52] MS Oxford – Bodl. heb. d. 20 reads, "Greek language," but all other witnesses read, "Greek wisdom."

[53] MSS Munich and Vatican 110 read, "That day." MS Oxford – Bodl. heb. d. 20 and printed editions read, "The next day."

[54] "Shrieked" is found only in MS Munich 95. See further at Vidas, "Greek Wisdom in Babylonia," 289 n. 5.

[55] MS Munich 95 reads, "learn," but I have followed all other witnesses that read, "teach."

[56] MS Oxford – Bodl. heb. d. 20 and printed editions add a line here that I have omitted based on other MSS.

[57] MS Vatican reads, "Rava."

[58] MS Munich 95 adds, "language," before "Greek wisdom." This appears to be a scribal error, although, "language of wisdom," does appear at B. Eruvin 53b.

> Gamaliel: "What does Scripture mean, 'My eyes have brought me grief over all the maidens of my city' (Lam 3:51)? There were one thousand children in my father's house; five hundred studied Torah and five hundred studied Greek wisdom and none of them are left except for me here and my cousin in Asia."
> Those of the house of Gamaliel are different for they are close to the government, as it was taught: They permitted the house of Gamaliel to learn Greek wisdom because they are close to the government.[59]

The Bavli details the origins of a ban dating to the Hasmonean civil war in the 60s BCE that covered not Greek language but rather Greek wisdom. It is not clear whether the Bavli describes a separate ban in addition to the one mentioned in the Mishnah[60] or whether the Bavli projects the Mishnaic ban back to Hasmonean times, considering that the curse is absent from parallel stories about the Hasmonean civil war in Josephus and the Yerushalmi.[61] Be that as it may, the Bavli makes a clear distinction between Greek language, which is permitted, and Greek wisdom, whose teaching is prohibited except at the patriarch's house.[62]

Scholars have puzzled over the meaning of the term "Greek wisdom." Moulie Vidas insightfully compares this Bavli phrase to parallels in Greek and Syriac Christian literature from both the Roman and Persian Empires, where the formulation, "wisdom of the Greeks," refers most commonly to Greek philosophy as well as to Aristotelian logic, paganism, and other aspects of classical education.[63] In the Roman Empire, the teaching of Greek language and culture went hand in hand,[64] which is why Palestinian rabbinic sources speak only of "Greek." However, in the Persian Empire, Greek works of philosophy

59 This section of the Bavli seems to expand upon T. Soṭah 15:8 by combining it with Y. Ta`anit 4:6, 69a; see further at Vidas, "Greek Wisdom in Babylonia," 299–303.

60 Saul Lieberman, *Hellenism in Jewish Palestine* (New York: The Jewish Theological Seminary, 1962), 100–2, writes that this ban came first and prohibited Greek wisdom while the ban in the Mishnah came later during the Kitos war and further prohibited Greek language. Sacha Stern, *Jewish Identity in Early Rabbinic Writings* (Leiden: Brill, 1994), 177, also takes the two bans as complementary following medieval commentators. Y. Shabbat 1:4, 3c, mentioned yet another ban against "their language" as one of the eighteen enactments of Beth Shammai. See also Elimelekh E. Hallewy, "Concerning the Ban on Greek Wisdom," [Hebrew] *Tarbiz* 41, no. 3 (1972): 270.

61 See Hirshman, *Torah for the Entire World*, 141–3.

62 See also B. Menaḥot 99b on the time conflict of studying Greek wisdom rather than Torah, and analysis of this and parallel sources at Gerald Blidstein, "Rabbinic Judaism and General Culture: Normative Discussion and Attitudes," in *Judaism's Encounter with Other Cultures*, ed. Jacob J. Schachter (Northvale, NJ: Jason Aronson, 1997): 9–21.

63 Vidas, "Greek Wisdom in Babylonia," 290–305.

64 H. I. Marrou, *A History of Education in Antiquity*, trans. George Lamb (University of Wisconsin Press, 1956), 255–64.

were translated into Syriac and became part of the curriculum in Christian schools. Vidas explains that this "is precisely the context in which the Bavli's distinction between 'wisdom' and 'language' makes sense."[65]

The question remains, however, how did "Greek wisdom" help the elder communicate with the besiegers?[66] Dov Rappel proposes that "Greek wisdom" here actually refers to Greek rhetoric, in particular, pantomime.[67] Rhetors developed sophisticated hand gestures to express themselves, especially in large theaters where their voices could not project. This developed into the art practiced by silent mimes who could communicate without words.[68] The elder traitor within the walls may have used pantomime to send a message to the besieging enemy. This interpretation finds support in the continuation of the siege story in one Bavli version in which Mordechai interprets the symbolic charades of a mute.[69] The *baraita* regarding the 500 children also suggests that they were not studying advanced philosophy but rather rhetoric, the typical subject of study for a young teenager after learning grammar.[70] Furthermore, the art of rhetorical persuasion in particular would most directly help the house of the patriarch in its dealings with the government.[71]

[65] Vidas, "Greek Wisdom in Babylonia," 296.

[66] Rashi (B. Soṭah 49b s.v. "*ḥokhmat Yevanit*") explains it as the language spoken at the palace that the masses do not understand. Maimonides (*Commentary on the Mishnah* to Soṭah 9:14), continuing a Geonic line of interpretations, says it is a cryptic language used by the Greeks that has now been lost. Vidas, ibid., 298, conjectures that the Bavli *baraita* originally just had the elder speaking Greek and that the Bavli's Stam added "wisdom" to make it conform to its new geographical context where Greek was not spoken, even though "Greek wisdom" does not fit the plot of the story. Vidas, ibid., 298 n. 46, rejects Rashi and Maimonides but does not deny that "Greek wisdom" can refer to rhetoric. In fact, Vidas, ibid., 293 and 301, points out that the *Life of St. Ephrem* depicts him as a talented rhetor who is able to defeat the "wisdom of the Greeks." This does not suggest that Ephrem has a negative attitude towards rhetoric itself, but rather that he knows how to use rhetoric to effectively defend Christianity against the arguments of pagan rhetors.

[67] Dov Rappel, "Ḥokhmat Yevanit – retorica?," [Hebrew] *Meḥqere Yerushalaim bi-Maḥshevet Yisrael* 2, no. 3 (1983): 317–22. See also Lieberman, *Hellenism in Jewish Palestine*, 101 n. 12; Emmanuel Levinas, *Beyond the Verse: Talmudic Readings and Lectures* (Bloomington: Indiana University Press, 1994), 27; Raphael Jospe, "Yefet in the Tents of Shem: Attitudes towards 'The Wisdom of Greeks'," in *Tra Torah e sophia: orizzonti e frontiere della filosofia Ebraica* (Genova: Marietti, 2011): 129–30; and Vidas, "Greek Wisdom in Babylonia," p. 298 nn. 43–44.

[68] See further pp. 45–46.

[69] See B. Menaḥot 64b.

[70] See p. 131 n 2.

[71] That rhetoric best describes the particular aspect of "Greek wisdom" mentioned in B. Soṭah 49b does not prevent this phrase from having broader meaning elsewhere as per Vidas, such as at B. Menaḥot 99b where an advanced Torah sage, not a child, seeks to study חכמת יוונית.

In sum, the status of Greek language, style and culture was the subject of lively and continuing debate among the rabbis, one that we will see play out in many ways over the course of this book. The reasons for opposition are both political – it enables informants – as well as religious in that it distracts from Torah study and perhaps weakens Jewish identity.[72] The study of Greek language within the Roman Empire certainly included aspects of Greek values, literature and composition style, just as "Greek wisdom" in the Persian Empire also encompassed various elements of logic and rhetoric, such as pantomime. That the Talmud designates this learning as Greek and records various prohibitions against it underscores that the rabbis viewed this knowledge as coming from outside of their own society and in contrast or even opposition to their own Hebrew language and Torah curriculum. Nonetheless, the positive statements they make about Greek language and the explicit permission given to the house of the patriarch, and sometimes also to daughters, to study Greek, reveal a more complex reality. There must have been many Jews studying Greek language and rhetoric, whether formally or not, whether they did so with the knowledge and blessing of the rabbis or not. More importantly, many aspects of Greek style and public oratory were simply so embedded in popular culture that they inevitably permeated rabbinic society deeply and often even imperceptibly.[73]

PREVIOUS SCHOLARSHIP AND METHODOLOGY

Saul Lieberman has shown that various aspects of Greco-Roman culture were pervasive not only among the more Hellenized Jews of the first centuries CE, but that even "the Rabbis of Palestine were familiar with the fashionable style of the civilized world of that time. Many of them were highly educated in Greek literature ... They spoke to the people in their language and in their style."[74] It therefore comes as no surprise that the Talmudic sages developed literary genres and modes of

[72] See also B. Berakhot 28b where R. Eliezer advises his students, "Restrain your sons from *higayon*." Lieberman, *Hellenism in Jewish Palestine*, 103, understands this as "'the science of logic' (or dialectics and sophistry)." See also Jospe, "Yefet in the Tents of Shem," 132–7.

[73] This assessment echoes a similar conclusion regarding the rabbis and philosophy by Zev Warren Harvey, "Rabbinic Attitudes toward Philosophy," in *"Open Thou Mine Eyes...": Essays on Aggadah and Judaica Presented to Rabbi William G. Braude on His Eightieth Birthday and Dedicated to His Memory*, ed. H. Blumber et al. (Hoboken: Ktav): 101: "perhaps they [the rabbis] considered philosophy to be foreign to their concerns *not* because they did not know what it was, but rather because they *did* know." Italics in original.

[74] Lieberman, *Greek in Jewish Palestine*, 66–7.

persuasion that bear affinity to those of Greco-Roman declamation.[75] Previous scholarship has focused much attention on documenting examples of classical rhetoric in rabbinic literature. To cite some prominent examples, Henry Fischel analyzes parallels throughout rabbinic literature to numerous rhetorical literary forms, most significantly the chreia.[76] Eliezer Shimshon Rosental suggests that the phrase, "two things – שני דברים," which appears in a Yerushalmi story about two Roman officers who learn the Torah from Rabban Gamaliel, does not refer to two issues that they raise (since there are four) but rather to the double standard (*dissoi logoi*) in the oral law and a reference to the sophistic ability to offer opposing arguments.[77] Eli Yassif finds cases of Greek exempla and fables that are repeated, sometimes almost exactly, in rabbinic literature.[78] Saul Lieberman and David Daube investigate links between Hellenistic and rabbinic methods of interpretation.[79] Boaz Cohen compares discussions by Greco-Roman rhetoricians about letter versus spirit in legal interpretation with similar notions in the Talmud.[80] Rivka Ulmer demonstrates the resemblance between the dialogic form of midrash and the diatribe arguments of the Cynics.[81] Jacob Neusner analyzes the use of dialectics in rabbinic literature.[82]

[75] The following survey focuses specifically on aspects of the Greco-Roman rhetorical tradition in the Talmud. Also relevant to a wider discussion, of course, are the thousands of Greek loan words and phrases incorporated into rabbinic Aramaic and Hebrew, and the many folktales, mythologies, and philosophical ideas known from classical literature that are found in rabbinic texts. See further at Henry Fischel, ed. *Essays in Greco-Roman and Related Talmudic Literature* (New York: Ktav, 1977), xiii–lxxii; Catherine Hezser, "Interfaces between Rabbinic Literature and Graeco-Roman Philosophy," in *The Talmud Yerushalmi and Graeco-Roman Culture II*, ed. Peter Schäfer (Tübingen: Mohr Siebeck, 2000): 161–87; and p. 43 n. 17.

[76] See pp. 132–4.

[77] Eliezer Shimshon Rosental, "Shnei devarim," in *Sefer Yitshak Aryeh Zeligman: ma'amarim ba-Mikra uva-`olam ha-`atiq*, ed. Yair Zakovits and Alexander Rofe (Jerusalem: E. Rubenstein, 1983): 463–81; and see herein p. 3 n. 10.

[78] Eli Yassif, *The Hebrew Folktale: History, Genre, Meaning*, trans. Jacqueline Teitelbaum (Bloomington: Indiana University Press, 1999), 120–32, and 191–209. See also Haim Schwarzbaum, "Talmudic-Midrashic Affinities of Some Aesopic Fables," in *Essays in Greco-Roman and Related Talmudic Literature*, ed. Henry Fischel (New York: Ktav, 1977): 443–72.

[79] See analysis on pp. 174–215.

[80] Boaz Cohen, "Letter and Spirit in Jewish and Roman Law," in *Essays in Greco-Roman and Related Talmudic Literature*, ed. Henry Fischel (New York: Ktav, 1977): 138–64.

[81] Rivka Ulmer, "The Advancement of Arguments in Exegetical Midrash Compared to that of the Greek 'δΐατρίβε'," *Journal for the Study of Judaism* 28, no. 1 (1997): 48–91.

[82] Jacob Neusner, *Jerusalem and Athens: The Congruity of Talmudic and Classical Philosophy* (Leiden: Brill, 1997). See Neusner's bibliography, p. 156, for other works of his relating to this topic. Neusner, however, turns towards analytic dialectics,

Alan Avery-Peck examines the use of Greco-Roman modes of argumentation in rabbinic pronouncement stories.[83] Shlomo Naeh's research on the art of memorization, one of the five stages in the study of rhetorical oratory, points out fascinating parallels between rabbinic and classical literature.[84] Martin Jaffee, based on examples from the Yerushalmi, argues that Galilean rabbis practiced oral exercises similar to those described in the progymnasmata of Theon and Hermogenes.[85] David Brodsky traces the dialogical form of Tannaitic midrash and the Talmud

syllogism, and modes of scientific inquiry, rather than the rhetorical mode of dialectics, the enthymeme, and modes of persuasive argumentation, which form the basis of my approach in this book. See also Richard Cohen, "The Relationship between Topic, Rhetoric and Logic: Analysis of a Syllogistic Passage in the Yerushalmi," in *Judaic and Christian Interpretation of Texts: Contents and Contexts*, ed. Jacob Neusner (Lanham: University Press of America, 1987): 87–125; Jack N. Lightstone, *The Rhetoric of the Babylonian Talmud, Its Social Meaning and Context* (Waterloo: Wilfrid Laurier University Press, 1994); and Lightstone, *Mishnah and the Social Formation of the Early Rabbinic Guild: A Socio-Rhetorical Approach* (Waterloo, Ontario: Wilfrid Laurier University Press, 2002). Cohen and Lightstone argue that rabbinic literature does evince a rhetoric of its own but one that is not significantly related to Greco-Roman rhetorical modes.

Other rhetorical readings of rabbinic texts that are also not directly dependent upon Greco-Roman models can be found at David Kraemer, "Composition and Meaning in the Bavli," *Prooftexts* 8, no. 3 (1988): 271–91; Kraemer, "Rhetoric of Failed Refutation in the Bavli," *Shofar* 10, no. 2 (1992): 73–85; Jay Rovner, "Rhetorical Strategy and Dialectical Necessity in the Babylonian Talmud: The Case of Kiddushin 34a–35a," *Hebrew Union College Annual* 65 (1994): 177–231; Michael Satlow, "Rhetoric and Assumptions: Romans and Rabbis on Sex," in *Jews in a Graeco-Roman World*, ed. Martin Goodman (Oxford: Clarendon Press, 1998): 135–44; and the analyses in Richard Hidary, *Dispute for the Sake of Heaven: Legal Pluralism in the Talmud* (Providence: Brown University, 2010) of B. Eruvin 46b–47b in ch. 1, B. Yebamot 13a–16a in chs. 2 and 4, and of B. Sanhedrin 87a–88a in ch. 6. Kraemer, "Composition," 273, finds that "there is no evidence" of Greco-Roman rhetoric influencing the Talmud and concludes: "It seems unlikely, therefore, that rhetorical criticism of the Talmud would allow for more than coincidental reference to the categories of Hellenistic rhetoric." See, on the other hand, Vernon Robbins' rhetorical analysis of M. Giṭṭin 1:1–2:2 in Lightstone, *Mishnah*, 201–13, who does base his analysis on classical canons.

83 Alan Avery-Peck, "Rhetorical Argumentation in Early Rabbinic Pronouncement Stories," in *The Rhetoric of Pronouncement*, ed. Vernon Robbins (Atlanta: Scholars Press, 1994): 49–69.

84 Shlomo Naeh, "On Structures of Memory and the Forms of Text in Rabbinic Literature," [Hebrew] *Meḥqere Talmud* 3, no. 2 (2005): 543–89. See also José Faur, *Golden Doves with Silver Dots: Semiotics and Textuality in Rabbinic Tradition* (Bloomington: Indiana University Press, 1986), 89.

85 Martin Jaffee, *Torah in the Mouth: Writing and Oral Tradition in Palestinian Judaism 200 BCE–400 CE* (Oxford: Oxford University Press, 2001), 128–39; and Jaffee, "The Oral-Cultural Context of the Talmud Yerushalmi: Greco-Roman Rhetorical Paideia, Discipleship, and the Concept of Oral Torah," in *The Talmud Yerushalmi and Graeco-Roman Culture I*, ed. Peter Schäfer (Tübingen: Mohr Siebeck, 1998): 27–61.

back to advanced progymnasmatic exercises.[86] Yair Furstenberg finds precedent in sophistic education for the *agon* of halakhic midrash with Scripture.[87] Tzvi Novick cites examples of exegetical encomia and invectives in Tannaitic midrash.[88] Stephen Hazan Arnoff analyzes pedagogy, oral performance, memory and writing in Leviticus Rabbah through the lens of patristic and pagan rhetorical systems.[89] Daniel Boyarin finds jest and Menippean satires in the Bavli, especially in its biographical narratives.[90] One example that we will discuss further below is the Bavli's portrayal of R. Meir as a sophist who "said about what is impure that it is pure, and about what is pure that it is impure and would demonstrate it with reasons."[91]

Building on the findings of these scholars, this book will more systematically analyze numerous examples of parallel structures, modes of reasoning, techniques of persuasion, and educational models in order to demonstrate how the classical rhetorical backdrop can help us gain perspective on rabbinic literature. While rhetorical criticism has been generously and fruitfully applied to the New Testament generally and the Pauline corpus in particular,[92] rabbinic literature has received relatively little attention in this regard.[93] I make no claim that any of the rabbis or redactors read any ancient works relating to Greek rhetoric. Lieberman submits that the rabbis "probably did not read Plato and certainly not the pre-Socratic philosophers." He does, however, conclude that the rabbis' "main interest was centered in Gentile legal studies and their methods of rhetoric."[94] Rhetorical education and

86 David Brodsky, "From Disagreement to Talmudic Discourse: Progymnasmata and the Evolution of a Rabbinic Genre," in *Rabbinic Traditions between Palestine and Babylonia*, ed. Ronit Nikolsky and Tal Ilan (Leiden: Brill, 2014): 173–231; and see p. 134f.

87 Yair Furstenberg, "The 'Agon' with Moses and Homer: Rabbinic Midrash and the Second Sophistic," in *Homer and the Bible in the Eyes of Ancient Interpreters*, ed. Maren Niehoff (Leiden: Brill, 2012): 299–328.

88 Tzvi Novick, "Scripture as Rhetor: A Study in Early Rabbinic Midrash," *Hebrew Union College Annual* 82–83 (2011–12): 37–59.

89 Stephen Hazan Arnoff, "Memory, Rhetoric, and Oral-Performance in Leviticus Rabbah" (PhD diss., Jewish Theological Seminary, 2011).

90 Daniel Boyarin, *Socrates and the Fat Rabbis* (Chicago: University of Chicago Press, 2009), 349.

91 B. Eruvin 13b. See pp. 281–3.

92 See further p. 10 n. 41 and pp. 43–6, and 268–76.

93 Interestingly, Khiok-Khng Yeo, *Rhetorical Interaction in 1 Corinthians 8 and 10: A Formal Analysis with Preliminary Suggestions for a Chinese, Cross-Cultural Hermeneutic* (Leiden: Brill, 1995), 63–67, argues that New Testament scholars should look towards Jewish rhetoric to better understand early Christian rhetoric.

94 Saul Lieberman, *Texts and Studies* (New York: Ktav, 1974), 228. Lieberman, ibid., 227, suggests that the rabbis' knowledge of Gentile law and legal progymnasmata came from their proximity to the famous law school in Beirut; see p. 8.

declamation were so widespread throughout the Greco-Roman world and were such an integral part of its culture that there is no need to find evidence of a specific rabbi reading a particular rhetorical handbook. The rabbis would have easily picked up rhetorical techniques and methodology by listening to orators in the public square, watching lawyers in the courthouse, and in conversations with their neighbors.

Some earlier scholars tend to portray the rabbis as a relatively self-enclosed minority group that remained, for the most part, intellectually isolated from the larger Greco-Roman conglomerate of political and cultural dominance, but did sometimes consciously borrow some elements from it. This approach reflects a penchant for seeking out foreign influences on the rabbis, a standard methodology in the scientific study of Judaism since its beginnings in the nineteenth century.[95] In this approach, the researcher must constantly struggle to distinguish between genealogical versus analogical parallels.[96] In other words, in some cases, a parallel between two cultures suggests a genetic connection between the two such that one must be dependent on the other or on a common ancestor. In other cases, it seems more plausible that two groups came up with the same idea independently and can be compared only by way of analogy.[97] Proving genealogical dependence requires finding unique phrases or characteristics shared by two texts or cultures, which are often wanting. This earlier scholarship tended to presume genealogical relationships even in debatable cases, sometimes leading to diagnoses of parallelomania,[98] and counterclaims of parallelophobia.[99] Nevertheless, this approach did succeed in at least

[95] This is the thrust of the work of Lieberman, Fischel and others cited in nn. 74–90. For example, Lieberman, Hellenism in Jewish Palestine, 64, writes that the rabbis "would certainly not hesitate to borrow from them [the Greeks] methods and systems which they could convert into a mechanism for the clarification and definition of their own teachings." Henry Fischel, *Rabbinic Literature and Greco-Roman Philosophy* (Leiden: Brill, 1973), xi, similarly writes: "The entire midrashic output of a specific Tanna is shown to be of Greco-Roman rhetorical provenance." These scholars are certainly careful to distinguish between Greco-Roman and rabbinic ideas when they are different, but a primary objective of their work is to show the similarities.

[96] On this terminology, see Michal Bar-Asher Siegal, *Early Christian Monastic Literature and the Babylonian Talmud* (Cambridge: Cambridge University Press, 2013), 28–30, citing Adolf Deissmann, *Light from the Ancient East: The New Testament Illustrated by Recently Discovered Texts of the Graeco-Roman World*, trans. Lionel R. M. Strachan (New York: Harper & Brothers, 1927).

[97] See examples of analogical comparisons on p. 16 n. 82.

[98] Samuel Sandmel, "Parallelomania," *Journal of Biblical Literature* 81 (1962): 1–14.

[99] See Israel Yuval, "Christianity in Talmud and Midrash: Parallelomania or Parallelophobia," in *Transforming Relations: Essays on Jews and Christians throughout History in Honor of Michael A. Signer*, ed. Franklin Harkins (Notre Dame: University of

identifying the relevant texts and topics and demonstrating the manifold aspects of commonality between the two sets of literature.

This model, however, proves lacking in that it oversimplifies the complex web of interactions between the various forces within the Roman Empire. Rather than get stuck in a simplistic dichotomy of influence versus isolation, or genealogical versus analogical parallels, it is more useful and closer to reality to emphasize the cultural fluidity of different groups who inevitably and unselfconsciously intertwine to the point that they are, to some extent, "just the same culture in different variants."[100] Jews were but one of many provincial subcultures within the Empire that each navigated their changing identities both in response to hegemonic power and in relation to each other.[101] As Annette Yoshiko Reed and Natalie Dohrman write: "Strategies of Palestinian rabbis share much more than is commonly noted with Greek, Syrian, Egyptian, and other local sub-elites who simultaneously subverted, absorbed, and manipulated Roman norms."[102]

Even the term "Greco-Roman" is fraught with tension in that the Greek East never lost its sense of intellectual and cultural superiority and independence when Roman political preeminence grew.[103] In turn, for minorities within the Greek East such as Jews, Samaritans, and Christians, the various aspects of Greek culture, mythology, and philosophy were themselves a dominant and impressive force that pervaded every aspect of daily life. Significantly, Greek learning also penetrated the Persian Empire both as a remnant of ancient Hellenistic rule and from constant travel and communication by Christians, Jews, and others from the Greek East.[104] Ironically, but predictably, the politically

Notre Dame Press, 2010): 50–74; and Gerald Klingbeil, *Bridging the Gap: Ritual and Ritual Texts in the Bible* (Winona Lake, IN: Eisenbrauns, 2007), 62.

100 Daniel Boyarin, "Hellenism in Jewish Babylonia," in *The Cambridge Companion to the Talmud and Rabbinic Literature*, ed. Charlotte Fonrobert and Martin Jaffee (Cambridge: Cambridge University Press, 2007). See also Lapin, Rabbis as Romans; and Michael Satlow, "Beyond Influence: Toward a New Historiographic Paradigm," in *Jewish Literatures and Cultures: Context and Intertext*, ed. Anita Norich and Yaron Eliav (Providence: Brown Judaic Studies, 2008): 37–53.

101 See Lapin, Rabbis as Romans.

102 Natalie Dohrmann and Annette Yoshiko Reed, "Rethinking Romanness, Provincializing Christendom," in *Jews, Christians, and the Roman Empire: The Poetics of Power in Late Antiquity*, ed. Natalie Dohrmann and Annette Yoshiko Reed (Philadelphia: University of Pennsylvania Press, 2013): 2.

103 See Dohrman and Reed, ibid., 4–6; and Timothy Whitmarsh, "'Greece Is the World': Exile and Identity in the Second Sophistic," in *Being Greek under Rome: Cultural Identity, the Second Sophistic and the Development of Empire*, ed. Simon Goldhill (Cambridge: Cambridge University Press, 2001): 269–305.

104 See pp. 108–14.

dominant groups often underwent greater cultural change than the conquered minorities.[105] The Roman Empire appropriated the sophisticated science, art, and thought of the Greek world. Judaism spread to perhaps ten percent of the Roman world[106] and gave birth to Christianity. Turning from prosecuted to powerful, Christianity itself overtook the Roman Empire, and the Jews, who were once a protected minority under most Roman emperors, became a disdained adversary.

Appreciating the place of classical rhetoric in rabbinic society according to this more complex, but more realistic, web of interactions requires that we include the views of Jews, Greeks, Romans, Christians, and Persians and triangulate each with the others. We must further recognize and account for subdivisions within each of these groups considering that Greek-speaking Jews in Egypt differed from rabbis in the Galilee, who in turn varied from their colleagues in Babylonia. Greeks and Romans both quarreled among themselves on the value of philosophy versus rhetoric as well as the details of how to teach declamation.[107] Christians and Persians too included diverse ethnicities and multiple opinions on the place of rhetoric in religion and society.[108]

Accordingly, we will follow the methodology set forth by Michael Satlow that encourages analysis of both similarities and differences between cultures: "Given the significant and growing indications that Jews shared much with the larger cultures in which they lived, these similarities cease to require explanation. The thing that needs explaining is difference. How and why are a given group of Jews different from those around them?"[109] Regarding the topic of this book in particular, the rabbis could not have been isolated from the classical educational canon that formed the basis of thought and public discourse throughout the Roman Empire. The evidence analyzed in the upcoming chapters will demonstrate, rather, that the rabbis display significant integration with the wider sophistic tradition.[110] This book will therefore document and evaluate both the similarities and differences between the Greco-Roman and rabbinic uses and approaches to rhetoric.

105 See Greg Woolf, "Beyond Romans and Natives," *World Archaeology* 28, no. 3 (1995): 339–50.
106 Louis Feldman, *Jew and Gentile in the Ancient World: Attitudes and Interactions from Alexander to Justinian* (Princeton: Princeton University Press, 1993), 92.
107 See pp. 23–35 and 152.
108 See pp. 108–14 and 268–77.
109 Satlow, "Beyond Influence," 47.
110 See Henry Fischel, "Story and History: Observations on Greco-Roman Rhetoric and Pharisaism," in *Essays in Greco-Roman and Related Talmudic Literature*, ed. Henry Fiscel (New York: Ktav, 1977): 449 n. 31, for a similar approach.

In this model, the definition of "influence" of one group upon another must be broadened to include borrowing, rejecting, adopting, adapting, subverting, converting, combating and combining. Therefore, at least as important as determining whether a parallel indicates a genealogical or analogical relationship are the roles that a certain idea or method play within the two cultures. Subtle differences between the way a certain rhetorical technique is applied in two cultural contexts can reveal key distinctive features about each group. Even a genealogical connection can serve to highlight uniqueness as much as it indicates acculturation. Consequently, direct influence is just one question in a larger analysis of the comparative role that rhetoric plays within each subgroup as they respond to the same challenges. For example, we saw above that the Second Sophistic promoted Greek cultural dominance, history, and pride in the face of the Roman Empire – even if only in the imaginary world of declamation. Jews unsurprisingly took part in Greek paideia as an integrated subculture within the Greek East sharing the same antipathy to the Romans as their neighbors. At the same time, however, Jews also struggled to maintain their unique identity within the culture of the Greek East and so they rabbinized their imaginary world of declamation[111] and developed their own unique approach to truth, rhetoric, and interpretation.[112]

In a similar vein, the rabbis adopted many Greek techniques of exegesis and inference in their hermeneutical rules of midrash. Yet, they attributed these rules not to foreign origins but rather considered them to be part of the oral law revealed at Sinai.[113] The hermeneutical rules became an integral part of rabbinic thought and their historical Greek origins shrank down to irrelevance. Regardless of whether it was done consciously, this move transformed an aspect of acculturation into a mark of rabbinic distinctiveness and independence.[114]

[111] See Chapter 4.

[112] See pp. 23–35.

[113] B. Sanhedrin 99a reads: "Even if one says, 'all of the Torah is from heaven except for this detail, this *qal va-ḥomer*, or this *gezerah shavah*,' behold this fulfills 'For he has spurned the word of the Lord' (Num 15:31)." See parallel at Y. Sanhedrin 10:1, 27d.

[114] There are also other cases where the rabbis explicitly mark a certain idea as being a foreign import indicating that, at least in their own minds, they viewed such ideas as deriving from outside influences. For example, the phrase, "Greek wisdom," analyzed above as a reference to some aspect of classical rhetoric or philosophy, indicates a conscious awareness by the rabbis of a field of knowledge that was external to their culture and whose study they attempted to actively regulate. See, for example, Sifre Deut 343 on p. 257; and Satlow, "Beyond Influence," 41. Another example of an explicitly external marking is analyzed by Beth Berkowitz, *Execution and Invention:*

Viewing the rabbis as one of many neighboring provincials within a complex web of hegemonies opens the way to comparing various subcultures within the Empire that responded to the same challenges in different ways. For example, early church fathers explicitly distanced themselves from rhetoric even as they employed much of it in practice in their speeches and letters. Christianity developed a complex relationship with rhetoric and ultimately largely rejected its philosophical underpinnings.[115] The rabbis, on the one hand, shared aspects of this complex relationship but, as we will demonstrate throughout this book, also fundamentally acceded to some of the major foundations of rhetorical thought.[116] Regardless of whether these groups directly influenced each other, their comparison remains significant both because there were areas of overlap and because their convergences help to highlight their important points of contrast. The comparison between rabbis and church fathers defies any simple dichotomy between genealogy or analogy because the two groups worked within a common milieu, shared similar backgrounds and experiences, and had to work though parallel challenges. Both groups confronted the same cultural and political forces and negotiated overlapping but disparate solutions that worked best within their respective worldviews.

As a last point, situating the Jews as Roman provincials not only grants us perspective about the Jews and the writings of the rabbis, but also can mutually contribute to an understanding of the Roman Empire. Few ancient sources provide detailed evidence for the experience of provincial minorities and their relationship with the Empire as do Jewish writings from late antiquity. As long as we take into account the many differences between Jews and their neighbors, the example of the Jews can serve as a useful model for what other provincials experienced as well.[117]

PHILOSOPHY AND RHETORIC, TRUTH AND LANGUAGE

The scholars cited in the previous section have demonstrated that rabbinic literature is embedded within and shares characteristics with

Death Penalty Discourse in Early Rabbinic and Christian Cultures (New York: Oxford University Press, 2006), 159.

115 See pp. 268–76.

116 See pp. 266–87.

117 See Dohrmann and Reed, "Rethinking Romanness," 8–9; David Mattingly, *Imperialism, Power, and Identity: Experiencing the Roman Empire* (Princeton: Princeton University Press, 2011), 26 and 128; and Martin Goodman, ed. *Jews in a Graeco-Roman World* (Oxford: Clarendon Press, 1998), 1–14. See also further methodological considerations in the next section and p. 83.

many aspects of classical rhetoric. While these findings carry wide consensus, there remains the more fundamental question as to the extent to which the rabbis accepted the philosophical underpinnings of classical rhetoric. In order to penetrate into this issue, we must first review in broad strokes the history of the debates between philosophers and sophists on the issues of truth, subjectivity, language, and interpretation. The assessment of how much rhetoric there is in rabbinic literature is not merely a technical measure of how many times a certain Hellenistic genre or theme arises. Rather, as the following review will demonstrate, this analysis reaches into the innermost depths of the rabbinic thought process and thereby sheds light on many aspects of the rabbinic literary output and worldview.

Ancient epistemology offers two basic views about truth: Plato taught that truth is singular, objective and unchanging, while the sophists viewed reality as being multifaceted, relative and in constant flux.[118] These two epistemologies, in turn, dictate two radically different modes of reasoning: the sophists engaged in rhetorical argumentation with the assumption that the most convincing case would establish the best interpretation within a particular interpretive community. Plato and his followers, on the other hand, eschewed rhetoric in favor of logical proofs that reveal the absolute and immutable truth. The tension between the sophists and the philosophers continued for centuries as the schools of philosophy and those of rhetoric competed for students and prestige. Of course, Plato himself was the master rhetorician using the dialogic format to drive his interlocutors into paradoxes and self-contradictions, even as he argued for the dangers of such deceptive modes of argumentation. But Plato is in this sense typical of writers in both the philosophic and Christian traditions who at the same time polemicize against rhetoric even while applying its methodology.[119]

Plato's attack on rhetoric runs throughout his dialogues and is a central theme in the *Phaedrus* and *Gorgias*. Socrates equates rhetoric

[118] See Bruce McComiskey, "Neo-Sophistic Rhetorical Theory: Sophistic Precedents for Contemporary Epistemic Rhetoric," *Rhetorical Society Quarterly* 24, no. 3/4 (1994): 16–24; and his book, *Gorgias and the New Sophistic Rhetoric* (Carbondale: Southern Illinois University Press, 2002); Scott Consigny, "Nietzsche's Reading of the Sophists," *Rhetoric Review* 13, no. 1 (1994): 5–26; and Susan Handelman, *The Slayers of Moses: The Emergence of Rabbinic Interpretation in Modern Literary Theory* (Albany: State University of New York Press, 1982), 3–25. Predictably, not everyone agrees with this reading of the sophists; see Handelman, "Edward Schiappa's Reading of the Sophists," *Rhetoric Review* 14, no. 2 (1996): 253–69.

[119] See p. 275.

with demagoguery, using verbal tricks to convince the masses of what is beneficial to the speaker without any concern for justice or truth.[120] Rhetoric is not an art but merely a knack for producing pleasure and for imitating the persuasive effects of philosophy but without any substance.[121] Only philosophy, he argues, can rightly be called an art because the philosopher understands the truth about the subject he analyzes in all its particulars and definitions; only he is able to discern the nature of the soul of his audience and how to best form a speech that will lead the soul to attain the truth.[122] Only through philosophy can we rise above the world of illusions and bodies in order that our souls may understand the ideal forms, the realm of unchanging truth.[123]

This debate predates Plato and continues throughout the history of Western thought. Plato's belief that there exists one objective and unchanging truth follows the view of Parmenides before him.[124] Rhetoric, on the other hand, assumes the worldview of Protagoras that "man is the measure of all things, of the things that are that they are, and of the things that are not that they are not."[125] Because objective truth does not exist, or at least is inaccessible, truth must be defined subjectively as the common consent reached after both sides have been heard and weighed. This split between philosophy and rhetoric, between idea and word, between truth and trickery served as a foundation for Western metaphysics for centuries to come. Enlightenment thinkers strove to achieve, through human reason, absolute truth in language, logic, mathematics, and physical and social sciences.[126] Modern literary and post-structuralist theory eschews the possibility of objective interpretation and absolute truth that had formed the basis of Western philosophy since Plato. Instead, it embeds meaning in language and considers interpretation as a complex interaction between the reader and the text,

120 *Phaedrus* 260 and 272d–e.

121 *Gorgias* 462c–466b. See Jeremy Bell, "'Empeiria kai Tribe': Plato on the 'Art' of Flattery in Rhetoric and Sophistry," *Epoche: A Journal for the History of Philosophy* 15, no. 2 (2011): 379–94.

122 *Phaedrus* 270b–272b, 277b–c.

123 *Republic* 409d–513e, and *Phaedo* 66d–e.

124 Robert Wardy, *The Birth of Rhetoric: Gorgias, Plato and Their Successors* (London: Routledge, 2005), 9–14.

125 Plato, *Theaetetus* 152a; and *Cratylus* 385e. See Susan Jarratt, *Rereading the Sophists: Classical Rhetoric Refigured* (Carbondale, IL: Southern Illinois University Press, 1991), 49–50; Stanley Fish, *Doing What Comes Naturally: Change, Rhetoric, and the Practice of Theory in Literary and Legal Studies* (Durham: Duke University, 1989), 480; and Rosental, "Shnei devarim," 17.

126 See Dorinda Outram, *The Enlightenment* (Cambridge: Cambridge University Press, 2013); and p. 100 n. 98.

which is itself a product of prior intertexts without beginning or end. This instability of meaning does not deny the possibility of interpretation and understanding but rather prompts us to locate meaning in the contextual and persuasive power of language.[127]

Where do the rabbis fit into this controversy? That is a fundamental question running through this book and it is not easy to answer considering that the Talmud does not address this topic in any explicit and systematic way. However, a broad view of rabbinic literature suggests that the rabbis succeeded in charting a unique and sophisticated approach that denies the very dichotomy between truth and words. Susan Handelman assesses that the rabbis "never suffered this schism; their concepts of language and interpretation not only preserve but exalt the innate logic of language."[128] The rabbis, to some degree, remained on the fringes of the controversies between Platonists and sophists and thereby preserved the more ancient unity of thought and language that has only recently resurfaced in the linguistic turn in Western philosophy. Let us review some manifestations of the rabbinic viewpoint discussed in previous scholarship as a backdrop for the findings of this study.

Scholars have discussed various points of evidence that the rabbinic view of truth and language contrasts with Platonic conceptions. On a linguistic level, rabbinic Hebrew possesses no word for the Greek conception of truth (ἀλήθεια) as an absolute, universal and unchangeable

[127] See Friedrich Nietzsche, "On Truth and Lying in an Extra-Moral Sense (1873)," in *Friedrich Nietzsche on Rhetoric and Language*, ed. S.L. Gilman, C. Blair, and D.J. Parent (Oxford: Oxford University Press, 1989): 246–57; Ferdinand Saussure, *Course in General Linguistics*, trans. Wade Baskin (New York: The Philosophical Library, 1959); Jacques Derrida, *Of Grammatology*, trans. Gayatri Chakravorty Spivak (Baltimore: Johns Hopkins University Press, 1997); Michel Foucault, *The Archaeology of Knowledge and the Discourse on Language*, trans. A.M. Sheridan Smith (New York: Pantheon Books, 1972); and Anthony Reynolds, "The Linguistic Return: Deconstruction as Textual Messianism," *SubStance* 43, no. 1 (2014): 152–65.

[128] Handelman, *Slayers of Moses*, 11. See similarly Faur, *Golden Doves*, xxvi, cited p. 31 n. 147. Daniel Boyarin, *Intertextuality and the Reading of Midrash* (Bloomington: Indiana University Press, 1990), xii, rightly criticizes these works for making sweeping generalities about Jewish thinking across Jewish writers of all times and places, including medieval Spain and modern France. Nevertheless, Boyarin agrees that contemporary literary theory's "questioning of the Platonic-Aristotelian (ultimately Enlightenment) understanding of language makes possible a space for a more sympathetic reading of midrash as an interpretive act" (ibid., x). Despite their differences, these three writers agree that the Talmudic rabbis maintained a counter-culture to Platonist ideas and thus prefigured modern theory. See also Sergey Dolgopolski, *What Is Talmud?: The Art of Disagreement* (New York: Fordham University Press, 2009), 151.

rational order. Hebrew *emet* refers in legal contexts to procedural validity[129] and in other contexts means sincerity and trustworthiness; it rarely if ever means ontological truth.[130] José Faur demonstrates the alliance of the rabbis with the rhetorical tradition in this regard when he writes:

> The intellectual space of the sages is the realm of the verisimilar. It pertains to rhetoric rather than metaphysics. One will fail to find in the Talmud formal and analytical proofs, proceeding, as with the Scholastics, from syllogisms accompanied by axioms, premises and conclusions. Talmudic "proofs" are not "demonstrative" – structured from formal deductions and inductions. Talmudic dialectics deal with probable and improbable alternatives, inferences and analogue constructs, indeterminate and statistical knowledge, variables and quantitative differences. Let us note that the Talmudic lexicon does not register the words "rational" (מושכל) or "necessary" (הכרח). Its dialectic is expository: it proposes the "reasonable" (סברא), not the absolute. The divergent and contradictory opinions of the *emora'im* are not classified as "true" (אמת) and "false" (שקר).[131]

Faur here distinguishes between metaphysics, which aims at truth through logical proofs, and rhetoric, which debates probabilities through dialectics. He places the rabbis in the latter category and thus explains why Hebrew lacks a word for ontological truth. Throughout this book I will use the word "truth" in both senses to refer to universal ontological

[129] See Christine Hayes, *What's Divine about Divine Law?* (Princeton: Princeton University Press, 2015), 169–245; Christine Hayes, "Legal Truth, Right Answers and Best Answers: Dworkin and the Rabbis," *Diné Israel* 25 (2008): 73–121; and Chaya Halberstam, *Law and Truth in Biblical and Rabbinic Literature* (Bloomington: Indiana University Press, 2010), 90. Y. Sanhedrin 1:1, 18a, for example, makes the extraordinary statement that even God must follow procedure in order to achieve truth: "R. Yoḥanan said, The Holy One, blessed be He, does not do anything in his world without first consulting with the heavenly court. What is the source? 'The word is truth and a great army' (Dan 10:1) – when is the seal of the Holy One, blessed be He, true? When he consults the heavenly court."

[130] See, for example, Avot d'Rabbi Natan A 34, 36; Gen Rabbah 96; Y. Sanhedrin 11:5, 30c; and B. Sanhedrin 85b. There are some instances where *emet* may mean essence or absolute truth such as in Avot d'Rabbi Natan A 6; and B. Megilah 16b. See further at Anthony C. Thiselton, "Truth," in *The New International Dictionary of New Testament Theology*, ed. Brown Colin (Exeter: Paternoster Press, 1978), 3:874–902.

[131] José Faur, *The Horizontal Society: Understanding the Covenant and Alphabetic Judaism* (Boston: Academic Studies Press, 2008), 1:277. See similarly José Faur, "Retorica y hemeneutica: Vico y la tradicion rabinica," in *Pensar para el nuevo siglo: Giambattista Vico y la cultura Europea*, ed. E. Hidalto-Serna (Napoli: La Città del Sole, 2001): 928. Translation by David Ramirez available at http://moreshetsepharad.org/.

reality as well as to legally valid or prophetically authenticated statements, making sure that I clarify to which definition I refer whenever the context does not make it sufficiently evident. As we will see in the Conclusion, this definitional gap allows for the rabbis to maintain a multivocalic notion of truth that incorporates the subjectivity of human interpretation even as it ultimately derives from divine prophecy.[132]

Regarding the term for "word," there is also a significant contrast between Greek *logos* and Hebrew *dabar*, which both developed a complex web of meanings in various centuries. Citing Giambattista Vico, Faur contends that in primeval mythical times, *logos* meant both word and idea, reflecting the view that saw no distinction between knowledge and its articulation.[133] For the rest of history, however, Greek refers to a lexical word using the terms *lexis* or *onoma*. *Logos*, in contrast, refers to the meaning of words and can be variously translated: explanation, argument, theory, or rational discourse. As Hans-Georg Gadamer writes, "Greek philosophy more or less began with the insight that a word is *only* a name – i.e., that it does not represent true being."[134] Hebrew *dabar*, on the other hand, refers to word, event, and thing, which reflects a unity between the word and the world such that to interpret the word is to understand reality and vice versa.[135] Modern linguistic theory has now revived the ancient rhetorical view that rejects the possibility of purely conceptual ideas and instead insists that ideas are integrally dependent on words.[136] Both regarding conceptions of truth and

[132] See pp. 277–87.

[133] José Faur, "The Splitting of the Logos: Some Remarks on Vico and the Rabbinic Tradition," *Poiesis: New Vico Studies* 3 (1985): 87; and see Giambattista Vico, *The New Science*, trans. Thomas G. Bergin and Max H. Fisch (Ithaca: Cornell University Press, 1968), 401; and Sandra Rudnick Luft, *Vico's Uncanny Humanism: Reading the New Science between Modern and Postmodern* (Ithaca: Cornell University Press, 2003), 88–91.

[134] Hans-Georg Gadamer, *Truth and Method* (London: Continuum, 2004), 406. Italics in original.

[135] See also Thorleif Boman, *Hebrew Thought Compared with Greek* (New York: W. W. Norton, 1960), 67–9 and 184; Handelman, *Slayers of Moses*, 3–9, 32–3; and Daniel Boyarin, "Moslem, Christian, and Jewish Cultural Interaction in Sefardic Talmudic Interpretation," *Review of Rabbinic Judaism* 5, no. 1 (2002): 6.

[136] Saussure, *Course in General Linguistics*, 111–12 writes:

> Psychologically our thought – apart from its expression in words – is only a shapeless and indistinct mass. Philosophers and linguists have always agreed in recognizing that without the help of signs we would be unable to make a clear-cut, consistent distinction between two ideas. Without language, thought is a vague, uncharted nebula. There are no pre-existing ideas, and nothing is distinct before the appearance of language.

language, therefore, Hebrew never accepted the dichotomies introduced by Plato and the philosophers that followed in his wake.

The Hebrew conception of language can help explain the methods of midrashic hermeneutics. As Isaak Heinemann explains, rabbinic midrash assumes the "independence of the parts of speech" such that "one cannot describe the interpretive methodology of the rabbis using the rationalist hermeneutical structure that is based on the complete dominance of the *logos*."[137] By *logos*, Heinemann refers to the idea in the author's head and the conception of meaning in the reader's mind as he or she translates ink splotches into letters, words, sentences, and ideas. The rationalists of Western thought demote words to a mere vehicle to convey meaning, rendering them dispensable once the idea is understood. Organic thinking, on the other hand, denies that words are mere vessels for *logos* but rather imbues words with independent significance. Processing language requires the reader to enter a vicious hermeneutic circle of turning particular signs into a larger idea and at the same time using the larger context to interpret and negate the meanings of those signs. Since the production of meaning from words is in all cases subjective and uncertain, we should acknowledge the legitimacy of exploring alternate and even radical ways of reading. According to Heinemann, midrash does just that by performing a close and careful reading of the letters and words but still allowing for creativity in framing the context, multiplying possibilities in making connections, and freeing each word to act as an independent entity.

The logocentrism of Plato engenders a focus on ideal unchanging truths and relegates language to a mere image of reality.[138] That is why Plato can accuse the sophists of misusing language in a way that divorces it from truth.[139] For the rabbis, however, truth and meaning are integrally bound up with the words themselves. Words can be misunderstood but they can neither be dispensed with nor confined to just one correct interpretation. A word is an active dynamic force, especially when it is the word of God: "My word is like fire, declares the Lord, and like a hammer that shatters rock" (Jer 23:29). The rabbis derive from

[137] Isaak Heinemann, *Darkhe ha-'aggada* (Jerusalem: Magnes, 1970), 102. See also Daniel Boyarin, *Border Lines: The Partition of Judaeo-Christianity* (Philadelphia: University of Pennsylvania Press, 2004), 189.

[138] Plato, *Cratylus*, 439a–b; and see Viktor Ilievski, "Language and Knowledge in Plato's *Cratylus*," *Filozofija* 35 (2013): 7–25.

[139] Rachel Barney, *Names and Nature in Plato's Cratylus* (New York: Routledge, 2001), 161, writes that for Plato, "names are ontologically degenerate and therefore potentially deceptive."

here: "Just as a hammer disperses many sparks so does a single verse issue forth many senses."[140] Prophetic language does not point to just one idea in the mind of the author; rather, linguistic ambiguity necessarily and legitimately engenders interpretive polysemy.[141] Therefore, the full scope of the prophetic message can only be appreciated through unpacking its full diversity of possible meanings. As Emmanuel Levinas eloquently states: "Something would remain unrevealed in the Revelation if a single soul in its singularity were to be missing from the exegesis."[142]

The dynamic power of language also manifests itself in the role of speech in creation. As the Psalmist writes: "By the word of the Lord the heavens were made" (33:6). God forms each part of the cosmos with speech and provides them a name (Gen 1:5, 8, 10) just as humans can conceive of the world only through language (Gen 2:19–20). The words that God used to create the world, the rabbis explain, are none other than the Torah itself. The Torah preceded creation as a blueprint for the universe:

> In the usual way of the world, a king of flesh and blood does not build a palace with his own skill but with the skill of an architect. And the architect does not build it in his mind but he uses a record book or a pinax to know how to make rooms and mosaics. So too the Holy One, blessed be He, looks at the Torah and creates the world.[143]

The rabbis form their conception of the world primarily through the text of the Torah and for that reason can state that the Torah existed prior to

[140] B. Sanhedrin 34a. See analysis at Faur, *Golden Doves*, xiii; Handelman, *Slayers of Moses*, 67; Susan Handelman, "Fragments of the Rock: Contemporary Literary Theory and the Study of Rabbinic Texts – A Response to David Stern," *Prooftexts* 5 (1985): 89–90; David Stern, *Midrash and Theory: Ancient Jewish Exegesis and Contemporary Literary Studies* (Evanston: Northwestern University Press, 1996), 17–18; Stern, "Literary Criticism or Literary Homilies? Susan Handelman and the Contemporary Study of Midrash," *Prooftexts* 5 (1985): 101; Azzan Yadin, *Scripture as Logos: Rabbi Ishmael and the Origins of Midrash* (Philadelphia: University of Pennsylvania, 2004), 69–79; Boyarin, *Border Lines*, 189–92; Boyarin, "Shattering the Logos – or, The Talmuds and the Genealogy of Indeterminacy," in *The Talmud Yerushalmi and Graeco-Roman Culture III*, ed. Peter Schäfer (Tübingen: Mohr Siebeck, 2002): 273–99; Hidary, *Dispute*, 19 and 27; and Steven Fraade, "Response to Azzan Yadin-Israel on Rabbinic Polysemy: Do They 'Preach' What They Practice?," *AJS Review* 38 (2014): 353 n. 31.

[141] On polysemy in midrashic interpretation, see Stern, *Midrash and Theory*, 15–38.

[142] Levinas, *Beyond the Verse*, 171.

[143] Gen Rabbah 1:1. See also parallel at Tanḥuma to Gen 1:1.

the universe. This midrash has a likely ancestor in Plato's *Timeaus*, which explains that the Creator gazed at the eternal forms as a model for constructing the world.[144] Significantly, the midrash replaces the analphabetic ideal forms with the words of the Torah.[145] Conversely, when God threatens to destroy the Israelites for sinning with the golden calf, Moses demands that God forgive their sin: "And if not, then erase me from the book that you have written" (Exod 32:32). A person's existence depends on his being written in God's book and his being killed is an act of textual erasure. Here again, reality is inextricably bound with words and the former disappears when the latter is erased. As Faur writes: "In the mind of the Hebrews, the Universe is represented as the writing or active speech of God."[146]

Faur continues:

> In the West, "philosophy" stood in hierarchical opposition to "rhetoric" ... Rabbinic tradition is the only intellectual and cultural movement to have continued developing since antiquity without a primaeval rupture – an inaugural split – resulting in an endless series of hierarchical opposition.[147]

Handelman similarly writes: "The struggle between philosophy and rhetoric in Greece ended in philosophy's conquest," whereas the rabbis retained an ancient integrated worldview.[148] David Stern

[144] *Timaeus*, 27–9.

[145] See Faur, *Horizontal Society*, 1.8–12; Faur, *Golden Doves*, 138; and Hengel, *Judaism and Hellenism*, 171; Handelman, *Slayers of Moses*, 38; Henry Fischel, "The Transformation of Wisdom in the World of Midrash," in *Aspects of Wisdom in Judaism and Early Christianity*, ed. Robert Wilken (Notre Dame: University of Notre Dame Press, 1975): 80 and 95; Ephraim Urbach, *The Sages: Their Concepts and Beliefs* (Cambridge: Harvard University Press, 1975), 1.198–200; and George Foot Moore, *Judaism in the First Centuries of the Christian Era, the Age of the Tannaim* (1927; repr., New York: Schocken Books, 1971), 1.267. A conduit for this tradition from Plato to the rabbis may have been Philo, *On Creation*, 15–25, who repeats Plato's cosmology and adds a parable of a king hiring an engineer. His parable, however, lacks a written blueprint, thus highlighting the contrast with the rabbis who move from forms to text.

[146] Faur, *Golden Doves*, xxv.

[147] Ibid., xxvi. See further discussion at Howard Eilberg-Schwartz, "When the Reader Is in the Write," *Prooftexts* 7 (1987): 194–205.

[148] Handelman, *Slayers of Moses*, 11; and see p. 26, and further elaboration at David A. Frank, "Arguing with God, Talmudic Discourse, and the Jewish Countermodel: Implications for the Study of Argumentation," *Argumentation and Advocacy* 41 (2004): 71–86; and David A. Frank, "The Jewish Countermodel: Talmudic Argumentation, the New Rhetoric Project, and the Classical Tradition of Rhetoric," *Journal of Communication and Religion* 26 (2003): 163–94.

counters this strict dichotomy between the West and the rabbis in his critique of Handelman:

> The major thrust of scholarship about Rabbinics for the last century has been to demonstrate that Rabbinic Judaism adapted and transformed the ideas of Hellenistic civilization to serve its own purposes, sometimes to make them the fount of its religious system: an idea as central as that extolling the study of Torah as the greatest commandment, for example, can be traced to analogous claims made for the pursuit of philosophy in classical Greece.[149]

Stern takes Handelman to task for dismissing the relevance of Lieberman's *Hellenism in Jewish Palestine* and similar scholarship with the justification that she focuses on "*structural differences* between Rabbinic and Greek thought"[150] rather than historical influence. Handelman counters that Lieberman himself only claims that the terminology of the thirteen hermeneutical principles are borrowed from the Greek rhetors, but not the forms of reasoning themselves.[151] She does admit that there exist "real influences of Hellenistic culture on the rabbis" but she chooses to emphasize the differences between them that are manifest in "specific attitudes towards language."[152] Stern, however, accuses Handelman of "falling into disingenuous generalizations."[153] In the end both agree that there are similarities and differences between the two traditions, but neither ventures to carefully delineate what they are.

I agree to a large extent with Faur and Handelman that the rabbis retained elements of a primeval organic system of thought. At the same time, a stark opposition between the West and the rabbis cannot accurately capture the nuance and complexity of each group and of their

149 David Stern, "Moses-cide: Midrash and Contemporary Literary Criticism," *Prooftexts* 4 (1985): 196.

150 Handelman, *Slayers of Moses*, 51. Italics are in the original.

151 See further on this in Chapter 5.

152 Handelman, "Fragments of the Rock," 88.

153 Stern, "Moses-cide," 196. See also the criticism of Philip S. Alexander, "Quid Athenis et Hierosolymis? Rabbinic Midrash and Hermeneutics in the Graeco-Roman World," in *A Tribute to Geza Vermes: Essays on Jewish and Christian Literature and History*, ed. P. R. Davies and R. T. White (Sheffield: Sheffield Academic Press, 1990): 101–24; and Philip S. Alexander, "Hellenism and Hellenization as Problematic Historiographical Categories," in *Paul Beyond the Judaism/Hellenism Divide*, ed. Troels Engberg-Pedersen (Louisville: Westminster John Knox Press, 2001): 67 and 273 n. 79; William Scott Green, "Romancing the Tome: Rabbinic Hermeneutics and the Theory of Literature," *Semia* 40 (1987): 147–68; and discussion at Catherine Hezser, *The Social Structure of the Rabbinic Movement in Roman Palestine* (Tübingen: Mohr Siebeck, 1997), 17–19; and Hidary, *Dispute*, 17 n. 65.

interaction. In fact, "the West" includes many and varied voices (including those of the rabbis). Plato himself is inconsistent in his description of the *logos* and the relationship between rhetoric and philosophy.[154] Aristotle certainly did not denigrate rhetoric but rather considered it to be a counterpart or outgrowth of dialectic[155] and consequently closely related to philosophical proof. In contrast to Plato who describes rhetoric as a counterpart to cookery,[156] Aristotle sees a proper place for rhetoric in the pursuit of truth as a form of persuasion that is weaker than demonstration but still appropriate for given audiences and subjects.[157] Rhetoric does assist in achieving justice because "the true and the just are by nature stronger than their opposites" and will prevail through debate. Furthermore, he writes, "one should be able to argue persuasively on either side of a question, just as in the use of syllogisms, not that we may actually do both (for one should not persuade what is debased) but in order that it may not escape our notice what the real state of the case is and that we ourselves may be able to refute if another person uses speech unjustly."[158]

Students in the Roman Empire would typically study first in a rhetorical school and then some would continue to a philosophical school without needing to take sides regarding their epistemological assumptions but would instead be engaged in both. The two disciplines were deeply intertwined and mutually reliant to the extent that "the philosophers looked upon the art [of rhetoric] as a practical technique that was quite legitimate in its own way and had a perfectly proper place in culture as a preliminary study, like grammar or mathematics; and they had no compunction about teaching it."[159] We therefore find approaches to truth that depend on both sophistic and philosophic assumptions side by side within Greco-Roman intellectual discourse.

On the rabbinic front, we must acknowledge that the rabbis were embedded in a deeply Hellenistic world, not isolated from it. In some cases, the rabbis recognized a Hellenistic idea as external to themselves

154 In *Sophist* 263e, Plato identifies *logos* with *dianoia* (thinking) except that the latter refers to the "silent inner conversation of the soul with itself" whereas the former describes "the stream that flows from the soul in vocal utterance." In this articulation, thought and word are unified. Translation from Plato, *Theaetetus and Sophist*, trans. H. N. Fowler, Loeb Classical Library (Cambridge: Harvard University Press, 1921).

155 Aristotle, *On Rhetoric*, I.1.1.

156 McComiskey, *Gorgias* 464b.

157 See Brad McAdon, "Rhetoric Is a Counterpart of Dialectic," *Philosophy and Rhetoric* 34, no. 2, 113–50; and Aristotle, *On Rhetoric*, 31 n. 4.

158 Ibid., I.1.13. See also Fish, *Doing What Comes Naturally*, 478–9; and herein p. 235 n. 81.

159 Marrou, *History of Education*, 211.

and explicitly decided to adopt it, adapt it, or reject it.[160] But in most cases, as discussed above, Hellenistic modes of thought, style, stories, and values simply pervaded the shared environment. Greek expressions and values resonated with biblical and other ancient traditions and became absorbed into each other and merged into a Hebraic-Hellenistic conglomerate.

Most recently, Sergey Dolgopolski has shown that Talmud is not reducible to either philosophy or rhetoric. Rather,

> [the sages] have their own inevitable metaphysical, yet not philosophical position that enables the unique Talmudic approach to learning not merely as a repetition of tradition, but rather, in its highest form, as a process otherwise known in rhetoric as the process of (re)discovery of the past through a rational rhetorical (re)invention of it.[161]

Unlike philosophers who seek a contextless ultimate truth, the rabbis adhere to the oral and written Torah traditions for their worldview. Unlike the sophists (at least as portrayed by the philosophers) who deny the possibility of truth, the Talmud does seek out Divine truths from the Torah, even as the rabbis recognize that that past is "reachable only through the process of rational rhetorical reinvention."[162] For this reason, "the Talmudic masters intrinsically turn to both philosophy and sophistry/rhetoric without, however, conflating their position with either of them."[163] I largely identify with this assessment, as will become clearer throughout this book.

In sum, it would be erroneous to portray the rabbinic worldview as being either completely dependent on or completely different from Greek philosophy or rhetoric. Rather than adopting either of these extreme views, this book argues that a complex combination of adoption and adaptation can best explain Talmudic rhetorical structure and reasoning. We can speak of rabbinic thought as a counter-culture to the Greco-Roman intellectual world only to the extent that we take into account the significant diversity of opinions within the Greco-Roman tradition itself. Philosophy and rhetoric each maintained many proponents in a lively and continuous debate among Greek thinkers who often combined elements of each in various ways. Therefore, any opposition by the rabbis to metaphysical truths or resistance by them to

160 See p. 22 n. 114.
161 Dolgopolski, *What Is Talmud*, 154.
162 Ibid.
163 Ibid., 158.

rhetorical argumentation may not be counter-cultural so much as siding with one or another Greco-Roman school. At the same time, we must also explore the prospect that the rabbis maintained their own distinctive voice that combined elements of various aspects of their surrounding popular and intellectual culture and integrated them within their own textual, social and legal world.

The goal of this book is to analyze how the rabbis fused together the various elements of the biblical organic tradition with the ambient culture of rhetorical training and their own focus on the transmission of oral law. As we will see in the Conclusion, assessing questions of truth and argumentation through the lens of prophetic Scripture necessarily prompted the rabbis to create their own unique and instructive contribution to these enduring issues. The sages of the Talmud adopt neither a Platonic monistic truth, nor a skeptical view that rejects any objective truth as the sophists do. We will demonstrate that, instead, they conceive of a model of multiple truths embedded within the words of the prophets than can be accessed through human interpretation.

ON RHETORICAL ARRANGEMENT

Several chapters of this book[164] will analyze the structure of rabbinic sermons and sugyot in relation to the arrangement of sections taught in Greco-Roman handbooks, the most important being those of Aristotle, Cicero, Quintilian, the anonymous *Ad Herennium*, and *On Invention* attributed to Hermogenes of Tarsus (flourished second century CE).[165] This section will summarize the basics of rhetorical arrangement and thereby serve as a background for the upcoming analyses.

Cicero describes five stages in the study of rhetoric:

> Invention (*inventio*) is the discovery of valid or seemingly valid arguments to render one's case plausible. Arrangement (*dispositio*) is the distribution of arguments thus discovered in the proper order. Expression (*elocutio*) is the fitting of the proper language to the

[164] See pp. 61–67, 68–9, 95–101, 114–6, 122–6, and 190–3. Two New Testament examples are also analyzed pp. 44–6 and 270–1.

[165] I have used the following editions: Aristotle, *On Rhetoric* (full citation in n. 12); Cicero, *On Invention* (full citation in n. 12); Quintilian, *Institutes of Oratory* (full citation in n. 1); *Ad Herennium*, trans. Harry Caplan, Loeb Classical Library (Cambridge: Harvard University Press, 1954); and George A. Kennedy, *Invention and Method: Two Rhetorical Treatises from the Hermogenic Corpus* (Atlanta: Society of Biblical Literature, 2005).

> invented matter. Memory (*memoria*) is the firm mental grasp of matter and words. Delivery (*pronuntiatio*) is the control of voice and body in a manner suitable to the dignity of the subject matter and the style.[166]

Regarding the second stage of arrangement, Cicero identifies six typical parts of a rhetorical discourse: "exordium, narrative, partition (*divisionem*), confirmation, refutation (*confutationem*), [and] peroration (*conclusionem*)."[167] *Ad Herennium* lists the same stages and concisely explains the purpose of each:

> The Introduction (*exordium*) is the beginning of the discourse, and by it the hearer's mind is prepared for attention. The Narration (*narrationem*) or Statement of Facts sets forth the events that have occurred or might have occurred. By means of the Division (*divisionem*) we make clear what matters are agreed upon and what are contested, and announce what points we intend to take up. Proof (*confirmationem*) is the presentation of our arguments, together with their corroboration. Refutation (*confutationem*) is the destruction of our adversaries' arguments. The Conclusion (*conclusionem*) is the end of the discourse, formed in accordance with the principles of the art.[168]

In other words, the exordium secures the goodwill of the audience, the narration details the facts of the case in judicial deliberation, and the partition introduces the primary headings of the proofs to follow.[169]

166 Cicero, *On Invention*, I.9.

167 Ibid., I.19. Aristotle, *On Rhetoric*, III.13–19, discusses these parts in more or less the same way. *On Invention*, attributed to Hermogenes, discusses the following parts of the oration: *prooemion* (equivalent to Cicero's exordium), *prokatastasis* (introduces the narration), *diēgēsis* (narration), *prokataskeuē* (partition), and *kataskeuē* (proof); see Kennedy, *Invention and Method*.

168 *Ad Herennium*, I.4 and see also III.16–18.

169 I will use the term "partition" rather than "division" in the rest of this book. Aristotle, *On Rhetoric*, III.13.1–2, calls this section a *prothesis* and considers it an essential part of a speech: "There are two parts to a speech; for it is necessary [first] to state the subject with which it is concerned and [then] to demonstrate the argument. It is ineffective after stating something not to demonstrate it and to demonstrate without a first statement; for one demonstrating demonstrates *something*, and one making a preliminary statement says it first for the sake of demonstrating it. Of these parts, the first is the statement [*prothesis*], the other the proof [*pistis*]."
Here is a sample partition from Cicero, *The Speeches*, trans. John Henry Freese (Cambridge: Harvard University Press, 1945), 153, *Pro Sexto Roscio Amerino* §35:

> As far as I can judge, there are three obstacles by which Sextus Roscius is faced to-day: the accusation brought by his adversaries, their audacity, and their power. The accuser Erucius has undertaken the fabrication of the charge; the

Significantly, Cicero discusses three example partitions, all of which list exactly three arguments.[170] Quintilian also cites a number of sample partitions, including two from Cicero's speeches, in which three arguments are listed.[171] *Ad Herennium* states explicitly that the number of points to be discussed "ought not to exceed three."[172] *On Invention* attributed to Hermogenes similarly cites examples from Demosthenes' orations that enumerate three upcoming arguments.[173] After the partition, the confirmation presents the arguments for one's point of view based on evidence or probabilities while the refutation presents arguments against the opposing point of view. Finally, the peroration recapitulates the main points of the speech.

While these six divisions represent the proper arrangement for a typical speech, certain types of oratory and different circumstances require the order to be changed or certain parts to be omitted. In fact, Tisias, the reputed fifth century BCE founder of rhetoric, is cited as teaching only four parts: prooemion/exordium, narration, confirmation, and epilogue.[174] Plato mentions a slightly expanded form of this arrangement even as he disparages it.[175] Aristotle writes that one can use as few as two parts: the statement (*prosthesis*) and the proof (*pistis*). However, he also lists the typical four-part structure and observes that other writers include further divisions.[176] Although the six-part structure became the standard during the Roman period, orators would deviate from its exact strictures more often than not and would sometimes revert to the four-part division. Clifton Black articulates this point most clearly:

> Roscii have claimed the role of the audacious villains; but Chrysogonus, who has the greatest influence, uses the weapon of power against us. I feel that it is my duty to discuss each of these three points.

Cicero continues to take up each of these three points in turn. See further at Friedrich Solmsen, "Cicero's First Speeches: A Rhetorical Analysis," *Transactions and Proceedings of the American Philological Association* 69 (1938): 542–56; and pp. 96–97 and 116.

170 Cicero, *On Invention*, I.32–33.

171 Quintilian, *Institutes of Oratory*, 4.5.9–12. In the last case, Cicero explicitly states that he will address three issues.

172 *Ad Herennium*, I.17.

173 Kennedy, *Invention and Method*, 64–5.

174 See Michael de Brauw, "The Parts of the Speech," in *A Companion to Greek Rhetoric*, ed. Ian Worthington (Malden, MA: Blackwell Publishing, 2007): 187–202; and Kennedy's appendix, "The Earliest Rhetorical Handbooks," in Aristotle, *On Rhetoric*, 293–306. For an argument that rhetorical theory does not originate earlier than the fourth century, see Edward Schiappa, *The Beginnings of Rhetorical Theory in Classical Greece* (New Haven: Yale University Press, 1999).

175 *Phaedrus* 266c–267d.

176 Aristotle, *On Rhetoric*, III.13–19.

> The organization of a speech varied with respect to its components and their degree of elaboration, depending on the species of rhetoric to which the address belonged and on the particulars of the rhetorical situation. Therefore, the fact that Hellenistic Jewish and early Christian sermons do not exhibit the full-blown arrangement of judicial discourse should kindle no surprise: no species of classical, not even judicial oratory itself, was straitjacketed into this comprehensive *taxis*. Within broad constraints, structural modification and abridgement were the rule, not the exception.[177]

We will see further considerations and variations on this structure in the analysis of the examples throughout this book.[178]

To illustrate this arrangement, let us turn to the master orator, Demosthenes, whose works continued to be studied and emulated by rhetors for centuries after his death in 322BCE.[179] Here is an outline of his lengthy oration *Against Aristocratus* highlighting the major six sections:[180]

> Exordium (¶1–7): Encourages audience to pay attention to his speech because the speaker is sincere and the matter is very important.
>
> Narration (¶8–17): The events leading up to the law under consideration.
>
> Peroration (¶18): "As I have undertaken to prove three propositions, [1] first that the decree is unconstitutional, [2] secondly that it is injurious to the common weal, and [3] thirdly that the person in whose favor it has been moved is unworthy of such privilege."
>
> Confirmation (¶19–186)
>
> Refutation (¶187–195)
>
> Peroration (¶215–220)

While typical examples of ancient orations are many pages long and elaborate much more than the rabbinic examples that we will analyze

177 Clifton Black, *The Rhetoric of the Gospel: Theological Artistry in the Gospels and Acts* (Louisville: Westminster John Knox Press, 2013), 124. *Ad Herennium*, III.9–10, makes this very point and provides examples.

178 See p. 35 n. 164. For variations on and omission of the exordium, see pp. 53–4, 65 and 96; on the narration, see p. 53 n. 61; and on the partition, see p. 46 n. 25.

179 For instance, the treatise *On Invention* attributed to Hermogenes in the second century CE quotes from the orations of Demosthenes as a model for proper arrangement; see III.2 (Kennedy, *Invention and Method*, 65) where he specifically points to Demosthenes' *Against Aristocratus* as an example of a partition.

180 This outline is based on Heather Teixeira, "Poetry, Politics, Persuasion: The Rhetoric of Demosthenes and George W. Bush," (Honors Thesis, Wesleyan University, 2008).

in this book, the Talmudic texts may be only an outline of what would be a much longer lecture if presented to an audience.[181] Methodologically, it is difficult to determine whether the structure of these sugyot bear a genealogical relationship to classical arrangement or whether the comparison is merely analogical. Certainly, common sense dictates that one would logically make an argument by beginning with an introduction, narrating an event, providing proofs and offering a conclusion. However, it seems more likely that the presence of a partition and other specific features that we will highlight for each case suggests, at the very least, a rhetorical sensibility that prodded the rabbis to give conscious attention to the structure of the argument. If, furthermore, we assume their familiarity with the general contours of Greek oratory, even if only from hearing many examples of it in courts and public spaces, then we can reasonably propose that these selected sugyot conform to the standards of classical rhetorical arrangement.

OUTLINE OF THE BOOK

Chapter 1 studies the role of the rabbi as public orator and reviews the basic forms of midrash aggadah. We show that the proem and *yelamdenu* forms conform to the structures recommended in Greco-Roman rhetorical handbooks. We further analyze extended examples including the sermon of Paul at Antioch and the Passover Haggadah.

The next five chapters turn to legal material. Chapter 2 reconstructs the role of the rabbis as school instructors and continues with a detailed source-critical and rhetorical analysis of a sugya from the Yerushalmi, extrapolating how it makes use of classical rhetorical techniques. Chapter 3 applies the same methodology to several legal sugyot from the Talmud Bavli, exploring how such Hellenistic models may have come to the Persian Empire.

Chapter 4 first compares progymnasmatic school exercises with midrash halakha and other Talmudic sugyot. It then probes parallels between the more advanced declamations called controversiae with similar sets of arguments on both sides of theoretical legal cases in rabbinic literature.

[181] On the relationship between literary versions of rabbinic texts and their performance, see Joseph Heinemann, "The Proem in the Aggadic Midrashim – A Form-Critical Study," in *Scripta Hierosolymitana* (1971): 100–22. In the case of the proem, however, the literary versions seem to be longer and more complex than their performative versions.

Building on previous analyses by Saul Lieberman and David Daube, Chapter 5 delves deeper into the system of hermeneutical reasoning employed in halakhic midrash. We here chart the various stages in the development and application of these rules and the political and cultural contexts of each stage. I argue here and in subsequent chapters that the rabbis not only incorporated much of Greco-Roman rhetoric but that they also resisted many of its sophistic aspects.

Considering the requirement of rhetorical training for becoming a lawyer and the considerable role that sophistical argumentation had in courts, the next two chapters analyze the rabbinic approach to rhetoric by comparing the roles of lawyers in rabbinic and Roman courtrooms – both on earth and in heaven. Chapter 6 contrasts Roman courts, which followed an adversarial system in which lawyers played an important role, with rabbinic courts, in which lawyers had almost no role. This discussion prompts the question considered in Chapter 7 as to why rabbinic aggadah portrays heavenly courts as being full of lawyers. As these two chapters demonstrate, the rabbis were fully aware of both the power and pitfalls of lawyerly rhetoric. Accordingly, they constructed careful safeguards to ensure justice and mercy in their own earthly and heavenly courts.

Having built a better appreciation for the rabbinic attitudes towards rhetoric, the Conclusion summarizes this study's key findings and then appraises the use of rhetoric by Christian writers from the New Testament to Augustine. These writers certainly utilize rhetorical techniques in their oratory and letters, even as they denigrate eloquence and claim to speak in a simple lowly style. We will contrast the antipathy of the church fathers towards the sophists with the rabbinic embrace of the idea of multiple truths and interpretations. The book closes with a proposal for the rabbis' theological justification that reconciles their devotion to prophetic truth with their concomitant celebration of forty-nine ways to declare the reptile to be pure.

1 Rabbis as Orators: The Setting and Structure of Rabbinic Homilies

> Speech sweeter than honey flowed from his tongue.[1]
>
> Anyone who speaks words of Torah in public that are not sweet to his listeners as this honey that comes from the comb, it would be better if he had not spoken them.[2]

Before writing his work *On Rhetoric*, Aristotle compiled a history of rhetoric in Greece based on earlier handbooks entitled *Synagōgē Technōn* (literally, collection of techniques).[3] While others have attempted to reconstruct that lost work,[4] this chapter imagines what a collection of *rabbinic* synagogue technai might have looked like, that is, what went into the craft of delivering a synagogue sermon? What techniques and structures did rabbinic orators use in their lessons and lectures to their students and to wider audiences? What similarities or contrasts can we draw between them and their Roman counterparts, and how might this help us understand works of midrash aggadah?

Roman orators presented speeches for public entertainment in theaters, temples, council chambers, and specially built lecture halls.[5] The Talmud similarly relates many instances of rabbis delivering public

1 *Iliad* 1.249, describing Nestor. See the negative attitude to this at Plato, *Republic*, 607a, and discussion at Fish, *Doing What Comes Naturally*, 476.

2 Shir ha-Shirim Rabbah 4:11. This parallel is noted by Boaz Cohen, *Law and Tradition in Judaism* (New York: Jewish Theological Seminary of America, 1959), 163.The midrash is likely based on Ps 19:11, which also inspired the title of Judah Messer Leon, *The Book of the Honeycomb's Flow*, trans. Isaac Rabinowitz (Ithaca: Cornell University Press, 1983). See also B. Shabbat 30b and Boyarin, *Socrates and the Fat Rabbis*, 10.

3 See Kennedy, *New History*, 11.

4 Leonard Spengel, *ΣΥΝΑΊΟΊΗ ΤΕΧΝΩΝ sive Artium Scriptores ab initiis usque ad editors Aristotelis de Rhetorica libros* (Stuttgart, 1828).

5 Donald A. Russel, *Greek Declamation* (Cambridge: Cambridge University Press, 1983), 76; and Christopher Johnstone, "Greek Oratorical Settings and the Problem of the Pnyx: Rethinking the Athenian Political Process," in *Theory, Text, Context: Issues in Greek Rhetoric and Oratory*, ed. Christopher Johnstone (Albany: State University of New York Press, 1996): 97–127.

lectures and sermons in study houses (*batei midrash*),[6] synagogues,[7] and other public venues.[8] Masses of Jews ran to the study house in order to hear R. Yoḥanan preach on aggadah.[9] R. Eliezer is said to have lectured for many hours on the laws of festivals to a diverse audience, though few participants had the patience to stay for the whole lesson.[10] That some prominent rabbis attracted large crowds derives support from the practice of hiring younger preachers to lecture while the crowd was gathering. They would then turn the floor over to the main speaker once the room was filled.[11]

This background invites us to compare the role of the rabbis with that of the sophists. Seth Schwartz correctly assesses that, "the roles the rabbis played in their society are not precisely comparable to those played by such contemporary urban types as sophists, *iurisprudentes*, philosophers or 'holy men.'"[12] Tropper goes a step further in judging that although the rabbis shared a "penchant for scholasticism and

[6] T. Soṭah 7:9–11 and n. 31.

[7] Rabbinic literature points to a few cases of rabbinic preaching in second-century CE synagogues, such as T. Megilah 2:18; Y. Soṭah 1:4, 16d; B. Megilah 28b; and Deut Rabbah 7:8. There are, however, many more such examples regarding rabbis of the third and fourth centuries: Pesiqta d'Rav Kahana 18:5; Y. Bikkurim 3:3, 65d; Y. Ta`anit 1:2, 64a; Lev Rabbah 32:7 and 35:12. See further at Lee Levine, *The Ancient Synagogue: The First Thousand Years* (New Haven: Yale University Press, 2005), 486–89. Levine, ibid., and Marc Hirshman, "The Preacher and His Public in Third-Century Palestine," *Journal of Jewish Studies* 42 (1991): 111, uncritically cite Samuel Krauss, "The Jews in the Works of the Church Fathers," *Jewish Quarterly Review* o.s. 6 (1894): 234, regarding evidence from Jerome about rabbinic preachers. Krauss's research, however, has been debunked by Hillel Newman, "Jerome and the Jews" (PhD diss., Hebrew University, 1997); and Gary Porton, "Midrash and the Rabbinic Sermon," in *When Judaism and Christianity Began: Essays in Memory of Anthony J. Saldarini*, ed. Alan Avery-Peck, Daniel Harrington, and Jacob Neusner (Leiden: Brill, 2004): 470–3.

[8] Gen Rabbah 10:7 reports that R. Yannai sat and preached at the gate of his city, presumably to a public audience. Avot d'Rabbi Natan A 4 praises sages who "sit and preach in a congregation (בקהל)." Several sages preach to the public (*ṣibbura*), though the venue is not specified; see Y. Terumot 2:1, 41c (=B. Ḥulin 15a); Y. Pe'ah 8:7, 21b; Y. Shabbat 14:4, 14c; Y. Beṣah 1:7, 60c; Gen Rabbah 28:3; and Ruth Rabbah 5:12 and 6:4. In B. Shabbat 59b, Levi teaches (*darash*) a certain leniency, which is then followed by the women of the town. Lieberman, *Greek in Jewish Palestine*, 161–2, argues that the rabbis spoke to a wide-ranging audience as suggested by the audience laughing in disapproval at a sermon of R. Abbahu (Gen Rabbah 28:3) and the congregation falling asleep during Rabbi's lecture (Song of Songs Rabbah 1:15:3). See, however, the correction of Hirshman, "The Preacher and His Public," 108–9, regarding Lev Rabbah 18:1. See also Porton, "Midrash and the Rabbinic Sermon," 466–8.

[9] Y. Horayot 3:4, 48b = Y. Baba Meṣi`a 2:11, 8d. See further at Hirshman, "The Preacher and His Public," 108–14.

[10] B. Beṣah 15b.

[11] See Y. Sukkah 5:1, 55a = Gen Rabbah 98:11.

[12] Seth Schwartz, "Gamaliel in Aphrodite's Bath: Palestinian Society and Jewish Identity in the High Roman Empire," in *Being Greek under Rome: Cultural Identity, the*

classicism" with the sophists, they also differed in that the rabbis "were jurists rather than popular entertainers, and they are portrayed as low-profile scholars rather than as powerful and egotistical public figures."[13] I agree that the rabbis differed from sophists in many respects. Nevertheless, considering the evidence of rabbis as popular orators who sought to educate, edify, and even entertain their audiences, it is worth exploring their similarities as well.

Rabbinic preachers, as Saul Lieberman has shown, often incorporated Greek words – sometimes in order to create rhymes[14] – and allusions to Greek laws and culture. Even Gentiles apparently found rabbinic sermons engaging and convincing: "When the elder sits and preaches many proselytes become converted at the same time."[15] Lieberman adds: "[The rabbis] were able to compete even with Gentile Christians, including those who got their education in Greek schools, in winning proselytes."[16] Previous scholarship has traced hundreds of references to Greek mythology and thought in rabbinic literature.[17] Rather than focus on content, however, this chapter will concentrate on the commonality between rabbinic sermons and Greco-Roman rhetoric in terms of style and structure.[18]

THE SETTING OF RABBINIC DECLAMATION: THE SABBATH SERMON

Probably the most public and important setting for rabbinic speeches was the Sabbath and festival sermon. Evidence for a sermon given during morning services exists from Second Temple times, as noted by Philo.[19]

Second Sophistic and the Development of Empire, ed. Simon Goldhill (Cambridge: Cambridge University Press, 2001): 338.

13 Tropper, *Wisdom, Politics, and Historiography*, 150–1.

14 Lieberman, *Greek in Jewish Palestine*, 60–3.

15 Song of Songs Rabbah 1:15:2.

16 Lieberman, *Greek in Jewish Palestine*, 66–7.

17 See Elimelekh E. Hallewy, *`Erkhe ha-aggadah veha-halakhah le'or meqorot Yevaniim ve-Latiniim*, 4 vols. (Tel-Aviv: Dvir, 1979); Elimelekh E. Hallewy, *`Olamah shel ha-aggadah: ha-agadah le-'or meqorot Yevaniim* (Tel-Aviv: Dvir, 1972); and see also herein p. 16 n. 75.

18 Even as late as the seventeenth century, Dutch rabbis were applying classical rhetorical techniques to their sermons; see Shlomo Berger, *Classical Oratory and the Sephardim of Amsterdam: Rabbi Aquilar's "Tratado de la retorica"* (Hilversum: Verloren, 1996).

19 Philo, *Special Laws*, II.62 in *The Works of Philo*. On ancient Hellenistic sermons, see Folker Siegert, "The Sermon as an Invention of Hellenistic Judaism," in *Preaching in Judaism and Christianity: Encounters and Developments from Biblical Times to Modernity*, ed. Alexander Deeg, Walter Homolka, and Heinz-Gunther Schottler (Berlin: Walter de Gruyter, 2008): 25–44.

Luke 4:16–30 describes Jesus delivering a sermon in Nazareth after a Haftarah reading from Isaiah, though the text of the sermon is not recorded.[20] Acts 13:14–41, however, does record the sermon that Paul delivered in the synagogue of Pisidian Antioch after the Torah reading and is worthy of its own rhetorical analysis:

> And on the Sabbath day they went into the synagogue and sat down. [15] After the reading of the law and the prophets, the officials of the synagogue sent them a message, saying, "Brothers, if you have any word of exhortation for the people, give it." [16] So Paul stood up and with a gesture began to speak:
>
> **[Exordium]**
> You Israelites, and others who fear God, listen.
>
> **[Narration]**
> [17] The God of this people Israel chose our ancestors and made the people great during their stay in the land of Egypt, and with uplifted arm he led them out of it. [18] For about forty years he put up with them in the wilderness. [19] After he had destroyed seven nations in the land of Canaan, he gave them their land as an inheritance [20] for about four hundred fifty years. After that he gave them judges until the time of the prophet Samuel. [21] Then they asked for a king; and God gave them Saul son of Kish, a man of the tribe of Benjamin, who reigned for forty years. [22] When he had removed him, he made David their king. In his testimony about him he said, "I have found David, son of Jesse, to be a man after my heart, who will carry out all my wishes."
>
> [23] Of this man's posterity God has brought to Israel a Savior, Jesus, as he promised; [24] before his coming John had already proclaimed a baptism of repentance to all the people of Israel. [25] And as John was finishing his work, he said, "What do you suppose that I am? I am not he. No, but one is coming after me; I am not worthy to untie the thong of the sandals on his feet."
>
> **[Proposition]**
> [26] My brothers, you descendants of Abraham's family, and others who fear God, to us the message of this salvation has been sent. [27] Because the residents of Jerusalem and their leaders did not recognize him or understand the words of the prophets that are read

[20] Jesus also preached in synagogues on the Sabbath at Mark 1:21 and Acts 16:13.

every Sabbath, they fulfilled those words by condemning him. [28] Even though they found no cause for a sentence of death, they asked Pilate to have him killed. [29] When they had carried out everything that was written about him, they took him down from the tree and laid him in a tomb. [30] But God raised him from the dead; [31] and for many days he appeared to those who came up with him from Galilee to Jerusalem, and they are now his witnesses to the people. [32] And we bring you the good news that what God promised to our ancestors [33] he has fulfilled for us, their children, by raising Jesus.

[Proof]

[1] As also it is written in the second psalm, "You are my Son; today I have begotten you" (Ps 2:7).

[2] [34] As to his raising him from the dead, no more to return to corruption, he has spoken in this way, "I will give you the holy promises made to David" (Isa 55:3).

[3] [35] Therefore he has also said in another psalm, "You will not let your Holy One experience corruption" (Ps 16:10). [36] For David, after he had served the purpose of God in his own generation, died, was laid beside his ancestors, and experienced corruption; [37] but he whom God raised up experienced no corruption.

[Conclusion]

[38] Let it be known to you therefore, my brothers, that through this man forgiveness of sins is proclaimed to you; [39] by this Jesus everyone who believes is set free from all those sins from which you could not be freed by the law of Moses. [40] Beware, therefore, that what the prophets said does not happen to you: [41] "Look, you scoffers! Be amazed and perish, for in your days I am doing a work, a work that you will never believe, even if someone tells you."[21]

Various elements of this speech identify it as a good example of Greco-Roman oratory. For example, Paul begins his speech with a gesture. Although the exact nature of the gesture is not spelled out, Cicero and Quintilian discuss rhetorical gestures in some detail.[22] Quintilian in particular writes that a suitable gesture for the opening of a speech is

[21] NRSV translation.

[22] See Dorota Dutsch, "Towards a Roman Theory of Theatrical Gesture," in *Performance in Greek and Roman Theatre*, ed. Georgy Harrison and Vayos Liaps (Leiden: Brill, 2013): 409–32; Jon Hall, "Cicero and Quintilian on the Oratorical Use of Hand Gestures," *The Classical Quarterly* 54, no. 1 (2004): 143–60; and Fritz Graf, "Gestures and Conventions: The Gestures of Roman Actors and Orators," in *A Cultural History*

to place the middle finger against the thumb, extend the other three fingers, move the hand forward and wave it to the left and the right.[23]

Besides the gesture, the structure of the speech also follows rhetorical arrangement:[24] it begins with an exordium (16b) calling for the audience's attention and continues with a narration (17–25) reviewing the history of Israel from the choosing of the patriarchs until the prediction of John the Baptist. Paul then offers a proposition (26–33a) that the promise to the ancestors has been fulfilled in the gospel and[25] he presents proof (33b–37) from three verses. He concludes with an epilogue (38–41) summarizing his main point together with an exhortation.[26] Since Paul was acquainted with the rhetorical conventions of Roman society and was able to put them into effective practice,[27] there is good reason to suspect that other Jews – including Pharisees and rabbis – did so as well.[28] An overview of the settings and forms of rabbinic sermons will help identify these elements in their *derashot*.

While the Sabbath sermon originates in the Second Temple era, there is ample evidence that the rabbis continued to deliver Sabbath and festival sermons in subsequent centuries. The Yerushalmi reports

of Gesture, ed. J. Bremmer and H. Roodenburg (Ithaca: Cornell University Press, 1986): 36–58.

[23] Quintilian, *Institutes of Oratory*, 11.3.92, and cf. 11.3.158.

[24] See pp. 35–9.

[25] Quintilian, *Institutes of Oratory*, 4.5.22, writes that the tripartite partition "is not always necessary or even advantageous" and that a single clear proposition suffices to introduce the proof section.

[26] For rhetorical analysis of this chapter, see George A. Kennedy, *New Testament Interpretation through Rhetorical Criticism* (Chapel Hill: The University of North Carolina Press, 1984), 124–5; Lawrence Wills, "The Form of the Sermon in Hellenistic Judaism and Early Christianity," *Harvard Theological Review* 77 (1984): 278–9; Clifton Black, "The Rhetorical Form of the Hellenistic Jewish and Early Christian Sermon: A Response to Lawrence Wills," *Harvard Theological Review* 81, no. 1 (1988): 8–11; Black, *Rhetoric of the Gospel*, 125–7; and David Aune, ed. *The Westminster Dictionary of New Testament and Early Christian Literature and Rhetoric* (Louisville: Westminster John Knox Press, 2003), 219–21.

J. W. Bowker, "Speeches in Acts: A Study in Proem and Yelammedenu Form," *New Testament Studies* 14 (1967): 96–111, explores the possibility that this and other speeches in Acts conform to the proem and *yelamdenu* forms. However, he relies on the research of Jacob Mann, *The Bible as Read and Preached in the Old Synagogue* (Cincinnati: Mann-Sonne Publication Committee, 1940–66; repr., Ktav, 1970), which has been heavily criticized. See B. Z. Wacholder's "Prolegomenon" to the 1970 reprint of Mann and further references and discussion at Marc Bregman, "The Triennial Haftarot and the Perorations of the Midrashic Homilies," *Journal of Jewish Studies* 32 (1981): 74–84.

[27] See Ryan Schellenberg, *Rethinking Paul's Rhetorical Education: Comparative Rhetoric and 2 Corinthians 10-13* (Atlanta: Society of Biblical Literature, 2013).

[28] On the possibility of Paul studying rhetoric in Jerusalem, see p. 6 n. 23.

that "Maisha the grandson of R. Yehoshua ben Levi was carried in a litter to go up and preach in public on the Sabbath."[29] When R. Yohoshua met two of his students, he inquired, "Whose Sabbath was it?" That is, who lectured on the Sabbath in the *bet midrash* of Yavneh? They respond that R. Eleazar ben Azariah lectured and they proceed to recount his sermon.[30] Various sages are similarly reported as expounding on the Sabbath in synagogues or *batei midrash*.[31] In the Bavli, one type of public lecture, the *pirqa*, was given before *musaf* on Sabbath mornings[32] and festivals.[33] The *pirqa* included both halakhic and aggadic topics: "When R. Meir used to preach in his *pirqa*, he would preach one third halakha, one third aggadah, and one third parables."[34] While the *pirqa* was directed at a large lay audience,[35] students and fellow sages were also expected to attend and could face excommunication if they failed to show up without a good excuse.[36] Questions from the students interrupting the lecture were highly discouraged lest the rabbi get stumped and be embarrassed in front of his audience.[37]

Earlier twentieth-century historians assumed that the rabbis controlled the synagogues and maintained a strong influence on the Jewish populations of both Palestine and Babylonia.[38] More recent scholarship,

[29] Y. Beṣah 1:7, 60c. Polemo (c. 88–144 CE) also arrived to declaim in a litter; see Reader, *Severed Hand*, 19; and Russel, *Greek Declamation*, 81.

[30] See T. Soṭah 7:9–11. Similarly, Y. Soṭah 1:4, 16d, reports that R. Meir would expound in the synagogue on Friday nights and Y. Ḥagigah 2:1, 77b, states that R. Meir expounded in the study house of Tiberias on the Sabbath.

[31] Hezser, *Social Structure*, 208–9, 212–13; and Gil Hüttenmeister, "Bet ha-kneset u-vet ha-midrash veha-ziqah benehem," *Catehdra* 18 (1981): 38–44. See also p. 42 n. 7, for references to sermons that do not specify the day they are given but are also likely to have taken place on the Sabbath.

[32] B. Berakhot 28b clearly describes a *pirqa* given before *musaf*. Other sources show it was given on the Sabbath without specifying the exact time: B. Berakhot 6b, 30a; B. `Eruvin 36b, 44b; B. Yoma 78b, 84a = B. Abodah Zara 28a (according to some MSS); and see David Goodblatt, *Rabbinic Instruction in Sasanian Babylonia* (Leiden: Brill, 1975), 182–4.

[33] B. Yoma 77b. See Isaiah Gafni, "`Al derashot be-ṣibur be-Bavel ha-talmudit: ha-pirqa," in *Kneset Ezra: sifrut ve-ḥayim be-bet ha-keneset*, ed. Shulamit Elitzur et al. (Jerusalem: Yad Yitzḥak ben Zvi, 1994): 126.

[34] B. Sanhedrin 38b. MS Munich 95 switches the order of the first two sections. See also Goodblatt, *Rabbinic Instruction*, 177, who cites twelve *pirqa* references that include halakhic material and ten that discuss aggadic topics.

[35] B. Ḥulin 15a.

[36] B. Berakhot 28b; B. Shabbat 148a; and B. Yoma 78a. See Gafni, "`Al derashot be-ṣibur," 126–7.

[37] Ibid., 127.

[38] See Gedaliah Alon, *The Jews in Their Land in the Talmudic Age (70–640 C.E.)*, trans. Gershon Levi (Jerusalem: Magnes Press, 1984), 22, 28, 33, 232–7, and 249.

however, has challenged this assumption, based on archaeological findings of synagogue art that violates rabbinic halakha as well as the scant mention of rabbis in synagogue inscriptions.[39] While it is difficult to determine the extent of rabbinic influence beyond a core group of adherents to a broad Jewish populace, it is nevertheless evident that various rabbis regularly spoke to wide-ranging audiences in synagogues and other venues.[40] In any case, because this chapter will focus on the rhetorical style of the rabbis as reflected in their extant compositions – especially the works of midrash aggadah – it matters little whether these sermons were actually performed for large public audiences, spoken only to a cadre of students, or never performed at all. Since redactors necessarily have in mind some projected audience, we will analyze the rhetorical techniques employed in these texts to persuade those real or imagined auditors. By comparing the rabbis' use of rhetoric with that of their Roman counterparts, we will be able to assess the rabbinic self-perception about the art of rhetoric generally, its usefulness, and its problems. Considering that little evidence exists for Tannaitic *derashot*, the following discussion will focus on *derashot* from the amoraic period when the major works of midrash aggadah were compiled.

THE STRUCTURE OF RABBINIC DECLAMATION: THE PROEM FORM

The most important form of midrash aggadah, and therefore the best place to begin examining the structure of the sermon is the proem (Hebrew, *petiḥa*).[41] Classical works of aggadic midrash from the amoraic

[39] See Levine, *Ancient Synagogue*, 466–98; and Seth Schwartz, *Imperialism and Jewish Society, 200 B.C.E. to 640 C.E.* (Princeton: Princeton University Press, 2001), 103–76. Fine, *Art and Judaism*, 98, 120–1, on the other hand, argues that the rabbis were generally tolerant of synagogue mosaic art and that their attitudes were "conditioned by a deep understanding of the Roman world" (p. 120).

[40] See nn. 7 and 8.

[41] Academic scholarship generally calls this form a *petiḥa* (plural *petiḥot*, Aramaic *petiḥta*). However, this term is not used in Tannaitic or amoraic sources but rather first appears in headings of medieval manuscripts. See Paul Mandel, "`Al 'pataḥ' ve`al ha-petiḥah: `iyun ḥadash," in *Higayon le-Yonah* (Jerusalem: Magnes Press, 2006): 73–5. It is true that the proem form is often introduced with the phrase, "R. X *pataḥ*," and so "*petiḥa*" is not an incorrect designation as a noun form derived from the verb. Also, the noun פיתחא does occasionally appear, as in B. Megilah 11a and B. Makkot 10b. However, since this form of *derasha* occurs even more often without the introductory verb *pataḥ*, we have decided here to simply use the Greek-derived term "proem" in accordance with the rhetorical usage of this form, as we will discuss below. This follows the careful analysis of Burton Visotzky, "The Misnomers

period, such as Lamentations Rabbah and Pesikta d'Rav Kahana,[42] generally begin each chapter (*parasha/pisqa*) with a series of proems.[43] While some early scholars assumed that the more than two thousand proems recorded in works of midrash aggadah are transcripts of actual synagogue sermons,[44] most recent scholars agree that they are literary creations of rabbinic schools, even if some of them partially derive from oral performances.[45] Be that as it may, it is worthwhile analyzing the

'*Petihah*' and 'Homiletic Midrash' as Descriptions for Leviticus Rabbah and Pesikta De-Rav Kahana," *Jewish Studies Quarterly* 18 (2011): 19–31, who writes: "We must eschew calling the first part of each L[eviticus] R[abbah] chapter a *petihah*, it does behoove us to use the Hellenistic term 'proem' for this aggregate of textual materials" (p. 27).

42 Scholars divide aggadic collections of midrash into two types: exegetical and homiletic. Exegetical midrashim, such as Genesis Rabbah and Lamentations Rabbah, provide a running commentary on most of the biblical text without regard for building thematic connections from one gloss to the next. Homiletic midrashim, such as Lev Rabbah and Pesikta d'Rav Kahana, on the other hand, focus on only the first verse of each lectionary and often present a thematically unified set of proems and glosses on that verse; see Strack and Stemberger, *Introduction*, 276–314. More recently, scholars have questioned the usefulness of this division; see Günter Stemberger, "The Derashah in Rabbinic Times," in *Preaching in Judaism and Christianity: Encounters and Developments from Biblical Times to Modernity*, ed. Alexander Deeg, Walter Homolka, and Heinz-Gunther Schottler (Berlin: Walter de Gruyter, 2008): 18–20; Visotzky, "Misnomers," 22–4; and herein p. 52 n. 56.

43 Proems permeate amoraic midrashic works but are hardly found in Tannaitic literature. For the beginnings of the proem form in the Tannaitic period, see Heinemann, "Proem," 112–22.

44 Judah Theodor, "Zur Komposition der agadischen Homilien," *Monatschrift für Geschichte und Wissenschaft des Judenthums* 29 (1881). Mann, *Bible as Read*, 27, writes concerning a particular section of Tanḥuma that it was a record of an actual sermon, even if touched up by a copyist.

45 See Visotzky, "Misnomers," 19–31; Stemberger, "The Derashah in Rabbinic Times," 7–21; Porton, "Midrash and the Rabbinic Sermon," 461–82; Martin Jaffee, "The 'Midrashic' Proem: Towards the Description of Rabbinic Exegesis," in *Approaches to Ancient Judaism IV: Studies in Liturgy, Exegesis and Talmudic Narrative*, ed. William Scott Green (Chico, CA: Scholars Press, 1983): 95–112; Richard Sarason, "The Petiḥot in Leviticus Rabba: Oral Homilies or Redactional Constructions," *Journal of Jewish Studies* 33 (1982): 557–67; and Siegmund Maybaum, *Die ältesten Phasen in der Entwicklung der jüdischen Predigt* (Berlin, 1901). This view finds support in artificial proems that are reworked by an editor from earlier non-proem parallels; see Hanoch Albeck and Judah Theodor, *Midrash Bereshit Rabbah: Critical Edition with Notes and Commentary* (Jerusalem: Shalem Books, 1996), III.15–17.

For a middle position see Heinemann, "Proem," 100, who writes: "It appears that the compilers of the Midrashim used for each of their homilies a variety of actual sermons, fully or in part, and combined them into a new entity, which we may perhaps call 'the literary homily.'" See also Joseph Heinemann, "Ha-petiḥot be-midreshe aggadah: meqoran ve-tafqidan," *World Congress for Jewish Studies* 4, no. 2 (1969): 43–7; Joseph Heinemann, "The Amoraim of the Land of Israel as Artists of the Sermon," [Hebrew] *Hasifrut* 25 (1977): 69–79; Joseph Heinemann, "'Omanut ha-kompoziṣia

rhetoric of this form and the effect it would have on its audience, regardless of the exact setting.

The proem begins with a biblical verse – most often from Psalms or other wisdom books – and proceeds to expound upon that verse. The verse usually lacks an obvious connection to the Torah lectionary and thus raises the curiosity of the audience. The audience is kept in this state of suspense until the speaker finally manages to connect the opening verse with the first verse of the Torah lectionary, thus delivering his main point with a memorable punch line. A proem from Leviticus Rabbah on Leviticus 1:1 will serve as a representative example:

> R. Tanḥuma expounded (*pataḥ*):[46] "Gold is plentiful, jewels abundant, but wise speech is a precious object" (Prov 20:15). In the way of the world, a person who has gold, silver, precious stones, pearls, and every desirable good in the world but who has no knowledge, what benefit does he have? The proverb states: If you have knowledge, what do you lack? If you lack knowledge, what do you have? "Gold is plentiful": Everyone brought his gift of gold for the Tabernacle, as it is written, "This is the gift…" (Exod 25:3). "Jewels abundant": This is the gift of the chieftains, as it is written, "The chieftains brought" (Exod 35:27). "But wise speech is a precious object": Moshe's soul was grieved saying, "Everyone brought their gifts for the Tabernacle but I did not bring anything." So the Holy One, blessed be He, said to him, "By your life, your speech is more beloved to me than all of these." Know that this is so for out of all of them, Scripture only called Moses, as it is written, "He called to Moses" (Lev 1:1).[47]

R. Tanḥuma begins with a verse from Proverbs that seemingly has no connection to Leviticus 1:1. He then continues with a popular proverb on the superiority of knowledge, still without any connection to Leviticus 1:1 in sight. Next, the preacher proceeds to atomize the verse he cited, applying each phrase to the various donations given by the Israelites and their chieftains to the Tabernacle. This relates directly to the end of the book of Exodus, but the audience must be itching to find out

be-midrash Vayikra Rabbah," *Hasifrut* 2, no. 4 (1971): 808–43; Lieberman, *Greek in Jewish Palestine*, 59; Arnon Atzmon, "'The Same Fate Is in Store for the Righteous and the Wicked:' Form and Content in Midreshei Aggadah," *Journal for the Study of Judaism* 43 (2012): 58–77; and Arnoff, "Memory," 3–5 and 37–9.

46 Mandel, "'Al 'pataḥ,'" shows that the word *pataḥ* in the standard opening of proems should be translated as "expounded" not "began." See also herein n. 68.

47 Lev Rabbah 1:6.

how this could possibly bear upon the beginning of Leviticus. The speaker now brings into the picture Moses, who regrets that he did not have the opportunity to donate any materials to the Tabernacle. God's consolation brings us back to the opening of the proem on the superiority of knowledge over material objects. Yet, even at this point, the audience still waits in suspense for the relevance of this message to Leviticus 1:1. Only upon reaching the very last sentence, which highlights the significance of God calling out *only* to Moses, do we finally appreciate the artful steps the orator has taken in leading his audience to its final destination.

The format of the proem reveals two fundamental rabbinic assumptions about the nature of the Bible. First, as God's prophetic text, every letter and word of the Bible is omnisignificant,[48] thus prompting the midrashist to atomize verses down to their smallest components and derive a message from each part. Second, the entire Bible is a single harmonious expression of Divine will such that one verse can hyperlink to another "most disparate and seemingly unrelated verse in order to create new and overreaching nexuses of meaning."[49] This unity explains the particular sense of joy at successfully linking verses together from different sections of the Bible to thereby recreate a pristine revelatory experience. The midrash therefore praises the greatness of various rabbis who would "connect (*maḥriz*) Torah to the Prophets and the Prophets to the Hagiographa," thereby causing fire to burn around him and make the words of Torah "as joyous as they were on the day they were given at Mount Sinai."[50] This method likely serves as the basis for the proem form.[51]

The proem seems to have been the opening of the typical amoraic sermon.[52] Midrashic literature does not preserve any original verbatim

48 See James Kugel, *The Idea of Biblical Poetry: Parallelism and Its History* (Yale University Press: New Haven, 1981), 103–4.

49 Stern, *Midrash and Theory*, 29; and see Rachel Anisfeld, *Sustain Me with Raisin-Cakes: Pesikta deRav Kahana and the Popularization of Rabbinic Judaism* (Leiden: Brill, 2009), 110; and James Kugel, *The Bible As It Was* (Cambridge: Harvard University Press, 1997), 17–23.

50 Lev Rabbah 16:4, Song of Songs Rabbah 1:53; and Y. Ḥagigah 2:1, 77b. See further at Boyarin, *Intertextuality*, 109–10; and Arnoff, "Memory," 154–8.

51 For another theory, see Paul Mandel, "Midrashic Exegesis and Its Precedents in the Dead Sea Scrolls," *Dead Sea Discoveries* 8, no. 2 (2001): 163–8, who proposes that the proem form is a polemic against Christian *pesher*-like contemporizing interpretation. Even if there is some truth in Mandel's proposal about the origins of this form, the above explanation nevertheless represents what later rabbinic practitioners viewed as the theoretical basis for this technique.

52 See p. 54 n. 68.

orations,[53] but scholars have derived what the format of amoraic sermons might have looked like from the structure of each chapter of midrash aggadah. Each *parasha* of Leviticus Rabbah, for example, begins with a series of proems on the first verse of the lectionary, followed by exegetical glosses, the last of which usually ends on a messianic note or some message of consolation.[54] The exegetical commentaries in the center are often introduced in manuscripts with the word *gufa* (body), indicating that they are the body of the sermon.[55] The ending note of comfort or hope serves as a peroration or epilogue. Other works of midrash also typically, though not consistently, follow this tripartite structure.[56] The amoraic sermon in its literary form – most likely reflecting its original oral form as well – was thus fashioned as a well-structured oration with an exordium, a body of exegetical material, and a messianic epilogue.[57]

Burton Visotzky has previously compared the proem and *gufa* sections to Hellenistic writing. Specifically, he points to Lucian, a sophist and satirist who lived in the second century CE and was active in the Greek East. Lucian's essay, "How to Write History," criticizes the unsophisticated popularizing style of contemporary history writers; the

[53] See p. 60 for the most well-preserved complete, though not verbatim, *derashot* and further discussion at p. 83.

[54] See Mordechai Margulius, ed. *Midrash Vayikra Rabbah* (Jerusalem: Bet Midrash Le-Rabbanim Be-Amerika, 1993), vol. 5, ix–xii; and Heinemann, "'Omanut ha-kompozișia," 810. Burton Visotzky, *Golden Bells and Pomegranates: Studies in Midrash Leviticus Rabbah* (Tübingen: Mohr Siebeck, 2003), 20–1, estimates that almost half of the chapters in Lev Rabbah do not end on a peroration. He concludes that the peroration is therefore "not an essential feature of the chapter structure" (ibid., p. 24 n. 3). While it may not be essential, I think its presence in most of the chapters indicates that it is a typical part of the *derasha* (oral or literary) that for whatever reason was not always recorded.

[55] See Margulius, *Midrash Vayikra Rabbah*, vol. 5, x–xi; and Visotzky, *Golden Bells*, 28.

[56] Visotzky, "Misnomers," 29, calculates that roughly half of the chapters in Pesikta d'Rav Kahana include some type of peroration. Genesis Rabbah also begins almost every chapter with proems and continues with exegetical material, though it rarely includes a peroration. See Albeck and Theodor, *Bereshit Rabba*, III.11–19. Genesis Rabbah differs from the so-called homiletic midrashim in that only 25 percent of its material consists of proems, as opposed to 39 percent of Lev Rabbah (Visotzky, ibid., 28). See p. 49 nn. 42 and p. 55 n. 70.

[57] For more detailed analyses of the forms of homiletic midrashim, see Norman Cohen, "Structure and Editing in the Homiletic Midrashim," *AJS Review* 6 (1981); Arnold Goldberg, "Form-Analysis of Midrashic Literature as a Method of Description," *Journal of Jewish Studies* 36 (1985); and Doris Lenhard, *Die Rabbinische Homilie. Ein formanalytischer Index* (Frankfurt: Gesellschaft zur Förderung judaistischer Studien, 1998).

essay itself is a spoof of the idea that one could learn to write history from a list of rigid rules in a manual.[58] Despite its sarcastic tone, however, the essay accurately portrays a typical two-part structure: a proem that draws the interest of the audience, followed by the body, which narrates the events. Accordingly, Visotzky looks to Lucian's essay as a heuristic model for the proem and body in each chapter of midrash.[59] We can extend Visotzky's argument by noting that Lucian's structure is merely a subset of general rhetorical arrangement. Visotzky minimizes the importance of the messianic epilogues.[60] However, if we include that section and remind ourselves of the flexibility of classical arrangement,[61] then the tripartite structure of midrashic chapters emerges as standard Hellenistic oratory.[62] Indeed, in epideictic discourse, which is the most fitting label for most midrash aggadah,[63] the full arrangement is usually "severely truncated" to just "proem, amplified topics, [and] epilogue."[64]

We find a model for the structure of the midrashic proem in Greco-Roman rhetoric in the form of the exordium, the opening section of a declamation also known as the *prooimion* in Greek. Aristotle writes that the *prooimion* of epideictic speeches should begin with an unrelated subject and then transition into the main topic of the speech. He likens this to the *proaulion* of flute players who, "first playing whatever they

58 See Clare Rothschild, *Luke-Acts and the Rhetoric of History: An Investigation of Early Christian Historiography* (Tübingen: Mohr Siebeck, 2004), 81–6.

59 Visotzky, *Golden Bells*, 29.

60 See p. 52 n. 54.

61 On the optional nature of the partition, see p. 46 n. 25. Although there is no separate section for narration in these sermons, we might consider the Torah verses of the lectionary to be the narration. In fact, Aristotle, *On Rhetoric*, III.16.1, writes that in epideictic orations, the narration could be distributed among the parts of the proof. If so, the various exegetical comments that formed the body of the sermon could be considered the joint narration and proof. As for a section of disproof, Joseph Heinemann, "Profile of a Midrash: The Art of Composition in Leviticus Rabba," *Journal of the American Academy of Religion* 31 (1971): 149–50, notes that sometimes a single midrash will include complementary or even contradictory teachings in the spirit of "adducing forty-nine reasons for declaring a thing unclean and forty-nine for declaring it clean." Of course, the rabbinic homily need not conform exactly to rhetorical arrangement in order to have been recognized as an example of Greco-Roman oratory; after all, Greco-Roman declamations themselves often veered from the prescriptions of the rhetorical handbooks. See n. 64.

62 Edmund Stein, "Die homiletische Peroration im Midrasch," *Hebrew Union College Annual* 8–9 (1931–2): 353–71, notes the relationship between the midrashic peroration and classical rhetoric. Goldberg, "Form-Analysis," 162, objects to describing midrash in terms of rhetoric, but I do not think his concerns are relevant here.

63 The example cited on p. 50, Lev Rabbah 1:6, is part of a long praise of Moses.

64 Black, *Rhetoric of the Gospel*, 123. See also p. 38.

play well, lead into the opening note of the theme."[65] An example of this structure can be found in Dio Chrysostom's *Olympicus*, which opens with Dio comparing himself to an owl in contrast to showy sophists who are like peacocks. Only after a few paragraphs does Dio eventually land on his main theme: human understanding of divinity.[66] Quintilian similarly writes:

> In panegyrics, he [Aristotle] thinks that the exordium may be allowed the utmost latitude, since it is sometimes taken from something foreign to the subject, as Isocrates has taken his in his oration in praise of Helen, or from something bordering on the subject, as the same orator, in his *Panegyric*, complains that "more honor is paid to the good qualities of the body than to those of the mind," and as Gorgias, in his oration at the Olympic games, extols those who first instituted such meetings. Sallust, doubtless following the example of these orators, has commenced his histories of the Jugurthine War and the Conspiracy of Catiline with introductions having no relation to his narratives.[67]

Just as the *prooimion* would introduce the declamation with a foreign subject, so does the proem begin the amoraic sermon with a distant verse.[68] The recognition that the midrashic proem conforms to the Greco-Roman rhetorical *prooimion* may provide a key to discovering its function and placement. The majority of scholars since the nineteenth century agreed that the proem served to introduce the sermon, which would take place after the weekly lectionary.[69] This consensus view, however, could not easily explain the presence of multiple proems for the same verse within a single chapter. One would expect one short proem followed by a long body for each sermon.

[65] Aristotle, *On Rhetoric*, III.14.1. See also Quintilian, *Institutes of Oratory*, 4.1.1–3. On the relationship between rhetoric and music, see G. J. Buelow, "Rhetoric and Music," *The New Grove Dictionary of Music and Musicians* 15 (1980): 793–808.

[66] Kennedy, *New History*, 234–5.

[67] Quintilian, *Institutes of Oratory*, 3.8.9.

[68] This assessment of the proem as the opening of the sermon is not based on the verb *pataḥ*, which can sometimes mean to begin but in this context means to reveal, explain or expound; see p. 48 n. 41. Rather, it is the consistent placement of all proems at the beginning of each chapter of midrash that primarily underpins this theory – as well as the similarity between its structure and the Greek *prooemia*. Mandel, "ʿAl 'pataḥ,'" 72–3, comes to basically the same conclusion except that he places the *Sitz im Leben* of these *derashot* in the rabbinic study session rather than in the public sermon.

[69] Sarason, "Petihot in Leviticus Rabba," 557 n. 2, lists these scholars.

Instead, one finds that proems comprise almost half of the material in each chapter.[70] There is not nearly enough exegetical material in each chapter of Leviticus Rabbah to fill the body of every sermon that allegedly followed each proem. Judah Theodor, who assumed that the literary form of the midrashim accurately reflected their original oral presentations, proposed that the preacher would offer multiple proems in order to illuminate the subject from different angles.[71] In contrast, Siegmund Maybaum rejected the idea that the literary form was a transcript of an oral sermon and instead thought of each chapter as an anthology of many original sermons. In order to explain why there were so many proems but relatively little material for the body of each sermon, Maybaum assumed that the exegetical material was standardized and used repeatedly by orators whereas only the proem offered the orator the opportunity to practice his creativity.[72] Joseph Heinemann, in turn, thought it would be anti-climactic for a preacher to begin with a new and artful proem only to continue with the same old interpretive material that he had taught repeatedly before. Instead, Heinemann proposed that the proem was originally a short sermon in itself[73] that preceded the weekly lectionary.[74] Others, however, reject Heinemann's view because of the dearth of evidence that a sermon was delivered before the Torah reading.[75]

70 Visotzky, "Misnomers," 28, finds that 39 percent of the sub-units in Lev Rabbah and 44 percent of the sub-units in Pesikta d'Rav Kahana are proems. He further reports (*Golden Bells*, 29 n. 42) that the number of lines in each chapter of Lev Rabbah devoted to proems equals on average the number devoted to the body of the sermon.

71 Theodor, "Zur Komposition der agadischen Homilien," 505. Theodor seems not to have placed much trust in his own theory considering that he makes no mention of it in his later article, "Midrash Haggadah," *Jewish Encyclopedia* (1906), 8:553–4, where he writes: "In some homilies the proems are equal in length to the interpretations proper, while in others they are much longer. Even if the editors of the midrashim combined the proems of different authors from the various homilies they had at hand, it yet seems strange that they should have been able to select for each homily several proems, including some very long ones, while they could find only a limited number of interpretations to the lessons, these interpretations, furthermore, covering only a few verses. The disproportion between the proems and the interpretations has not yet been satisfactorily explained, in spite of various attempts to do so." See also Heinemann, "'Omanut ha-kompozișia," 809 n. 10, who notes that Jacob Mann also assumes that the preacher delivered multiple proems.

72 Maybaum, *Die ältesten Phasen*, 35–44.

73 For a list of all scholars who agree that the proem was a self-standing homily, see Sarason, "Petihot in Leviticus Rabba," 557 n. 2.

74 Heinemann, "*Proem*," 104–11. Heinemann also admits to the possibility that, at a later stage of development, proems were used as introductions for more complex sermons.

75 Peter Schäfer, "Die Peticha - ein Proömium?," *Kairos* 12 (1970): 216–19.

By situating the proem within the context of Greco-Roman rhetoric, we discover that the inclusion of multiple proems within one sermon may not have been so out of the ordinary after all. In fact, ancient rhetoricians prescribe that a declamation that includes several different arguments may be introduced by several *prooemia* corresponding to each argument. Anonymous Seguerianus, for example, writes: "Some have said that on the same hypothesis there can be both many *prooemia* and one *prooemion* ... When, then, they say the proofs are different, the *prooemia* will be multiple."[76] Sopatros (early third century CE), accordingly, included six in one of his speeches,[77] and Libanius regularly integrated multiple *prooemia* into his declamations.[78] Consequently, the many proems found in a given chapter of midrash may not be the result only of anthologizing multiple homilies.[79] Rather, a single homily may have included multiple proems in order to introduce multiple themes that would come up over the course of the sermon.[80]

For example, Pesikta d'Rav Kahana 2 focuses on the commandment in Exodus 30:11–16 to take a census of Israel through the contribution of the half-shekel. This homily contains two basic themes: (1) the giving of the half-shekel atones for the sin of the golden calf and (2) God loves Israel and makes minimal demands on them. As noted by Norman Cohen, the first theme is introduced in the first proem, which praises God for forgiving and lifting Israel after the sin of the golden calf.[81] The second proem relates to the second theme of God's love by contrasting Rome's harsh taxes with God's pleasantly worded decree. Interestingly, neither proem explicitly mentions the half-shekel or the counting of the people. The next three proems return to the first theme and the last

76 Apsines 1.14–15 similarly discusses in more detail how to include multiple *prooemia*. See Dilts and Kennedy, *Two Greek Rhetorical Treatises from the Roman Empire: Introduction, Text and Translation of the Arts of Rhetoric Attributed to Anonymous Segeurianus and to Apsines of Gadara*, 15 and 81.

77 Russel, *Greek Declamation*, 54, citing C. Walz, *Rhetores Graeci I–IX* (Stuttgart, 1832–6), 8.110–24, p. 33.

78 See Mikael Johansson, *Libanius' Declamations 9 and 10* (Göteborg: Acta Universitatis Gothoburgensis, 2006), 23. See also Kennedy, *New Testament Interpretation*, 117, who shows that Peter's speech in Acts 2 also includes two proems.

79 Interestingly, Visotzky, *Golden Bells*, 31–40, argues that the anthological character of Lev Rabbah itself follows "the tradition of hellenistic encyclopedic miscellanies" (p. 40).

80 For a related theory that multiple speakers would offer a series of proems before the chief homilist rose to offer the main body of the sermon, see Tzvi Novick, *Rabbinic Poetry: Late Antique Jewish Liturgical Poetry and Rabbinic Midrash* (Göttingen: Vandenhoeck & Ruprecht, forthcoming).

81 Cohen, "Structure and Editing," 7–12.

proem oscillates back to the message of the second proem. The exegetical section that forms the body of the homily then comments on each phrase of the opening verses, first relating to the theme of forgiveness and then on the theme of God's love for Israel. The two themes are finally brought together in the last section: God forgives Israel through the minimal demand of a half-shekel because he loves them.[82] In a live performance of this sermon, the preacher may have presented only a selection of the proems recorded here, but the inclusion of multiple proems would not be unusual in the context of classical oratory. On the contrary, this example underscores how multiple proems on different themes can be artfully woven together in the body of the sermon, enhancing its rhetorical power.

The major works of aggadic midrash should therefore be seen as anthologies of homiletic material arranged in sections following the structure of a typical sermon: proem, amplifying exegesis, and epilogue. Preachers may have presented only one proem on some occasions and multiple proems on other occasions. In either case, the editors of the midrashim would have found it natural to gather a series of proems at the beginning of each chapter, since live orations already incorporated this feature. The rabbinic sermon in amoraic times – and perhaps beforehand as well – thus consisted of a standard tripartite structure that parallels what a typical epideictic oration would have sounded like. The proems that opened the sermon functioned in a similar way to classical *prooemia* that would begin with a foreign topic and weave its way back to the primary theme. The midrashic proem became a focus for rabbinic creativity and skill, both in the speaker's ability to connect the opening proem verse with the lectionary verse as well as in integrating the proem theme with the exegetical body and peroration that would follow. Amoraic *derashot* surely had their own unique characteristics and internal development, but their basic structure and style would have fit right into their Greco-Roman context.

THE YELAMDENU FORM

Besides the proem, another common form of midrash aggadah is the *yelamdenu* opening. This form is found often in Midrash Tanḥuma in its various versions as well as in parts of other post-amoraic works such as Exodus Rabbah, Numbers Rabbah, Deuteronomy Rabbah, and Pesikta

[82] See ibid. I have changed what Cohen lists as the second theme to more accurately reflect the text of the midrash as I understand it.

Rabbati.[83] These midrashim typically open with the phrase "*yelamdenu rabbenu* – let our master teach us," followed by a legal question.[84] The answer that follows is generally a quote from a Mishnah or *baraita*. These questions are usually simple and easily answered, suggesting that this form was directed to a popular uneducated audience. Alternatively, the question may have been a necessary formal part of the structure that had to be included even when the answer was obvious.[85] The preacher would then transition from the legal answer to the subject of the lectionary and in this way the *yelamdenu* form parallels the exegetical proem form.[86] After the *yelamdenu* opening, each section of the Midrash Tanḥuma generally continues with other proems and exegetical material and concludes on a messianic note.[87] Like the proem, then, the *yelamdenu* form parallels the Greco-Roman *prooimion* in that it introduces the rest of the sermon by opening with a seemingly unrelated point about a detail of halakha before transitioning into the body of the sermon.[88]

Like other midrashim, it is difficult to assess the extent to which the homilies in Midrash Tanḥuma are literary creations or reflect live sermons. In either case, rabbinic sources indicate that a forum did exist in which students would ask legal questions to which the rabbi would respond.[89] While it is possible that these questions were sometimes planted beforehand,[90] it is evident that the format of such gatherings would call for the speaker to be able to answer the legal question and

[83] See Marc Bregman, "Tanhuma Yelamdenu," *Encycopaedia Judaica* (2007); Strack and Stemberger, *Introduction*, 304; and Hananel Mack, *The Aggadic Midrash Literature* (Tel-Aviv: MOD Books, 1989), 104–6.

[84] M. Stein, "Le-ḥeqer midreshe yelamdenu," in *Sefer ha-yovel li-khevod Professor Moshe Shor* (Warsaw: Ha-ḥevrah le-hafaṣat mada`e ha-Yahadut be-Polania, 1935): 89.

[85] Joseph Heinemann, *Derashot be-ṣibbur bi-tqufat ha-Talmud* (Jerusalem: Bialik Institute, 1970), 18; and Mack, *The Aggadic Midrash Literature*, 103.

[86] See Heinemann, *Derashot be-ṣibbur*, 17–18; and Allan Kensky, "New Light on Midrash Yelammedenu," *Shofar* 13, no. 3 (1995): 51. Some scholars call the *yelamdenu* form a halakhic *petiḥa* as opposed to the aggadic *petiḥot*. See, for example, Stein, "Le-ḥeqer midreshe yelamdenu," 98; and Mack, *The Aggadic Midrash Literature*, 101.

[87] Anat Raizel, *Mavo la-midrashim* (Alon Shevut: Tevunot – Mikhlelet Herzog, 2010), 237–8; and Strack and Stemberger, *Introduction*, 304–5.

[88] Stein, "Le-ḥeqer midreshe yelamdenu," 97, argues further that the *yelamdenu* form is Hellenistic in its use of questions and answers. For example, Philo composes an exegetical work in this format in his *Questions and Answers on Genesis*.

[89] See T. Berakhot 4:16 and Gen Rabbah 81:2 = Y. Yebamot 12:6, 13a.

[90] Mack, *The Aggadic Midrash Literature*, 103; and Stein, "Le-ḥeqer midreshe yelamdenu," 94–7. Interestingly, in T. Berakhot 4:16, R. Ṭarfon first asks his students a question and only then do they respond, "*yelamdenu rabbenu*."

compose a related homily on the spot.[91] Traveling preachers, likewise, needed the ability to extemporize on the spot since they did not always know beforehand where the congregation would begin their lectionary.[92]

As Avraham Epstein points out, the expectation that rabbis were able to improvise parallels the style of the contemporary Greek sophists who similarly delivered extemporized orations on a topic chosen by the audience.[93] To be sure, Aelius Aristides, the Roman orator, refused this challenge and even told Marcus Aurelius, "Propose the theme today and come hear it tomorrow. I am a perfecter of speeches, not a vomiter."[94] Nevertheless, aside from exceptions like this, the ability to improvise effortlessly was generally expected and most highly regarded.[95] When it comes to rabbinic literature, however, some midrashim warn preachers to thoroughly prepare their homilies[96] – despite the pressure to extemporize in some cases and the prestige one could receive by doing so. In fact, the rabbis prohibited audience members from asking questions not related to the subject matter at hand.[97] These sources prefer a well-thought-out response by someone engrossed in the topic over a show of ingenuity and quick wit. To the extent that the questions in the *yelamdenu* midrashim were literary additions or planted questions, this

[91] See Heinemann, *Derashot be-ṣibbur*, 19–20, who points to many *yelamdenu* midrashim wherein the question is connected only tenuously to the body of the sermon. In such cases, it is more likely that the rabbi did not know the question from beforehand.

[92] See, for example, Lev Rabbah 3:6. Traveling preachers are also mentioned in B. Shabbat 31b, 80b, 88a, B. Soṭah 40a, B. Baba Qama 52a, B. Sanhedrin 113a, and B. Makkot 23a. See also B. Sanhedrin 70a and B. Ḥulin 27b where עובר can either mean "an itinerant" or be the preacher's name, `Ubar. If the latter, it would indicate a non-rabbinic preacher. See Zechariah Frankel, *Mavo ha-Yerushalmi* (Breslau: Schletter, 1870), 51b; Marc Bregman, "The Darshan: Preacher and Teacher of Talmudic Times," *The Melton Journal* 14 (1982); and Hosea Rabinovits, "Ḥamesh derashotav shel ha-hu Gelila'a," *Hagige Giv`ah* 3 (1995): 53–64. See also M. Eruv 3:5 on sages who would visit a city on the Sabbath, presumably to preach, though this is not explicit.

[93] Abraham Epstein, *Miqadmoniot ha-Yehudim* (Jerusalem: Mosad Harav Kook, 1964), 59; and Epstein's letter in Eleazar ha-Levi Grinhut, *Sefer ha-liqutim: qoveṣ midrashim yeshanim u-ma'amarim shonim* (Jerusalem, 1967), 24–5. See also Reader, *Severed Hand*, 28.

[94] Translation from Whitmarsh, *The Second Sophistic*, 25. For more on Aristides, see Kennedy, *New History*, 239–41.

[95] See ibid.; Russel, *Greek Declamation*, 79–80; and Reader, *Severed Hand*, 28–9.

[96] Exod Rabbah 40:1. The embarrassment caused by a speaker not knowing the answer to his audience's questions is dramatized in Gen Rabbah 81:2 = Y. Yebamot 12:7, 13a, where Levi ben Sisi is appointed to be the rabbi of Simonia but forgets his learning when put on the spot and is forced to leave.

[97] T. Sanhedrin 7:7; and M. Avot 5:7.

form was produced only after careful preparation, even if it does portray itself as improvisation.[98]

Epstein further compares the rabbinic orators with the sophists in several other respects. The rabbis, for instance, often cited and repeated *derashot* of earlier rabbis, just as later sophists would perform orations of earlier orators. Additionally, rabbinic orators spoke in poetic Hebrew and refrained from using commonly spoken Aramaic, just as sophists imitated Attic Greek and were called Atticists for that reason.[99] Rabbinic sermons sought to grab the attention of the audience by asking questions such as, "Can this be?" and "What does this mean?" They utilized dialogic form and highly poetic style similar to that of the sophists.[100] These similarities indicate that Greco-Roman rhetorical methods greatly impacted rabbinic sermons. Epstein suggests that this influence occurred during the fifth century CE in Caesarea, where the Jews lived alongside Christian schools and academies of rhetoric.[101]

While scholars debate when the *yelamdenu* form first originated,[102] Bavli Shabbat 30a records a relatively early example of the use of a halakhic question to introduce an aggadic midrash. Unlike the typical *yalamdenu* form in which the halakhic question is answered immediately and only then followed by further homiletic material, in this example, the aggadic material precedes the answer and builds up to it. The sermon concludes with the response to the original question thus forming a halakhic inclusio around the aggadic center.[103] Scholars have singled out this pericope as the best candidate for an original complete sermon.[104]

[98] See Stein, "Le-ḥeqer midreshe yelamdenu," 97.

[99] This claim is partially contradicted by Marc Bregman, "Revadei yeṣirah va-`arikha be-midreshei Tanḥuma-yelamdenu," *Proceedings of the Tenth World Congress for Jewish Studies* C.1 (1990): 117–18, who shows that early versions of Tanḥuma midrashim in the Cairo Geniza do include Aramaic. On the other hand, this makes the shift to Hebrew in later versions all the more significant.

[100] Epstein, *Miqadmoniot ha-Yehudim*, 59–60. Epstein suggests further that the more complex forms of midrash represented in the *yelamdenu* midrashim derive from Caesarea where the influence of Greeks and Christians was greater. See also Wilhelm Bacher, *Agadat Amora'e Ereṣ Yisrael,* trans. A. Z. Rabinovits (Tel-Aviv: Dvir, 1930), 3.3, 118–20.

[101] While Epstein finds these parallels in the *yelamdenu* midrashim, much of the same applies to other midrashim as well.

[102] See Strack and Stemberger, *Introduction*, 305–6; and Marc Bregman, "Mesorot u-meqorot qedumim be-sifrut Tanḥuma-yelamdenu," *Tarbiz* 60 (1991): 269–74.

[103] This is similar to the structure of the Geonic genre of She'iltot; see Jason Rogoff, "The Compositional Art of the She'iltot of R. Aḥa: Creating a Babylonian Homiletic Midrash" (PhD diss., Jewish Theological Seminary of America, 2010), 2–4 and 67–70.

[104] Heinemann, *Derashot be-ṣibbur*, 18; and Heinemann, "Proem," 100 n. 2. David Rosental, "The Torah Reading in the Annual Cycle in the Land of Israel," [Hebrew]

For that reason, as well as for its structure and beauty, it deserves its own analysis.[105] This sermon conforms with the structure of rhetorical arrangement,[106] as indicated by the bracketed subheadings.[107]

[Narration]
This question was asked before R. Tanḥum of Newai: May one extinguish a lit lamp for a sick person on the Sabbath?

[Exordium]
He expounded (*pataḥ*) and said: You, Solomon, where is your knowledge? Where is your wisdom? Is it not enough that your words contradict those of David your father, but your words even contradict themselves!

[Partition]
[1] David your father said: "The dead cannot praise the Lord" (Ps 115:17).
[2] But you said: "I praise the dead who have already died" (Eccl 4:2).
[3] Then you went back and said: "Even a live dog is better than a dead lion" (Eccl 9:4).

[Proof]
This is not a difficulty.[108]

Tarbiz 53, no. 1 (1983): 146, also singles out B. Abodah Zarah 2a–3b (=Tanḥuma *Shoftim* 9) as a "seemingly complete *derasha*." The Buber edition is the shortest and perhaps most original version of this *derasha* and it follows a neat rhetorical structure, beginning with a question and followed by three challenges from the nations and God's response to each in turn. Marc Hirshman, *A Rivalry of Genius: Jewish and Christian Biblical Interpretation* (Albany: State University of New York Press, 1996), 76-81, cites instances of tannaitic sermons that feature a direct appeal to a specific audience and thus point to a live setting.

Yet another candidate for the oldest complete sermon is a Geniza fragment that consists of one folded sheet containing a single homily; see further at Marc Bregman, *The Tanhuma-Yalammedenu Literature: Studies in the Evolution of the Versions* (Piscataway, NJ: Gorgias Press, 2003), 72, 163–5 and 180. Bregman (p. 165) makes the important observation that many of the rhetorical elements preserved in this Geniza fragment disappear in later versions of the homily. This raises the distinct possibility that there were many more rhetorical techniques in sermons recorded in various works of midrash aggadah that have been lost irrecoverably without extant early fragments.

105 See also the analysis of Heinemann, *Derashot be-ṣibbur*, 52–4, who notes the "excellent rhetorical artistry" of this sermon.

106 See pp. 35–9.

107 B. Shabbat 30a–b. Translation follows Geniza fragment MS Friedberg 9-002 at the University of Toronto, unless otherwise noted. Only significant variants are pointed out.

108 MS Friedberg reads, "Rather, this is a difficulty." The translation follows all other MSS.

[1] That which David said, "The dead cannot praise the Lord": This is what he meant: a person should always engage in Torah and commandments before he dies, for once he dies he idles from Torah and commandments[109] and the Holy One, blessed be He, has no praise from him.[110] This is what R. Yoḥanan said:[111] What does this verse mean: "In death is freedom" (Ps 88:6)? Once a person dies, he becomes free from Torah and commandments.

[2]

[a] That which Solomon said, "I praise the dead who have already died": When Israel sinned in the desert, Moses stood before the Holy One, blessed be He, and recited many prayers and supplication before Him but he was not answered. But when he said, "Remember Abraham, Isaac, and Israel" (Exod 32:13), he was immediately answered. Has Solomon not said correctly, "I praise the dead who have already died"?

[b] Another interpretation:[112] In the way of the world, when a king[113] of flesh and blood issues a decree, it is doubtful whether people will fulfill it or not. And even if you wish to say that they fulfill it during his lifetime, once he dies they do not fulfill it. However, Moses, our rabbi, issued many decrees and made many enactments on his own[114] and they remain in force forever. Has Solomon not said correctly, "I praise the dead who have already died"?

[c] Another interpretation: "I praise the dead..." As Rav Yehuda said in the name of Rav, for Rav Yehuda said in the name of Rav, what does the verse mean, "Show me a sign of Your favor..." (Ps 86:17)? David said before the Holy One, blessed be He: "Master of the World, forgive me for that sin." He replied, "You are forgiven." He said to Him, "Show me a sign of Your favor."[115] He replied, "I will not make it known during your lifetime; I will make it

109 MS Friedberg omits from here to "commandments" at the end of the paragraph due to homoioteleuton. I have included it based on all other MSS.

110 See parallel at Pesikta Rabbati, *hosafah* 1:3.

111 This statement is found in Y. Kilayim 9:3, 32a = Y. Ketubot 12:3, 34d. It is there stated anonymously but the Bavli often attributes traditions from Palestine to R. Yoḥanan as he is the most prominent sage there.

112 MS Friedberg reads, "For he said," which is a mistaken expansion of the abbreviation ד"א. The translation follows all other MSS.

113 Printed editions read, "officer."

114 Printed editions lack, "on his own."

115 Printed editions read, "in my lifetime."

known during the life of your son Solomon." When Solomon built the Temple and he wanted to bring the Ark into the innermost chamber,[116] the gates stuck together. Solomon recited twenty-four prayers but he was not answered ... Once he said, "Lord, God, do not reject your anointed one; remember the loyalty of Your servant David" (2 Chronicles 6:42), he was immediately answered ... Has Solomon not said correctly, "I praise the dead..."?

[3] That which Solomon said: "Even a live dog is better than a dead lion": As Rav Yehuda said,[117] for Rav Yehuda said in the name of Rav, what does the verse mean, "Tell me, O Lord, when my end is..." (Ps 39:5). David said before the Holy One, blessed be He: "Master of the World, tell me God my end." The Holy One, blessed be He, replied, "There is a decree before me that we do not make known the end of flesh and blood." [David said,] "What is the measure of my days?" (ibid.) [He replied,] "There is a decree before me that we do not make known the measure of days of humans." [David said,] "Let me know how fleeting my life is" (ibid.). He replied, "You will die[118] on the Sabbath." [David said,] "Let me die on Sunday." [He replied,] "The kingdom of Solomon your son has already come and no kingdom can touch the next one even so much as a hairbreadth." [David said,] "Let me die before the Sabbath." He replied, "'Better is one day in your courts than a thousand' (Ps 84:11). Better to me is one day of you engaging in Torah before me than a thousand burnt offerings that Solomon your son will sacrifice upon the altar."

Every Sabbath day from then on, [David] would sit and recite [Torah] all day long. On that Sabbath day that his soul was destined to rest (*menaḥ*), the angel of death came and stood before him but was unable to [kill] him because he did not cease from recitation.[119] There was a garden behind his [David's] house. He [the angel of death] made a noise among the trees.[120] David said, "Let me go

116 Also Cambridge T-S NS 161.172, and Munich 95. Printed editions and MS Oxford Opp. Add. fol. 23 read, "Holy of Holies."

117 MSS Friedberg and Cambridge T-S NS 161.172 lack, "in the name of Rav," as present in printed editions and MSS Munich 95, and Oxford Opp. Add. fol. 23.

118 MS Friedberg lacks, "You will die," but it appears in all other MSS.

119 Printed editions and MSS Munich 95, and Vatican 127 add: "He [the angel of death] said, 'What can I do to him?'"

120 Also MS Oxford Opp. Add. fol. 23. Printed editions and MSS Munich 95 and Vatican 127 read instead, "[The angel of death] came and was shaking the trees."

> out to see what this is."[121] He was climbing up the step, the step fell from under him, he went silent,[122] and his soul rested (*naḥ*).
>
> Solomon sent to the House of Study, "My father died and is lying in the sun and the dogs of my father's house are hungry. What should I do?" They sent to him, "Cut up a dead animal and leave (*hanaḥ*) it for the dogs. As for your father, place (*hanaḥ*) a loaf of bread or a baby on him and carry him." Has Solomon not said correctly, "Even a live dog is better than a dead lion"
>
> **[Epilogue]**
> Regarding the question that I asked you,[123] a lamp is called a lamp and the soul of a person is called a lamp. It is better that the lamp of flesh and blood should be extinguished before the lamp of the Holy One blessed be He.

The audience asks whether one may extinguish a lamp on the Sabbath in order to allow a sick person to rest and thereby save his life.[124] Historically, this was an important issue since Second Temple period sects prohibited violation of the Sabbath even to save a life. For example, some Jews at the time of the Maccabees chose to be killed by the Seleucids rather than take up arms to defend themselves on the Sabbath.[125] However, by the time of R. Tanḥum in the fourth century CE,[126] violating the Sabbath to save a life would have been permitted by all rabbinic opinions and obvious to the audience.[127] Nevertheless,

[121] Also MS Oxford Opp. Add. fol. 23. Printed editions and MSS Munich 95 and Vatican 127 read instead, "He went out to see."

[122] He stopped reciting Torah.

[123] As a gesture of modesty, R. Tanḥum places himself in the position of questioner before his audience even though it was they who asked him the question.

[124] The assumption that this question deals with a sick person in danger of dying derives from the answer, which contrasts life with death. See also Rabbenu Ḥananel *ad loc.* Extinguishing a lamp for a sick person who is not in danger of dying, by contrast, would depend on whether extinguishing a flame not for the sake of preparing the wick but only because one wants it to be dark is considered a biblical violation (R. Yehuda's opinion) or only a rabbinic violation (R. Shimon); see M. Shabbat 2:5.

[125] See 1 Maccabees 2:32–41; Jubilees 50:12; Shlomo Goren, *Torat ha-Shabbat veha-mo`ed* (Jerusalem: Ha-histadrut ha-Zionit ha-`Olamit, 1982), 36–105; Shmuel Safrai, ed. *The Literature of the Sages, Part One* (Philadelphia Fortress Press, 1987), 144–5; and Shmuel Safrai and Ze'ev Safrai, *Mishnat Eretz Israel* (Jerusalem: E.M. Liphshitz College Publishing House, 2008), Shabbat, 1:21–22, and further references there.

[126] Bacher, *Agadat Amora'e Ereṣ Yisrael*, 3.3, 116, argues that R. Tanḥum of Newai is the same person as the famous *darshan* R. Tanḥuma bar Abba.

[127] Josephus, Antiquities 15:63. T. `Eruvin 3:5–7.

R. Tanḥum responds to (and perhaps even plants) this simple question as a means to explore the value of life and death in general.

If we place this *derasha* within the genre of judicial oratory, then the opening question would be the narration, which retells the case that the speaker will discuss. However, since the audience has already posed the question, the orator does not need to restate it. Quintilian in fact writes that the narration may be omitted when the audience is already acquainted with the case.[128] R. Tanḥum's sermon begins with an exordium, whose goal in general is to make the auditor "well-disposed, attentive, and receptive."[129] In this case, R. Tanḥum grabs the attention of the audience with a striking – even blasphemous – indictment against Solomon's wisdom and a charge that he contradicts his father and himself. Quintilian states that the exordium commonly attacks the adversarial party and so this opening indictment fits standard judicial oratory.[130] While it is far from obvious at this point how Solomon can fulfill the role of the adversarial party regarding a question of ritual Sabbath law, this divergence from the expected pattern itself arouses the curiosity of the audience. By the end of the *derasha*, the connection between the halakhic and aggadic portions of this midrash will eventually become clear.

Following the exordium, R. Tanḥum cites three verses that illustrate how Solomon contradicts both his father and himself. These three verses will each be subject to its own treatment in the body of the sermon and so this section serves as a partition – introducing the three parts of the proof to follow.

The body of the sermon does not actually prove the opening accusation to be true, as we might expect in a typical judicial oration. Rather, it shows that Solomon did not contradict himself or his father but actually spoke with subtlety and deep wisdom. Once again, this sermon follows common rhetorical arrangement but also deviates from it, thereby increasing the interest and satisfaction of the listener who is now relieved to hear that the tension between Solomon and David has been resolved.[131] R. Tanḥum explains that when David said, "The dead cannot praise the Lord," the praise refers not to prayer, as we might expect,[132] but rather to the praise God receives when a person studies Torah and fulfills its commandments. This theme will reappear in part [3].

[128] Quintilian, *Institutes of Oratory*, 4.2.5.

[129] Cicero, *On Invention*, I.20. See herein p. 36.

[130] Quintilian, *Institutes of Oratory*, 4.1.14.

[131] See discussion of form criticism at Robert Alter, *The Art of Biblical Narrative* (New York: Basic Books, 1981), 47–62.

[132] See Midrash Tehillim, 146.

Part [2] deals with the most problematic verse, which praises the dead over the living. Three solutions are provided, each of which concludes with the refrain, "Has Solomon not said correctly…" Solution [a] explains that the dead refers to the forefathers whose merit pacifies God in contrast to Moses whose prayers were ineffectual even during his lifetime.[133] Solution [b], in turn, praises Moses, whose decrees remained in effect even after his death. Solution [c] repeats the theme of solution [a] but here it is Solomon whose repeated prayers are ineffective; by contrast, God responds only to the invocation of Solomon's dead father, David.

Part [3] explains that the dead lion of Ecclesiastes 9:4 refers to David while the live dogs refer to the palace dogs who are about to eat David's carcass. The sages of the house of study permit Solomon to handle animal carcasses for the purpose of feeding the live dogs but would not permit him to violate the rabbinic prohibition of *muqṣe*[134] in order to handle David's body to keep it from decay. Only by discovering a loophole – placing a permitted item on top of the body, and handling the body as a basis for the permitted item – did the sages permit moving the body. The story leading up to this conclusion artistically picks up on elements from each of the previous sections. Part [1] focused on the inability of the dead to learn Torah, which becomes a central theme in part [3], thus creating a chiasm. First, God does not allow David to die on Friday because each day of his learning Torah is better than Solomon's sacrificial offerings.[135] Then, it is the power of Torah study that protects David from the grasp of the angel of death.[136] The theme of prayers going

[133] Roman rhetoricians also invoked the deeds of one's ancestors in defending litigants; see Mason, *Flavius Josephus: Translation and Commentary, Volume 9: Life of Josephus*, xxxix, citing James May, *Trials of Character: The Eloquence of Ciceronian Ethos* (Chapel Hill: University of North Carolina Press, 1988), 6–7.

[134] *Muqṣeh* refers to a set of vessels and items that are "set aside" and may not be moved on the Sabbath because they have no use. See further at Richard Hidary, "'One May Come to Repair Musical Instruments': Rabbinic Authority and the History of the Shevut Laws," *Jewish Studies, an Internet Journal* 13 (2015): 4 n. 21.

[135] On comparative statements in rabbinic literature arguing for the supremacy of Torah over priestly rituals, see Richard Hidary, "The Rhetoric of Rabbinic Authority: Making the Transition from Priest to Sage," in *Jewish Rhetorics: History, Theory, Practice*, ed. Michael Bernard-Donals and Janice Fernheimer (Lebanon, NH: Brandeis University Press, 2014): 16–45. As noted above, part [1] substitutes the praise mentioned in the verse with Torah study and fulfillment of commandments, which emphasizes the value of Torah over prayer or sacrificial service. In part [3] also, Solomon, the builder of the Temple, must go to the house of study to inquire about the law while David is portrayed as himself a Torah scholar.

[136] On the symbolism of the circumstances of David's death, see Boaz Spiegel, "Madua` ni`nea` mal'akh ha-mavet et ha-'ilanot bi-ftirat David ha-melekh," *Shma`tin* 150 (2003): 286–311.

unanswered in [2][a] and [c] repeats here with the refusal of David's request to know the date of his death. Part [2][c] and part [3], besides both being statements of Rav Yehuda in the name of Rav, also both discuss the transition from David to Solomon: in [c] a sign of forgiveness for David's sin with Bathsheba cannot come in his lifetime but must wait until Solomon builds the Temple; in part [3], God cannot delay David's death to Sunday because that would impinge on Solomon's reign. Finally, the theme of issuing decrees that remain in effect from [b] above appears again here in God's response that there is a decree prohibiting the revelation of the date of one's death. Part [3] ends with the same refrain as part [2], "Has Solomon not said correctly…."

The epilogue returns to the opening question of the audience, who now realize the relevance of the intervening discussion to their query. Both David and Solomon have taught us that life is preferable to death because only the living can learn Torah and perform commandments. Although it is true that the merit of the dead surpasses that of the living, that merit is only earned through the Torah study and good deeds performed while alive. Given the great value of life, the sermon builds the case that saving a life is more important than refraining from a violation of the Sabbath. The audience members asking a question of R. Tanḥum are themselves represented in the sermon by Solomon who sends a question to the house of study. The house of study responds that the sanctity of the Sabbath outplays the honor due to a dead body; however, the needs of a live being, even a dog, trump the sanctity of the Sabbath. In short, there is no glory in death because only one who is alive can study Torah and serve God. This response, in turn, paves the way for the final answer: one may, and even must, violate the sanctity of the Sabbath by extinguishing the lamp (the human lamp) in order to save a human life (God's lamp).

This analysis shows R. Tanḥum to be a skilled rhetorician who not only mastered the ability to weave together a complex, artful, and engrossing oration on the model of Greco-Roman arrangement but was also able to do so spontaneously in response to an audience-generated (or planted) question. While this Talmudic text is a contender for the oldest recorded rabbinic sermon, there is another text that has been nominated to be the oldest aggadic midrash – the Passover Haggadah.[137] The next section argues that the Passover liturgy also fits the pattern of classical rhetorical structure.

137 See Louis Finkelstein, "The Oldest Midrash: Pre-Rabbinic Ideals and Teachings in the Passover Haggadah," *Harvard Theological Review* 31, no. 4 (1938): 291–317.

THE PASSOVER HAGGADAH

Mishnah Pesaḥim 10 details the ceremony and liturgy of the Passover meal, which scholars have compared with the Roman symposium. A classic description of a symposium comes from Plato's dialogue by that name: "Socrates took his seat after that and had his meal, according to Aristodemus. When dinner was over, they poured a libation to the god, sang a hymn, and – in short – followed the whole ritual. They then turned their attention to drinking. At that point Pausanias addressed the group."[138] Both the Roman symposium and the Passover meal, Barukh Bokser observes, include "the use of waiters to bring in the food, reclining at the meal, dipping the food, *hors d'oeuvres*, the use of wine before, during, and after the meal, being festive, the pedagogic use of questions and intellectual discussion, singing and praise to God, and games to keep children awake."[139] As Siegfried Stein points out, the participants at the symposium would offer speeches after the meal in response to introductory questions and the theme of the conversation sometimes revolved around the food that was served.[140] While both scholars add that the rabbis took great care to differentiate the Passover meal from some of the more frivolous and indulgent aspects of the symposium, there is no doubt as to the strong affinity between the two ceremonies.[141] It is thus fitting to analyze the discussion that dominates the ceremony against the background of classical rhetoric. Mishnah Pesaḥim 10:4–10 outlines the oration that accompanies the second cup of wine:[142]

> **[Exordium]**
> They pour for him the second cup and here the child asks. If the child has no understanding, then his father teaches him: "What is different about this night from all other nights:

[138] John Cooper, ed. *Plato: Complete Works* (Indianapolis: Hacket Publishing, 1997), *Symposium* 176a.

[139] Baruch Bokser, *The Origins of the Seder: The Passover Rite and Early Rabbinic Judaism* (Berkley: University of California Press, 1984), 52. I have omitted Bokser's sources and his enumeration.

[140] Siegfried Stein, "The Influence of Symposia Literature on the Literary Form of the Pesaḥ Haggadah," *Journal of Jewish Studies* 8 (1957): 32–3; and Joseph Tabory, *JPS Commentary on the Haggadah: Historical Introduction, Translation, and Commentary* (Philadelphia: The Jewish Publication Society, 2008), 7 and 14.

[141] See Bokser, *Origins*, 62–6.

[142] Follows MS Kaufman. Translation follows the preferred explanation of Richard Steiner, "On the Original Structure and Meaning of *Mah Nishtannah* and the History of Its Reinterpretation," *Jewish Studies, an Internet Journal* 7 (2008): 163–204.

[a] "that on all other nights we dip only once[143] but on this night twice;
[b] "that on all other nights we eat leavened bread and unleavened bread but on this night it is all unleavened bread;
[c] "that on all other nights we eat broiled, boiled, or cooked [meat] but on this night it is all broiled?"

[Narration]
According to the understanding of the son does the father teach him. He begins with disgrace and concludes with praise and he expounds from "My father was a wandering Aramean" (Deut 26:5) until he finishes the entire pericope.

[Partition]
Rabban Gamaliel says: Whoever did not explain these three things on Passover has not fulfilled his obligation: [a] Passover, [b] unleavened bread, and [c] bitter herbs.

[Confirmation]
[a] Passover – because the Omnipresent passed over the houses of our forefathers in Egypt.
[c] Bitter herbs – because the Egyptians made the lives of our forefathers bitter.
[b] Unleavened bread – because they were redeemed.

[Epilogue]
Therefore we are obliged to thank, laud, praise, glorify, exalt, and extol He who has done for us and for our forefathers all of these miracles and has released us from slavery to freedom and we will recite before Him, "Haleluyah."

The final word "Haleluyah" introduces the recitation of the Hallel at Psalms 113–18. Hallel, which concludes the Mishnaic Haggadah,[144] is actually the earliest component of the Passover liturgy, having been recited to accompany the preparation and consumption of the Passover sacrifice.[145] Everything else in the Haggadah progressively and artfully builds up the feeling of gratitude among the participants in order to

143 Following MS Parma.

144 The liturgy of the Passover symposium is not called the Haggadah until amoraic times (B. Pesahim 115b), but I use the term here anachronistically for convenience and as an application of Exodus 13:8.

145 M. Pesaḥim 5:7 and 9:3. Philo, *The Special Laws*, II.138 in *The Works of Philo: Complete and Unabridged*, describes his contemporary Jews gathering in houses to

prepare them to sing the Hallel with a full heart. In fact, I contend that the creators of the Mishnaic Haggadah structured it as a work of Greco-Roman rhetorical oratory, the most common and effective means of persuasion available in their culture, precisely in order to achieve this liturgical goal. Through a combination of *logos* (the telling of the history of the Exodus and the expounding of verses), *pathos* (feeling the suffering of slavery and the joy of redemption), and *ethos* (citations from the Bible and from sages like Rabban Gamaliel),[146] the audience experiences the magnitude of the Exodus at a personal level and so cannot help but break into a song of gratitude.

The Haggadah proceeds step by step through a deliberate rhetorical plan. It opens with questions in an effort to involve and raise the curiosity of the children – "here the child asks."[147] However, the Talmud also teaches: "The rabbis have taught: If his son is a sage, he [the son] asks him [the father]. If he is not a sage, then his wife asks him. If not, he asks himself. Even two sages who know the laws of Passover must ask each other."[148] In other words, opening questions constitute a formal requirement of the Haggadah that one must recite even if all present are sages. I propose that the opening section of questions not only parallels the symposium, but further that the Haggadah is an early form of a *yelamdenu* midrash that must begin with questions from the audience. As discussed above, in both Greco-Roman and Jewish contexts these questions would sometimes be planted in advance. Here too, the child would ideally present questions on his own and only if he did not ask does the father teach him what to ask.[149] Opening with an audience question also serves, as in this case, to involve the listeners and motivate them to pay attention to the answer. An audience will be more interested and inclined to hear the speaker out if they themselves asked the

feast on the Passover sacrifices while reciting prayers and Hallel. See Stein, "Influence of Symposia," 21.

146 On pathos and ethos, see Quintilian, *Institutes of Oratory*, 6.2.8–17.

147 B. Pesaḥim 115b relates that when Abaye was sitting before Rava and saw the table being taken away, he asked, "Have we already eaten?" Rava responded, "You have exempted us from reciting, 'How is this night different.'"

148 B. Pesaḥim 116a.

149 It would make the most sense to expect the child to ask questions if this discussion took place after the meal – as was the order in Roman symposia – and the child had already witnessed these curious activities. See Tabory, *JPS Commentary on the Haggadah*, 10–11. Unlike the modern Seder where the discussion precedes the meal, the Mishnah dictates that the food is served and presumably eaten before the discussion. On the other hand, if the Tannaitic order did have the discussion first, then it would be more understandable why the child would have to be taught to ask about the foods that have not yet been eaten.

question in the first place. In the Haggadah, these questions, whether asked by the child or prompted by the father, thus serve the purpose of the exordium.

While modern Haggadot include four questions, the Haggadah found in Mishnah manuscripts, the Yerushalmi and the Cairo Geniza list only three.[150] Since Jewish law requires that the Passover sacrifice be roasted, the original Haggadah includes a question [c] about why the participants eat only roasted meat on this night. This question would have been relevant during the Second Temple period and for some time afterwards when people still retained the practice of eating roasted meat.[151] However, by the Geonic era, this practice had been stamped out and the question was therefore dropped.[152] Regarding the first question [a], people in Roman times generally dipped vegetables before the meal and so this query wonders why on this night they also dipped the *maror* after the meal began. In the original Haggadah as preserved in Mishnah manuscripts, the question about dipping twice would have clearly referred to the dipping of the *maror*. However, once the common practice of dipping before the meal ceased, this question was changed to: "On all other nights we do not dip even once." Because the question now concentrated on the act of dipping itself, it became less obvious that the question concerned the eating of the *maror*. Therefore, a new question was added about why *maror* is eaten on this night.[153]

In Talmudic times, after the children had asked the question, the patriarch, sage, or father of the household would deliver the rest of the Haggadah to all present.[154] The patriarch's presentation accords with

[150] Y. Pesaḥim 10:4, 37b; E. D. Goldschmidt, *Haggadah shel Pesaḥ: meqoroteha vetoldoteha* (Jerusalem: Mosad Bialik, 1969), 10–13; and see Jay Rovner, "An Early Passover Haggadah according to the Palestinian Rite," *Jewish Quarterly Review* 90, no. 3/4 (2000): 350–1.

[151] Bokser, *Origins*, 101–6. Robert Brody, *The Geonim of Babylonia and the Shaping of Medieval Jewish Culture* (New Haven and London: Yale University Press, 1998), 204–5.

[152] As a replacement for the question about roasted meat, Haggadot from the Geonic period ask why only on this night do we eat while reclining. In Roman times, when reclining was the common position for formal dining, this question could not have been asked and so must have been added later. See Tabory, *JPS Commentary on the Haggadah*, 29–30.

[153] See ibid., 29; and Menachem Kasher, *Haggadah shelemah* (Jerusalem: Makhon Torah Shelemah, 1967), 112–16.

[154] This is evident from B. Pesaḥim 116b: "Meremar said, I asked the sages of the house of Rav Yosef, 'Who recites the Haggadah in the house of Rav Yosef?' They said, 'Rav Yosef.' 'Who recites the Haggadah in the house of Rav Sheshet?' They said, 'Rav Sheshet.'"

the structure of Greco-Roman oratory by opening with a narration of past events. The Mishnah provides two guidelines for how to retell this narrative: the patriarch should speak on a level that the child understands, and he should begin by recounting the shame of Israelite bondage and conclude by acclaiming the glory of their redemption. Since the goal of the oration is to bring the audience to heartfelt gratitude and praise, it is essential that he speak at their level. Furthermore, the audience must first empathize with the suffering of their ancestors in order to better appreciate the grandeur of their redemption. Stein notes that this formula accords with the elements "praise and blame" that comprise epideictic orations wherein one recounts a person's humble beginnings in order to highlight their achievement.[155]

The Mishnah then points to Deuteronomy 26:5–10 as the text that fulfills these very requirements.[156] Since every farmer bringing first fruits to the Temple recited this text, it would have been well known and easily repeated by heart. According to the Mishnah, one should expound this text with midrashic commentary and Scriptural cross references such that this simple text could be taught to a small child or explored in depth for the benefit of advanced sages. The text reviews the entire history of the nation from the time of the forefathers who had no homeland or national identity, through the period of slavery and redemption from Egypt, until the day when the farmer comes to live securely in Israel on his productive land. This text and its midrashic exposition makes up the narration section of the oration.

Following the narration section comes a pronouncement by Rabban Gamaliel that one must discuss three food items, which he first enumerates and then explains.[157] These three food items remind the participants

[155] Stein, "Influence of Symposia," 36–7; and Quintilian, *Institutes of Oratory*, 4.3.9–12. Stein also proposes Greco-Roman parallels to other parts of the Haggadah that are not found in the Mishnah. However, those sections are later additions that do not necessarily conform to the Mishnah's original structure, and so I have focused only on the Mishnaic liturgy for its structure and rhetorical effect. See also Furstenberg, "The 'Agon' with Moses and Homer," 324.

[156] Tabory, *JPS Commentary on the Haggadah*, 33–7. By amoraic times, Rav and Samuel had introduced two other texts to fulfill the requirement of starting with shame and ending with glory (ibid., 32).

[157] Rabban Gamaliel may have stated this pronouncement independently from the order of the Haggadah as set forth in the Mishnah. Even if that is the case, however, once his statement became incorporated into the Haggadah, it could serve as the partition and confirmation when combined with the rest of the orational elements. See also Israel Yuval, "Easter and Passover as Early Jewish Christian Dialogue," in *Passover and Easter: Origin and History to Modern Times*, ed. Paul F. Bradshaw and Lawrence A. Hoffman (Notre Dame: University of Notre Dame Press, 1999): 106–7, who reads

of three distinct historical events: the Egyptian enslavement of the Israelites, God's protection of the Israelites and punishment of the Egyptians, and God's redemption of the Israelites. Each of these experiences contributes to the final point of the Haggadah, i.e., that we ought to praise God for His deliverance. Rabban Gamaliel's three subjects parallel the three questions that begin the Haggadah and provide the response to them.[158] The intervening narration fills in the background needed to make these three points effectively. The enumeration, "Passover, unleavened bread, and bitter herbs," serves as a partition that introduces the three points that are then elaborated upon to form the confirmation for the oration.[159] Confirmation sections, in fact, typically consist of three points.[160] While the Mishnaic gloss on each item is rather short, each explanation might have served only as a talking point upon which the live presenter would have elaborated for many minutes.[161] In any case, once the patriarch effectively convinces his audience of the greatness of God's redemption of the Israelites, he can then move into the peroration calling upon those assembled to break into a heartfelt Hallel. And so, although the style of this oration and so much of the ceremony of the night appears just like any other Roman drinking party, its content and goal make this symposium very different from all other symposia.

CONCLUSION

The major forms of the rabbinic sermon as recorded in amoraic midrashim – both their overall tripartite structures, and the proem and *yelamdenu* openings – parallel similar structures set forth in classical rhetorical handbooks and practiced in Greek orations. Furthermore, a couple of the oldest *derashot* follow a more complete rubric of classical

Rabban Gamaliel's requirement as a counter to early Christians who imbued these three foods with Christological symbolism.

158 Shmuel Safrai and Ze'ev Safrai, *Hagadat Ḥazal* (Jerusalem: Karta, 1998), 26–7; and Tabory, *JPS Commentary on the Haggadah*, 14.

159 The order of the partition differs from the order of the confirmation in MSS Kaufman and Parma and Geniza fragments T-S E1.57 and T-S E2.53. (All are equivalent to MS Kaufman as translated above.) It seems that the partition follows the order of appearance in Num 9:10–11. In the confirmation, perhaps in order not to end on a bitter note, the bitter herbs are placed in the middle, and the redemption, symbolized by the unleavened bread, is saved for the end. In printed editions, the confirmation follows the order of the partition.

160 See p. 37.

161 In fact, from Geonic times on, Haggadot include a full paragraph for each food item complete with biblical citations. See Rovner, "An Early Passover Haggadah," 377–8.

arrangement by including a narration, partition, and three-part proof. Although the rabbis most likely never read a handbook of Greek rhetoric, it is clear that they did incorporate many Hellenistic techniques into their own sermons and lessons. Public speaking was a significant part of city life throughout the Empire, and the Jews took part, contributed, and felt at home in that milieu. Jews attended the theaters and circuses along with everyone else and the rabbis were very familiar with what went on there as well.[162] Even without enrolling in a school of rhetoric, any rabbi who attended an oration in a theater or public square would have easily and unselfconsciously applied similar techniques to his own speeches. His audiences would have appreciated that as well. The rabbis also adapted the forms of popular oration to fit their own worldview by promoting prepared lectures over extemporizing and by developing forms that expressed their view of the Bible as a self-referencing harmonious and unified composition.

As noted in the introduction, public oratory during the Second Sophistic not only served as entertainment but also instilled in Greek-speaking Romans a sense of identity and pride about their own history and culture.[163] The rabbis similarly gave public sermons that entertained the audience and that ironically also used Greek rhetoric to instill Torah knowledge and Jewish identity. In fact, the rabbis even compared their own *derashot* with pantomime theatre. Pantomime, which was closely related to rhetorical oratory,[164] was a popular Roman form of entertainment in which male actors would silently re-enact tragic myths and risqué plays.[165] Pantomimes also offered political criticism of the emperor and the government.[166] Officials tolerated these

[162] Martin Jacobs, "Theatres and Performances as Reflected in the Talmud Yerushalmi," in *The Talmud Yerushalmi and Graeco-Roman Culture I*, ed. Peter Schäfer (Tübingen: Mohr Siebeck, 2002): 327–47; Berkowitz, *Execution and Invention*, 153–79; and Zeev Weiss, "Theaters, Hippodromes, Amphitheatres, and Performances," in *The Oxford Handbook of Jewish Daily Life in Roman Palestine*, ed. Catherine Hezser (Oxford: Oxford University Press, 2010): 623–40.

[163] See p. 5.

[164] Dutsch, "Towards a Roman Theory of Theatrical Gesture," 419, writes: "Theatrical and rhetorical delivery were viewed in antiquity as similar enough to allow an exchange of knowledge between those proficient in one type of performance and those studying the other." See also William Slater, "Pantomime Riots," *Classical Antiquity* 13, no. 1 (1994), 135 n. 86.

[165] Edith Hall, "Pantomime: Visualising Myth in the Roman Empire," in *Performance in Greek and Roman Theatre*, ed. George Harrison and Vayos Liaps (Leiden: Brill, 2013): 451–73; and Jacobs, "Theatres," 335.

[166] Hall, "Pantomime," 452; and Jacobs, "Theatres," 345. See also ibid., 338–9, on the opportunity for the people to appeal to the emperor or other authorities in theaters and during chariot races.

performances because they served as an outlet for the population's frustrations and thereby prevented them from taking action against the rulers.[167] As Moshe David Herr notes, one midrash not only refers to this phenomenon but also draws a parallel to the rabbinic sermon:[168]

> Yose of Ma`on declaimed in the synagogue of the Maonians: Hear this, "O priests, attend, O House of Israel, and give ear, O royal house, for right conduct is your responsibility" (Hosea 5:1).[169] In the future, the Holy One, blessed be He, will make the priests stand in judgment, "Why have you not toiled in Torah? Did you not enjoy twenty-four gifts from my sons?" They respond, "They have not given us anything."
>
> "Attend, O House of Israel: Why haven't you given them twenty-four priestly gifts as I wrote in the Torah?" They respond that those of the house of the patriarch have taken all of them.
> "Give ear, O royal house, for right conduct is your responsibility. It was up to you [to fulfill] 'This shall be the priests' due' (Deut 18:3). Therefore, the attribute of justice will turn against you."
>
> Rabbi [Yehudah Nesi'ah] heard and became angry. Before evening, R. Shimon ben Laqish came to visit him and pacify him on behalf of [R. Yose]. He said to him, "Rabbi, we have to have gratitude for the nations of the world because they invite mimes into their theaters and circuses who entertain them so that they do not sit and speak to each other. Yet, Yose of Ma'on speaks words of Torah and you become angry at him?"[170]

Yose of Ma`on offers a sermon on God's inquiry into why the priests do not study Torah. The priests shift the blame to the rest of the Jews who are not paying the priestly dues, who in turn blame the patriarch for taking these gifts for himself. The patriarch, Rabbi Yehudah Nesi'ah, is incensed. R. Shimon ben Laqish, who according to Talmudic legend was himself a gladiator and intimately familiar with the details of Greek

[167] Jacobs, "Theatres," 346; and Moshe David Herr, "Synagogues and Theaters (Sermons and Satiric Plays)," [Hebrew] in *Knesset Ezra – Literature and Life in the Synagogue: Studies Presented to Ezra Fleischer*, ed. S. Eliezer et al. (Jerusalem: Yad Izhak Ben-Zvi, 1994): 111.

[168] Ibid., 105–19; and see similarly Jacobs, "Theatres," 345–6. David Stern also sees a subtle criticism of the patriarch Rabban Gamaliel in the *derasha* of R. Eliezer. See Stern, *Midrash and Theory*, 35–8. See also Lam Rabbah, *petiḥa* 17; Y. Berakhot 4:2, 7d; and Pesikta d'Rav Kahana, 28:1.

[169] MS London inserts here, "He said," which I have omitted following MSS Paris, Oxford, and Munich.

[170] Gen Rabbah 80:1. Follows MS London unless otherwise noted.

forms of entertainment,[171] comes to pacify the patriarch. He compares Yose to the Roman pantomimes, explaining that the patriarch should tolerate Yose at least as much as the Roman government tolerates the mimes. It is not immediately clear in the midrash how Romans conversing with each other would be detrimental; nor is it apparent how Yose's teaching Torah and being better than the pantomimes relate to the insult that he directed at the patriarch. However, once we remember that pantomimes would also sometimes mock the Emperor and satirize the government, we can then readily understand the midrash. The government preferred people to vent their frustration through pantomime – over which they had some control – rather than hold conversations and meetings in private that could lead to riots and revolts. If the Emperor tolerated such mockery, then certainly the patriarch could tolerate the criticism of Yose, who was, after all, teaching Torah and keeping people from watching lewd dances. The rabbinic sermon thus fulfills a similar role in Jewish society as does the Roman oration in relation to the greater empire. Pantomime artists were the pop stars of their day[172] and the rabbis strove to gain some of the same attraction to their own teachings. At the same time, they also imitated the pantomimes in using their own rhetorical form to criticize not the emperor but the highest Jewish leader, the patriarch.

The Yerushalmi similarly explicitly parallels the activity of the synagogue with that of the theater:

> Upon his departure [from the study house] what would [R. Naḥunia ben ha-Qanah] say? "I give thanks before you Lord, my God and God of my fathers, that you have placed my lot among those who sit in the study house and synagogues and you did not place my lot in the theaters and circuses. For I toil and they toil; I am industrious and they are industrious. I toil to inherit the Garden of Eden; they toil for the nethermost pit.[173]

Beth Berkowitz comments on this: "The Rabbis pair the study houses with the theater in order to show the study house's superiority, but in the process they inextricably link the two. Buried in their rejection of Rome but also perpetuated by it is an anxiety about rabbinic distinctiveness. Living in the thick of paganized Jewish Palestine, the Rabbis are preoccupied with creating an alternative to the dominant Roman

[171] B. Giṭṭin 47a.
[172] Slater, "Pantomime Riots," 128.
[173] Y. Berakhot 4:2, 7d.

culture."[174] The rabbis feel competitive with and overpowered by Roman civilization, but at the same time they believe that the Jewish people are ultimately superior. They therefore speak in the style of Greek oration, showing that they are no less sophisticated or learned than the declaimers and actors who represent Roman culture. The rhetors of the Second Sophistic turned to Attic oratory to revive Greek pride in the face of Western Roman political domination; the rabbis distinguished themselves from both Roman domination and Greek culture by applying the rhetorical technique of the Greeks to their teaching of Torah.

For the rabbis, rhetorical skill served a somewhat different function than it did for the Greeks. At least ideally, rabbinic *derashot* were not about the personal ingenuity of the speaker but rather aimed to demonstrate the perfection of Scripture. Connecting verses from across the Bible assumes that all verses share a common prophetic source and therefore all speak with one voice and can mutually explain each other. Atomizing a verse, moreover, emphasizes the significance of each and every word or phrase. Daring, imaginative, and skillful exegesis had the goal not of promoting the speaker but of reading between the lines of Scripture to reveal its internal and eternal message. The sense of suspense and joy achieved at its resolution affirmed time and again the transcendent connectivity of all of biblical prophecy and the ability to unpack some of its divine depth. For the rabbinic sermonizer, in contrast to the sophists, the goal of delivering a speech that would be "as sweet to his listeners as honey,"[175] was not merely aesthetic; rather, he strove to recreate nothing less than an experience of the Sinaitic revelation.[176] We will return in the Conclusion to the rabbinic use of rhetoric as a means for retrieving Sinaitic prophecy. In the meantime, let us further explore the application of rhetorical structures and argumentation in rabbinic literature.

[174] Berkowitz, *Execution and Invention*, 158.
[175] See epigraph at the beginning of this chapter.
[176] See p. 51.

2 Rabbis as Instructors: Rhetorical Arrangement and Reasoning in the Yerushalmi

> [If one can return] the lost item of his father or the lost item of his rabbi, that of his rabbi takes precedence, for his father brought him to this world but his teacher who taught him wisdom brought him to the world to come.[1]

> Isocrates the orator used to advise his acquaintances to honor teachers ahead of parents; for the latter have been only the cause of living, but teachers are the cause of living well.[2]

The rabbis not only presented homiletic sermons in synagogues, as we analyzed in the previous chapter, they also taught law and legal interpretation to students in schools and to wider audiences in other public spaces. In order to better appreciate rabbinic legal texts and the role of the rabbis as teachers, this chapter will first compare them with the Greek instructors of rhetoric and explore the instructional settings that inspired these legal discussions. We will then perform a rhetorical analysis of one legal pericope from the Talmud Yerushalmi with an eye towards identifying its structure as an example of classical rhetorical oratory, and analyzing how the rhetorical moves in each line contribute to its overall message.

THE SETTING OF RABBINIC INSTRUCTION

Talmudic literature grows out of a long tradition of rabbinic discussion and instruction that took place in various settings. The sages of the Talmud generally taught in small study circles[3] wherein each rabbi

1 M. Baba Meṣi`a 2:11.

2 *The Exercises of Aelius Theon*, 99; translation from George A. Kennedy, *Progymnasmata: Greek Textbooks of Prose Composition and Rhetoric* (Leiden: Brill, 2003), 18. See also Ronald Hock and Edward O'Neil, *The Chreia in Ancient Rhetoric: Volume I. The Progymnasmata* (Atlanta: Scholars Press, 1986), 324.

3 Jeffrey Rubenstein, "Social and Institutional Settings of Rabbinic Literature," in *The Cambridge Companion to the Talmud and Rabbinic Literature*, ed. Charlotte

attracted a number of devoted students who would meet in a study house (*beit midrash*),[4] in the rabbi's home,[5] in the private home of a patron,[6] in a synagogue,[7] or outdoors in fields, marketplaces, and at city gates.[8] Students would sit before the master and listen to him explain a tradition and then respond with questions. At other times, the students would recite traditions or provide explanations while the master listened and added corrections.[9] When their teacher died, the students would disperse to find other teachers as there was no ongoing institution that outlived the master.[10] This description applies also to Greek rhetorical schools, such as those of Athens and Gaza where individual teachers each attracted a circle of pupils.[11]

Fonrobert and Martin Jaffee (Cambridge: Cambridge University Press, 2007): 59, explains that the rabbis did not generally teach in large institutional schools that included "hierarchies of positions, administrative bureaucracies, curricula, or requirements." On post-amoraic yeshivot in Palestine, see Hezser, Social Structure, 225–7. For an earlier attempt to assess the nature of Talmudic educational oratory, see Gerald Phillips, "The Practice of Rhetoric at the Talmudic Academies," *Speech Monographs* (1959): 37–46; and Gerald Phllips "The Place of Rhetoric in the Babylonian Talmud," *Quarterly Journal of Speech* 43, no. 4 (1957): 390–3, who concludes: "the whole Jewish culture of the Talmudic period rested upon the art of rhetoric in use, and rhetoric represented the core of the whole religious, judicial and educational system of the people."

4 This term can refer to the study circle itself or to a physical building. Evidence in Palestine for the latter grows in amoraic times; see Haim Shapira, "Beit ha-Midrash (the House of Study) during the Late Second Temple Period and the Age of the Mishnah: Institutional and Ideological Aspects" [Hebrew] (PhD diss., Hebrew University, 2001), 129–45. In Palestine, the term used most often for these schools is *beit midrash*, while in Babylonia the primary designation is *bei rav*. See Goodblatt, *Rabbinic Instruction*, 106–7. Other nearly synonymous terms found in the Yerushalmi are *beit va`ad* and *sdar*; see Rubenstein, "Social and Institutional Settings," 63.

5 Hezser, *Social Structure*, 224.

6 M. Avot 1:4 and Rubenstein, "Social and Institutional Settings," 60–1.

7 Lee Levine, *The Rabbinic Class of Roman Palestine in Late Antiquity* (Jerusalem: Yad Izhak Ben-Zvi Press, 1989), 29 n. 17.

8 Adolf Büchler, "Learning and Teaching in the Open Air in Palestina," *Jewish Quarterly Review* 4 (1914): 485–91; Shapira, "Beit ha-Midrash," 132–3; Shmuel Safrai, "Education and the Study of Torah," in *The Jewish People in the First Century: Historical Geography, Political History, Social, Cultural and Religious Life and Institutions*, ed. S. Safrai and M. Stern (Amsterdam: Van Gorcum, 1976): 953; and Faur, *Golden Doves*, 95 and 183 n. 62.

9 Goodblatt, *Rabbinic Instruction*, 199–259; Hezser, *Social Structure*, 337–8; M. Gewirtsmann, "Ha-munaḥ 'yatib' u-mashma`uto," *Sinai* 65 (1969): 9–20.

10 Rubenstein, "Social and Institutional Settings," 58–74; Hezser, *Social Structure*, 195–224; and Goodblatt, *Rabbinic Instruction*, 108–54.

11 See Kennedy, *New History*, 243; N. G. Wilson, *Scholars of Byzantium* (London: Gerald Duckword and Co., 1983), 29–31; and Robert Penella, ed. *Rhetorical Exercises from Late Antiquity: A Translation of Choricius of Gaza's Preliminary Talks and Declamations* (Cambridge: Cambridge University Press, 2009), 1–2.

In addition to these smaller local study circles, Tannaitic literature bears witness to more formal bodies of learning and adjudication at Yavneh, Lydda, and in the Lower Galilee that may have been headed by the patriarch.[12] Larger groups of rabbis also occasionally met in the upper stories of capacious houses belonging to laypeople.[13] The court – referred to as *beit din*, *yeshiva* or *metivta* – furnished yet another setting that engendered lively rabbinic discussion.[14] Whether they met regularly or ad hoc, court sessions provided rabbis with the opportunity to discuss practical matters of halakha and convey them to the public. Besides their homiletic sermons, the rabbis also delivered public lectures that addressed halakha. As mentioned in the previous chapter, the *yelamdenu* form often included some legal material as did the *pirqa* in Babylonia. Because the audiences at such public lectures included many unlearned people, the rabbis were careful not to teach any esoteric teachings or halakhic leniencies that the lay audience might misapply.[15] More nuance in halakhic teaching was possible in classes geared to advanced audiences that included not only students but also learned laymen and colleagues. In Babylonia, the most prominent advanced study session was called the *kallah*, which met for a few days during the year, during which people would gather for intense study with a master.[16]

During their public lectures, the rabbi would sit[17] and speak softly, while a student or colleague would stand, listen, and then repeat the words of the lecturer in a loud voice.[18] This human loudspeaker, called an *amora* or *meturgeman*,[19] was present in both

[12] Shapira, "Beit ha-Midrash," 171–225; Hezser, *Social Structure*, 185–200; David Goodblatt, *The Monarchic Principle: Studies in Jewish Self-Government in Antiquity* (Tübingen: Mohr Siebeck, 1994), 232–76; Levine, *Rabbinic Class*, 76–83; and Hidary, *Dispute*, 7 nn. 21 and 22. In the early Tannaitic period before 70 CE, the two schools of Shammai and Hillel dominated Pharisaic/rabbinic legal discussion, but neither is portrayed as having a leader or a building. Rather, these were most likely two loosely organized groups of sages. See further at Hidary, *Dispute*, 163–6, especially n. 3.

[13] T. Shabbat 2:5; T. Soṭah 13:3; and Rubenstein, "Social and Institutional Settings," 60.

[14] Goodblatt, *Rabbinic Instruction*, 63–107; and Hidary, *Dispute*, 7 n. 21.

[15] B. Pesaḥim 50a = B. Kiddushin 71a; B. Ta`anit 26b; B. Nedarim 23b; and Y. Terumot 2:1, 41c = B. Ḥulin 15a. See Gafni, "`Al derashot be-ṣibur," 121–5.

[16] Goodblatt, *Rabbinic Instruction*, 155–70.

[17] Gen Rabbah 98:13 (Theodor-Albeck ed., p. 1261).

[18] Safrai, "Education and the Study of Torah," 968.

[19] These two terms are used interchangeably in B. Sanhedrin 7b. The term *meturgeman* refers originally to the one who recites the Targum after each verse of the Torah reading as in M. Megilah 4:4. The title was then transferred to the *amora* who similarly spoke after each statement of the lecturer, although he was not translating but simply repeating in a louder voice.

Palestine[20] and Babylonia.[21] It was considered undignified for a speaker to have to raise his own voice, and the presence of a *meturgeman* not only promoted the prestige of the speaker but also formally marked an official session wherein the speaker's rulings held legislative authority.[22] The *meturgeman* was expected to repeat precisely the message of the sage.[23] Occasionally, however, the *meturgeman* would insert his own interpretations, much to the consternation of the speaker.[24] This choreography contrasts sharply with Roman orators who would stand while declaiming,[25] pay careful attention to their voice intonations, and accompany their orations with elaborate hand gestures.[26] We cannot be sure when and where the institution of the *meturgeman* was most prevalent and whether it was commonly used for lectures on legal topics, synagogue sermons, or other settings.[27] Nevertheless, the *meturgeman*, whenever he was present, removed the possibility for the sage to make use of intonation, gestures, and other rhetorical effects. While the *meturgeman* could have added some rhetorical effects of his own, his presence would have the effect of highlighting the content of the lecture over its delivery.

How do the various roles of the rabbi as a teacher and public speaker compare with those of the Greek rhetor? Procopius and Choricius of Gaza emphasize that the rhetor should be a "respectful teacher as well as a successful orator."[28] Rhetors had to lead young men in their education and also charm audiences in public displays of their oratory power. As Robert Penella observes: "Students were not the only auditors of sophists' declamations in antiquity; adults also heard them, at least in

20 See Y. Berakhot 4:1, 7c–7d; Y. Megilah 4:10, 75c; Exod Rabbah 8:3; and Eccl Rabbah 9:17. B. Sanhedrin 7b also involves Palestinian *amoraim* but see the parallel story at Y. Bikkurim 3:3, 65d, which includes the same interpretation in a different context.

21 B. Ḥulin 15a, where the *amora* presents during the *pirqa*.

22 Y.M. Kosovsky, "Ha-meturgeman ba-derasha ha-ṣiburit (pirqa) be-bet ha-keneset," *Sinai* 45 (1959): 233–43.

23 T. Megilah 3:41; Y. Megilah 4:10, 75c; B. Kiddushin 31b.

24 Gen Rabbah 70:17; B. Sanhedrin 7b; B. Soṭah 40a.

25 Some speakers would sit for the *dialexis*, an informal introduction to the main speech, but then stand for the oration itself. See Russel, *Greek Declamation*, 77; Stanley F. Bonner, *Roman Declamation in the Late Republic and Early Empire* (Liverpool: Liverpool University Press, 1969), 51; and Penella, *Rhetorical Exercises*, 28.

26 See n. 22.

27 Although most references to a *meturgeman* suggest a legal lesson, some refer to an aggadic context, as in Gen Rabbah 70:17 and B. Ta`anit 8a. At least some of the references to the *meturgeman* place him in the *pirqa*, which often combined halakha and aggadah; see B. Ḥulin 15a.

28 Litsas, "Choricius of Gaza," 24–5 and 33.

some cities, whether in the school or outside it, whether in select groups or as part of a large audience."[29] The rhetor was widely respected in public. In fact, whenever Procopius "appeared in the marketplace everyone immediately rose."[30] In their role as teachers, rhetors would present compositions to students both to serve as models and for their feedback, and students would also present their speeches to the master for criticism.[31] The master would take his students under his wing like a father; Choricius writes of his teacher: "Procopius had become a father to whoever he taught, loving his students equally as his own children."[32] In return, the students respected and looked after the welfare of their master.

This description of the rhetor matches that of the Talmudic rabbis who similarly presented public orations to the wider community as well as trained students. Likewise, when a rabbinic sage entered a room, all present were expected to rise.[33] The rabbis considered their students to be equivalent to their own sons.[34] In turn, a student was expected to show respect and serve the master[35] to an even greater extent than to a parent. This parallel between the roles of the rabbi and the rhetor helps explain the nearly matching prescriptions cited in the epigraph to this chapter for why respect for a teacher trumps that of a father.[36]

[29] Penella, *Rhetorical Exercises*, 13.

[30] "Funeral Oration to Procopius" from Litsas, "Choricius of Gaza," 219.

[31] Kennedy, *New History*, 45; and Cribiore, *The School of Libanius*, 149–50.

[32] Litsas, "Choricius of Gaza," 39. See also Cribiore, *The School of Libanius*, 138–41; and Jaffee, *Torah in the Mouth*, 207 n. 64.

[33] T. Sanhedrin 7:8; Y. Bikkurim 3:3, 65c; B. Horayot 13b and B. Kiddushin 32b–33b.

[34] Sifre Deut 34; Y. Sanhedrin 10:2, 28b; and B. Sanhedrin 19b.

[35] On the expectation of service in the master–disciple relationship, see Jaffee, *Torah in the Mouth*, 147–51; Shaye Cohen, "The Rabbis in Second-Century Jewish Society," in *The Cambridge History of Judaism. Vol. 3: The Early Roman Period*, ed. W. Horbury, W. D. Davies, and J. Sturdy (Cambridge: Cambridge University Press, 1999): 952–4; Hezser, *Social Structure*, 332–46; Levine, *Rabbinic Class*, 59–61; Safrai, "*Education and the Study of Torah*," 964; Moshe Aberbach, *Ha-ḥinukh ha-Yehudi bi-tqufat ha-Mishnah veha-Talmud* (Jerusalem: Rubin Mass, 1982), 93–212; and further citations at Stuart Miller, *Sages and Commoners in Late Antique Eretz Israel* (Tübingen: Mohr Siebeck, 2006), 372 n. 96.

[36] One the relationship between sages and students, see further at Cribiore, *The School of Libanius*, 138–43; and Barry Wimpfheimer, *Narrating the Law: A Poetics of Talmudic Legal Stories* (Philadelphia: University of Pennsylvania, 2011), 96–121. On the general parallels between the roles of rabbis and rhetors, see Fischel, "Greek and Latin," 8:58, who writes:

> the *tannaim* and many leading Palestinian *amoraim*, as well as their Pharisaic predecessors, belong to a group of 'technocrat' experts who could administer, legislate, interpret, edit law and literature, theologize, moralize, and console – precisely the abilities and functions of their Greco-Roman counterparts, the

If the rabbis fulfilled a role similar to that of the rhetors then perhaps they also shared similar techniques and models of public presentation. Making the comparison between Greek and rabbinic orations is fraught with methodological difficulties. While neither group preserved verbatim transcripts of oral presentations, their two sets of literature still differ significantly. Greek orators usually wrote down their own orations shortly before or after their performance and so their written lectures bear close affinity to their oral presentations. In contrast, the great distance between the original rabbinic presentations of late antiquity and the Talmudic literature that has been preserved in medieval manuscripts raises fundamental issues of redaction and transmission history.[37] While the Mishnah and other Tannaitic collections were published and transmitted nearly verbatim by professional memorizers, this was not the case for amoraic discussions and teachings. Often, only the legal conclusions of an amoraic lecture would be submitted for official transmission while the orator's proofs and explanations would, at best, be repeated by future students in a severely truncated form.[38] The Talmud Yerushalmi, compiled c. 400 CE, mainly consists of these apodictic amoraic legal pronouncements together with summaries of amoraic discussions and minimal editorial additions.[39] The more elaborate Talmud Bavli results from two or more added centuries of redactional activity in which anonymous sages termed Stammaim[40] worked to fill in those summary traditions by reconstructing amoraic discussions and lectures.

Despite these considerable methodological challenges, I propose that a comparison between Talmudic sugyot and classical rhetoric remains possible and valuable. First, because even the truncated form of lectures that serve as the basis for many sugyot still may retain a kernel of the structure and lines of argumentation from the original oral presentation. Second, and more importantly, the final work of the

rhetorician-scholar-bureaucrats, from Cicero to Seneca (once practically vice-emperor), from Dio Chrysostom to Plutarch (a priest-magistrate). The rabbis' idealization of the Sage – the characteristic ideology of hellenized bureaucracies – their popular ethics and their uses of Hellenic myth, literary forms, and hermeneutics, their academic institutions and efforts at preserving tradition, suggest knowledge of their Greco-Roman colleagues.

[37] See also pp. 49 and 52 on the recording of oral sermons in midrash aggadah.

[38] Halivni, *Formation*, 3–4.

[39] Ibid., 193–5; and Leib Moscovitz, "The Formation and Character of the Jerusalem Talmud," in *The Cambridge History of Judaism IV*, ed. S. Katz (Cambridge: Cambridge University Press, 2006): 663–77.

[40] Plural of Stam, the anonymous redactors of the Talmuds. See p. 8 n. 35.

redactors is worthy of study on its own, regardless of whether it accurately portrays amoraic teachings. The methods by which the Stammaim reconstruct arguments and persuasive orations reflects well on their own rhetorical knowledge, which we can then compare with Greek rhetorical structure. As I will argue in this chapter and the next, many sugyot can be fruitfully analyzed as persuasive speech. This chapter will identify and analyze one Yerushalmi sugya that has a more polished style and structure than most of the Yerushalmi and is thus a good candidate for rhetorical analysis – whether it is the work of an Amora or an anonymous redactor. Academic Talmud scholarship usually focuses on source criticism – breaking down a sugya into its chronological layers to reveal the original meanings of its sources.[41] By adding rhetorical criticism to our toolbox, we can better succeed in recovering the goals of the redactors in constructing the sugya as it stands. As I shall demonstrate, the composers or redactors[42] of this sugya utilized some of the style and goals of oratorical composition that were common in their environment.

RABBAN GAMALIEL'S NONCONFORMITY

Yerushalmi Berakhot 1:1 discusses the deviance in halakhic practice of Rabban Gamaliel of Yavneh compared with other Tannaim.[43] Rabban Gamaliel served as patriarch[44] and as such would have received more

[41] Halivni, for example, uses source criticism in order to recover the original meaning of amoraic traditions that were misunderstood by the Stammaitic redactors. He writes: "The reason for these forced explanations of Amoraic traditions is that the Stammaim lacked the complete version of the sources or the correct order of traditions; in order to complete them or correct the order they had no choice but to offer forced explanations" (ibid., 12).

[42] Since I have no access to the prehistory of this sugya, I cannot tell whether it was originally composed with its current structure or whether later redactors reworked an earlier proto-sugya into its current format. I will use the term redactors throughout this chapter to be safe. I also do not know whether it was put together by one person or by a group; I use the plural here only out of convention.

[43] Previous versions of this analysis appeared in Richard Hidary, "Classical Rhetorical Arrangement and Reasoning in the Talmud: The Case of Yerushalmi Berakhot 1:1," *AJS Review* 34, no. 1 (2010): 33–64; and Hidary, *Dispute*, 241–59.

[44] I make no claim here concerning the historical role of Rabban Gamaliel of Yavneh as patriarch. My goal is to analyze how the Talmud represents and remembers Rabban Gamaliel; for this purpose, his purported role as patriarch is significant. On the history of the patriarchate in general see Martin Goodman, *State and Society in Roman Galilee, A.D. 132–212* (Totowa, NJ: Rowman & Allanheld, 1983), 111f.; Martin Goodman, "The Roman State and the Jewish Patriarch in the Third Century," in *The Galilee in Late Antiquity*, ed. Lee Levine (New York: The Jewish Theological

Greek education than most of his colleagues.[45] Tannaitic sources retell many narratives that portray Rabban Gamaliel of Yavneh as someone who occasionally diverged from the practice of the majority of sages. In some cases, Rabban Gamaliel acted more stringently than his colleagues;[46] in other cases, more leniently.[47] He not only practiced according to his own opinion against the majority consensus, but he is even reported to have applied his power as patriarch to pressure others to adopt his own view.[48]

The historical accuracy of this portrayal makes little difference here since my interest lies neither in the historical Rabban Gamaliel nor even

Seminary of America, 1994): 107–19; Shaye Cohen, "Patriarchs and Scholarchs," *Proceedings of the American Academy for Jewish Research* 48 (1981): 57–85; Levine, *Rabbinic Class*, 134–91; Levine, "The Status of the Patriarch in the Third and Fourth Centuries: Sources and Methodology," *Journal of Jewish Studies* 47, no. 1 (1996): 1–32; Seth Schwartz, "The Patriarchs and the Diaspora," *Journal of Jewish Studies* 51, no. 2 (2000): 208–318; Schwartz, *Imperialism*, 103–28, and see references there at p. 111 n. 20; Paul Heger, *The Pluralistic Halakhah: Legal Innovations in the Late Second Commonwealth and Rabbinic Periods* (Berlin: Walter De Gruyter, 2003), 289–309; and David Goodblatt, "The End of Sectarianism and the Patriarchs," in *For Uriel: Studies in the History of Israel in Antiquity Presented to Professor Uriel Rappaport*, ed. M. Mor et al. (Jerusalem: Zalman Shazar Center for Jewish History, 2005): 32.

45 See p. 13 n. 59.

46 See M. Berakhot 2:5, M. Beṣah 2:6, M. Sukkah 2:5, T. Berakhot 4:15, T. Beṣah 2:12 and T. Shabbat 1:22.

47 See M. Berakhot 1:1 and herein p. 89 n. 67. All of these narratives are collected and analyzed in Ben-Zion Wacholder, "Sippure Rabban Gamaliel ba-Mishna uba-Tosefta," *World Congress for Jewish Studies* 4, no. 1 (1967): 143–4; Shamai Kanter, *Rabban Gamaliel II: The Legal Traditions* (Ann Arbor: Brown University Press, 1980), 238–42, 246–51; Hanah Kohat, "Ben 'aristoqratyah le-demoqratyah – Rabban Gamaliel ve-Rabbi Yehoshua," in *Sefer yeshurun*, ed. Michael Shashar (Jerusalem: Shashar Publishing, 1999): 213–28; Jacob Neusner, "From Biography to Theology: Gamaliel and the Patriarchate," *Review of Rabbinic Judaism* 7 (2004): 52–97; and Alexei Siverstev, *Households, Sects, and the Origins of Rabbinic Judaism* (Leiden: Brill, 2005), 218–31. Rabban Gamaliel is also portrayed as feeling himself above the rules regarding learning Greek studies (B. Soṭah 49b). Cf. M. Abodah Zarah 3:4; Azzan Yadin, "Rabban Gamliel, Aphrodite's Bath, and the Question of Pagan Monotheism," *Jewish Quarterly Review* 96, no. 2 (2006): 149–79; and Lapin, *Rabbis as Romans*, 129–32. Similarly, Rabban Gamaliel I is portrayed as maintaining special halakhic privilege in the Temple; see M. Sheqalim 3:3 and 6:1.

48 See M. Rosh Hashanah 2:8–9, Y. Berakhot 4:1, 7c-d = Y. Ta`anit 4:1, 67d, B. Berakhot 27b–28a, and B. Bekhorot 36a. For similar portrayals, see Louis Ginzberg, *A Commentary on the Palestinian Talmud*, 4 vols. (New York: Jewish Theological Seminary of America, 1941), 1:91; David Stern, "Midrash and Hermeneutics: Polysemy vs. Indeterminacy," in *Midrash and Theory: Ancient Jewish Exegesis and Contemporary Literary Studies* (Evanston, IL: Northwestern University Press, 1996): 34; and Heger, *Pluralistic Halakhah*, 309–34. For a different view of Rabban Gamaliel, see Goodblatt, "End of Sectarianism," 32–6, who bases his stance on historical assumptions and trends rather than on rabbinic texts.

his portrayal in Tannaitic sources, but rather in how the Yerushalmi interprets one particular Tannaitic report. I will first present a source-critical analysis of the sugya followed by a second analysis using rhetorical criticism. As we will see in the source-critical analysis, the Yerushalmi reads M. Berakhot 1:1 and other sources against the grain in order to prove that Rabban Gamaliel and other Tannaim always conformed to the majority opinion. Such forced interpretations reveal that the Yerushalmi's conclusions derive from some preconceived ideology of its redactors. The rhetorical analysis will focus on the arrangement of the parts of the sugya and will highlight its similarity to classical rhetorical structures and methods. By joining together the historical/source-critical and rhetorical aspects of this sugya, we will gain insight into how the sugya's redactors may have reflected on their own activity and how we should read their work generally.

SOURCE-CRITICAL ANALYSIS

The Yerushalmi passage under discussion comments on M. Berakhot 1:1, which reads as follows[49]:

[A] From what time may one recite *shema* in the evenings? From the time that the priests enter to eat their *terumah*.[50]

[B] [One may continue to recite *shema*] until the end of the first watch (i.e., the fourth hour of the night); these are the words of R. Eliezer. But the sages say until midnight. Rabban Gamaliel says until dawn arrives.

[C] It happened that his [Rabban Gamaliel's] sons came from the banquet hall. They told him, "We did not recite *shema*." He responded, "If dawn has not yet arrived you may[51] recite.[52]

[49] Translation follows MS Kaufman.

[50] That is, priests who had been impure and had to bathe and wait until dark to become pure in order to eat from their priestly gifts of produce.

[51] MSS Kaufman, Parma, Geniza TS E 2.3 and 2.4, and Bavli MS Paris read "מותרין." Geniza TS E 2.2 reads "חייבין," which is changed to "מותרין" in the margin. The Mishnah in the Bavli printed edition and MSS Munich and Florence read "חייבין." See Ginzberg, *Commentary*, 1:92 n. 11.

[52] The Mishnah continues with another sentence that essentially eliminates the controversy between Rabban Gamaliel and the sages by explaining that the sages actually agree with Rabban Gamaliel that one may recite even until dawn from Torah law but they encourage people to recite before midnight as a safeguard. As we will see, however, the Yerushalmi assumes that the sages invalidate recitation of shema after midnight, even from Torah law. The Yerushalmi's redactors may have interpreted the continuation of the Mishnah as Rabban Gamaliel's explanation for why the sages

Line B records three opinions about the latest time for reciting *shema*: R. Eliezer says only until the first watch, the sages say only until midnight, and Rabban Gamaliel says even until dawn. Line C recounts a story in which Rabban Gamaliel instructed his sons to follow his own opinion, even though the sages invalidate recitation after midnight. Rabban Gamaliel's nonconformity in allowing his sons to recite after midnight against the view of his colleagues troubles the Yerushalmi, which reads[53]:

[I. Question]

[A. Narration]

It happened that his [Rabban Gamaliel's] sons came from the banquet hall. They told him, "We did not recite *shema*." He told them, "If dawn has not yet arrived, you are obligated[54] to recite."

Does Rabban Gamaliel disagree with the rabbis and did he perform a deed according to his own opinion?

[B. Partition]

[1] Behold R. Meir disagrees with the rabbis but did not perform a deed according his own opinion.

[2] Behold R. Akiva disagrees with the rabbis but did not perform a deed according to his own opinion.

[3] [Behold R. Shimon disagrees with the rabbis but did not perform a deed according to his opinion.][55]

[C. Confirmation]

[1] Where do we find that R. Meir disagrees with the rabbis but did not perform a deed according to his own opinion? As it was taught: One may annoint a sick person with a cloth on the Sabbath only when he has mixed it with wine and oil from before the Sabbath. But if he had not mixed it from before the Sabbath, it is forbidden.

added a rabbinic safeguard against reciting after midnight – but a safeguard with which Rabban Gamaliel himself disagrees. The Yerushalmi therefore makes its own attempt at reconciling Rabban Gamaliel with the sages. See further at Hidary, *Dispute*, 243–5.

53 Translation follows Venice edition, unless otherwise noted.

54 MS Leiden and printed editions read "חייבין." See, however, n. 51.

55 This line is missing in printed editions due to homoioteleuton. The base text of MS Leiden does have this line for R. Akiva and R. Shimon but omits it for R. Meir. An attempt is made to correct this between the lines, which results in the text found in the printed editions.

It was taught: R. Shimon ben Eleazar said, R. Meir used to permit one to mix wine and oil and to anoint a sick person on the Sabbath. It once happened that [R. Meir] became sick and we wanted to do so for him but he did not let us. We told him, "Rabbi, your ruling will become nullified in your lifetime." He responded, "Even though I am lenient for others, I am stringent upon myself for behold my colleagues disagree with me."[56]

[2] Where do we find that R. Akiva disagrees with the rabbis but did not perform a deed according to his own opinion? As we have learned there: The spine or the skull from two corpses, a quarter [of a *log*[57]] of blood from two corpses, a quarter [of a *qab*[58]] of bones from two corpses, a limb severed from a dead person from two corpses, or a limb severed from a live person from two people, R. Akiva declares impure and the sages declare pure.[59]

It was taught: It happened that a basket full of bones was brought from Kefar Ṭabi and placed in the open air[60] of the synagogue of Lydda. Theodorus the doctor entered and all the doctors entered with him. Theodorus the doctor declared, "There is neither a spine from one corpse nor a skull from one corpse here." They [the rabbis] said, "Since there are some who declare pure and some who declare impure here let us put it to a vote." They began with R. Akiva who declared pure. They said, "Since you used to declare impure and now you have declared it pure, it is pure."[61]

[3] Where do we find that R. Shimon disagrees with the rabbis but did not perform a deed according to his own opinion? As we have learned there: R. Shimon says, All the aftergrowths are permitted [during the seventh year] except for the aftergrowths of cabbage for other vegetables of the field are not similar to

[56] See T. Shabbat 12:12; and B. Shabbat 134a.

[57] A *log* is a liquid measurement of approximately 0.3 liters.

[58] A *qab* is a dry measure of approximately 1.2 liters.

[59] M. 'Ohalot 2:6 and cf. T. Eduyot 1:7.

[60] The basket was placed in the open-air courtyard where there was no roof to create a problem of *ohel*. However, see commentary of R. Eleazar Azikri (Safed, 1533–1600), Perush mi-ba`al sefer ḥaredim, s.v. "והניחוהו," (printed in standard editions of the Yerushalmi) who says it was hung inside the synagogue so that nobody would touch it, which would cause impurity according to all opinions. See also Saul Lieberman, *Tosefeth rishonim* (New York: The Jewish Theological Seminary of America, 1999), 3:102.

[61] T. 'Ohalot 4:2 and B. Nazir 52a–b.

> them.[62] But the sages say all aftergrowths are prohibited.[63] R. Shimon ben Yoḥai was passing[64] by during the seventh year. He saw someone gathering aftergrowths of the seventh year. He told him, "Isn't this prohibited? Aren't they aftergrowths?" He responded,[65] "Aren't you the one who permits?" He told him, "Don't my colleagues disagree with me?" R. Shimon applied to him the verse, "One who breaches a fence will be bitten by a snake" (Eccl 10:8). And so it happened to him.

[D. Peroration]

Does Rabban Gamaliel disagree with the rabbis and did he perform a deed according to his own opinion?

[II. Response]

Here it is different for it [the recitation of *shema*] is simply repetition [a form of learning]. According to this, [his sons should be allowed to recite *shema*] even after the sun has risen?

Others explain that there [in all three cases involving other Tannaim], they were able to fulfill the opinion of the sages. Here, however, midnight had already passed and they were not able to fulfill the opinion of the sages [in any case]. [Therefore, Rabban Gamaliel] told them to perform a deed according to his own opinion.[66]

The sugya has two parts: [I] the question, which includes a well-structured argument based on three proofs, and [II] the response. The opening question of the sugya focuses on and questions only one instance of Rabban Gamaliel's dissident practice, even though other sources portray multiple instances of his nonconformity.[67] The sugya

[62] Cabbages do not generally grow unattended in the wild. Therefore, even R. Shimon bar Yoḥai prohibits picking them during the seventh year.

[63] M. Shevi`it 9:1.

[64] Following Geniza and Y. Shevi`it 9:1, 38d. See Louis Ginzberg, *Yerushalmi Fragments from the Genizah: Vol. I, Text with Various Readings from the Editio Princeps* (Jerusalem: Jewish Theological Seminary of America, 1909), 2, line 8. MS Leiden here reads "עבד עובדא" instead of "עבר."

[65] Following Geniza, which has "א'." MS Leiden reads, "אמרי." See also Ginzberg, *Commentary*, 1:90, regarding the placement of this verb.

[66] Y. Berakhot 1:1, 3a.

[67] Y. Pesaḥim 7:2, 34b, asks a similar question about M. Pesaḥim 7:2, "רבן גמליאל חלוק על חכמים ועושה הלכה כיוצא בו – Rabban Gamaliel disagrees with the sages and practices halakha accordingly!" Similarly, Y. Beṣah 3:2, 62a, comments on Rabban Gamaliel's alleged nonconformity in M. Beṣah 3:2. Similar phrases also appear at Y. Abodah Zarah 3:10, 43b, and Y. Demai 3:3, 23c. Also relevant is Y. Pesaḥim 4:1, 30d, which

reveals at the outset its driving motivation: to make the case that sages never practiced in opposition to the majority. The agenda of this sugya is further made apparent by analyzing its proofs, each of which rely on subtle sophistic reasoning. The Yerushalmi cites three cases in which various other Tannaim who held minority opinions nevertheless followed the majority ruling in practice. However, upon analysis, each of these examples is easily refuted or even used to argue against halakhic conformity. Let us analyze each in turn.

[1] R. Meir

The first case reports that the sages prohibited the preparation of a wine and oil ointment for a sick person on the Sabbath but R. Meir permitted it. Nonetheless, on one occasion when R. Meir was himself sick and his students offered to prepare this ointment, R. Meir replied, "Even though I am lenient for others, I am stringent upon myself for behold my colleagues disagree with me." The sugya focuses on the second half of R. Meir's statement, "I am stringent upon myself," in order to prove that R. Meir conformed to the majority opinion. However, R. Meir also says, "I am lenient for others." That R. Meir issued practical decisions based on his own opinion is confirmed earlier in this source, which states, "R. Meir used to permit." This source contains elements of both conformity (R. Meir for himself) and nonconformity (R. Meir for others). In fact, the discussion of this *baraita* in the Bavli explicitly emphasizes R. Meir's leniency for others, an interpretive possibility not taken by the Yerushalmi.[68]

In short, this *baraita* does not fit well into the overall argument of the Yerushalmi sugya. The sugya is trying to prove that other rabbis conformed to the majority in order to question how Rabban Gamaliel could have taught his sons to contradict the majority. However, if R. Meir taught others to follow his own opinion, even if he was stringent for himself, then he poses no problem for Rabban Gamaliel who is also lenient for others. Yet, the Yerushalmi includes this as a proof for R. Meir's conformity and a challenge to Rabban Gamaliel without further comment.[69]

assumes that Beth Shammai did not practice its own opinion but rather agreed that halakha follows Beth Hillel. The combination of these texts shows a consistent tendency by at least some redactors of the Yerushalmi to read uniformity into the past. See further at Hidary, *Dispute*, 259–64.

[68] B. Shabbat 134a. See further at Hidary, "Classical," 44 n. 43.

[69] R. Eleazar Azikri (1533–1600), Perush mi-ba`al sefer ḥaredim, s.v. "חלה וכבר," appropriately asks:

[2] R. Akiva

In the previous case, R. Meir had a more lenient view than the rabbis and so he could act stringently without compromising his own principle. However, in this case, R. Akiva has a more stringent view than the majority regarding how much of a corpse suffices to cause impurity. Such a case came up before the rabbis in Lydda. They decided to take a vote and called upon R. Akiva first, knowing that he disagreed with the majority. To their surprise, he followed the majority view and voted pure, whereupon the vote immediately ended. This shows that R. Akiva voted publicly according to the majority opinion even though he privately opined that the basket was impure. This seems like a straightforward proof – until we examine the full context of the story as presented in the Tosefta. T. 'Ohalot 4:2[70] surrounds the narrative with a discussion by two of R. Akiva's disciples:

> R. Yehudah said: Regarding six issues, R. Akiva used to declare impure but then changed his mind.
>
> It happened that baskets of bones were brought from Kefar Ṭabi and placed in the open air of the synagogue of Lydda. Theodorus the doctor entered together with all the doctors. They declared, "There is neither a spine from one corpse nor a skull from one corpse here." They [the rabbis] said, "Since there are some who declare pure and some who declare impure here let us put it to a vote." They began with R. Akiva who declared pure. They said, "Since you used to declare impure and now you have declared it pure, let them be pure."
>
> R. Shimon said: R. Akiva declared impure until the day of his death. If he changed his mind after he died, I am not aware of it.

> This is highly problematic. Did they [R. Meir's students] not know that [in a dispute between] an individual and the majority the law follows the majority? Furthermore, that which R. Meir responds, "Even though I am lenient...," is a story that contradicts [what the Talmud sets out to prove], for the sages oppose him yet he practices in a case according to his own opinion and even teaches it to the public?

Azikri answers that R. Meir did not actually permit others to rely on his leniency but did not protest if they did rely on it because this is a matter of health. This, however, does not fit well with the words of the *baraita*, which suggest that R. Meir permitted it for others outright. See further discussion at Ginzberg, *Commentary*, 1:81–6; and Hidary, "Classical," 43–6.

70 The Tosefta also appears in B. Nazir 52b.

According to R. Yehudah, R. Akiva had changed his mind from his original position and now actually agreed with the majority. His vote supporting the majority was not an expression of conformity but rather a reversal of opinion. This fact spoils the entire argument of the Yerushalmi. According to R. Shimon, this entire story never occurred and so it certainly cannot serve as a proof for anything. Even if the Yerushalmi redactors did not know of the comments by these two Tannaim as cited in the Tosefta, the anecdote still does not serve as a solid proof. Perhaps R. Akiva only conformed to the majority because it was a public vote and he would have lost the vote anyway.[71] We cannot prove from here that Rabban Gamaliel, who was deciding alone and in private, could not have decided against the majority.[72]

[3] R. Shimon bar Yoḥai

R. Shimon bar Yoḥai is more lenient than his colleagues concerning picking the aftergrowth of vegetables during the Sabbatical year when farming is prohibited. Nevertheless, a story relates that R. Shimon told a farmer to follow the stringent view of the sages despite his own lenient position. The Yerushalmi presumes that he would act stringently himself as well. However, there is good reason to believe that R. Shimon himself would eat from the aftergrowth and was simply making a point in his harsh treatment of this farmer. This story is repeated at Y. Shevi`it 9:1, 38d, where another story follows in which R. Shimon bar Yoḥai also rebukes and curses someone, and the second story also ends with "and so it was."[73] In that context, the story is one example of R. Shimon bar Yoḥai's intensity and zeal; he is portrayed in these stories as impatient and impulsive.[74] Furthermore, the tone of the story – with its repeated use of sarcasm, introduced by the words "Isn't ... Aren't ... Aren't ... Don't..." – suggests that this story involves a personal tiff rather than an earnest halakhic discussion. R. Shimon bar Yoḥai was offended by this farmer's actions and cursed him. Had he seen a rabbinic colleague

[71] See further analysis at Hidary, "Classical," 47–8.

[72] Ginzberg, ibid., asks this question and concludes that the Yerushalmi only compares one aspect of the cases even though they are fundamentally different. Ginzberg, ibid., 91, is forced to say that "the cases of R. Akiva and R. Shimon were only cited here as a mere example since they also were particular to honor their colleagues, but the main question to Rabban Gamaliel is from R. Meir."

[73] The order of the stories is reversed in Bereshit Rabba, *Va-yishlaḥ, par.* 79:6, to Gen 38:18 (ed. Theodor-Albeck, 2:945).

[74] See further at Jeffrey Rubenstein, *Talmudic Stories: Narrative Art, Composition, and Culture* (Baltimore: Johns Hopkins University Press, 1999), 121f.

gathering vegetation, he might have been more tolerant. In this case, however, R. Shimon bar Yoḥai seems to have been particularly upset because the farmer was an ignoramus who was simply taking advantage of R. Shimon's leniency on this issue. Even though the story only describes an exceptional case of an impatient rabbi dealing with an opportunistic layperson, the Yerushalmi nevertheless cites it as proof that no rabbi may follow a minority opinion.

Compare this story with the following report in B. Pesaḥim 51a–b:

> For Rabbah bar bar Ḥannah said: R. Yoḥanan ben Eleazar told me, "One time I followed R. Shimon ben R. Yose ben Laqunia into a garden. He took an aftergrowth of cabbage, ate it,[75] gave it to me and told me, 'My son, you may eat in my presence but you may not eat when outside my presence. I saw R. Shimon bar Yoḥai eating and R. Shimon bar Yoḥai is worthy to rely on in his presence and outside his presence. You [who only saw me eat] may eat in my presence but may not eat when outside my presence.'"

According to the Bavli, R. Shimon does in fact follow his own opinion and even advises his student to do so. Strangely, this directly contradicts the Yerushalmi story. Wondering about this contradiction, Tosafot insightfully explain that in the Yerushalmi case, the source of R. Shimon's anger is not the lenient practice itself, but rather the character of the ignoramus farmer who simply follows the leniency blindly.[76] Of course, we cannot assume that the Yerushalmi's redactors knew of this Bavli story.[77] As noted above, however, even if they did not know of it, a literary reading of the Yerushalmi story itself implies that R. Shimon was particularly upset by the farmer because he was a layman who was simply taking advantage of R. Shimon's leniency. One could easily imagine an alternative sugya trying to prove the opposite view by

[75] The Bavli subsequently cites a *baraita* stating that R. Shimon bar Yoḥai prohibits aftergrowth of all vegetation except the cabbage, which is the opposite of M. Shevi`it 9:1. The Bavli story about R. Shimon bar Yoḥai eating of the cabbage concurs with the Bavli *baraita*. See Tosafot to B. Nazir 51a, s.v. "כל."

[76] Tosafot to B. Pesaḥim 51b, s.v., "אני." Another resolution is that a rabbi may follow his own opinion for himself (which may include his students while in his presence) but must follow the majority when ruling for others. See further at Moshe Halbertal, *People of the Book: Canon, Meaning, and Authority* (Cambridge: Harvard University Press, 1997), 83–4. The case of R. Meir, however, does not fit into this model.

[77] Duberush Ashkenazi, *Sha`are Yerushalmi* (Warsaw: Drukerni N. Schriftgisser, 1866), 2b, in fact takes the position that the Yerushalmi did not know of the Bavli story in order to resolve the difficulty that the Bavli story would pose to the Yerushalmi argument.

citing this story and concluding, "an ignoramus (*`am ha'areṣ*) is different," just as Tosafot does.[78]

Furthermore, as was the case for R. Meir, R. Shimon's stringency does not cause him to violate any of his own rulings. While these examples can prove that a rabbi should be stringent in consideration of the majority, it cannot prove that a rabbi may act leniently following the majority where he believes the law requires stringency. Thus, the R. Shimon story cannot prove the right or the need for Rabban Gamaliel to forgo what he considers an obligation to recite *shema*.[79] The Yerushalmi's use of this source as a precedent that no rabbi may practice against the majority rests on shaky grounds.

Response

After repeating its initial question, the Yerushalmi offers two solutions. The first is that Rabban Gamaliel instructed his sons to read even though he did not think they could fulfill their obligation, i.e., he completely agreed with the sages that recitation after midnight is not valid and only permitted his sons to read the *shema* as a form of study. The Yerushalmi rejects this explanation because Rabban Gamaliel provides a time limit, "If dawn has not yet arrived," but one may certainly study *shema* even after dawn. The second response is that Rabban

[78] On the relationship between rabbis and *`amei ha'areṣ*, see Levine, *Rabbinic Class*, 112–17.

[79] See Aryeh Leib Gunzberg, *Sha'agat'aryeh* (New York: Israel Wolf, 1958), siman 4, p. 11, who writes:

> The main question of the Yerushalmi is only from the case of R. Akiva, for there is no question from R. Meir and R. Shimon who act stringently according to the majority who disagree with them, since there is no stringency that leads to a leniency in their controversies. Therefore, they acted according to the majority and were stringent. However, regarding the recitation of *shema* after midnight, since according to Rabban Gamaliel this is still the time for the recitation of *shema* and they may recite, therefore they are necessarily obligated to recite. If they would act stringently according to the sages, even if the majority prohibits him from reading as a rabbinic enactment, this would be a stringency that would lead to a leniency.... The cases of R. Meir and R. Shimon were only dragged in incidentally by the Yerushalmi. Since it cited that R. Akiva did not perform an act according to his own opinion it cites the cases of R. Meir and R. Shimon as well who did not perform acts according to their own opinions even though the main question is only from R. Akiva. This is the way of the Yerushalmi in all places to drag in many things that are similar even though they are not very relevant to the topic of the sugya and this is clear to whomever is acquainted with the Talmud Yerushalmi.

Cf. n. 72. These comments indicate the extent to which the proofs in this sugya remain indecisive and problematic.

Gamaliel did rely on his opinion *ex post facto* and ruled that they could fulfill their obligation. This solution allows for diversity of practice only where it is, in any case, impossible to fulfill the law according to the majority. Still, Rabban Gamaliel would not have opposed his colleagues before the fact.

In sum, all three proofs of the Yerushalmi present problems in that they rely on unnecessary assumptions and are readily refutable. That the Yerushalmi nevertheless depends on these three sources to prove halakhic conformity within the Tannaitic community reveals the Yerushalmi's push to read uniformity into the past. Evidently, it is uncomfortable with diversity of practice among the Tannaim and interprets examples of it out of existence.[80]

RHETORICAL ANALYSIS

The above source-critical analysis leads to the question of how the redactors thought about or justified what they were doing. Did they think that these sources definitively proved their point? Why did they not point out the difficulties in applying these three cases to the Rabban Gamaliel story? Even if they thought these sources were comparable with the case of Rabban Gamaliel, just because three other rabbis conformed in certain cases does not necessitate that Rabban Gamaliel also must have done so on every occasion. If we analyze this sugya in strict logical terms or try to translate it into syllogisms, it will be found wanting. With that in mind, I suggest that we view this sugya within the genre of rhetoric rather than logic. The most clearly evident use of classical rhetoric is in the structure of the sugya.

On Arrangement

The question section of this sugya, part [I], displays a highly organized structure: it has a beginning, middle and end; it repeats the primary query at the opening and at the conclusion; it includes a short introductory summary of its three more lengthy proofs; and it begins each proof with a similarly formed question. The arrangement of sections within the sugya is purposefully and carefully chosen. In fact, it follows the model of Greco-Roman rhetorical arrangement, as indicated by the emboldened subheadings I have added in the sugya above.

[80] See Hidary, *Dispute.*

The sugya contains four of the six parts of a suggested judicial oration but is missing the exordium and the refutation. According to Cicero, the exordium, whose purpose is to "commend the speaker to his audience,"[81] can be skipped if the case is likely to be easily accepted by the audience.[82] Hence, the composers of this sugya may have felt that their audience of fellow rabbis or students would be readily receptive to the arguments about to be presented, either because they also supported uniform behavior, or because they implicitly accepted the authority of whomever first presented this sugya publicly. Alternatively, a live presentation of this oration would have included an exordium suitable for the audience and the occasion, but this introduction was not preserved by the Yerushalmi redactors.[83]

Next comes the narration section. Aristotle teaches that the content of the narration depends on the type of oration.[84] In judicial oratory, the narration describes the case to be adjudicated, while in deliberative oratory, the narration recounts "events in the past, in order that by being reminded of those things the audience will take better counsel about what is to come (either criticizing or praising)."[85] This sugya bears much similarity to judicial oratory in that it judges whether or not Rabban Gamaliel is "guilty" of nonconformity. The narration presents the case and the charge, while the proof section establishes that all rabbis do and must follow the majority. The sugya also has a deliberative aspect in its seeking to establish a general principle that all rabbis should conform to the majority practice. Note that the exclamatory tone in the narration ("Does Rabban Gamaliel disagree...?!") already assumes that Rabban Gamaliel must have conformed, and the proof section does not address Rabban Gamaliel's actions but rather provides examples that corroborate the general principle. In this reading, the narration presents a case from the past not in order to judge it but rather to establish future policy.[86]

Following the narration comes the partition, wherein "the matters which we intend to discuss are briefly set forth in a methodical way. This leads the auditor to hold definite points in his mind."[87] Cicero

[81] Cicero, *On Invention*, I.15.
[82] Ibid., I.21.
[83] See also p. 115.
[84] See p. 3.
[85] Aristotle, *On Rhetoric*, III.16.11.
[86] Of course, the sugya need not fit neatly into Aristotle's categories. Nevertheless, it is useful to apply the categories in order to gain a sharper assessment of the function of each part of the sugya.
[87] Cicero, *On Invention*, I.31. See further p. 36 n. 167.

suggests that the partition "have the following qualities: brevity, completeness, conciseness."[88] Part B of the sugya fulfills all of these requirements.

The next section contains the body of the argument and includes three proofs, following the typical style of classical oratory.[89] The sugya contains only a confirmation and lacks a separate refutation section of counter arguments. However, as we saw in the source-critical analysis, each of the sources in this section could potentially serve as examples of nonconformity: R. Meir rules leniently for others against the majority; R. Akiva only voted with the majority because he either changed his mind or saw that he would lose the vote in any case; and R. Shimon bar Yoḥai actually did follow his own opinion in similar cases and simply lost his temper at an ignoramus in this case. Perhaps the redactors chose these difficult sources rather than clear-cut stories of conformity, such as M. Rosh Hashanah 2:9, precisely in order to refute them and take them off the table. In this sense, the sugya accomplishes both confirmation and refutation at the same time.

When citing multiple arguments, classical rhetoric recommends placing a strong argument first, the weakest argument in the middle, and the strongest argument last "since what is said last is easily committed to memory."[90] This sugya seems to follow this pattern. The middle argument, concerning R. Akiva, is the weakest since his vote was not going to be followed in any case. The first argument, regarding R. Meir, contains a problematic line within the source itself, which states that R. Meir ruled according to his opinion for others. This

[88] Ibid., I.32.

[89] See p. 37. Tripartite sugyot are common in both Talmuds, as shown by Shamma Friedman, "Some Structural Patterns of Talmudic Sugyot," [Hebrew] *Proceedings of the Sixth World Congress of Jewish Studies* 3 (1977): 391–6; and Jeffrey Rubenstein, "Some Structural Patterns of Yerushalmi Sugyot," in *The Talmud Yerushalmi and Graeco-Roman Culture III*, ed. Peter Schäfer (Tübingen: Mohr Siebeck, 2002). The context of classical rhetoric may help explain why tripartite structures are so prevalent.

[90] *Ad Herennium*, III.18. See similarly, Cicero, *Orator*, xv.50. This scheme may be the basis for the order of the verses cited in the *musaf* prayer on Rosh Hashanah. For each of the three central blessings relating to the themes of kingship, memory, and *shofar*, one must cite verses from Torah, Prophets, and Writings. However, M. Rosh Hashanah 4:6 teaches that "one begins with the verses from the Torah and ends with the verses from the Prophets." The verses of the lowest status from Writings are placed in the middle. Although rhetors recommend placing the strongest arguments at the end, unlike the first opinion in the Mishnah, R. Yose there adds that one may place the Torah verses at the end. I thank my sons David and Ronnie for bringing this Mishnah to my attention.

example is still strong, though, since it contains a genuine example of conformity. The third argument, about R. Shimon, offers the strongest proof since it is an actual ruling for someone else – not a vote and not his own action – and therefore most similar to Rabban Gamaliel's case. As this arrangement of examples demonstrates, the redactor assessed the relative strength of each source and arranged them for maxim rhetorical effect.

Finally, the peroration repeats the main argument of the questioner. The purpose of the peroration, or epilogue as Aristotle terms it, is "to remind the audience of what has been said earlier ... [I]n the epilogue one should speak in recapitulation of what has been shown. The starting point [of the epilogue] is to claim that one has performed what was promised."[91] While a peroration in classical rhetoric can sometimes be rather complex, the peroration of this sugya simply repeats the opening question verbatim. Nevertheless, if indeed this sugya is based on a live oration, then the original speech may have been more elaborate. In that case, this sugya may simply serve as a literary outline for a real or imagined oral presentation.

The three examples used in this sugya regarding three other Tannaim have no direct bearing on the practice of Rabban Gamaliel. The sugya's argument does not follow syllogistic logic nor even an enthymeme to prove that all rabbis always act with the majority. Rather, the sugya employs inductive reasoning, generalizing from examples: since we have stories about three prominent Tannaim who each submitted to the authority of the majority opinion when it came to practical rulings, we can assume that Rabban Gamaliel should have done so as well.[92]

If we read this sugya as a judicial speech, then its goal is to accuse Rabban Gamaliel of breaking ranks with the majority. In this interpretation, the anonymous prosecutor adduces various legal precedents of conformity in order to generalize from them a norm that would impute Rabban Gamaliel's actions. The anonymous defender accepts that

[91] Aristotle, *On Rhetoric*, III.19.3–4. See also Cicero, *On Invention*, I.98.

[92] These three examples do not actually prove anything about Rabban Gamaliel's conduct or attitude since they are examples from other occurrences that bear no relation to the story under discussion. This, however, is typical of the argument by example. As Corbett and Connors, *Classical Rhetoric*, 62, write: "An argument by example does not really prove anything, for like the rhetorical enthymeme, the example leads, most of the time, to a mere probability. But because a probability is what usually happens or what is believed to happen, the example has persuasive value." On the rhetorical power of rabbinic stories as legal precedents, see Moshe Simon-Shoshan, "Halakhic Mimesis: Rhetorical and Redactional Strategies in Tannaitic Narrative," *Diné Israel* 24 (2007): 101–23.

Rabban Gamaliel did act against the majority but finds a reason why the norm does not apply to this case and Rabban Gamaliel is acquitted.

If, on the other hand, we consider the sugya as deliberative oratory, then it seeks to read conformity into the past as a paradigm to be followed in the future. Consider Aristotle's assessment of the use of inductive reasoning from prior stories in persuasive speech: "Paradigms [i.e., proof from examples] are most appropriate to deliberative oratory, enthymemes more suited to judicial; for the former is concerned with the future, so it is necessary to draw examples from the past."[93] The unstated upshot of the Yerushalmi's examples is to encourage the audience to also take heed to conform to the majority practice.

What can the careful arrangements of the parts of this sugya tell us about its redactors' goals and methods? A logician who wishes to present a formal demonstration of a geometric theorem or to prove a postulate based on syllogistic logic will be bound to arrange his or her argument according to strict logical requirements. Such arguments are static and remain valid independent of their audience. Attention to the order of proofs, introductions, repetitions, and summaries, on the other hand, places a composition outside the realm of formal logic and into the genre of persuasive rhetoric. This sugya must therefore be categorized as rhetoric whose goal is not absolute truth or objectivity, but rather the presentation of a certain point of view in a way that will persuade an intended audience.[94] Rhetorical analysis of the sugya not only helps us uncover its structure but also its redactors' very mode of reasoning.

In general, the method of rhetorical composition starts with a given thesis and then proceeds to invent and formulate the most convincing arguments for it, regardless of whether the thesis is actually correct. Rhetorical training thus demands the ability to argue effectively for both sides of a proposition. As Thomas Sloane writes, "The first principles of whatever might be considered rhetoric's intellectual habit stem from the discipline's openness to contrariness, even to perversity, and from the ancient dialogic practice of generating arguments on both sides of the question."[95] The rhetorical mode of reasoning implies a hermeneutic of its own in how it selects and interprets its sources.

93 Aristotle, *On Rhetoric*, III.17.5.

94 See Chaim Perelman, *The Realm of Rhetoric*, trans. William Kluback (Notre Dame: Notre Dame Press, 1982), 146–52.

95 Thomas Sloane, *On the Contrary: The Protocol of Traditional Rhetoric* (Washington, D.C.: The Catholic University of America Press, 1997), 11.

Chaim Perelman elaborates on the choices that the rhetorician makes when formulating his or her argument:

> Every argument implies a preliminary selection of facts and values, their specific description in a given language, and an emphasis which varies with the importance given them. Choice of elements, of a mode of description and presentation, judgments of value or importance – all these elements are considered all the more justifiably as exhibiting a partiality when one sees more clearly what other choice, what other presentation, what other value judgment could oppose them. An affirmation and presentation that at first seem objective and impartial appear one sided – deliberately or not – when confronted with evidence from the other side.[96]

Our Yerushalmi sugya seems, on the surface, like an impartial argument based on three objective sources that each displays uniformity of practice. However, the source-critical analysis uncovered a very different presentation that the redactors could have chosen using the very same sources. For the first proof, the Yerushalmi emphasizes one line in the story, R. Meir's stringency upon himself, and ignores another line, R. Meir's leniency for others. The interpretation not taken in the Yerushalmi, i.e., to emphasize R. Meir's nonconformity, is in fact found in the Bavli.[97] The second source finds in R. Akiva's vote an act of normative conformity despite theoretical disagreement. The Yerushalmi could have taken an interpretive strategy similar to that of R. Yehudah in the Tosefta or rejected its applicability because it occurred in a public vote, and R. Akiva would have lost anyway. The third proof applies a story about R. Shimon's rebuke of a farmer to Rabban Gamaliel's instruction to his sons rather than rejecting this comparison on account of their different contexts. These alternate interpretive possibilities that were not taken reveal the Yerushalmi's partiality.

Cicero similarly describes how an orator should utilize laws and other documents to support his thesis: "A controversy turns upon written documents when some doubt arises from the nature of writing. This comes about from ambiguity, from the letter and intent, from conflict of laws, from reasoning by analogy, [and] from definition."[98] He then

96 Perelman, *The Realm of Rhetoric*, 34.

97 See p. 90 n. 68.

98 Cicero, *On Invention*, II.116. Modern writers recognize not only the ambiguity of given texts but even the indeterminacy built into all language. Perelman, *The Realm of Rhetoric*, 43–4, writes:

continues to show how an orator can argue for either side of a case using the same source

> by converting something in the written document to his own case or by showing that it contains some ambiguity; then on the basis of that ambiguity he may defend the passage which helps his case, or introduce a definition of some word and interpret the meaning of the word which seems to bear hard upon him, so as to support his own case, or develop from the written word something that is not expressed.[99]

By identifying ambiguities, contradictions, and gaps in a text, one can utilize that source in opposite directions. This understanding of the hermeneutical strategy assumed by rhetorical reasoning can help explain some of the difficulties raised by the source-critical analysis of the Yerushalmi sugya. The Yerushalmi begins with the thesis that all Tannaim conformed to a uniform majority opinion. It then continues to adduce three sources in favor of this thesis. While the sugya's redactors do not make explicit how they interpret each of these sources, their application of these sources to the Rabban Gamaliel narrative already suggests a limited range of interpretations, as discussed above. Each of these three sources is rather ambiguous and the interpretations of them assumed by the sugya are far from necessary. Despite these difficulties, or perhaps even because of them (assuming that it wants to refute them[100]), the Yerushalmi employs them in its effort to make the best case possible. Another orator might utilize these same sources to argue for the opposite point of view and present alternative interpretations of them. A debate would thus ensue as to which interpretation is the most probable; but that debate would remain within the realm of probability, which is the jurisdiction of rhetoric, rather than definitive proof, the jurisdiction of logic.

> For centuries, under the influence of rationalistic thinkers who considered mathematical language the model to be followed by ordinary language, and especially by philosophers, we have lived under the impression that messages, in principle, are clear and that multiple interpretations are the result of their authors' negligence or the interpreter's bad faith .... Today it is generally recognized that mathematics and for that matter all formal systems constitute artificial languages that we subject to numerous restrictions in the attempt to eliminate ambiguity ... In natural languages, ambiguity – the possibility of multiple interpretations would be the rule.

99 Cicero, *On Invention*, II.142.
100 See p. 97.

In an attempt to pry into the minds of the redactors a bit further, we may wonder how conscious they were of their interpretive choices. Were they aware that their interpretations were at best contingent and sometimes rather weak or even forced? If yes, how did they justify these choices? If not, how could these manifestly intelligent sages miss these seemingly obvious objections?[101]

One possibility is that the redactors were aware that their sources do not prove their thesis but they were more interested in teaching a halakhic/homiletic lesson regarding uniformity of practice than in presenting a historical and exegetically accurate account of the past.[102] That is, for didactic/rhetorical purposes, they deliberately included these sources and interpreted them according to their chosen agenda. This approach would put these Palestinian redactors well within the tradition of Greco-Roman rhetoric, which emphasized achieving the persuasive goal over the integrity of the process of getting there.

In this case, however, I prefer a second possibility that the redactors were truly convinced of the correctness of their interpretations. They believed that these sources really do support their thesis regarding uniformity of practice because they held certain assumptions that directed their interpretive choices. Working within the rhetorical mode, the authors of this sugya recognized that received texts and traditions can be ambiguous or otherwise problematic and that they sometimes need to be explained, limited to a given circumstance, emended, reconciled, or even rejected. They therefore believed that the plain contextual

[101] I would reject the possibility that the redactors were not at all aware of alternate sources or readings and created the most impartial argument they could, based on a monolithic understanding of the sources they had. Regarding the Rabban Gamaliel story of M. Berakhot 1:1, for example, the question of the sugya reveals an awareness that one reading of the story can find in it non-uniformity of practice. The two explanations at the end of the sugya are clearly deliberate and conscious re-readings. Rather, I assume that the redactors were in command of their sources and were able to lay out a range of interpretive possibilities for them. For support of this assumption, see Ishay Rosen-Zvi, "Midrash and Hermeneutic Reflectivity: *Kishmu`o* as a Test Case," in *Homer and the Bible in the Eyes of Ancient Interpreters*, ed. Maren Niehoff (Leiden: Brill, 2012): 329–44. My question is only whether they thought that their interpretive decisions accurately reflected the thrust of these sources or were simply apologetic or creative uses of them.

[102] This is similar to the reworking of narrative sources performed by the Bavli's redactors. See Rubenstein, *Talmudic Stories*, 15–21. While Rubenstein attributes this activity to the Babylonian Stammaim, similar activity may be found in the Yerushalmi as well, even if much less frequently. Rubenstein, ibid., 92, points to Y. Ḥagigah 2:1, 77b–c, as "among the most artful and complex of all rabbinic stories." In the area of non-narrative sugyot, the sugya analyzed in this chapter may be among the most carefully structured and rhetorically conscious of all rabbinic compositions.

interpretation of some sources could be faulty in light of their larger convictions regarding Tannaitic diversity of practice. Consequently, they sometimes preferred forced interpretations of certain sources to readings that might be more literal but still less accurate.

I prefer this possibility because, as I have previously argued at length, the Yerushalmi generally holds the conviction that uniformity of halakhic practice is not only ideal but also that it was a reality in past generations. This viewpoint follows a common tendency throughout the Yerushalmi to avoid factionalism, prosecute dissent, systematize rules of codification, and maintain unified community norms.[103] By reading these stories about Tannaitic activity with the basic assumption of uniformity already in mind, the sugya regards these interpretations as the most plausible. In other words, the redactors considered it appropriate to select a possible interpretation of a text, even if it may not have been its most straightforward reading, over another interpretation that would contradict a larger conviction fundamental to their worldview and built into their characterization of rabbinic society.[104] Recognizing that texts are inherently ambiguous, the redactors read these sources in the best light they could, based on their historical and sociological assumptions regarding uniformity of practice.[105]

[103] See Hidary, *Dispute*.

[104] The Yerushalmi similarly reads uniformity of practice into the past regarding disputes between the Houses of Shammai and Hillel. See ibid., 99–100 and 163–223.

[105] This hermeneutical stance accords with what W. V. O. Quine, *Word and Object* (Cambridge: MIT Press, 1960), 58–9, calls the principle of charitable reading. See further discussion on this concept by Ronald Dworkin, *Law's Empire* (Cambridge: Belknap Press, 1986), 53, and Halbertal, *People of the Book*, 27–32.
The following quote from Martin Heidegger also describes accurately the interpretive mode of the authors/redactors of our sugya:

> An interpretation is never a presuppositionless apprehending of something presented to us. If, when one is engaged in a particular kind of interpretation, in the sense of exact textual interpretation, one likes to appeal [beruft] to what 'stands there', then one finds that what 'stands there' in the first instance is nothing other than the obvious undiscussed assumption [Vormeinung] of the person who does the interpreting. [Martin Heidegger, *Being and Time*, trans. John Macquarrie and Edward Robinson (New York: Harper & Row, 1962), 191–2, cited at Gerald Bruns, *Hermeneutics Ancient and Modern* (New Haven: Yale University Press, 1992), 4.]

The Being-in-the-world of the redactors necessitated halakhic uniformity and so any texts on this subject would be understood in that light. It was inconceivable to them that the past could be otherwise and so readings that from our perspective may seem forced were for them much less problematic than overturning their most basic assumptions.

CONCLUSION

The previous chapter analyzed the forms of rabbinic homiletic sermons and found them to follow the basic tripartite arrangement of rhetoric with an exordium, body, and epilogue. We also found some examples of sermons that include narration, partition, and three proofs. This chapter extends this rhetorical analysis to rabbinic legal presentations. Much of the rabbis' legal instruction occurred in small study circles in which the teacher would recite traditions and provide explanations. These discussions, which form the basis of many sugyot, may not reflect rhetorical arrangement because they were not delivered as orations but rather as individual lessons.[106] However, the rabbis also offered public lectures on legal subjects that likely would have conformed to rhetorical arrangement and style. The Talmudic sages officially transmitted only the legal conclusions and barebones summaries of these lectures, making it difficult to reconstruct the content and form of these presentations. Nevertheless, I believe that Yerushalmi Berakhot 1:1 preserves the outline and major arguments of one such lecture.[107]

Considering the advanced rhetorical techniques in this sugya's arrangement and its subject matter regarding the behavior of the patriarch Rabban Gamaliel of Yavneh, one could venture a guess that the author of the sugya may have been a later patriarch who received a proper education in rhetoric[108] and wanted to exonerate his ancestor's

A similar idea is developed in the analysis by Gadamer, *Truth and Method*, 336, of "historically effected consciousness [that] is at work in all hermeneutical activity." Gadamer himself points out the connection between his project and that of classical rhetoric (ibid., p. 18). Moshe Halbertal, *Interpretive Revolutions in the Making: Values as Interpretive Considerations in Midrashei Halakhah* [Hebrew] (Jerusalem: Magnes Press, 1999), 193–5, applies Gadamer's description of the hermeneutical enterprise to midrashic readings of certain biblical passages in which the rabbis radically reinterpret these biblical laws to conform to moral principles. This chapter follows a similar methodology. While Halbertal deals with how the midrash interprets biblical verses in light of moral considerations, this chapter discusses how the Yerushalmi redactors interpret Tannaitic sources in light of social/political considerations. Halbertal, ibid., 197–203, concludes that the rabbis may have shared some of the interpretive methods described by Gadamer and other similar theorists but that their motivations and underlying assumptions for doing so were very different from those of these postmodern writers. He is led to this conclusion based, in part, on the divinity of the biblical texts, a consideration that is less significant in amoraic interpretations of tannaitic texts.

106 See further in Chapter 4 on rabbinic lessons as rhetorical exercises.

107 We cannot be sure whether this sugya derives from a live oration or was composed only for study. But even in the latter case, it still reflects what its author imagined would have been appropriate in a live oration.

108 See p. 7 n. 32.

behavior. Alternatively, the author could have been any Palestinian sage who wanted to instruct his audience on the need for halakhic conformity. In either case, the compiler of this sugya shows familiarity with Greco-Roman rhetorical arrangement and style and is able to apply that knowledge to create a well-designed persuasive composition.

Academic Talmud study tends to focus on source criticism by dissecting the chronological layers and sources of a sugya in an effort to rewind the work of the redactor. However, scholars do not always continue to put the pieces back together and view the sugya as a literary whole. Performing rhetorical criticism on Talmudic sugyot can help uncover the persuasive goal of the redactor and illuminate how each step of the sugya's argumentation leads one to that target. In order to demonstrate this methodology, this chapter first subjected the sugya to a source-critical analysis and then combined those results with a rhetorical analysis of the text as a literary unit.[109] Reading the Talmud against the background of Greco-Roman rhetoric provides an essential tool to help place the Talmud's forced explanations into contextual perspective, unpack the sugya's meaning, and even appreciate its beauty. The next chapter will apply the same methodology to the Bavli.

[109] For further examples of rhetorical readings, see the sugyot listed at Hidary, *Dispute*, 39 n. 149 and analyzed therein.

3 The Agonistic Bavli: Greco-Roman Rhetoric in Sasanian Persia

Like an athlete he undertook a contest with heresies,
And as if with his finger, he showed their powerlessness.
He resembled a wrestler in his retorts,
And he beat falsehood to the ground before the eyes of the onlookers.
The various ways of fighting were regarded by him as a theatre,
And in his whole life he never allowed himself to be conquered.[1]

R. Yoḥanan said, "I have cut off the legs of that child."[2]

Even more than their Palestinian colleagues, the Amoraim of Babylonia were known for their contentious argumentation. These rabbis shared this agonistic spirit both with their Syriac-speaking Christian neighbors and with the wider Hellenistic culture of rhetoric that penetrated beyond the Roman Empire into Persia as well. For the Greeks, persuasive speech rose to an art form and further became the focus of intense competition on a par with sporting events and gladiatorial battles. As Walter Ong writes, "Oratory has deep agonistic roots. The development of the vast rhetorical tradition was distinctive of the West and was related, whether as cause or effect or both, to the tendency

This chapter is a modified version of Richard Hidary, "The Agonistic Bavli: Greco-Roman Rhetoric in Sasanian Persia," in *Shoshannat Yaakov: Jewish and Iranian Studies in Honor of Yaakov Elman*, ed. Shai Secunda and Steven Fine (Leiden: Brill, 2012): 137–64. I thank Brill for permission to re-publish it.

[1] A panegyric to Theodore in Narsai's mēmrā on the Three Nestorian Doctors, published in F. Martin, "Homélie de Narsès sur les trois docteurs Nestoriens," *Journal Asiatique*, ix, 14–15 (1899): 446–92 and 469–525. English translation from Kathleen McVey, "The Mēmrā on the Three Nestorian Doctors as an Example of Forensic Rhetoric," in *III Symposium Syriacum*, ed. R. Lavenant (Rome: 1983): 94.

[2] B. Me`ilah 7b. See further at Jeffrey Rubenstein, *The Culture of the Babylonian Talmud* (Baltimore, MD: Johns Hopkins University Press, 2003), 57.

among the Greeks and their cultural epigoni to maximize oppositions."[3] In fact, Greek orators often compared argumentation to warfare.[4] It is within this atmosphere that Narsai, one of the most prominent theologians of the Eastern Church, could write a homily praising his teacher in the manner cited in the epigraph to this chapter as a wrestler who beats his adversaries to the ground.

The Bavli similarly records R. Yoḥanan calling his younger colleague a child and boasting about the severing of his legs as a metaphor for winning an argument.[5] In fact, the Bavli often compares halakhic debate with battle and refers to "those who give and take in the war of Torah."[6] The hostility aroused by these debates extends so far that the Bavli can state: "Three hate each other, and these are they: dogs, fowl, and [Zoroastrian] priests. And some say: prostitutes. And some say, the scholars of Babylonia."[7] R. Oshaia contrasts the scholars in Palestine, who "are gracious to each other in legal [debate]," to the scholars in Babylonia, who "damage (*meḥablin*) each other in legal [debate]."[8] Yaakov Elman proposes that "the most striking thing about the Bavli is its nature as a continual and unending *dialogue*, from beginning to end – its *agonistic* nature."[9] Jeffrey Rubenstein similarly shows that the thematization of hostility and violence in the Talmud as a metaphor for halakhic argumentation is more prevalent in the Bavli than in the Yerushalmi.

Elman and Rubenstein attribute the agonistic character of the Bavli to two related factors: the oral culture of the Bavli and the redactional activity of the Stammaim that continued about two centuries after that of the Yerushalmi.[10] Unlike writing, which creates some distance

3 Walter J. Ong, *Orality and Literacy: The Technologizing of the World* (London: Routledge, 1982), 108–9.

4 See Rubenstein, *Culture*, 179 n. 33.

5 Although R. Yoḥanan is a Palestinian sage, the epigraph cited from B. Me`ilah 7b is likely not the original words of that sage but rather an elaboration of the Bavli redactors. Rubenstein, *Culture*, 54–9. Severing legs also appears in B. Baba Qama 81b, and see also Rashi "*qafḥinhu*" to B. Giṭṭin 29b. Most battle wounds were made to the legs because they were not protected by armor; see Brian Campbell and Lawrence Tritle, eds., *The Oxford Handbook of Warfare in the Classical World* (Oxford: Oxford University Press, 2013), 297.

6 B. Megilah 15b. See Rubenstein, *Culture*, 59–61; and Ishay Rosen-Zvi, "The Rise and Fall of Rabbinic Masculinity," *Jewish Studies, an Internet Journal* 12 (2013): 13–14.

7 B. Pesaḥim 113b. Translation from Rubenstein, *Culture*, 54.

8 B. Sanhedrin 24a. See further at Rubenstein, ibid., 55–6; and Hidary, *Dispute*, 25.

9 Yaakov Elman, "Orality and the Redaction of the Babylonian Talmud," *Oral Tradition* 14, no. 1 (1999): 84.

10 See Elman, "Orality," 84; Rubenstein, *Culture*, 61–4; and Hidary, "Agonistic Bavli," 137–9.

between interlocutors and provides more time for reflection and nuance, oral debate encourages a more competitive, heated, and personalized exchange. The Stammaim redacted, recreated, and transmitted the Bavli within such an oral atmosphere where one's personal honor or shame depended on dialectical skill and victory in verbal polemics.[11] Rubenstein finds that it is particularly the Stammaim, the fifth- to seventh-century redactors of the Bavli, who portray the rabbinic academy as "a competitive environment characterized more by struggle than by mutual collaboration. Combine the valorization of argumentation and the competitive spirit with the 'agonist' ethos of the oral milieu and you have a hostile climate."[12] While I agree with this assessment, I see both of these factors as themselves part of the environment of classical rhetoric[13] that increasingly pervaded Persia in the late amoraic and Stammaitic periods. The glamorization of oratory, live debate, and verbal agon are the hallmarks of the Hellenistic sophistic culture that gave rise to the agon of the Bavli.

The previous chapters demonstrated the presence of Greco-Roman rhetorical reasoning and arrangement in Palestinian amoraic midrashim as well as in the Yerushalmi.[14] This chapter will analyze examples of rhetorical persuasion and structure in the Bavli as well. Before delving into this analysis, however, it will first be necessary to explore possible conduits by which the classical rhetorical tradition could have entered the Babylonian rabbinic purview.

GRECO-ROMAN RHETORIC IN SASANIAN PERSIA

Scholars have long assumed that there was little Hellenistic influence in the Babylonian Talmud, except perhaps through communication with Palestinian rabbis. This is symptomatic of the more general "tendency of many scholars to underestimate the philosophical exchange between Byzantium and Sasanian Iran."[15] Joel T. Walker instead argues

[11] Rubenstein, *Culture*, 67–79.

[12] Rubenstein, *Culture*, 64.

[13] On the close relationship between orality, oratory, and agon, see Ong, *Orality and Literacy*, 43–5; and Ong, "The Agonistic Base of Scientifically Abstract Thought: Issues in Fighting for Life: Contest, Sexuality, and Consciousness," in *An Ong Reader: Challenges for Further Inquiry*, ed. Thomas Farrell and Paul Soukup (Cresskill: Hampton Press, 1982): 480.

[14] Another example of rhetorical arrangement in the Yerushalmi is at Pesaḥim 6:1, 33a, analyzed on pp. 190–2.

[15] Joel T. Walker, "The Limits of Late Antiquity: Philosophy between Rome and Iran," *Ancient World* 33, no. 1 (2002): 46.

for a "much broader pattern of cultural exchange."[16] In the Jewish context, Charlotte Elisheva Fonrobert points to this permeable border to explain how "neo-Platonism would have made inroads at least into the Sasanian royal world in Ctesiphon, a city which, in turn, had a strong presence of rabbinic sages."[17] Similarly, Daniel Boyarin has more recently argued for "extensive cultural contact and interaction between the Rabbis of late Babylonia and the Greco-Christian cultural world,"[18] whether through a common Hellenistic culture in Persia or through direct contact between the Syriac Christians and late Babylonian rabbis.

Shaye Cohen shows significant parallels between the Babylonian Talmud's portrayal of the patriarch and the description of the scholarch in Greek sources, which relate to further similarities between the Bavli's depiction of the rabbinic academy and the Greek evidence of the workings of the philosophical schools. Cohen, however, provides no mechanism for this "Hellenization of Babylonian Jewry in the fourth and fifth centuries."[19] In fact, Greek traditions could have entered the Bavli by means of many possible conduits, such as itinerant sophists visiting Babylonia, traveling rabbis importing what they learned in the West (from Palestinian colleagues or from the general milieu), or Jews with some Greco-Roman education conversing with rabbis. Moreover, the pursuit of "influence" is hardly necessary considering that many aspects of Hellenism pervaded Sasanian Persia. As Eva Riad writes, "Even the most genuine Syriac writers, considered most free from Greek influence, like Afrem and Afrahat, lived in a milieu imbued with Hellenistic

[16] Ibid. Walker's argument centers on the flight of Damascius and his colleagues to the court of Khosrow in 532 CE after Justinian closed the School of Athens. Although Damascius' stay in Persia lasted only one year, the story reflects the "the richness of intellectual life at the late Sasanian court, as well as the intensity of its contacts with Greek and Syrian intellectuals" (ibid., p. 68).

[17] Charlotte Elisheva Fonrobert, "Plato in Rabbi Shimon bar Yohai's Cave (B. Shabbat 33b–34a): The Talmudic Inversion of Plato's Politics of Philosophy," *AJS Review* 31, no. 2 (2007): 295.

[18] Boyarin, *Socrates and the Fat Rabbis*, 140. See also Boyarin, "Hellenism in Jewish Babylonia," 336–63. Even if Boyarin stretches the application of this hypothesis beyond the evidence, the basic claim that the Babylonian Talmud reflects a significant degree of Hellenism can hardly be denied. See Adam Becker, "The Comparative Study of 'Scholasticism' in Late Antique Mesopotamia: Rabbis and East Syrians," *AJS Review* 34, no. 1 (2010): 107 n. 84; and Adam Becker, "Positing a 'Cultural Relationship' between Plato and the Babylonian Talmud," *Jewish Quarterly Review* 101, no. 2 (2011): 255–69.

[19] Cohen, "Patriarchs and Scholarchs," 85.

thought patterns."[20] The Babylonian Amoraim lived in the same Hellenized environment and rabbinic Judaism, in all its forms, is in many ways a manifestation of Hellenism.[21]

While these considerations can account for Hellenistic elements in the amoraic layer of the Bavli dating from the third to fifth centuries, a connection between the Syriac Christian schools and their contemporary Stammaitic academies can be most useful in explaining the extraordinary leap in dialectics and specific rhetorical methods that we find in the redactional layers of the Bavli.[22] For example, one possible conduit for the penetration of Greco-Roman literature into Sasanian Persia is the relocation of the School of the Persians in Edessa to Nisibis, several hundred miles eastward.[23] The School of Nisibis was founded by Narsai (died c. 503), one of the most important writers and theologians of the Eastern Church, and continued until the seventh century.[24] In addition to this famous school, the School of Seleucia was founded in the mid-sixth century in Seleucia-Ctesiphon, the capital of the Sasanian Empire and an important center of rabbinic learning, known in the Bavli as Meḥoza.[25] Besides these schools, many other monastic and independent schools as well as smaller village schools were founded throughout Mesopotamia in the sixth century CE.[26]

[20] Eva Riad, *Studies in the Syriac Preface* (Uppsala: Uppsala University, 1988), 40. See also the literature cited at Richard Kalmin, *Jewish Babylonia between Persia and Roman Palestine* (New York: Oxford University Press, 2006), 6.

[21] See Boyarin, *Socrates and the Fat Rabbis*, 29; Levine, *Judaism and Hellenism*, 96–138; and Wimpfheimer, *Narrating the Law*, 106.

[22] The growing Hellenization of Syriac culture, especially from the fourth century to the fifth and sixth centuries, is documented by Sebastian Brock, "From Antagonism to Assimilation: Syriac Attitudes to Greek Learning," in *East of Byzantium: Syria and Armenia in the Formative Period*, ed. Nina Garsoian, Thomas Mathews, and Robert Thomson (Washington D.C.: Dumbarton Oaks, Center for Byzantine Studies, 1982): 17–34. See also Richard Kalmin, *Migrating Tales: The Talmud's Narratives and Their Historical Context* (Oakland, CA: University of California Press, 2014), 1–11.

[23] The school was forcibly closed by the Emperor Zeno in 489 CE because of Christological disputes. See Adam Becker, *Fear of God and the Beginning of Wisdom: The School of Nisibis and the Development of Scholastic Culture in Late Antique Mesopotamia* (Philadelphia: University of Pennsylvania, 2006), 2 and 77–8.

[24] See Sebastian Brock, "A Guide to Narsai's Homilies," *Journal of Syriac Studies* 12, no. 1 (2009): 21–40.

[25] Becker, *Fear of God*, 157–8; and Becker, "Comparative Study," 4. See also Pinchas Hayman, "From Tiberias to Mehoza: Redactional and Editorial Processes in Amoraic Babylonia," *The Jewish Quarterly Review* 93, no. 1–2 (2002): 117–48, who locates Meḥoza as a primary location for the editing of some Bavli material during the fourth century CE.

[26] Becker, *Fear of God*, 159–68.

Isaiah Gafni has noted the similarities between these Eastern Christian schools and the Babylonian yeshivot, especially in post-amoraic times.[27] Syriac Christians and Aramaic-speaking rabbis, for instance, shared terminology such as *rav, metivta, siyyuma*, and *qam be-resh*. Furthermore, both schools had a two-semester schedule such that students could go earn a living by working in the fields during the summer and winter harvest seasons.[28] Both communities also maintained public lectures, called the *pirqa* by the rabbis[29] and *'elltha* by the Eastern Christians,[30] and the office of the *resh galuta* had its parallel in the East Syrian Catholicos.[31] In addition, many stories, interpretations, and ideas made their way from Christian sources into the Babylonian Talmud.[32]

Most significantly, as Adam Becker argues, both communities followed a scholastic program of study that included systematic textual interpretation, and both held such study to be a transformative act of piety and devotion.[33] Using José Ignacio Cabezón's model of activities representative of scholasticism,[34] Michael Swartz shows that the rabbis, especially in the Bavli, display many characteristics of scholasticism, including upholding the authority of tradition, contributing to that tradition through commentary, participation in dialectic, and reconciliation of disparate sources.[35] Swartz elaborates:

[27] Isaiah Gafni, "Nestorian Literature as a Source for the History of the Babylonian *Yeshivot*," [Hebrew] *Tarbiz* 51 (1982): 567–76. See also Rubenstein, *Culture*, 35–8; and Becker, "Comparative Study," 101–2 and 105 n. 77. Scholars now recognize that these descriptions apply only to the Babylonian yeshivot during post-amoraic times when the Talmud was redacted, but that is in any case the period that is most relevant to the subject of this chapter; see Jeffrey Rubenstein, "The Rise of the Babylonian Rabbinic Academy: A Reexamination of the Talmudic Evidence," *Jewish Studies, an Internet Journal* 1 (2002): 56–68.

[28] Rubenstein, *Culture*, 36–7; Becker, *Fear of God*, 106; and Becker, "Comparative Study," 101–2.

[29] See p. 47.

[30] Becker, "Comparative Study," 102.

[31] Geoffrey Herman, *A Prince without a Kingdom: The Exilarch in the Sasanian Era* (Tübingen: Mohr Siebeck, 2012), 15.

[32] See Bar-Asher Siegal, *Early Christian Monastic Literature.*

[33] Becker, "Comparative Study," 104–6. See also Rubenstein, *Culture*, 37.

[34] José Ignacio Cabezón, ed. *Scholasticism: Cross-Cultural and Comparative Perspectives* (Albany: State University of New York Press, 1998), 4–6.

[35] Michael Swartz, "Scholasticism as a Comparative Category and the Study of Judaism," in *Scholasticism: Cross-Cultural and Comparative Perspectives*, ed. José Ignacio Cabezón (Albany: State University of New York Press, 1998): 91–114. Swartz, ibid., 101–2, has difficulty locating the use of a process of abstraction by the rabbis, which is one of the characteristics of scholasticism according to Cabezón. However, Leib Moscovitz, *Talmudic Reasoning: From Casuistics to Conceptualization* (Tübingen: Mohr Siebeck, 2002), demonstrates that the Stammaim do engage in abstraction.

> [T]he Gemara often takes the form of an ongoing conversation among sages, many of whom lived centuries apart from each other. This conversation is moderated, as it were, by an anonymous Aramaic text (called the "*stam*") that can take the role of a skeptical observer – asking questions regarding opinions presented, pointing out contradictions and logical inconsistencies, and arranging source materials for comparison. This method of presentation can be considered a kind of dialectical argumentation about traditional sources for exegetical purposes. It is thus in the Talmud that many of the characteristics we can identify with scholasticism are best expressed in Judaism.[36]

Since the scholastic activities identified by Cabezón and Swartz were practiced by both Eastern Christians and by the Bavli's Stammaim, it stands to reason that methods of rhetorical composition found in the former would similarly find expression in the latter. In fact, the use of Greco-Roman rhetoric by Syriac writers is well established. As John Watt explains, "There is every reason to suppose that Greek literature and rhetoric were studied by philhellenes of Syria and Mesopotamia just as much as Greek grammar, philosophy, and medicine."[37] Despite the lack of extant rhetorical treatises in Syriac prior to that of Anton of Tigrit (ninth century CE), there are indications that rhetoric was being studied and used in Persia since the fifth century.[38] As an example of the use of Greek rhetoric, Riad points to the inclusion of prefaces by Syriac writers, a genre that emerged from classical forensic speech.[39] Such prefaces are found already in the fourth century and became increasingly customary in the fifth and sixth centuries.[40]

In the remainder of this chapter, I will focus on classical rhetorical arrangement as found in both Syriac writings and in the Bavli. Many Syriac writers seem to have been aware of the divisions of Greco-Roman arrangement,[41] whether they read rhetorical handbooks or only learned

[36] Swartz, "Scholasticism," 94.

[37] John Watt, "Eastward and Westward Transmission of Classical Rhetoric," in *Centers of Learning: Learning and Location in Pre-Modern Europe and the Near East*, ed. J.W. Drijvers and A. A. MacDonald (Leiden: Brill, 1995): 3.

[38] See Robert Murray, "Some Rhetorical Patterns in Early Syriac Literature," in *A Tribute to Arthur Vööbus: Studies in Early Christian Literature and Its Environment, Primarily in the Syrian East*, ed. Robert Fischer (Chicago: The Lutheran School of Theology at Chicago, 1977): 109–31.

[39] Riad, *Studies in the Syriac Preface*, 13–14.

[40] Ibid., 19–23.

[41] See pp. 35–9.

it by imitation, and utilized it in their own compositions.[42] Balai of Qennesrin, who may have been chorbishop in Qennesrin and in nearby villages, was active in the late fourth and early fifth centuries and wrote, among other things, a work titled *Sermons on Joseph*. In analyzing this work, Robert Phenix has found many techniques used by Balai to be in common with the Greco-Roman rhetorical tradition. Significantly, Phenix has shown that at least two of Balai's prefaces to his sermons follow precisely the order of sections recommended in *Ad Herennium*,[43] thus demonstrating "the plausibility of the influence of classical rhetoric on the arrangement of some of the speeches" in *Sermons on Joseph*.[44]

Alexander Böhlig has analyzed the anonymous Syriac treatise *Liber Graduum*, also written in the late fourth or early fifth century. He classifies this work as deliberative rhetoric and has similarly found that many of its sermons follow the more basic four parts of arrangement – exordium, narration, argument, and peroration – though the structure varies depending on the subject matter.[45] Similarly, Jost Blum shows that the sermons of Jacob of Sarug also follow the same arrangement.[46] To return to Narsai, Kathleen McVey analyzed one of his mēmrē that probably dates to 489 CE when Zeno closed the School at Edessa. She discovered that it is "a piece of forensic rhetoric in the Greco-Roman style" and that it "conforms to the definition of the forensic speech as given by Quintilian,"[47] following the very same arrangement into six parts listed in the rhetorical handbooks. McVey concludes: "The influx of Greek learning into Syriac theological education in the fifth century A.D. and the context of the fifth century Christological controversies provide a plausible setting for the introduction of this rhetorical form into Syrian literature."[48] In sum, there exists sufficient evidence that

[42] Although these treatises were written centuries earlier than the Amoraim and Syriac writers discussed below and hundreds of miles apart, the fundamentals of rhetorical theory remained relatively static over time, with only minor variations from one writer to the next. Since no Syriac rhetorical handbook is extant from late antiquity, the early Latin and Greek handbooks must serve as the best approximation to the instruction taught at Syriac schools. See p. 8 n. 37.

[43] Robert Phenix, *The Sermons on Joseph of Balai of Qenneshrin: Rhetoric and Interpretation in Fifth Century Syriac Literature* (Tübingen: Mohr Siebeck, 2008), 192–7.

[44] Ibid., 198.

[45] Alexander Böhlig, "Zur Rhetorik im Liber Graduum," in *IV Symposium Syriacum*, ed. H.J.W. Drijvers et al. (Rome: Pontificium Institutum Studiorum Orientalium, 1987): 397–405.

[46] Jost G. Blum, "Zum Bau von Abschnitten in Memre von Jacob von Sarug," in *III Symposium Syriacum*, ed. R. Lavenant (Rome: 1983): 307–21.

[47] McVey, "Mēmrā," 87.

[48] Ibid.

various aspects of Hellenism, including classical rhetoric and arrangement of orations, were well known in Babylonia, were put into practice by Syriac writers, and would have been readily available for use by their rabbinic neighbors as well.

MUST A FATHER FEED HIS DAUGHTER?

We are now in a position to analyze a set of Bavli sugyot whose structure follows the arrangement advocated by classical rhetoric. Significant aspects of classical rhetoric, including arrangement, arguing both sides of an issue, and creation of suspense, are evident in B. Ketubot 49a, which comments on M. Ketubot 4:6. The Mishnah teaches[49]:

> A father is not obligated to feed his daughter. This is the interpretation that R. Eleazar ben Azariah presented before the sages in the vineyard of Yavneh: [The *ketubah* reads:] "The sons will inherit and the daughters will be fed." Just as the sons do not inherit until after the death of their father, so the daughters are fed only after the death of their father.

The Gemara comments[50]:

> **[Narration]**
> "A father is not obligated in feeding his daughter." He is not obligated in feeding his daughter but he is obligated in feeding his son. Even for his daughter, there is no obligation but there is a *miṣvah*.[51]
>
> **[Partition]**
> Who is the author of our Mishnah?
> [A] It is not R. Meir.
>
> [B] It is not R. Yehudah.
>
> [C] It is not R. Yoḥanan ben Beroqa.

[49] Translation follows the text of MS Kaufman.

[50] Translation generally follows the text of MS Vatican 487. See Hidary, "Agonistic Bavli," 146–53, for textual notes. See further variants at Moshe Hershler, ed. *Tractate Ketubot: The Babylonian Talmud with Variant Readings* (Jerusalem: Mekhon haTalmud haYisre'eli haShalem, 1972), 1:361–5 and a chart of all manuscript traditions at http://rabbinics.org/charts.

[51] The word *miṣvah* cannot be translated literally as "commandment" because in this context it is distinguished from obligation. Rather, it means a praiseworthy deed that the father ought to do but is not legally obligated to do.

[Proof]

[A] As it was taught: There is a *miṣvah* to feed the daughters, all the more so sons who study Torah, the words of R. Meir.[52]

[B] R. Yehudah says: There is a *miṣvah* to feed the sons, all the more so daughters because of their disgrace.

[C] R. Yoḥanan ben Beroqa says: There is an obligation to feed the daughters after the death of their father but during the lifetime of the father he need not feed either these [the sons] or those [the daughters].

[Peroration]

Who is the author of our Mishnah?

[A] If it is R. Meir, but he said one ought to feed sons.

[B] If it is R. Yehudah, but he said one ought to feed sons.

[C] If it is R. Yoḥanan ben Beroqa, he said there is not even a *miṣvah*.

The sugya includes four of the six recommended parts of arrangement. As noted in the previous chapter, the exordium may be omitted when the audience is already favorably disposed to the speech.[53] We cannot know if this sugya was ever performed in front of an audience, but it is likely that the projected audience would be a group of students and colleagues who would already have accepted the authority of the speaker. Another possibility is that in a live delivery, the rabbi would have opened his lecture with an exordium; however, this section was not recorded in the sugya since it lacks any substantive value beyond its performative setting. Each performance required a different exordium to fit the speaker, audience, and occasion.[54]

The sugya, therefore, begins with the narration, which is made up of the Mishnah under discussion, as well as two laws deduced from it.

[52] Rashbam to B. Baba Batra 141a comments that the words "who study Torah" are not part of the *baraita* but rather explanatory glosses by the Talmud.

[53] See p. 96, citing Cicero, *On Invention*, I.15.

[54] There is some evidence of rabbinic use of exordiums in the report that Rava regularly began his lectures with words of humor (B. Shabbat 30b; B. Pesaḥim 117a), even though the Talmud did not feel his jokes worthy of preservation. See further on the rhetorical value of humor in Quintilian, *Institutes of Oratory*, 6.3 and Boyarin, *Socrates and the Fat Rabbis*, 4–12. Other sages would begin their lectures with homilies in honor of their hosts (B. Berakhot 63b). Yet another possibility is that the place of the exordium may have been filled with an introductory prayer in praise of God giving the Torah; see Joseph Heinemann, *Prayer in the Talmud: Forms and Patterns* (Berlin: de Gruyter, 1977), 251–6.

Since the Mishnah says only that daughters need not be fed,[55] the Talmud derives that the law must be different for sons, whom the father is obligated to feed. Furthermore, even for daughters, although the Mishnah states only that there is no obligation, the Talmud infers that there is a *miṣvah* for the father to feed his daughters; otherwise, the Mishnah should have said that he does not even have that lower level of responsibility. The Mishnah, along with these two starting interpretive assumptions, comprises the case that will be under discussion.

Cicero advises that in the partition, "the matters which we intend to discuss are briefly set forth in a methodical way. This leads the auditor to hold definite points in his mind."[56] In line with this advice, the partition in this sugya outlines the three-part structure of the upcoming argument that the Mishnah cannot be authored by any of the three Tannaim who rule on this issue.[57]

Next comes the body of the tripartite proof from a *baraita*. Both R. Meir and R. Yehudah agree with the second derived assumption in the narration that fathers ought to feed their daughters. However, they both disagree with the assumption that there is an absolute obligation to feed sons, stating instead that it is only a *miṣvah*. Therefore, they cannot be the authors of the Mishnah. R. Yoḥanan ben Beroqa, meanwhile, opines that there is no responsibility whatsoever for the father to feed his children during his lifetime, so he certainly cannot be the author of the Mishnah.

The next section revisits each opinion in turn and makes explicit why each Tanna cannot be the author of the Mishnah. To the extent that this was clear from the *baraita* itself, this review can be considered the peroration, whose purpose in general is to "speak in recapitulation of what has been shown."[58] This completes the first half of the sugya, which presents the challenge that apparently no Tanna can be the author of the Mishnah. Note that there is no refutation section here, perhaps because the second half of the sugya will in fact refute the

[55] In fact, this entire chapter of Mishnah only speaks of the rights and obligations of daughters and does not relate at all to sons, for whom the law may very well be the same. Nevertheless, the Talmud interprets the Mishnah with the principle of omnisignificance in a similar manner to the way midrash interprets Scripture. For background on inheritance law for daughters in tannaitic and comparative literature, see Jonathan Milgram, *From Mesopotamia to the Mishnah: Tannaitic Inheritance Law in its Legal and Social Contexts* (Tübingen: Mohr Siebeck, 2016), 105–31.

[56] Cicero, *On Invention*, 1.31. See further p. 36 n. 167.

[57] See p. 37 and p. 97 n. 89.

[58] Aristotle, *On Rhetoric*, III.19.4.

arguments presented so far. The second half of the sugya resolves the challenge of authorship:

> [A] If you want I can say it is R. Meir.
>
> [B] If you want I can say it is R. Yehudah.
>
> [C] If you want I can say it is R. Yoḥanan ben Beroqa.
>
> [A] If you want I can say it is R. Meir. This is what [the Mishnah] says: The father is not obligated to feed his daughter and the same is true for his son. But there is a *miṣvah* for his daughter and all the more so for his sons. The reason [the Mishnah] includes only the daughter is that even though there is no obligation there is still a *miṣvah*.
>
> [B] If you want I can say it is R. Yehudah. This is what [the Mishnah] says: The father is not obligated to feed his daughter and the same is true for his son. But there is a *miṣvah* for his son and all the more so for his daughters. The reason [the Mishnah] includes only the daughter is that there is no obligation even for the daughter.
>
> [C] If you want I can say it is R. Yoḥanan ben Beroqa. This is what [the Mishnah] says: The father is not obligated to feed his daughter and the same is true for his son and the same is true that there is not even a *miṣvah*. [The reason the Mishnah specifies only non-obligation for daughters is that] since it already teaches the obligation to daughters after their father's death, [the Mishnah] also teaches that he is not obligated [before death].

While the first half of the sugya proved that no Tanna could possibly be the author of the Mishnah, the second half argues the opposite: any of the three Tannaim mentioned in the *baraita* could potentially be the author of the Mishnah. This is a wonderful example of arguing both sides of an issue, which, as we noted above, was a central feature of both rhetorical and rabbinic discourse. The speaker would show great dialectical skill in first creating a problem by proving no possible authorship and then rebutting every one of his own arguments to open a full range of possible authors. By rejecting all possibilities, the Bavli sugya creates a sense of suspense – yet another technique of classical rhetoric.[59] The suspense is fully resolved, however, when all possible authors are resurrected. Quintilian describes a technique similar to that used in this sugya: "The orator often prepares his

[59] Quintilian, *Institutes of Oratory*, 9.2.22, provides an example and names this technique *sustentatio*.

way, dissembles, lays traps, and says things in the first part of the speech which will prove their value at the end."[60]

To be sure, the Bavli's style differs in some respects from the typical orations of Roman writers. Greco-Roman speeches fit into categories of forensic, deliberative and epideictic[61]; this sugya can be categorized only tenuously as forensic: "who is responsible for authoring the Mishnah?" Classical orators based their arguments on reason and emotion while the rabbis primarily sought proof from tradition and textual interpretation. In terms of length, Cicero's orations, at least in their written form, typically fill dozens of pages and are much more complex than the minimal outline that he recommends in his own handbook. This sugya, in contrast, is quite simple and weighs in at under 400 words. We can account for some of these differences: this sugya may be only an outline of what would have been a more elaborate presentation – after all, a lecture must have been more than just a few minutes long.[62] We should also remember that the use of rhetorical form by the Bavli's redactors likely derives from loose imitation rather than formal rhetorical training and the rabbis also may have adapted the form to fit their needs.

Therefore, even accounting for differences, the sugya nonetheless displays significant Hellenistic aspects. The first half of the sugya is highly structured and follows the general pattern of arrangement recommended by classical rhetoric, thus defining itself as a unit. The response in the second half is also highly structured and shares the feature of the partition, which announces the outline of the argument that will be made. These three features: following a structured outline, arguing on both sides of the issue, and creating suspense, together reveal the Hellenistic imprint on this sugya.

As aesthetically and intellectually pleasing as these rhetorical techniques may be, however, the lingering question remains: what is ultimately their persuasive goal? At face value, the Bavli aims to reconcile the Mishnah with the *baraita* by identifying which of the three opinions in the *baraita* could match the law of the Mishnah. However, had this been the Bavli's only goal, the answer could have been simple and straightforward: the Mishnah fits perfectly with the opinion of R. Yoḥanan ben Beroqa who says that the father is not obligated to feed his daughters

60 Ibid., 10.1.21.

61 See p. 3.

62 See n. 54. On the relationship between literary versions of rabbinic texts and their performance, see Heinemann, "Proem," 100–22. In the case of the proem the literary versions seem to be longer and more complex than their performative versions.

during his lifetime. R. Yoḥanan ben Beroqa's distinction between during and after the father's lifetime is also found in R. Eleazar ben Azariah's exegesis of the language of the *ketubah*, itself provided as evidence for the anonymous opinion in the Mishnah. This is, in fact, the third possible resolution in the sugya [C]. Most Bavli sugyot that introduce the question, "מתניתין מני – Who is the author of our Mishnah?," simply provide one answer.[63] That this sugya problematizes what could have been a simple solution suggests that the redactors had an additional motivation.

The redactors may have been bothered by the morality of the law of the Mishnah, which seems overly lenient on the responsibility of a father to feed his young children as common decency obligates. They therefore did not want such a view to be stamped with the authority of the Mishnah.[64] This ethical consideration is made explicit in the continuation of the Gemara quoted below. The responsibility of a father to feed his daughters even during his lifetime is required by the plain sense of the language of the *ketubah* and it is only R. Eleazar ben Azariah's midrash that rereads this line.[65] In fact, the version of this *baraita* found in Tosefta Ketubot 4:8 quotes R. Yoḥanan ben Beroqa as ruling that a father is obligated to feed his daughters[66]:

> There is a *miṣvah* to feed one's daughters and all the more so one's sons. R. Yoḥanan ben Beroqa says there is an obligation to feed one's daughters.

[63] See B. Shabbat 150a, B. Pesaḥim 79a, 86a, B. Rosh Hashanah 33a, B. Yoma 78b, 81b, B. Sukkah 23a, 54a, B. Megilah 7b, B. Ḥagigah 19b, B. Yebamot 64b, B. Ketubot 97b, B. Nedarim 16a, 87a, B. Baba Qama 33a, B. Sanhedrin 67a, 75a, 105a, B. Makkot 13a, B. Horayot 3a, 7a, B. Menaḥot 93a, B. Temurah 13a, B. Me`ilah 8a and 19b. While most of these sugyot are Stammaitic, B. `Eruvin 71a, B. Giṭṭin 71b and B. Shabbat 150b cite this type of sugya in the name of R. Yoḥanan, Rav Ḥisda and Abaye, respectively. This simple structure may be the earlier amoraic form of what the Stammaim later develop into the form of classical arrangement.

[64] See Rashbam to B. Baba Batra 141a who finds a source for this sentiment in Isa 58:7. The same verse is similarly used in Gen Rabbah 17 (ed. Theodor-Albeck, p. 154), Lev Rabbah 34 (ed. Margulius, p. 882), and B. Ketubot 52b.

[65] See M. Ketubot 4:11 and Milgram, *From Mesopotamia to the Mishnah*, 112, citing Mordechai A. Friedman, *Jewish Marriage in Palestine: A Cairo Genizah Study* (Tel-Aviv: Tel-Aviv University, 1980).

[66] The Tosefta seems to be more original, since R. Yoḥanan ben Beroqa did not generally apply midrashic methods of interpretation to human language. See Saul Lieberman, *Tosefta ki-fshutah* (New York: The Jewish Theological Seminary of America, 1955–1988), Ketubot, 245, citing Tosafot to B. Ketubot 53b. The same conclusion is reached by David Weiss Halivni, *Meqorot u-mesorot*, 6 vols. (Tel Aviv: Dvir, and Jerusalem: Jewish Theological Seminary of America and Magnes, 1968–2003), Nashim, 192. The obligation of the father to feed his daughters is also assumed in Mekhilta d'R. Shimon bar Yoḥai 21:3, cited by Ramban to Exod 21:3.

The Yerushalmi cites this version of the Tosefta and makes no attempt to reconcile it with the Mishnah, thus recognizing that the Mishnah's ruling differs from and is more lenient on the father than both of the opinions in the Tosefta. The Bavli's version of the *baraita*, in contrast, places R. Yoḥanan ben Beroqa's view at the opposite extreme, saying that the father is not obligated to feed his children during his lifetime, thus presenting the Bavli's redactors with a ready identification of the Mishnah.[67] The Bavli's redactors, however, do not take this easy path. Rather, in order to distance the Mishnah from the extreme view of R. Yoḥanan ben Beroqa, the Bavli introduces the category of *miṣvah* into the Mishnah. It finds this category in the first two opinions in the *baraita* and, preferring that there be at least a *miṣvah* to feed one's daughters, reads it back into the Mishnah.

By rejecting all possibilities in the first half of the sugya, the redactors wipe the slate clean and make room for alternative interpretations to be introduced. Had the sugya stated up front that the Mishnah follows R. Meir and R. Yehudah without having first rejected R. Yoḥanan ben Beroqa as the author, then its conclusion would not have been as persuasive. By postponing the arrival at the most obvious answer and creating a sense of suspense, the sugya opens up the space necessary to consider various other possibilities as well.

The continuation of the Gemara brings to the fore the frustration of the Amoraim with how leniently this law treats the responsibility of the father:

> R. Ila said in the name of R. Shimon ben Laqish in the name of R. Yehudah bar Ḥanina: It was decreed at Usha that a father must feed his young sons and daughters.

Does the law follow him [R. Ila] or does the law not follow him?

[1] Come and hear: When they [people with a case against a father] came to Rav Yehudah, he told them, "A jackal gave birth and throws [his child] upon the people of the town."

[2] When they would come before Rav Ḥisda, he told them, "Turn over a mortar in public and let someone stand up and announce, 'A raven wants its child but this man does not want his child'..."

[67] If the *baraita* is not simply the result of a transmission error of the original Tosefta (see previous note), then perhaps it is an emendation by a tradent who wanted to reconcile the Mishnah with the Tosefta. The Bavli redactors, receiving this emended text, then had the task of further reconciling, or perhaps un-reconciling, the two sources.

[3] When they came before Rava, he told him [the father], "Are you satisfied that your children should be fed from charity?"

We only apply [this law] to someone not wealthy but a wealthy person, we force him [to pay] against his will. As the case of Rava who forced Rav Natan bar Ami [to pay] and expropriated from him four hundred *zuz* for charity.

Although there is a tradition of a decree at Usha to rectify the original ethically problematic law, this tradition is not followed because, as the Yerushalmi similarly says, we do not know who voted at that session.[68] The authenticity of R. Ila's statement is in doubt and his tradition may be more wishful thinking than real. Instead, various Amoraim must use extra-legal means of coaxing, pressuring, and shaming stingy fathers to fulfill their moral obligations to feed their children.[69] The Yerushalmi cites another similar case[70]:

Uqba came before R. Yoḥanan. [R. Yoḥanan] told him, "Uqba, feed your children." He replied, "From where does the master [derive this law]?" He said, "Uqba you wicked person, feed your children."

These narratives highlight the problem that the Mishnah provides no legal ruling that requires recalcitrant fathers to feed their daughters. The Bavli solves this difficulty by reading the opinions of R. Meir and R. Yehudah, who at least legislate that there is a *miṣvah* for the father to feed his daughters, back into the law of the Mishnah. The sugya achieves its goal by temporarily ruling out the most likely candidate, R. Yoḥanan ben Beroqa, from being a possible author of the Mishnah and raising our curiosity so that we are more willing to accept all of the answers proposed in the resolution. The rhetorical structure of the sugya that explores all possible interpretations thus not only serves as a scholastic exercise but also aims to persuade the audience towards a practical halakhic position.

[68] Y. Ketubot 4:8, 28d.

[69] The combination here of law and narrative creates what Wimpfheimer, *Narrating the Law*, 16, calls a "thick" sugya wherein the various competing cultural forces at play within rabbinic society are all represented. This creates a truly dialogical text that defies simple codification. Only the combination of considerations stemming from marriage law, ethics, shame punishment, and charity law can comprehensively portray the rabbis' thought about this issue.

[70] Y. Ketubot 4:8, 28d.

READING FOUR PORTIONS IN SECOND ADAR

The technique and structure that we identified above are also utilized in B. Megilah 6b commenting on M. Megilah 1:4[71]:

[Narration]
Mishnah: If they read the Scroll [of Esther] in the first Adar and the year was intercalated, they read it in the second Adar. There is no difference between the first Adar and the second Adar except for reading the Scroll and gifts to the poor.

Gemara: Therefore, regarding reading the series of [four Pentateuchal] portions, this [first Adar] and the other [second Adar] are the same.

[Partition]
Who is the author of our Mishnah?
[A] It is not the first Tanna.

[B] It is not R. Eleazar the son of R. Yose.

[C] It is not Rabban Shimon ben Gamaliel.

[Proof]
[A] As it was taught[72]: If they read the Scroll in the first Adar and the year was intercalated, they read it in the second Adar, for all commandments that can be practiced in the second can be practiced in the first except for reading the Megilah.

[B] R. Eleazar the son of R. Yose says in the name of R. Zekhariah the son of the butcher, we do not read it in the second Adar for all the commandments that can be practiced in the second can also be practiced in the first.

[C] Rabban Shimon ben Gamaliel says in the name of R. Yose, we read it again in the second Adar for all commandments that can be performed in the second cannot be performed in the first.
But they are agreed regarding eulogizing and fasting, which are prohibited in this [first Adar] and the other [second Adar].

Rav Papa said, the series of portions differentiates between Rabban Shimon ben Gamaliel and the first Tanna. For the first Tanna opines that [the portions] should be read ideally in the second [Adar] but if

[71] Translation generally follows MS Kaufmann for the Mishnah and MS Göttingen 3 for the Gemara. See Hidary, "*Agonistic Bavli*," 154–5, for textual notes, and for a chart of all manuscript variants see http://rabbinics.org/charts/.

[72] See parallel at T. Megilah 1:6.

they already did [read them] in the first they did so [legitimately] excluding reading the Scroll for even if they read [the Scroll] in the first [Adar] they must read in the second [Adar]. R. Eleazar the son of R. Yose opines that even reading the Scroll should ideally be in the first [Adar]. And Rabban Shimon ben Gamaliel opines that even regarding the series of portions, even if they read [them] in the first [Adar] they must read [them] in the second [Adar].

[Peroration]

[A] If it is the first Tanna, there is a question from gifts to the poor.

[B] If it is R. Eleazar the son of R. Yose, there is a question from reading the Scroll.

[C] If it is Rabban Shimon ben Gamaliel, there is a question from the series of portions.

[Resolution]

[A] It is actually the first Tanna who taught regarding reading the Scroll but the same law applies to gifts to the poor, for one is dependent on the other.

[C] Or if you want I can say, it is actually Rabban Shimon ben Gamaliel and [the Mishnah] is lacking and this is how it should be taught: There is no difference between the fourteenth of the first Adar and the fourteenth of the second Adar except for reading the Scroll and gifts to the poor. Therefore, regarding eulogies and fasting this one and that one are the same. But it does not deal with the series of portions.

Rav Ḥiyya bar Ashi said in the name of Rav, the halakha follows Rabban Shimon ben Gamaliel who spoke in the name of R. Yose.

This sugya follows a similar structure as that in B. Ketubot 49. Although B. Megilah 6b includes an amoraic elaboration in the proof section and only two possibilities in the resolution section, both sugyot otherwise follow the outline of classical rhetorical arrangement. Moreover, the two sugyot utilize this rhetorical style for similar goals: to reinterpret the Mishnah in accordance with what the redactors believe should be the halakha. M. Megilah 1:4 states that only the recitation of Esther and gifts to the poor need to be performed in the second Adar, implying that everything else, including the reading of the four portions,[73] can be

[73] Four portions are recited on various Sabbaths during and just before Adar: *sheqalim* (Exod 30:11–16), *zakhor* (Deut 25:17–19), *parah* (Num 19:1–22), and *haḥodesh* (Exod 12:1–20).

performed in the first Adar. The final sentence of the sugya, however, decides the halakha in accordance with Rabban Shimon ben Gamaliel in the *baraita* that the four portions must be recited in the second Adar. The Talmud must therefore reinterpret the Mishnah to be compatible with Rabban Shimon ben Gamaliel.

As David Weiss Halivni argues, the Mishnah corresponds best with the first Tanna.[74] Compare how the language of the first phrase of the Mishnah matches that of the first Tanna almost word for word. Furthermore, the explanation given in the first resolution [A] – that the requirement to provide gifts to the poor depends on the reading of the Scroll – is already established by Rav Yosef at B. Megilah 4b: "because the eyes of the poor look towards the reading of the Scroll." Therefore, the exclusion formula in the second half of the Mishnah, that the two months are similar in all respects except two, would likely place the series of portions in the first Adar. This being the case, had the Gemara simply stated up front that the Mishnah follows Rabban Shimon ben Gamaliel and that the Mishnah must be interpreted to refer only to the fourteenth of the month, the listeners would not have been convinced. On the contrary, they would have rightly objected that there is a better option, namely, that the Mishnah follows the first Tanna. The sugya must therefore reject all possible attributions at the outset so that the listener will be more receptive to accepting any and all possible solutions. Here again, the rhetorical structure serves to persuade the audience towards a given legal conclusion.

LEAVEN OWNED ON PASSOVER

Yet another example of using rhetorical arrangement for the goal of reconciling the Mishnah with the halakha can be found at B. Pesaḥim 28b–29a, commenting on M. Pesaḥim 2:2[75]:

[74] Halivni, *Meqorot u-mesorot*, Megilah, 473–4. Halivni also points to the Scholium to Megilat Ta`anit, which cites the second half of M. Megilah 1:6 followed by Rabban Shimon ben Gamaliel, suggesting that they are in opposition.

[75] Translation generally follows MS Vatican 109 for the Mishnah and MS Oxford 366 for the Gemara. See textual notes at Hidary, "Agonistic Bavli," 158–9, and a complete manuscript chart at http://rabbinics.org/charts/. I have skipped a number of lines in the middle of the sugya that are not relevant to my argument. Halivni, *Meqorot u-mesorot*, Pesaḥim, 350–1, additionally argues that these lines are Stammatic additions to the original amoraic sugya.

[Narration]

Mishnah: Leaven belonging to Gentiles that was owned during Passover is permitted for use [after Passover]. [Leaven] belonging to Jews is prohibited, as Scripture says, "No [leaven] shall be found with you" (Exod 13:7).

[Partition]

Gemara: Who is the author of our Mishnah?

[A] It is not R. Yehudah.

[B] It is not R. Shimon.

[C] It is not R. Yose the Galilean.

[Proof]

What is it? For it was taught[76]:

[A] Leaven, both before its time [from noon on the 14th of Nisan] and after its time [after Passover], one transgresses a negative prohibition. During its time [during Passover], one transgresses a negative prohibition and is liable to *karet*. These are the words of R. Yehudah.

[B] R. Shimon says, leaven, both before its time and after its time, one does not transgress anything. During its time one transgresses a negative prohibition and is liable to *karet*.

[C] R. Yose the Galilean says, You should be astonished at yourself! How can leaven be prohibited for use all seven days?[77]

...

[Peroration]

Who is the author of our Mishnah?

[A] If it is R. Yehudah, he said leaven without qualification, [implying] even that of a Gentile [would be prohibited].

[B] If it is R. Shimon, even [leaven] of a Jew is permitted.

[C] If it is R. Yose the Galilean, even during its time, use is permitted.

[76] See T. Pesaḥim 1:8.

[77] Halivni, ibid., argues that the three opinions here are not all part of one *baraita* but rather the redactor concatenated one *baraita* containing the first two opinions with another that expresses R. Yose the Galilean's opinion. Indeed, R. Yose the Galilean's opinion is hardly required for the logic of this sugya. As noted in n. 88, many sugyot that follow classical rhetorical arrangement include only two possibilities. Adding R. Yose the Galilean allows the sugya to have three elements in its proof, which is more common in classical rhetoric; see p. 37 and p. 97 n. 89.

[Resolution]

[A] Rav Aḥa bar Yaakov said, it is actually R. Yehudah and he derives [the law of] eating leaven from [the law of] seeing leaven. Just as with seeing leaven, you may not see your own but you can see that belonging to others and that dedicated upon High [to the Temple], so too eating leaven, you may not eat your own but that belonging to others [on Passover] you may eat [after Passover]. Technically, the Mishnah should have taught that [leaven] owned by a Gentile is also permitted for eating but since it taught that [leaven] of a Jew is prohibited for use, it also taught that [leaven] of a Gentile is permitted for use. And technically, it should have taught that [leaven of a Gentile] is permitted [for use] even within its time, but since it taught about [leaven] of a Jew after its time, it also taught about [leaven] of a Gentile after its time.

[C] Rava said, it is actually R. Shimon. R. Shimon imposes a [rabbinically enacted] penalty since he violated the prohibition against seeing.

The Mishnah teaches that leaven that was owned by a Jew on Passover may not be eaten, sold, or used for any purpose forever, even after Passover. In support, the Mishnah cites Exodus 13:7: since one may not have leaven in one's possession, violation of this ban causes such leaven to be prohibited from use for all time. This opinion accords best with the view of R. Yehudah of the Bavli *baraita* that leaven owned on Passover is prohibited forever, a view not shared by R. Shimon. That the Mishnah cites a verse and R. Yehudah imposes a biblically authorized punishment shows that both understand the law as biblical. In fact, the Yerushalmi equates these two views: "Who taught, 'Do not see'? It is R. Yehudah."[78]

Rava, however, legislates an alternate ruling, "The halakha is that leaven … after its time, whether mixed with its kind or not with its kind, is permitted, in accordance with R. Shimon."[79] This ruling by Rava may have a more ancient source, considering that T. Pesaḥim 1:8 transmits R. Shimon's opinion as that of the Sages, whose opinion would be preferred over the minority opinion of R. Yehudah. Since Rava, as well as the redactors of this sugya, decided that the halakha should follow R. Shimon, it was necessary to reconcile R. Shimon with the Mishnah by interpreting the prohibition in the Mishnah to be of only rabbinic authority. As in the previous two examples, the redactors

[78] Y. Pesaḥim 2:2, 28d.

[79] B. Pesaḥim 30a.

accomplish this reinterpretation by first rejecting all possible attributions of the Mishnah so that the most obvious attribution to R. Yehudah would not dominate the field. Once the field is cleared, then two possibilities can be presented as equally persuasive[80] and the one preferred by halakha easily accepted. Methods of classical rhetoric such as arrangement, suspense, and arguing both sides of an issue, are again applied by the redactors[81] of this sugya for the persuasive goal of showing the Mishnah to be in line with the final halakha.

FURTHER EXAMPLES

Many other Bavli sugyot are structured, in whole or in part, according to classical rhetorical arrangement,[82] often for similar objectives to those in the examples above.[83] B. Rosh Hashanah 16a, for instance, includes a partition that rejects four possibilities, all of which remain rejected, while accepting only a fifth possible attribution. The context there is not legal but instead deals with the question of how often God judges the world. The aim of that sugya is to move away from the Mishnah's view that the world is judged once a year, to a more philosophically acceptable view that the world is judged every day. Both the Yerushalmi and Bavli challenge the Mishnah with questions such as, why does God wait

80 In fact, the sugya gives the impression that Rava's interpretation fits the Mishnah even more smoothly. For resolution [A], the Talmud inserts a lengthy line of reasoning to justify why the language of the Mishnah is restricted to permitting only the use of leaven owned by a Gentile and only after Passover. No such justification is provided for Rava, even though he would have to interpret the Mishnah in the same way. Furthermore, the continuation of the sugya, not cited here, states that the verse included in the Mishnah is easily explained according to Rava's reading but explained only with difficulty according to Rav Aḥa bar Yaakov's reading. The Talmud says this despite the fact that the prohibition is only rabbinic for Rava but biblical for Rav Aḥa bar Yaakov. These two glosses suggest that the redactors of the sugya want to show that Rava's explanation of the Mishnah is preferable, even on purely exegetical grounds, to that of Rav Aḥa bar Yaakov.

81 While Halivni, ibid., argues that the original sugya is amoraic, due to the amoraic attributions in the resolution, it is still possible, and I think likely, that the rhetorical structure of the overall sugya is Stammaitic.

82 For example, Rabban Gmaliel's response to the heretics at B. Sanhedrin 90b begins with a partition: "He replied from the Torah, from the Prophets, and from the Writings." The response continues with details of each proof as well as the refutations from the heretics, thus combining the proof and disproof sections (see a similar structure on p. 191–3). The conversation ends with final decisive proofs, which may constitute a peroration.

83 Other variations to מני מתניתין are: מתניתין דלא כר' פלוני, מאן תנא, הא מני, and כמאן. See Ezra Zion Melamed, *Pirqe mavo le-sifrut ha-Talmud* (Jerusalem, 1973), 72, 120 and 378–83. The use of these various terms requires a separate study.

until the end of the year to kill some people who deserve capital punishment if their sentences were already decided at the beginning of the year, and why should we pray for poor and sick people if they have already been judged for the year.[84] However, only the Bavli uses classical rhetorical arrangement to force the Mishnah into the position of a minority view, thus allowing for the promotion of other views.

Writing in the tenth century, Sherira Gaon already notes the tendency of the Talmud to assign names to anonymous views in the Mishnah in order to reject them:

> When Rabbi saw [to prefer] one view and the later rabbis did not see [to prefer] it, they explained it [in such a way] that they would not have to rely on it. For example, if [Rabbi] taught a minority view anonymously because it made sense to him [that halakha should follow that view], but it did not make sense to the later rabbis ... they would tell you it follows Rabbi or they would teach it as a minority view and we do not practice according to it.[85]

Thus, two different interpretive approaches were available to the Amoraim and Stammaim when they needed to disagree with the anonymous view of the Mishnah: to label the anonymous view as a minority opinion (B. Rosh Hashanah 16a and the sugyot cited by Sherira Gaon), or to expand the Mishnah to allow for multiple possible authors, including the one preferred by the redactors (the three sugyot analyzed above). The first form assigns the anonymous view to a minority and thus rejects the Mishnah, while the latter form allows the Mishnah to follow multiple views thus reconciling the halakha with the Mishnah, even though it does so at the expense of reinterpreting the Mishnah. The latter form is consequently the strategy used in B. Megilah 6b, analyzed above, where the plain Mishnah fits with the anonymous view of the *baraita*, which would represent the majority view. The latter form also fits the tendency in the Bavli to explore all interpretive possibilities and keep open as many options as possible.[86] In other cases, however, the language of the Mishnah may simply not allow for such reinterpretations to be accomplished convincingly, thus permitting only the first strategy.[87]

[84] See Y. Rosh Hashanah 1:3, 57a, and B. Rosh Hashanah 16a.

[85] Benjamin Lewin, ed. *Iggeret Rav Sherira Gaon* (Jerusalem: Makor, 1972), 53–4, French recension. A clear example of this phenomenon is at B. Beṣah 31a.

[86] See Hidary, *Legal Pluralism*, 22–6.

[87] Cicero, *On Invention*, II.142, writes that the orator should find any ambiguity present in a document in order to interpret that source towards his side of the argument. However, such ambiguity may not always be present.

In the three examples analyzed at length above, the latter form of argument is accomplished through the use of classical rhetorical arrangement. B. Rosh Hahsnah 16a, however, also follows the structure of classical rhetorical arrangement even though it uses the first form. That sugya could have simply assigned the Mishnah to the fifth view at the start without having rejected the first four possibilities. In that case, the rhetorical arrangement serves to introduce the alternative opinions so that they can be discussed and given more prominence later on.

Several other sugyot include all sections of classical arrangement but they entertain only two possibilities rather than the usual three.[88] B. Ta`anit 28a, however, settles on only one of three possibilities. The same is true in B. Baba Qama 86a where the final answer is already indicated in the partition.[89] B. Megilah 23a, meanwhile, settles on only one of two possibilities.[90] In yet other sugyot we find no separate sections for proof and peroration.[91] Further research is required to analyze the use and function of classical rhetorical arrangement across these variations.[92] With that in mind, one lesson that emerges already from this project is the extent to which many Bavli sugyot should be read rhetorically, that is, as persuasive compositions meant to lead the listener towards a particular legal, homiletical, or exegetical goal, rather than simply haphazard anthologies of sources and theoretical discussions. While this chapter has analyzed only a very small subset of the rhetorical techniques found in the Bavli, the next chapter will help to further reconstruct what the rabbis' textbook on the art of rhetoric may have looked like, were they to write such a work.

In sum, the strikingly agonistic nature of the Bavli derives not only from its oral setting, but also from the agonistic roots of Greco-Roman rhetoric as reflected similarly in the scholastic and rhetorical culture of

88 B. Beṣah 18a, B. Ketubot 64b, and B. Baba Qama 86a (bottom of page). B. Shabbat 37a, B. Baba Qama 36a, B. Baba Meṣi`a 51a and B. Shebu'ot 3a also include two possibilities but no separate sections for proof and peroration.

89 I refer to the sugya in the middle of the page. See similarly at B. Beṣah 12b.

90 See similarly at B. Ḥulin 26a. B. Baba Mesi`a 111a–b offers two possibilities but then concludes with a third, namely, that the Mishnah follows the school of R. Ishmael. The same strategy is used in B. Rosh Hashanah 16a, discussed on p. 127.

91 See n. 88.

92 Another form that includes a partition is found at B. Berakhot 4b: "If you want I can say from Scripture, if you want I can say from reason," as well as dozens of similar formulations.

the Syriac Christians. Narsai's agonistic panegyric[93] cited in the epigraph could easily describe many Babylonian Amoraim. The Bavli's use of classical rhetorical arrangement in its highly structured sugyot parallels similar usage by Narsai, Balai, and the anonymous author of *Liber Graduum*. The practice of arguing both sides of a dispute and the creation of suspense are also well-established rhetorical techniques. Clearly, the rabbis had a good sense for the art of public speaking. We cannot know whether the Babylonian Amoraim inherited concepts of rhetoric from their Palestinian counterparts, how often the Stammaim overheard Christian sermons, or to what extent Syriac writing style was itself a symptom of a larger Hellenistic atmosphere. Nevertheless, no matter how we reconstruct these lines of communication and cultural trends, it remains clear that the Bavli's agonism and rhetorical style owes much of its character and form to Greco-Roman rhetorical oratory.

[93] On the close relationship between agonism and panegyric, see Ong, *Orality and Literacy*, 45. Fulsome praise is but the flip side of antagonistic argumentation in the "highly polarized, agonistic, oral world of good and evil, virtue and vice, villains and heroes" (ibid.). Narsai beautifully combines the two by employing over-the-top praise to describe Theodore's ability to conquer his opponents in debate.

4 Progymnasmata and Controversiae in Rabbinic Literature

> There is a curious irony in the fact that the Jews, in seeking to save themselves from being overborne by the Greek culture, should have adopted the Hellenic institution of the school for their children and the Hellenic practice of disputation for their young men.[1]

A Roman boy who had the privilege of continuing his education past grammar school would enroll in a school of rhetoric during his teenage years.[2] There, the teacher would introduce him to the theory of oratory based on the rhetorical handbooks, which detailed the techniques of invention, arrangement, style, memory, and delivery.[3] Students would also practice written composition in a series of preparatory exercises called progymnasmata.[4] Having mastered the progymnasmata, advanced students would then go on to compose more elaborate practice speeches called controversiae.[5] This chapter will demonstrate that many of the techniques, forms, and even some of the content of these exercises find parallels throughout rabbinic literature. Previous chapters analyzed examples of fully developed rhetorical arrangement in Talmudic sugyot and midrashic forms, which suffice to show significant rabbinic familiarity with the oratorical standards of Hellenistic culture. The bulk of rabbinic literature, however, does not conform to such well-developed arrangement. I will argue in this chapter that tannaitic

[1] William Boyd, *The History of Western Education* (London: A. & C. Black, 1921), 61. See also Nathan Morris, *The Jewish School: An Introduction to the History of Jewish Education* (London: Eyre and Spottiswoode, 1937), 40.

[2] Raffaella Cribiore, *Gymnastics of the Mind: Greek Education in Hellenistic and Roman Egypt* (Princeton: Princeton University Press, 2001), 2; Marrou, *History of Education*, 265; and Stanley F. Bonner, *Education in Ancient Rome* (Berkley: University of California Press, 1977), 117 and 135. Aristocratic girls did attend grammar school but did not continue their education once they were married.

[3] See p. 36.

[4] The singular form is progymnasma. Kennedy, *New History*, 83; and Marrou, *History of Education*, 201.

[5] The singular form is controversia.

midrash and much of the Talmud still reflect the classical rhetorical tradition in their format, style, and hermeneutics once we expand our purview to include genres of Greco-Roman rhetorical education. Specifically, the penchant for arguing both sides of an issue, the use of a dialogic format, and the discussion of hypothetical cases that characterize rabbinic literature find close parallels in Roman school exercises. By placing rabbinic literature into this cultural context and noting both the similarities and differences with classical rhetorical education, we will better understand the thought and teachings of the rabbis, the structures of their compositions, and their educational methods.

Textbooks of progymnasmata survive from the first until the fourth centuries CE from Alexandria, Tyre, Athens, Tarsus, Antioch, and a fragment from Nepolis in Palestine.[6] Progymnasmata were popular not only throughout the Roman Empire but were also present in Syriac schools in Persia.[7] All of these progymnasmatic works include about fourteen standard exercises of increasing difficulty. As a typical example, Aphthonius, a student of Libanius, lists the following exercises from easiest to most challenging in his primer: fable, narrative, chreia (anecdote), maxim, refutation, confirmation, commonplace topics, encomium, invective, comparison (*syncrisis*), personification, description, thesis, and introduction of law.[8] Students would write out their compositions and then read them aloud to the teacher.[9] Each of the progymnasmatic exercises focuses on one aspect of a speech such that by the end of his training, the student would be on his way towards putting together all of the pieces of a full oration.

Having completed the progymnasmata, the student would advance to longer exercises called *gymnasmata* or, more commonly, declamations (Greek *meletai*).[10] These declamations, like the progymnasmata, also treated mostly theoretical issues as practice before the young rhetor went out to perform his skill in the real world. Declamations could be of two types: controversiae and sausauria. Controversiae were speeches written for an imaginary court case, usually one that was particularly

[6] Hock and O'Neil, *Chreia in Ancient Rhetoric*, 10–11; and Visotzky, *Golden Bells*, 52.

[7] Catherine Chin, "Rhetorical Practice in the Chreia Elaboration of Mara bar Serapion," *Hugoye: Journal of Syriac Studies* 9, no. 2 (2006): 145–71.

[8] Craig Gibson, *Libanius's Progymnasmata: Model Exercises in Greek Prose Composition and Rhetoric* (Atlanta: Society of Biblical Literature, 2008), xxi. Textbooks by other authors are included in Kennedy, *Progymnasmata*. See descriptions of each at Kennedy, *New History*, 203–7.

[9] Kennedy, *Progymnasmata*, x.

[10] Hock and O'Neil, *Chreia in Ancient Rhetoric*, 14–15.

paradoxical or even humorous. Sausauria were practice deliberative speeches placed in the mouth of an ancient figure deliberating between two courses of action.[11] Students would be asked to compose a declamation for either or both sides of each issue paying no attention to the actual law or historical outcome.

The first half of this chapter will analyze selected progymnasmata that serve as relevant and important points of comparison with various aspects of rabbinic literature. The second half of this chapter will explore the more advanced controversiae and their Talmudic counterparts. By analyzing how rabbinic texts use a dialogical format and how they approach theoretical cases in light of Greco-Roman parallels, we can assess both the extent of overlap and noteworthy distinctions between the rabbis and their surrounding culture.

PROGYMNASMATA

Of all the progymnasmatic exercises, scholars of rabbinic literature have devoted the most attention to analyzing the chreia (pl. chreiai). A chreia consists of an anecdote about a sage that includes a short narrative and/or a proverb meant "to capture and preserve the characteristic teaching and behavior" of the best philosophers.[12] Students would be given such an anecdote and then asked to develop it through various grammatical and rhetorical transformations. Henry Fischel demonstrates the presence of cynicizing chreiai among anecdotes about and sayings by Hillel.[13] For example, M. Avot 2:6 states: "He [Hillel] also saw a skull floating upon the water. He said to it, 'Because you have drowned [someone], they have drowned you and those who drowned you will also

[11] I have not found any rabbinic parallels to the sausauria. However, further research may uncover some similarity between this genre and the pseudepigraphic testament literature.

[12] Hock and O'Neil, *Chreia in Ancient Rhetoric*, 3. See also Kennedy, *Progymnasmata*, 15; and Kennedy, *New History*, 204. See the epigraph in Chapter 2 on p. 00 for a chreia of Isocrates.

[13] Henry Fischel, "Studies in Cynicism and the Ancient Near East: The Transformation of a 'Chria'," in *Religions in Antiquity: Essays in Memory of Edwin Ramsdell Goodenough*, ed. Jacob Neusner (Leiden: Brill, 1968): 372–411; and Fischel, "Story and History," 443–72. See also Catherine Hezser, *Form Function, and Historical Significance of the Rabbinic Story in Yerushalmi Neziqin* (Tübingen: Mohr Siebeck, 1993), 288–91; 306–9; Hezser, "Die Verwendung der hellenistischen Gattung Chrie in frühen Christentum und Judentum," *Journal for the Study of Judaism* 27 (1996): 371–439; Hezser, "Interfaces," 167–70; Marc Hirshman, "The Greek Fathers and the Aggada on Ecclesiastes: Formats of Exegesis in Late Antiquity," *Hebrew Union College Annual* 59 (1988): 160–1; and Visotzky, *Golden Bells*, 43–4, 52.

be drowned.'"[14] In fact, Mishnah Avot contains a series of chreiai structured within a succession list, a combination also attested in Hellenistic literature.[15] In many instances, aphorisms in Avot parallel not only the form but also the content of Greek chreiai.[16] Fischel is also careful to note, however, that the rabbis adapt the chreiai by naturalizing them to include Jewish sages, using them as halakhic precedents, and shifting them from addressing political matters to transcendental and ethical concerns.[17] Martin Jaffee further suggests that the rabbis reformulated chreiai and other rabbinic sources in a manner similar to rhetorical exercises.[18]

Besides the chreia, scholars have analyzed several other rhetorical exercises that inform the hermeneutical methods and dialogic formats of much of midrash halakha and the Talmud. Saul Lieberman and David Daube have linked the midrashic methods of *qal va-ḥomer* and *gezerah shavah* with the exercise of comparison called *synkrisis*, which will be the subject of the next chapter. Rivka Ulmer insightfully points out the resemblances between halakhic midrashim and the rhetorical diatribe, which both feature dialogue forms that incorporate the voices of imaginary objectors.[19]

Building on Ulmer, David Brodsky has convincingly shown the similarities between rabbinic literature and two of the more advanced progymnasmatic exercises.[20] Brodsky sets as his goal to trace the origin of the dialogue form in the Talmud Bavli and finds that despite the now extensive and productive body of research into the Persian background of the Bavli, there is still little parallel to its legal dialogical form.[21] Rather, the Bavli's dialogic form developed, in part, from shorter and simpler dialogue in Palestinian rabbinic texts such as the tannaitic midrashim and the Yerushalmi. All of these rabbinic texts, in turn, share

[14] See further at Judah Goldin, *Studies in Midrash and Related Literature* (Philadelphia: Jewish Publication Society, 1988), 208.

[15] Tropper, *Wisdom, Politics, and Historiography*, 182–8; and p. 5.

[16] Fischel, *Rabbinic Literature and Greco-Roman Philosophy*, 51–89.

[17] See Fischel, "Story and History," 469–70.

[18] Jaffee, *Torah in the Mouth*, 126–40. See also Arnoff, "Memory," 104–7, 139–43; and Tropper, *Wisdom, Politics, and Historiography*, 184 n. 93, who suggests that embellishments of Mishnah Avot in Avot d'Rabbi Natan result from such progymnasmatic exercises.

[19] Ulmer, "Advancement of Arguments," 48–91.

[20] Brodsky, "From Disagreement to Talmudic Discourse," 179–206.

[21] See Brodsky, ibid., 175, and references there, especially Yaakov Elman, "Toward an Intellectual History of Sasanian Law: An Intergenerational Dispute in 'Herbedestan' 9 and Its Rabbinic and Roman Parallels," in *The Talmud in Its Iranian Context*, ed. C. Bakhos and M. R. Shayegan (Tübingen: Mohr Siebeck, 2010): 21–57.

a common structure with the dialogue form that is typical of the progymnasmatic exercises of thesis and introduction of law. Brodsky finds that both rabbinic literature and the Greek exercises include a dialogic format that follows the same pattern: statement, support, challenge, resolution, challenge, resolution, conclusion.[22] I fully agree with Brodsky's assessment and would like to build upon his findings. Rather than repeat Brodsky's examples, I will analyze other representative texts of both the progymnasmata and parallel rabbinic sources in order to strengthen and expand upon the significant connections between the two sets of literature.

In the progymnasma on the introduction of a law, the student composes either a support of (*synegoria*[23]) or an attack on (*kategoria*[24]) a proposed or existing law. Attacks would show that the law is unclear, unjust, unnecessary, shameful or contradictory while supports would argue the opposite.[25] Aphthonius provides a typical example with a speech opposing a law that permits one to kill an adulterer when caught in the act:

> This present law has been advanced in opposition to all laws. You (members of the assembly) seem to me to scrutinize the law in a much better way if you judge it as you do all other public matters – appointment of generals, the priesthoods, the decrees. Almost everything that is done best in time of peace or war undergoes the scrutiny of judges.... How then is it not illogical for everything to be subject to scrutiny and for the law before us alone to remove the vote of judges?
>
> **[Antithesis]** "Yes," he says, "but the wrongs done by adulterers are great."
>
> **[Solution]** What? Are not those of murderers greater? And do we think traitors are less wicked than others, and are temple robbers of

22 Brodsky's labels, "statement" and "support," appropriately describe the beginnings of the rabbinic texts that he cites. The progymnasmatic introduction to law, on the other hand, opened with a formal prooemium; see Kennedy, *Progymnasmata*, 124 (Aphthonius, 54). It is possible that in a live lecture, the rabbi would have given a more elaborate introduction to his thesis that served as a prooemium. However, even without such an introduction, the persuasive value of presenting a law through a dialogic structure is enough to warrant a comparison of these two sets of compositions.

23 See p. 223 n. 31.

24 See p. 240 n. 4.

25 See Kennedy, *Progymnasmata*, 62–6, 124–7, and 171–2; Gibson, *Libanius's Progymnasmata*, 527; and Kennedy, *New History*, 206.

less account than traitors? Yet whoever is caught doing these things faces judges and neither does a traitor suffer punishment without the judge giving vote, nor does death come to a murderer unless the prosecutor proves the crime, nor do those who rob the higher powers suffer until there is an opportunity for the judges to learn about these matters...

[Antithesis] "What is the difference between killing an adulterer and handing him over to judges, if he will sustain death equally from both?"

[Solution] There is as much difference as between tyranny and law and between democracy and monarchy. It is characteristic of a tyrant to kill whomever he wants but of law to put to death justly one who has been convicted...

[Antithesis] "Yes," he says, "but falling immediately on the spot will be a harsher punishment; lapse of time before judgment will be an advantage to the adulterer.

[Solution] If brought to trial, he will have the opposite experience; for his life hereafter will be more unpleasant; for he will find the expectation more terrifying than the experience...

[Epilogue] An adulterer is a terrible thing, and he has exceeded the utmost degree of wrong. As a result, let him first be tried, then let him be executed.[26]

The declaimer here proves that the adulterer, even when caught in the act, should be brought to trial rather than killed on the spot. After introducing his position and its reason, the speaker quotes the opposing argument, refutes it, and continues that pattern twice more. This dialectical structure does not rise to the level of a dialogue, since the opposing side is not fully represented but is only quoted in order to be refuted.[27] Rather, the rhetor utilizes dialectic as a persuasive technique

[26] Kennedy, *Progymnasmata*, 124–6. The labels "Antithesis," "Solution," and "Epilogue" are not in the original Greek but are provided by Kennedy in his translation. I have borrowed these labels for the rabbinic texts below rather than Brodsky's labels, although they are basically synonymous. Kennedy's labels derive from the handbook of Nicolaus the Sophist; see ibid., 132–3.

[27] As Mikhail Bakhtin, *The Dialogical Imagination: Four Essays*, trans. Caryl Emerson and Michael Holquist (Austin: University of Texas, 1981), 325, observes: "Double-voiced discourse is very widespread in rhetorical genres, but even there – remaining as it does within the boundaries of a single language system – it is not fertilized by a deep rooted connection with the forces of historical becoming that serve to stratify language, and therefore rhetorical genres are at best merely a distanced echo of this

by preempting counterarguments and showing that all arguments to the contrary are false. The basic structure of this exercise typically comprises the proof section of a complete oration.[28]

Significantly, tannaitic midrash regularly structures its arguments in this same format. As Brodsky correctly notes: "The earliest rabbinic sources to contain such discourse [of give-and-take in one voice] are the various works of Midrash Halakhah."[29] Consider the example of Mekhilta d'R. Ishmael, Nezikin, 5[30]:

> **[Thesis]** "You shall not steal" (Exod 20:13): behold this is a warning for one who kidnaps.
>
> **[Antithesis]** You say it is a warning against kidnapping, but perhaps it only a warning against stealing money?
>
> **[Solution]** When it states: "You shall not steal, you shall not deal deceitfully or falsely" (Lev 19:11) behold this is a warning against stealing money. What, therefore, does "You shall not steal" (Exod 20:13) teach? This verse is a warning against kidnapping.

becoming, narrowed down to an individual polemic." On the extent to which Talmudic dialogue is similarly monological, see Boyarin, *Socrates and the Fat Rabbis*, 140–67; Wimpfheimer, *Narrating the Law*, 21–4; Brodsky, "From Disagreement to Talmudic Discourse," 184; and Moshe Simon-Shoshan, "The Talmud as Novel: A Bakhtinian Approach to the Bavli, or, How I Learned to Stop Worrying and Love the *Stam*," paper presented at the Association for Jewish Studies Conference, Chicago (2012). Boyarin and Wimpfheimer seek dialogism within the Bavli that goes against the grain of its normative legal world; they find it in, respectively, legal narrative and satiric stories. They deem the rest of the give and take of the Bavli to be monological dialogue. For a different view, see Marc-Alain Ouaknin, *The Burnt Book: Reading the Talmud* (Princeton: Princeton University Press, 1995), 85–6, and 161.

Be that as it may, it is also important to distinguish between monologue in the literal (non-Bakhtinian) sense that happens to make reference to other opinions in order to refute them and dialogue in the literal sense that presents two different views, even if both work within the same language and structure. Monological dialectic is found in the exercise on introducing law, as quoted above, in Midrash Halakha, as quoted below, in Plato's *Protagoras*, and in some Talmudic sugyot where the Stam has a strong hand in leading the argumentation towards a certain opinion. The dialogical format comprises much of the *ta shema* and other forms of give and take in the Talmuds that genuinely argue different legal points of view and come to no normative conclusion. It is found also in Plato's *Symposium* (see Boyarin, *Socrates and the Fat Rabbis*, 145–6). Neither of these formats may be dialogical in the Bakhtinian sense, but they are significantly different from each other in their forms of presentation.

28 For example, Libanius' Declamations 9 and 10 each include six such antitheses utilizing the same style as that of the progymnasmata. The structure of these orations is analyzed at Johansson, *Libanius' Declamations*, 131 and 231.

29 Brodsky, "From Disagreement to Talmudic Discourse," 182.

30 Translation follows MS Oxford.

[Antithesis] Or perhaps this verse (Exod 20:13) refers to stealing money and that verse (Lev 19:11) refers to kidnapping?

[Solution] You should say: three commandments were stated in this context. Two of them are apparent and one is obscure. Let us elucidate the obscure one from the apparent ones. Just as the apparent ones ["You shall not murder" and "You shall not commit adultery"] are commandments for which one is liable to death at the hands of the court, so too the obscure one ["You shall not steal"] is a commandment for which one is liable to death at the hands of the court.

[Epilogue] Therefore, you should not say the latter option but rather the former option: this (Exod 20:13) is a warning for kidnapping and that (Lev 19:11) is a warning for stealing money.[31]

The midrash explains the redundancy of the multiple Pentateuchal prohibitions against stealing by designating one as a law against monetary theft and the other as a rule against kidnapping. The question is, which verse is which? The midrash concludes that the context of the sixth and seventh commandments that demand capital punishment requires that the eighth commandment must prohibit kidnapping, which also demands capital punishment.

Note the dialectical structure of the midrashic argument: it first presents a thesis, then challenges it by suggesting the opposite view, then provides a solution and then repeats the cycle with further challenges and solutions until it arrives at a definitive conclusion. This form and the key phrases that it employs to demarcate its sections are typical of the standard formulas found throughout the midrashic literature of the Tannaim. The example here is from a midrash from the School of R. Ishmael, which deploys these terms: "do you say (אתה אומר) ... or perhaps it is only (או אינו אלא) ... behold (הרי) ... or perhaps (או הרי) ... you should say (אמרת) ... therefore, you should not say the latter option but rather the former option." Akivan midrashim include slightly different terminology such as: "can it be (יכול) ... therefore it teaches (תלמוד לומר)" but otherwise follow the same dialectical format.[32]

[31] See parallel at Mekhilta d'R. Ishmael, Ba-ḥodesh, 8. A variation of this interpretation is found at B. Sanhedrin 86a, which explains that since the previous two commandments regarding murder and adultery are sins committed against the bodies of other people and not just their money, so too "You shall not steal" must also be kidnapping the body of another and not his money. See further at Meir Ish Shalom, ed. *Mekhilta d'R. Ishmael ʿal sefer Shemot ʿim tosafot Me'ir ʿAyin* (Vienna: 1870), p. 70b n. 15.

[32] See Hanoch Albeck, *Mavo la-Talmudim* (Tel-Aviv: Dvir, 1987), 93–102; and Y. N. Epstein, *Mevo'ot le-sifrut ha-Tannaim, Mishnah, Tosefta, u-midreshe halakha*, ed. E.

This structure is strikingly similar in both form and purpose to the progymnasma on introducing a law. Note how both texts present a semblance of a dialogue even though it is actually a single voice quoting an imaginary interlocutor.[33] This strategy resolves potential questions that the audience might have and lends to the proposed law an air of being rigorously debated even while the presenter maintains full control over the arguments. When the rabbis who composed these midrashim wanted to convince their audience of the legitimacy of their legislation and interpretation, they followed the most effective and widespread means of persuasion in their culture. The exercise on introducing a law as taught to students and the forms it took when embedded in full orations at public assemblies set the standard for how best to present legislation. Midrash halakha follows this same standard and applies it to the derivation of the oral law from the Bible.[34]

This type of dialectical form that aims to prove a given point of view is also found in the Yerushalmi, although not as ubiquitously as in tannaitic midrash. For example, Mishnah Baba Qama 3:1 rules: "One who places a jug in the public thoroughfare, and someone else came along and tripped on it and broke it, [the passerby] is exempt." Y. Baba Qama 3:1, 3b–c, extends this to a related case that involves taking the law into one's own hands[35]:

> **[Theoretical Case]** All of the public thoroughfare was filled [with jugs].
>
> **[Thesis]** If a passerby removes them from here and replaces them elsewhere, he is creating a pit.[36] Rather, he may take a staff and break them, or pass over them and if they break then so be it.
>
> **[Proof]** Let us learn it from here: "If an ox arose upon another and the owner of the [bottom] ox comes to remove his ox or the ox removed

Z. Melamed (Jerusalem, 1947), 568–69. On the two schools of midrash, see Strack and Stemberger, *Introduction*, 247–75. On the differences between the schools related to *gezerah shavah* see herein pp. 207–212.

[33] Although, the progymnasmata cite the interlocutor in third person while midrash halakha does so in second person. See also Brodsky, "From Disagreement to Talmudic Discourse," 203–5, especially n. 64.

[34] See further discussion of midrash halakha and rhetorical *topoi* in the next chapter.

[35] Translation follows MS Leiden.

[36] One who leaves an object in the public thoroughfare falls under the category of one who digs a pit there and is responsible for any damage it causes to passersby. See M. Baba Qama 1:1 and 3:1. In this case, once the passerby moves the jug and places it elsewhere in the thoroughfare, the passerby becomes responsible for damages that the jug might cause.

itself and the [upper] ox fell and died, [the owner of the bottom ox] is exempt. If [the owner of the bottom ox] pushed it [the upper ox] and it fell and died, then he is liable."[37]

[Antithesis] Can he [the owner of the upper ox] not say to him [the owner of the lower ox], "If you had left him alone I would have paid you for your damage?"[38]

[Solution] In fact, it is he [the owner of the lower ox] who can say to him [the owner of the upper ox], "If I had left it alone you would have paid only for half of the damage."[39]

[Antithesis] Assume that it was a warned ox.

[Solution] "It is not up to you that I should have to litigate against you in court."

The Talmud presents a theoretical case of a thoroughfare filled with jugs and proposes that the passerby should be permitted to walk through the thoroughfare without being held responsible for breaking the jugs. As a proof for this position, it cites a Tosefta that exempts the owner of an ox who pulls it out from under another ox causing the upper ox to fall and die. In both cases, one is permitted to resort to self-help even though he would suffer no permanent loss; in the first case, the passerby would simply have to take a detour, and in the second case, the owner of the bottom ox would only have to collect damages from the owner of the upper ox. The Tosefta's ruling itself is then challenged precisely on the grounds that the owner of the upper ox would have paid the owner of the bottom ox; since the latter would have suffered no loss he should not be permitted to take the law into his own hands. The Talmud then finds support for the Tosefta's ruling in that if the upper ox had no prior history, its owner would only be liable to half of the damages inflicted upon the lower ox. Consequently, the owner of the lower ox would suffer loss and therefore would be allowed to resort to self-help. The Talmud's final challenge argues that since the Tosefta does not specify the status of the upper ox, we may presume that its ruling holds true even when the

37 T. Baba Qama 3:6.

38 In designating this line as a question about the proof above, I follow R. Yisrael Haim Daiches, *Netivot Yerushalaim* (Vilna, 1880), 22. R. Moshe Margaliot, *Pne Moshe*, understands this line as a continuation of the proof and the next line as a question such that the pericope ends with the conclusion that one may not resort to self-help in these cases. However, I think that the above translation and structure best fit the text.

39 The owner of an ox with no previous history of violence pays only for half of the damages. Once an ox causes damage three times it is considered forewarned and is responsible for full damages. See Exod 21:35–6 and M. Baba Qama 2:4 and 3:8.

upper ox does have a history and there would be no loss. The discussion concludes that since the owner of the lower ox would have to enter into litigation to collect damages, that effort itself is enough of a loss to permit his taking the law into his own hands to prevent damage to his ox. Now that the law of the Tosefta has been defended, it stands as proof for the original thesis that the passerby may break the jugs in the thoroughfare even though it would cause only minimal loss for him to take a different route.

Both of the examples above from the Mekhilta and the Yerushalmi follow a structure parallel to that of the progymnasma on introducing a law. They begin with a case and propose a thesis as to what the law should be. Then, they repeatedly challenge and resolve the original thesis. In all of these sources, the challenges are presented as quotations of a real or imagined opposing voice, thus imitating the rhythm of a dialogue. However, as in the progymnasma, the challenges only serve to bolster the persuasive power of the thesis by again and again resolving each antithesis.[40]

This dialectical structure also underlies the progymnasma on thesis, as Brodsky points out, as well as the progymnasmata that most directly trained students to argue for both sides of an issue: the exercises of refutation (*anaskeue*) and confirmation (*kataskeue*). The latter two exercises employ further techniques that also exemplify Talmudic sugyot, as we will see below. For the progymnasma of refutation, a student would be given a certain myth from classical poetry and would have to argue that the myth is not historical based on its being unclear, impossible, implausible, illogical, inappropriate, or inconsistent.[41] Libanius provides a sample refutation on the subject of the story of Chryses in Homer's Iliad. Agamemnon was said to have captured the daughter of Chryses during the Trojan War. Chryses, who was a priest of Apollo, went to ransom her, carrying money and holy objects, but was rebuffed. At Chryses' request, Apollo sent a plague through the Greek armies, after which Agamemnon agreed to return his prize to her father.[42] Libanius' refutation proceeds to argue that this story is fictional on account of its being implausible:

> [Homer] says that Chryses came to the Greek ships to ransom his daughter and made a two-part supplication... How would an old

[40] See p. 136 n. 27.

[41] See Kennedy, *Progymnasmata*, 40–2, 101–5, 144–7 and 199–206.

[42] Homer, *Iliad*, 1.1–52.

> man have dared to go to the enemy? Not even a young man would risk that.[43] These were people at whose approach he probably would have fled: how could he have been willing to go to them, knowing that they hated Troy and were plundering the surrounding peoples?
>
> **[Antithesis]** "Longing for his daughter forced him to do it."
>
> **[Solution]** But fear of the enemy prevented him ...
>
> **[Antithesis]** "Yes, by Zeus, but he could be confident in his scepter and ribbons."
>
> **[Solution]** And what stock did the Greeks put in the enemy's gods?[44]

Libanius goes on at some length, but this quotation should suffice to provide a sense of how a refutation would be written. Significantly, Libanius punctuates his oration with quotations from what his detractors might say, thereby adding a dialogical character to the composition. Hermogenes, in fact, prescribes this technique in his primer: "This is how you will argue in favor of the proposition and you will rebut it from the opposite arguments. You will also refute the arguments found on the other side of the issue."[45]

Libanius later proceeds to present a confirmation that argues that the myth is true because it is inappropriate to cast doubt on the poets, especially Homer. Furthermore:

> Is it not the law of nature to risk danger for one's children? Do we not take up arms on their behalf and go into battle and die with pleasure, having obtained their freedom with our own hands? Also, he was an old man, and he had no reason to expect a long life .... It was also of great assistance that he was in charge of sacred rites, displayed the scepter of the god, and carried ribbons; for he believed that the Greeks, being Greeks, would not easily despise these things.[46]

Notice how the confirmation addresses each point brought up in the refutation and spins it in the opposite direction. These exercises are thus doubly dialogical: the confirmation rejects each point in the refutation, while the refutation itself, anticipating the confirmation, cites and contradicts arguments from the opposite side. Progymnasmatic textbooks sometimes record compositions on only one side of an issue

[43] Note the use of comparisons from the lesser and greater here, the subject of the next chapter.

[44] Gibson, *Libanius's Progymnasmata*, 109.

[45] Kennedy, *Progymnasmata*, 88.

[46] Gibson, *Libanius's Progymnasmata*, 127.

and, in other cases, record exercises on one side followed by further compositions on the other. The students would apply skills they received from these two exercises to other progymnasmata as well. The first-century CE rhetor Theon, in fact, does not even count refutation and confirmation as independent exercises but rather includes them within the exercises of fable, narrative, chreia and maxim, description, and introduction of law.[47] In all of these exercises, a student would be asked to argue for one side or the other or both. Aphthonius explains that refutation and confirmation are so basic that they include within themselves "all the power of the art"[48] of rhetoric.

Many Talmudic sugyot follow similar patterns of proving or disproving both sides of an argument. For example, the Tosefta provides arguments on both sides of a debate recorded at M. Berakhot 8:1 regarding the order of blessings recited at *qiddush*[49] on the eve of the Sabbath and festivals. T. Berakhot 5:25 teaches[50]:

> Beth Shammai say one makes a blessing on the day and afterwards makes a blessing on the wine, for the day causes the wine to come and the day is already holy before the wine comes.
>
> Beth Hillel say one makes a blessing on the wine and then makes a blessing on the day for the wine causes the holiness of the day to be declared. Another reason, the blessing on the wine is frequent and blessing on the day is not frequent.[51]

Interestingly, the justifications for both sides draw on reason rather than tradition or legal precedent. Beth Shammai reason that since the Sabbath begins immediately at nightfall and precedes the recitation of *qiddush*, the holiness of the day causes the need for *qiddush* of the wine. While Beth Hillel acknowledge that the Sabbath becomes holy first, they reason that the recitation of a blessing about the holiness of the day depends on the presence of wine; from this perspective, the wine precedes because it brings about the possibility for *qiddush*. The inclusion of an additional

[47] Gibson, ibid., 107, citing the progymnasmata of Theon: ¶74 and ¶76–78 (fable), ¶93–96 (narrative), ¶101 and ¶103–106 (chreia and maxim), ¶120 (description), and ¶129–130 (introduction of law); and see Kennedy, *Progymnasmata*, 24–63.

[48] Kennedy, ibid., 101 and 104 (Aphthonius 28 and 30).

[49] *Qiddush* (lit. holiness of [the day]) is a set of blessings recited over wine to declare the onset of the Sabbath or festival. *Havdalah* (lit. differentiation) is also a set of blessings recited over wine to mark the end of the Sabbath or festival.

[50] Translation follows MS Vienna.

[51] In general, a ritual that occurs more frequently precedes another that occurs less frequently. See, for example, Y. Yoma 2:2, 40a, B. Sukkah 54b, et al.

alternate explanation for Beth Hillel – that whatever occurs more frequently should precede – suggests that these justifications likely do not derive from the original sages who first legislated the laws but rather come from the learned speculation of later students and sages. In this case and in so many others like it, the rabbis took upon themselves the task of providing arguments for both sides of a debate, just as students of progymnasmata did. Continuing this format, a later generation of Amoraim then built upon the reasons found in this Tosefta to draw implications for what the Houses might say regarding the order of blessings in *havdalah*. Y. Berakhot 8:1, 11d, reports[52]:

> R. Yose said: According to the words of both of them, when there is wine and *havdalah*, wine precedes. Isn't the reason of Beth Shammai that the holiness of the day causes the wine to come? But here, since *havdalah* does not cause the wine to come, the wine precedes. Isn't the reason of Beth Hillel that the wine is frequent and holiness is not frequent? Here too, since the wine is frequent and the *havdalah* is not frequent, wine precedes.
>
> R. Mana said: According to the words of both of them, when there is wine and *havdalah*, *havdalah* precedes. Isn't the reason of Beth Shammai that he was already obligated in the holiness of the day before the wine came? Here too, since he was obligated in *havdalah* before the wine came, *havdalah* precedes. Isn't the reason of Beth Hillel that the wine causes the holiness of the day to be declared? But here, since the wine does not cause *havdalah* to be declared, *havdalah* precedes.

The two Amoraim here discuss an issue about which the Houses recorded no ruling and try to derive a conclusion based on the arguments of the Tosefta. Both R. Yose and R. Mana agree that there is a consensus between the Houses regarding *havdalah*, but they come to opposite conclusions about what that consensus is. Both Amoraim also presume that *havdalah* differs from *qiddush* in that the primary recitation of *havdalah* occurred already in the prayers without wine, rendering *havdalah* less dependent on wine than is *qiddush*. R. Yose applies this distinction to Beth Shammai, while R. Mana applies the same distinction to Beth Hillel; each Amora thereby reverses the Houses' respective stances in the case of *havdalah*. This is fascinating in that the two sides prove two opposite positions based on the very same data point

[52] Translation follows MS Leiden.

interpreting the same Tosefta.[53] The progymnasmata cited above similarly make use of the very same data point – for example, that Chryses is old – to argue both ways.[54]

The form of the progymnasmata wherein arguments are drawn up on both sides of an issue can also help inform the *ta shema* sugya form. These sugyot, of which there are hundreds in the Bavli, follow a set structure: they begin with a law, present a problem (*ba`ya*), and then attempt various proofs for or against each side using the formula "come and hear" (*ta shema*) to introduce every source. These proofs are each rejected until the sugya either arrives at a definitive proof or – as is often the case – the sugya concludes, "let the question stand" (*tequ*), once the sources have been exhausted without a definitive conclusion in either direction.[55] Let us analyze a fairly typical example from B. Baba Qama 27b–28a[56]:

> Rav Yehuda says, "One may not take the law into his own hands." Rav Naḥman says, "One may take the law into his own hands." In a case where there would be loss, all agree that one may take the law into his own hands. They disagree when there is no loss. Rav Yehuda says, "One may not take the law into his own hands." Since there is no loss let him go stand before the judge. Rav Nahman says, "One may take the law into his own hands." Since he acts lawfully, he can say to him, "I do not have to burden myself."[57]
>
> **[Challenges to R. Yehuda]**
> **[Antithesis]** Rav Kahana challenged: Ben Bag Bag says, "Do not enter the courtyard of your fellow to take what is yours without his permission lest he perceive you as a thief. Rather, break his teeth and tell him, 'I am taking what is mine.'"[58]

[53] In this case, the two Amoraim are able to take advantage of the two sets of reasons provided for Beth Hillel, with each side choosing one or the other, as well as emphasizing one or the other of the two phrases in the explanation of Beth Shammai.

[54] See Hermogenes, *On Invention*, III.3 (Kennedy, *Invention and Method*, 82–5) who calls this type of refutation "*biaion*" wherein, "we can turn around the argument and catch the opponent with the very things he has boldly asserted." He describes it as "the most unexpected and strongest and most effective" refutation.

[55] Louis Jacobs, *Teyku: The Unsolved Problem in the Babylonian Talmud* (London: Cornwall Books, 1981), 13–14. See further herein pp. 162–170.

[56] Follows MS Hamburg 165. Significant variants are noted.

[57] MSS Escorial G.I.3 and Florence II.I.8 add, "to go to court."

[58] T. Baba Qama 10:38. See analysis at Irwin Haut, "Self-help in Jewish Law: Literary and Legal Analyses," *Diné Israel* 17 (1993–94): 75–82.

[Solution] He responded, "Kahana! Kahana![59] With you? With you?[60] Ben Bag Bag is a minority and we do not agree with him[61] and the rabbis disagree with him."

. . .

[Antithesis] Come and hear: "If an ox arose upon another to kill it and the owner of the [bottom] ox came to remove his ox or the [bottom] ox removed itself and the [upper] ox fell and died, [the owner of the bottom ox] is exempt."[62] Is the case not involving a warned ox and there is no loss?

[Solution] No, it is an unwarned ox and there is loss.

[Antithesis] If so, then cite the end [of the Tosefta]: "If he [the owner of the bottom ox] pushed the upper ox and it died, he is liable." If it is unwarned, then why is he liable?

[Solution] Because he should have pulled out [his own ox] and he did not pull it out.

[Antithesis] Come and hear: "One who fills the courtyard of his fellow with jugs of wine or jugs of oil, the owner of the courtyard may smash them to exit and smash them to enter."

[Solution] R. Naḥman bar Yiṣḥak,[63] "He smashes and exits to court, smashes and enters to retrieve his title documents."

[Antithesis] Come and hear: How do we know that a [slave whose ear has] been pierced whose days are complete[64] and whose master is prevailing upon him to leave and he does not leave[65] and he [the master] injured him and gave him a wound, how do we know that he

[59] Printed editions omit, "Kahana! Kahana!" MSS Florence, Munich 95, and Vatican 116 include "Kahana!" only once. MS Escorial mistakenly reads, "Rav Kahana, Kahana."

[60] This exclamation seems to be a short way of saying, "Is this argument passable with you? Do you yourself think you have a valid point?" It is inserted in the margin of MS Hamburg but appears twice in all other MSS and just once in printed editions.

[61] "And we do not agree with him," is omitted in all witnesses except MS Hamburg.

[62] This is a slightly different version of T. Baba Qama 3:6 compared with that cited in the Yerushalmi on p. 139–140.

[63] MS Florence omits, "bar Yiṣḥak."

[64] A Jewish slave may remain in servitude even after his prescribed six years by asking his master to pierce his ears. This pierced slave must go free at the Jubilee. The Talmud deals with such a slave who refuses to leave and whose master forces him out and injures him rather than bring him to court – thus taking the law into his own hands.

[65] Printed editions omit, "and he does not leave."

[the master] is exempt? Scripture states, "Do not take ransom . . . to return" (Num 35:32) – Do not take ransom for one who returns.[66]

[Solution] What are we dealing with here? A slave who is a thief.[67]

[. . .]

[Challenges to R. Naḥman]

[Antithesis] Come and hear: "One who places a jug in public domain and another person comes and trips on it and breaks it, [the passerby] is exempt."[68] The reason [he is exempt] is because he tripped on it but if he [purposely] smashed it, then he would be liable.

[Solution] Rav Zevid from Neharde`a[69] said in the name of Rabbah:[70] The same law applies even if he smashed it. The Mishnah teaches "tripped" because it wanted to teach the end of the Mishnah: "If he [the passerby] was injured by it then the owner of the jug is liable for his injury." That is only if he tripped but not if he smashed. What is the reason?[71] For he injured himself. Thus, the beginning of the Mishnah also says "tripped."

[Antithesis] Come and hear: "You shall cut off her hand – this refers to monetary [payment]." Is this not in a case when she was unable to save [her husband] by another means?

[Solution] No, it is when she was able to save by another means. But if she could not save by another means[72] then what?[73] She would be exempt.

. . .

[Antithesis] Come and hear: "If the public thoroughfare passed through his field and he removed it and gave them a [new] thoroughfare on the side [of his field], then what he had given is given and his

[66] The verse in its context legislates that an unintentional killer may not return home from the city of refuge by paying a ransom. The Talmud revocalizes a word and applies the verse to a Jewish slave whose period of slavery is over but who keeps returning to his master. This midrash teaches that even if the master injures the slave to force him out, the slave does not receive compensation.

[67] If the master allows the slave to enter his house, the slave might then steal something and cause a loss. In such a case, even R. Yehudah would agree that one may resort to self-help and injure the slave if necessary to keep him out.

[68] M. Baba Qama 3:1.

[69] All witnesses except MS Hamburg omit, "from Neharde`a."

[70] Following MS Hamburg. MS Florence reads, "Rav." All other witnesses read, "Rava."

[71] All witnesses except MS Hamburg omit, "What is the reason?"

[72] MSS Escorial and Munich omit, "by another means."

[73] Printed editions omit, "what?"

own [land on which he made the new path] does not return to his property."[74] If you say that one may take the law into his own hands, then let him take an iron tool and sit [guarding the path he retook].

[Solution] Rav Zevid said in the name of Rabbah,[75] "It is a safeguard lest he provide for them a roundabout path."

...

[Antithesis] Come and hear: If a homeowner left *pe'ah*[76] from one side and poor people came and took from another side – both this and that are *pe'ah*." But if you say that one may take the law into his own hands, then why are this and that *pe'ah*? Let him take an iron tool and sit.

[Solution] Rava[77] said, what does, "this and that are *pe'ah*" mean? That it is[78] exempt from tithes.

All of the challenges here, except for the first one, are Stammaitic. They are also neatly structured with four attempted proofs against R. Yehudah, which are all deflected, followed by four attempted proofs against R. Naḥman, which again are all deflected. This sugya is thus also doubly dialogical in that it presents a dialectical argument for one side and pits it against a dialectical argument for the other side. Other *ta shema* sugyot do not typically separate the arguments for each side but rather swing back and forth between each side. Nevertheless, *ta shema* sugyot evince a concerted effort to challenge both sides with more or less equal rigor.

A significant difference between the two sets of literature is that progymnasmata strive to prove one side or the other while the goal of most *ta shema* sugyot is to uphold both sides by rejecting proofs for either side. More specifically, each progymnasma offers a series of arguments for a given position that succeeds in proving one side and disproving the other side; sometimes a second progymnasma follows, arguing the opposite case. These exercises typically follow a dialogic form with quotes from a dissenting voice, but each of those challenges will necessarily be parried. The dissenting quotations by the speaker in the

74 M. Baba Batra 6:7.

75 Following MS Hamburg. All other witnesses read, "Rava," except MS Vatican, which omits the name altogether.

76 Leviticus 19:9 requires a farmer to leave unharvested a corner (*pe'ah*) of the field for the poor to take from it.

77 MS Florence reads, "Rav Papa."

78 MSS Hamburg, Escorial, Florence and Vatican read this in the singular. MS Munich and printed editions read, "they are."

progymnasmata serve to preempt arguments from the opposing camp. *Ta shema* sugyot, in contrast, typically present a series of disproofs against either side and reject each one with a view to demonstrating that both opposing positions can be reconciled with various tannaitic sources. Sometimes these sugyot conclude by proving one side but, more often than not, they end without a definitive conclusion. These sugyot do not generally strive to decide the practical halakha. Rather, they present an argumentative exercise demonstrating how each side of the debate can explain and be reconciled with all prior authoritative sources.

This strategy reflects fundamentally different assumptions about truth and tradition. The sophists denied the existence of any objective truth and therefore prided themselves on being able to convince an audience of any position. The goal of the progymnasmata was therefore to demonstrate one's skill in making anything seem true by conclusively proving one side and disproving the other. The rabbis, in contrast, believed that *both* sides of the debate contained truth value because both are part of the oral tradition of the Torah. As Daniel Boyarin writes, "[F]or the anonymous redactorial voice of the Babylonian Talmud it is most often the case that such an apparent proof of one view is considered a difficulty (*qushia*) requiring a resolution which, in fact, shows that there is no resolution."[79] Consequently, the ultimate resolution for the Stammaim was to persuade their audiences that neither view could be rejected and both are valid.

A second related difference between the Greek and Rabbinic rhetorical exercises is that the Greeks used reason to prove one side or the other while the rabbis mostly resorted to proofs from authoritative sources. A third difference is that progymnasmata are written compositions that provide a sustained persuasive argument in the voice of a single speaker who occasionally cites other views; the Talmud orally compiles relatively short sources and arguments held together by anonymous interjections. Despite these differences, however, the similarity between the progymnasmata and the rabbinic literary forms discussed here suffice to show that the rabbis did take part in a shared culture of rhetoric. Both the progymnasmata and the rabbinic texts offer arguments for and against each side; both employ a dialogic format to cite and preempt possible objection; and both demand great ingenuity on the part of the student/sage to muster all of his powers of persuasion and display his dialectical skills. This is a good example of how the rabbis

[79] Boyarin, *Border Lines*, 152. For more on polysemy and multiple truths in rabbinic thought, especially in the Bavli, see Hidary, *Dispute*, 17–31.

both adopt a widespread pedagogical method and adapt it to their own epistemological and religious framework of multiple truths that derive from their prophetic tradition.[80]

CONTROVERSIAE AND HYPOTHETICALS

Once a student had mastered the progymnasmatic exercises, he would be ready to move on to compose more elaborate declamations called controversiae. Controversiae have almost the same form as the advanced progymnasmata, except that they deal with specific cases rather than general principles. A student was presented with a law and a theoretical case and was asked to compose a declamation that applied the law to the case in one way. The student might then be tasked with composing another declamation to the opposite effect, following a pattern similar to that of the progymnasmata of confirmation and refutation. Most often, these involved very outlandish hypothetical cases. Examples of complete controversiae are extant from the hands of Polemon of Laodicea, Aelius Aristides, Lucian, Libanius, Choricius of Gaza and many others.[81] A set of full major declamations is attributed to Quintilian but were probably written by a later rhetor; another set of minor declamations were more likely penned by Quintilian, but they record only the cases and his lecture notes.[82] Seneca the Elder similarly collected dozens of controversiae that he remembered hearing in his youth. For each, he provides the law, case, snippets of arguments offered on each side by the various masters of his time, and his own analysis of their arguments, called *coloures*.

In this section, I will analyze the similarities and differences between Talmudic sugyot and the genre of controversiae. I will show that both the Greeks and the rabbis used hypothetical scenarios to sharpen the analytical skills of their students. Talmudic hypotheticals tend to be less convoluted and paradoxical than their Greek parallels, though the rabbis concocted many outlandish examples as well. Furthermore, the form and goal of many Talmudic sugyot become clearer when compared to the form of the controversiae. As we will see in the next section, the epitomes of controversiae resemble the style of *ta*

80 See further on this theme on pp. 277–87.

81 This literature is surveyed in Russel, *Greek Declamation*, 3–9; and Penella, *Rhetorical Exercises*, 8–26.

82 See Quintilian, *The Major Declamations Ascribed to Quintilian*, trans. Lewis Sussman (New York: Verlag Peter Lang, 1987); and Quintilian, *The Lesser Declamations*, trans. D. R. Shackleton Bailey (Cambridge: Harvard University Press, 2006).

shema sugyot, and the development and purpose of the former can help us appreciate that of the latter.

Here is one sample controversia that provides a feel for this genre. Seneca presents a law: "A girl who has been raped may choose either marriage to her ravisher without dowry or his death."[83] This law is an oversimplification of the actual practice under Greek and Roman legal systems. While marriage with the rapist may have been practiced when agreeable to the victim, the death penalty would have been applied only in extreme cases when the culprit refused to pay a fine.[84] Presenting the law as such a stark choice, however, adds to the dramatic tension in the case that follows. Seneca reports that the orators of his youth debated this scenario: "On a single night a man raped two girls. One demands his death, the other marriage." The law thus produces contrary results. Seneca cites a number of orators who argue that the man should die because his multiple offenses make him a greater criminal and perhaps the second girl was complicit with the rapist to get him out of the death penalty. Others defend the man on the grounds that since there are two equal claims, mercy should prevail. It is doubtful that such a case ever occurred, but this hypothetical offers the orator a rich palette of arguments from which to build his case and exercise his creativity.

Donald Russel coined the term "Sophistopolis" to describe the imaginary world that combined aspects of ancient Athens with contemporary conditions and served as the setting for these theoretical cases.[85] This is a world constantly at war, where tyrants are ever ready to seize power, where the innocent poor continually struggle with the unjust rich, where fathers disown their sons for all sorts of reasons, and where the rhetor was heralded a hero. It was in this imaginary world that citizens of the Greek East could maintain their culture and history in the face of Roman power as well as providing a setting in which to work out the issues of the day.[86] The same can be said of the rabbis who lacked political autonomy and held only limited judicial jurisdiction over their own adherents, but nevertheless legislated an elaborate set

[83] Seneca, *Declamations*, II.167, controversia 8.1.

[84] See Bonner, *Roman Declamation*, 89–91; and Russel, *Greek Declamation*, 33–4.

[85] Russel, *Greek Declamation*, 21–39.

[86] Whitmarsh, *The Second Sophistic*, 70–3. See also p. 5. Although controversiae originally served to create this political virtual reality in the Greek East, they eventually became popular in the Latin West for their educational and cultural benefits. See further in Penella, *Rhetorical Exercises*, 12–13, on the important social and cultural role of declamation in Roman society.

of ritual and civil laws – some applicable and some only theoretical – as if they were the sovereign rulers of a nation.[87]

Besides the political and cultural value of this imaginary world, the hypothetical and paradoxical cases in the controversiae provided a testing ground for students to develop their wit, ingenuity, and rhetorical skill. As engaging and fun as these theoretical scenarios were, however, they also became the target of criticism by contemporary writers for being too outlandish. Tacitus, for example, voices his criticism in the mouth of Messala:

> Good heavens! What strange and astonishing productions are the result! It comes to pass that subjects remote from all reality are actually used for declamation. Thus the reward of a tyrannicide, or the choice of an outraged maiden, or a remedy for a pestilence, or a mother's incest, anything, in short, daily discussed in our schools, never, or but very rarely in the courts, is dwelt on in grand language.[88]

Petronius similarly complains that since students never experience these issues in ordinary life, all of their theoretical training leaves them unfit to enter a real court.[89] Synesius too mocks the elderly Libanius for devoting all of his energy to vigorous and serious debate about impossible cases involving people who never existed.[90] Despite these voices of criticism, however, such hypothetical cases continued to be the staple of education in the schools of rhetoric for centuries.[91]

In order to best compare the place of such hypothetical deliberations in the Greco-Roman and rabbinic contexts, let us analyze three issues that come up in both sets of literature: self-help, surrendering an individual to an enemy, and conflicting filial obligations. Regarding the first topic, many declamations and Talmudic sugyot involve cases of taking the law into one's own hands. We saw above the sample progymnasma debating whether one can kill an adulterer when discovered in the act. Such cases surely occurred in real life and, in fact, Roman law at

[87] For a description of the world as portrayed in the Bavli, see Ruth Calderon, *A Bride for One Night: Talmudic Tales* (Philadelphia: Jewish Publication Society, 2014), xvii–xx.

[88] Tacitus, *Dialogue on Oratory*, 35; translation from A. J. Church and W. J. Brodribb, *The Agricola and Germany of Tacitus and the Dialogue on Oratory* (London: Macmillan, 1911), 188–9. See further at Bonner, *Roman Declamation*, 71–83; and Michael Winterbottom, *Roman Declamation* (Bristol: Bristol Classical Press, 1980), 1–8.

[89] Petronius, *Satyricon*, 1.

[90] Synesius, *On Dreams*, 27. See Russel, *Greek Declamation*, 21.

[91] For a defense of the use of imaginary cases, see Penella, *Rhetorical Exercises*, 11–12.

first permitted and then prohibited such vigilante justice.[92] The cases proposed in declamations, however, introduce new levels of complication. Libanius, for example, writes a speech for the following paradoxical case: "There was a rumor that a father was seducing his son's wife. The father proposed a law that it should be permitted to kill one's son without trial. The son now proposes a law to allow adulterers to be killed without trial."[93] Or take the case discussed by Quintilian in his lecture notes entitled, "The adulterer-priest," which I quote here in full:

> **[Law]** Let a priest have power to release one person from punishment. Let it be lawful to kill adulterers.
>
> **[Theoretical Case]** A man caught a priest in adultery and when he [the priest] claimed immunity for himself under the law, [the man] killed him. He is charged with murder.
>
> **Discussion**
>
> Was the person caught still a priest, that is, at the moment he was caught, did he lose his rights as a priest? If he was still a priest, could he ask for himself in this offence? Can he exercise his option anywhere but in public?
>
> **Declamation**
>
> I caught an adulterer, which is enough for me. For no person is excepted, and adultery is more disgraceful in a priest.
>
> **[Antithesis]** "He had a law," says the prosecutor.
>
> **[Solution]** That is like a general turned traitor or a guardian who abuses his female ward asking to be let off. But imagine I went to law with him from suspicion of adultery; if he had been found guilty, I suppose he would have forfeited his priesthood.
>
> Add that the law grants power to save somebody else. It is written that he who saves the life of a citizen be honored; can someone who saves his own life receive the reward? Or can someone who beats himself be found guilty of injury?
>
> Furthermore, the law of adultery has priority over the priest's law; for the priest opts in public, and if the adulterer gets that far, he has escaped. Besides, he was claiming for two; for the adulteress

[92] Bonner, *Roman Declamation*, 119–21.

[93] Donald A. Russel, *Imaginary Speeches: A Selection of Declamations* (London: Gerald Duckworth, 1996), 170.

could not be killed without the adulterer; then I should indeed have committed murder.[94]

I will return to analyze the structure of this controversia in the next section,[95] but for now let us focus on the case itself. If we compare the cases in the controversiae to the discussions of self-help in the Yerushalmi and Bavli, which we have already cited and analyzed,[96] we note both their similarities as well as several important differences. The Roman writers use examples of adultery and homicide while the rabbis mostly discuss damages and theft. The declamations revel in logical paradoxes created by such outlandish cases; the typical cases discussed by the Talmuds, on the other hand, are more run of the mill occurrences like oxen attacking one another and people blocking up the thoroughfare. Even the most bizarre Talmudic scenarios do not reach the level of paradox that was typical in the Roman curriculum.

As a second example, both the declamations and the Talmud discuss similar ethical dilemmas regarding surrendering a citizen, but the former includes various improbable situations not found in the latter. Consider Libanius' declamation on a case of filicide: "A tyrant demanded a handsome boy from a neighboring city, threatening war if he did not get him. The city chose war. The tyrant attacked. During the siege, the boy's father killed him and threw him from the wall. The tyrant departed, and the father is now charged with murder."[97] Libanius composes a speech in the voice of the father defending his action on account that he loved his son and only killed him in order to save the city. The father cites various objections that his prosecutor might say, such as: "The people had resolved to go to war" and refused to submit to the tyrant. The imaginary father responds, "As it was right for you to do these things for me, so it was right for me to do for you what I did."[98] The speech continues with logical and emotional pleas convincing the audience of his blamelessness and courage. Further complicating this case, Choricius proposes that the murdered boy has a girlfriend who commits suicide when she hears of the boy's death. The father of the girlfriend sues the father of the boy for killing his daughter.[99]

[94] Quintilian, *The Lesser Declamations*, I.312–15, declamation 284. The headings, "Discussion," and "Declamations" are in the original text; I have added the other headings in brackets. See also ibid., declamations 244 and 347; and Seneca, *Declamations*, I.104–21 and II.214–35, controversiae 1.4 and 9.1.

[95] P. 166.

[96] Pp. 139 and 145.

[97] Russel, *Imaginary Speeches*, 179.

[98] Ibid., 184.

[99] Penella, *Rhetorical Exercises*, 177.

The rabbis debate a similar case in M. Terumot 8:12: if an enemy demands the surrender of one woman to be raped or else they will rape all the women in the group, the group may not surrender anyone. T. Terumot 7:20 similarly rules that if the enemy demands the surrender of one person from a traveling group or else they will kill everyone, then the group may not surrender anyone. However, the Tosefta adds, "if they specified him like they specified Sheva ben Bikhri,[100] then they should give him up rather than all die." The Tosefta cites other opinions that disagree and the Yerushalmi retells an actual case of a surrendered refugee in Lydda.[101] While the Talmud does not record any full declamations on this subject, it is unlikely that the rabbis uttered no more than the pithy one-line rulings cited in rabbinic literature. Rather, I assume that they offered lengthy lectures on this and similar subjects that may have resembled the lengthy orations preserved by Libanius. Although there is no reason to think that the rabbis would have composed an imaginary speech in the mouth of a defendant or prosecutor, there is every reason to presume that they would have used the dialogic format that is ubiquitous throughout the Talmud to build arguments for both sides of these dilemmas.

That both sets of literature discuss the same topic helps highlight an important difference between the Talmudic and Roman genres. The Roman orators propose variations on this case that border on the absurd, as in the case proposed by Choricius cited above. The rabbis, on the other hand, debate only the simple case as found in Libanius. They likely derived the idea for this case from 2 Samuel 20, as well as from real-life occurrences – as seen in the case cited in the Yerushalmi – rather than from the Greek exercises. They debated this issue not just as a thought exercise but also because it could and did actually happen.

The contrast between Talmudic discourse and the Greek declamations regarding hypothetical cases comes to bear more clearly in a third comparison regarding conflicting filial obligations. One controversia of Seneca discusses the case of a son torn between obligations to his father and mother. Again, I will quote it at length so that I can return to analyze its structure:

> **[Law]** Children must support their parents, or be imprisoned.
>
> **[Theoretical Case]** A man with a wife and a son by her set out abroad. Captured by pirates, he wrote to his wife and son about a

[100] Sheva ben Bikhri rebelled against David and ran for refuge in the city of Abel Beth-maacah; see 2 Sam 20.

[101] Y. Terumot 8:4, 46b; see further analysis at Lieberman, *Tosefta ki-fshutah*, Zera`im, 1.420–3; Michael Harris, "Consequentialism, Deontologism, and the Case of Sheva ben Bikhri," *The Torah u-Madda Journal* 15 (2008–9): 72–94.

ransom. The wife's weeping blinded her. She asks support from her son as he goes off to ransom his father; she demands that he should be imprisoned because he will not stay.

[Epitomes of Declamations]

For the mother

Cestius Pius. You should not judge the woman's emotions by the law she is using to threaten her son; she is doing everything she can to avoid her son being imprisoned ...[102]

Albucius Silus . . .

Triarius . . .

Marcellus Aeserninus. If you persist drag me too to the pirates: I will get support from them – they are feeding my husband too.

Fulvius Sparsus. The mother will die if she is not fed; the father is being fed, even without a ransom.

Julius Bassu. Your father still has eyes, and food.

The other side

Cestius Pius. I want to do the same as my mother; she taught me to love my family. – [s]he binds two with the chains of one. – If I wish to be as loving as my mother's precedent suggests, I owe even my eyes to my father.

Arellius Fuscus Senior . . .

Varius Geminus . . .

Fulvius Sparsus . . .

Bueso . . .

[Divisions and Coloures][103]

Seneca continues to cite snippets from the arguments of dozens of declaimers on each side. In favor of the mother, he quotes Fulvius Sparsus who says, "The mother will die if she is not fed; the father is being fed, even without a ransom." Latro adds, "Not even the father wanted the son to go – surely, if he knew the mother was in such a plight, he would not allow it." Cestius Pius, on the other hand, argues

[102] That is, by the pirates.

[103] Seneca, *Declamations*, II:84–7, controversia 7.4. I have added the headings in brackets. I have also added ellipses in place of the arguments for each speaker that appear in Seneca's text. Divisions and *coloures* are Seneca's own comments about the various arguments he has quoted; see further on p. 167.

that helping the father is consonant with the mother's own love for her family: "If I wish to be as loving as my mother's precedent suggests, I owe even my eyes to my father."[104]

Compare this with the rabbinic law that although one must equally respect one's mother and father, when the two obligations conflict, "the father precedes the mother in all cases because both he [the son] and his mother are both obligated to respect his father."[105] B. Kiddushin 31a discusses both this law and its application to a hypothetical case:[106]

> A certain son of a widow asked R. Eliezer, "If my father says, 'Give me to drink,' and my mother says, 'Give me to drink,' who of them precedes?" He replied, "Leave the honor of your mother and perform the honor of your father for you and your mother must honor your father."
>
> He came before R. Joshua. He responded the same way. He asked, "Rabbi, what if she was divorced?" He replied, "From between your eyelids it is evident that you are the son of a widow. Put water in a bowl and cackle for them like hens do."

If the parents are divorced, then the mother has no obligation to respect the father. In such a case, the reasoning of the law giving priority to the father would not apply and the conflict between serving his father and mother would come to a head. R. Joshua recognizes that the questioner's father has died and that his question does not derive from an actual occurrence but is merely a theoretical case. Perhaps sensing that the questioner is mocking the basis of the Mishnaic law, R. Joshua offers a sarcastic and dismissive response to invite the parents with a hen's cackle to drink from a common bowl. In this instance, at least, the sage has little patience for impractical hypothetical cases.

These comparisons to the controversiae reveal that the Talmudic examples are somewhat more straightforward than their Greek parallels. The controversiae seek out logical paradoxes and ironies that offer rich ingredients to prepare a creative and entertaining oration; in contrast, rabbinic cases – even if not always realistic – generally focus on details that can illuminate a legal principle. This is not to say, however, that there are no bizarre cases in rabbinic literature as well; in fact, there are many. Rabbinic literature is replete with theoretical cases that could never occur, and some read like entertaining riddles meant to engage and

[104] Ibid., II.86–9.

[105] M. Keritot 6:9 and Sifra, *Ḥoba, parashah* 7, 10:10 and *Qedoshim, parasha* 1, 9.

[106] Translation follows Geniza fragment Oxford Heb. b. 1/8–9.

amuse students and audiences. Even if the rabbis are overall more conservative than their Roman counterparts in the hypotheticals that they discuss, this difference is only relative and the Mishnah and both Talmuds include very outlandish cases.[107] Here are examples from each work of rabbinic literature starting with M. Nazir 5:7:

> If one sees a *koy*[108] and says, "I will be a Nazirite if this is a wild animal." [Another says,] "I will be a Nazirite if this is not a wild animal." [Another says,] "I will be a Nazirite if this is a domestic animal." [Another says,] "I will be a Nazirite if this is not a domestic animal." [Another says,] "I will be a Nazirite if this is a wild animal and a domestic animal." [Another says,] "I will be a Nazirite if this is neither a wild animal nor a domestic animal." [Another says,] "I will be a Nazirite if one of you is a Nazirite." [Another says,] "I will be a Nazirite if none of you is a Nazirite." [Another says,] "I will be a Nazirite if all of you are Nazirites." Behold all of these are Nazirites.

The Mishnah presents this set of paradoxes[109] in order to illustrate the principle that even in a case of doubt, if there is some possibility that the condition is true, then the vower becomes a Nazirite. A simpler example surely could have sufficed to underscore this principle, but this playful paradox more memorably demonstrates the extent to which this principle applies. As Elizabeth Shanks Alexander demonstrates, the Mishna's oral transmission and structure presumes a didactic feature of challenging students with successively more difficult casuistic cases.[110]

[107] For further discussion of theoretical cases in the Talmud, see Hershey Friedman, "Talmudic Humor and the Establishment of Legal Principles: Strange Questions, Impossible Scenarios, and Legalistic Brainteasers," *Thalia: Studies in Literary Humor* 21, no. 1 (2004): 14–28; Yechiel Guttmann, "She'elot 'akademiot ba-Talmud," *Devir* 1 and 2 (1923): 38–87 and 101–63; and Hanina Ben-Menahem, *Judicial Deviation in Talmudic Law* (New York: Harwood Academic Publishers, 1991), 33–40.

[108] A type of bearded deer or antelope that the rabbis were unsure whether to categorize as a domestic or wild animal, since it evinces characteristics of both. See M. Bikkurim 2:8–11. It can also be pronounced "khevi"; see Hanoch Yelin, "Le-shitat ha-niqud shel ha-Mishnah" in Hanoch Albeck, *Six Orders of Mishnah*, 6 vols. (Jerusalem: Mossad Bialik, 1959), Mo`ed, 20 n. 24.

[109] On the rhetorical figure of paradox, see Mark Moore, "Seeking Knowledge from the 'Container and Thing Contained'," *Rhetoric Society Quarterly* 18, no. 1 (1988): 15–30, and also Fischel, *Rabbinic Literature and Greco-Roman Philosophy*, 70–3, on paradoxes in rabbinic literature.

[110] See Elizabeth Shanks Alexander, *Transmitting Mishnah: The Shaping Influence of Oral Tradition* (New York: Cambridge University Press, 2006), 117–73.

Y. Baba Qama 3:1, 3c, cited earlier on the case of one who fills the public thoroughfare with jugs, continues its discussion with several hypothetical cases:

> If one placed his stone in the public thoroughfare and another came and placed another beside it and someone else comes, trips on one and hits the other, who is liable, the first [person who placed a stone] or the second?
>
> Let us learn it from here: "If an ox pushed another and it fell into a pit, the owner of the ox is liable and the owner of the pit is exempt. R. Natan says, if the ox is warned, then this one [the owner of the pit] pays half and this one [the owner of the ox] pays half."[111]
>
> ...If one placed his stone in the public thoroughfare and wind comes and blows it into [his own] private property and someone else comes and trips on it, then is he liable for his damage?[112]
>
> If one placed his stone in the public thoroughfare and another person came and tripped on it and caused it to fly into [the first person's] private property and then yet another person came and tripped on it, is he [the first person who placed the stone] liable for his damage?

These three cases progress from the most realistic to the most outlandish, with each step introducing a new complication. The Yerushalmi offers a resolution only to the first case and leaves the following two cases open. It seems likely, however, that this list of cases derived from a study session in which the various sides were argued and fleshed out; perhaps this sugya simply outlines a real or proposed lecture in which the teacher would present the two sides of each case one after another in order to amplify the legal principles at play.

Hypotheticals that reach the absurd are especially prevalent in the Bavli, as in the following examples. Can a priest marry a pregnant

111 T. Baba Qama 6:1 and Mekhilta d'R. Shimon bar Yoḥai 21:33. According to the first anonymous opinion, since the ox only fell into the pit on account of the other ox that pushed it, the owner of the ox that pushed it takes complete liability; so too in the case at hand, the person who placed the second stone would be liable since he caused the person to trip and hit the other stone. According to R. Natan they would share responsibility in both cases.

112 If the stone had been in private property all along, then the owner of the stone would be exempt. In this case, however, now that the wind has moved it to private property, is the owner no longer liable? Or, should we reason that since the irresponsible placement of the stone in the public thoroughfare was the original cause of the chain of events that resulted in damage, he is therefore liable? The Talmud leaves the question open.

virgin?[113] Does impurity on the ground reach up to a tower flying in the air?[114] Can one ritually slaughter a flying bird with an arrow?[115] If a weasel extracts an animal fetus from the mother and inserts it into the womb of another animal, does it lose its status as firstborn?[116] If a man says to his wife, "Here is your divorce document but the paper is mine," the divorce is not valid; but if he says, "Here is your divorce document but the paper between the lines and words is mine," is that valid?[117] One may not yoke together two different species of land animals; but may one have a goat and a fish pull a wagon together?[118] If meat falls from heaven, is it kosher?[119] If wheat falls from the clouds, can it be used for a bread offering?[120] Does one have to send away the mother bird to take an egg if the nest is on someone's head?[121]

At the same time, the Bavli also displays intolerance for absurd theoretical cases in many other instances where the context reveals that the question is meant as a challenge or personal insult rather than the test of a legal principle. For example, Rav Adda asks a visiting sage, R. Dimi, whether an impure basket that is swallowed by an elephant and excreted through its rectum remains impure or is considered a new object and becomes pure.[122] R. Dimi was duly offended by this hypothetical, which was in fact meant to insult him and was not a sincere query. Similarly, when studying the law that a bird found less than fifty cubits from a dovecote belongs to the owner of the dovecote, but if found more than fifty cubits away then the finder can keep it, R. Jeremiah asks, "If one of its feet was within fifty cubits and the other foot was outside of fifty cubits, then what is the law?" For asking this question, R. Jeremiah was kicked out of the *bet midrash*.[123] In another instance, when Polemo asks Rabbi: "If a man has two heads, upon which of them should he don *tefilin*?", Rabbi responds: "Either get up and go into exile or accept upon

[113] B. Ḥagigah 14b.
[114] B. Ḥagigah 15b; see Rashi.
[115] B. Ḥulin 30b.
[116] B. Ḥulin 70a.
[117] B. Giṭṭin 20b.
[118] B. Baba Qama 55a.
[119] B. Sanhedrin 59b.
[120] B. Menaḥot 69b.
[121] B. Ḥulin 139b.
[122] B. Baba Batra 22a.
[123] B. Baba Batra 23b. Presumably, the answer could simply have been that they split the value of the bird, as legislated in a similar case at M. Baba Batra 2:6. But perhaps R. Jeremiah asked with a mocking tone and therefore it was felt that he must step outside, measure for measure like the bird. See also Jacobs, *Teyku*, 298–9; and Albeck, *Mavo la-Talmudim*, 342.

yourself excommunication."[124] Rabbi's strong reaction shows that he must have felt that Polemo was not asking from sincere curiosity but as a challenge to the halakha generally. The next line, however, reports that just then, a father of an actual two-headed baby walked in to ask the same question and Rabbi offered a learned answer to the second questioner. Evidently, it was more the insincerity of the questioner rather than the strangeness of the case that angered Rabbi.

These examples suggest that the rabbis show intolerance to hypothetical questions specifically when they sense that the questioner seeks to undermine the authority of Jewish law by mocking its method of reasoning and attention to detail.[125] Theoretical cases are more than welcome, however, when they contribute to unpacking the subtleties of a given topic. As a last example, the following extended set of theoretical questions demonstrates how the Bavli builds one dilemma on top of another to gain ever increasing accuracy in a style similar to that of Y. Baba Qama 3:1, 3c. The Mishnah rules that one must check one's house for *ḥameṣ* (leaven) on the night before Passover, but one need not check any place where one never brings *ḥameṣ*, and one need not worry that a weasel may have brought *ḥameṣ* to those places.[126] Based on this law, the Talmud wonders about various theoretical cases where there is reason to suspect that a weasel or a mouse did bring in *ḥameṣ*[127]:

> Rava stated: If a mouse enters with a loaf in its mouth and someone enters after it and finds crumbs, it requires checking because it is not the way of a mouse to make crumbs.[128] If a baby enters with a loaf in his mouth[129] and someone enters after it and finds crumbs then it does not require checking because it is the way of a baby to make crumbs.
>
> Rava asked: If a mouse enters with a loaf in its mouth and a mouse exits with a loaf in its mouth, what is the law? Do we say the one that entered is the one that exited? Or, is it a different one?

124 B. Menaḥot 37a.

125 See challenges from heretics to the hermeneutical rules discussed in the next chapter, pp. 200–2.

126 M. Pesaḥim 1:1–2.

127 B. Pesaḥim 10b. Follows MS Oxford Opp. Add. fol. 23, unless otherwise noted.

128 MS Oxford adds, "האי עייליה למזייה ופירורין דאחריני נינהו." Rabbinovicz, *Dikduke Soferim*, notes that he does not know what למזייה means and suggests that it is a scribal error. I have omitted this line based on all other witnesses. Printed editions insert here, "And Rava said."

129 So also MS Vatican 134. Other MSS read, "hand."

> And if you should say, "The one that entered is the one that exited," then if a white mouse enters with a loaf in its mouth and a black mouse exits with a loaf in its mouth, what is the law? Do we say this is surely a different one or perhaps [the black mouse] lifted it[130] from [the white mouse]?
>
> And if you should say, "Mice do not take[131] from each other," then if a mouse enters with a loaf in its mouth and a weasel exits with a loaf in its mouth, what is the law? [Do we say] that the weasel surely took it from a mouse, or perhaps[132] if indeed it took it from the mouse then the mouse should be found in its mouth.[133]
>
> And if you should say that if it is the same [loaf] then it [the weasel] would have taken all of it [including the mouse],[134] then [if the mouse entered with a loaf in its mouth and a weasel exited][135] with the loaf and the mouse in the weasel's mouth, what is the law? [Do we say] that here certainly this is the same one?[136] Or, perhaps if this is the same one then the loaf should have been found in the mouth of the mouse. Or, perhaps it fell [from the mouth of the mouse] because of fright and [the weasel] took it?
>
> Let it stand (*tequ*).

These cases have no practical application but rather challenge students to analyze the limits of legal presumptions in increasingly unlikely scenarios. This sugya does not record any of the arguments for and against each side, but it is likely that students would be invited to present arguments at each stage, as we find in conversations recorded in many other Talmudic texts.[137] This sugya ends with *tequ*, signifying that the debate over the question is more important than actually finding an answer.

[130] Following all witnesses that read, "ארמויי ארמייה," except for MS Oxford, which reads, "אדמוייה אדמיה."

[131] Following all MSS that read, "מרמו" or מרמייה," except for MS Oxford, which reads, "מדמו." Printed editions read, "שקלי."

[132] Printed editions add here, "it is a different one for."

[133] See Rabbinovicz, *Dikduke Soferim* for manuscript variants here.

[134] Printed editions read, "If indeed it took it from the mouse then the mouse should be found in its mouth."

[135] The bracketed words, "[if the mouse entered with a loaf in its mouth and a weasel exited]," appear in MS JTS and printed editions. I have included them here for clarity.

[136] MS Oxford inserts, "רמיניה שקלתיה," which I have omitted based on all other witnesses.

[137] See discussion of Y. Shebu`ot 3:7, 34d on p. 170.

CONTROVERSIAE AND THE *TA SHEMA* FORM

Having analyzed the educational use of hypothetical cases in the controversiae and Talmudic texts, we can now return to, and gain a better appreciation for, the *ta shema* form. Many *ta shema* sugyot focus on theoretical cases and also end with *tequ*. We showed above the similarity between the *ta shema* sugya structure and the progymnasmata.[138] However, the *ta shema* sugya is even closer in form to the controversiae. Controversiae in their full written form follow this structure: law, hypothetical case, and declamation. This matches the typical *ta shema* sugya, which also begins with a citation of a Mishnah or another early law, asks a question about a theoretical case, and then follows with various proofs and disproofs. Louis Jacobs sets forth the structure of the *ta shema* sugya in algebraic form as follows[139]:

Let the law or statement be A and the definition either x or y.

then *ba'ya*: which correct Ax or Ay?

ta shema`: authority states that Ax (or Ay) is correct.

Jacobs analyzes the 300 plus instances of *tequ* sugyot in the Bavli and concludes that "the Talmudic *ba`ya* is not simply a 'question' but a formal problem, even one of a contrived nature" that is proposed by a teacher to his students as an academic challenge.[140] In fact, "the whole point of the *ba`ya* is that it is a purely theoretical exercise, an attempt at discovering two ways of looking at the matter either one of which may be correct."[141] I agree and think it is evident that the *ta shema* sugya parallels the controversiae in both form and purpose. Both propose a theoretical problem related to an established law and both continue to

[138] See pp. 145–9.

[139] Jacobs, *Teyku*, 13–14.

[140] Jacobs, *Teyku*, 15.

[141] Ibid., 294. Many proposed *ba`yot* in the Bavli lack a *ta shema* section and instead go directly to *tequ*. However, I imagine that these problems too were the subjects of vigorous debate by various sages offering arguments on each side that have simply not been recorded. Even full *ta shema* sugyot are, to some degree, a creation of the Bavli's editors. Jacobs, ibid., 290, writes: "The editors had before them only the bare problems set by the various teachers and, probably, the solutions that had been offered or, at least, some of these. They reworked all this material." But even though the details of the student responses were not transmitted for the most part, I assume that they did once exist and that the Bavli editors reconstructed such arguments based on the outlines and snippets that were passed down. See Rubenstein, *Talmudic Stories*, 244; and Hidary, *Dispute*, 37–8, on how the Bavli creates sugyot from the outlines of earlier Palestinian traditions.

offer arguments for one side or another. Both also use this form to explore far-fetched hypothetical cases that test the limits of the laws, refine legal principles, and challenge the creativity and ingenuity of students.

If we look back at the structures of the sugyot cited above, we notice how well they match. For example, Y. Baba Qama 3:1, 3b–c, works off of the law of M. Baba Qama 3:1, presents a theoretical case, and then a declamation in dialectical form.[142] Similarly, in B. Pesaḥim 10b, Rava extends the law of the Mishnah about where one must check for *ḥameṣ* into a series of theoretical cases, although the declamations that might have been presented for each are not extant.[143]

Let us analyze one last example of a *ta shema* sugya, showing how it fits within the genre of controversiae. M. Menaḥot 12:4 states that one may donate three, four, or six *lugim*[144] of wine to the Temple because those numbers have precedents in the libations that accompany a lamb, ram, and bull, respectively.[145] However, one may not donate one, two or five *lugim* of wine because they have no corresponding sacrifice, and even a self-standing libation offering cannot be made unless it equals an amount already biblically prescribed. The Bavli at Menaḥot 104a then wonders whether the donation of an improper amount can be divided up and partially offered or whether the donation amount is fixed and cannot be divided. This is debated through a theoretical example of a five *log* donation that would be invalid if amounts are fixed but could be divided into four and one if amounts are not fixed.[146]

> **[Law]** Mishnah: One may not donate one, two or five *lugim* [of wine to the Temple], but one may donate three, four, six, or more than six [*lugim*].
>
> **[Theoretical Case]** Gemara: The question was asked of them: Is there a fixed amount for libations or is there no fixed amount for libations? How so? For example, if he brings five, if you say there is no fixed amount for libations then he can pour and sacrifice four of them as fit for a ram and the rest will be a voluntary offering. But if you say there is a fixed amount for libations then it is not offered until he completes the amount. What [is the law]?

[142] See p. 139.
[143] See p. 161.
[144] Plural of *log*, defined on p. 88 n. 57.
[145] Num 15:1–16.
[146] Text follows the Venice *editio princeps*.

[Proof for Fixed Amount] Abaye said: Come and hear (*ta shema*): "There are six [containers in the Temple] for voluntary offerings ... [to collect surplus funds of various kinds]."[147] If indeed [there is no fixed amount for libations] then there should be another container for the surplus of libations.

[Antithesis] Those [surplus funds] go to voluntary communal offerings [which are not common]. These [surplus libations] are common. It is readily possible to combine [the surplus] of this master and that master together and offer them.

[Proof Against Fixed Amount] Rava said[148]: Come and hear (*ta shema*): "'Citizen' (Num 15:13) – this teaches that one may offer self-standing libation offerings. How much? Three *lugim*. How do you know that if he wishes to add to the amount that he may do so? Scripture teaches, 'It shall be' (ibid. 15:15 and 16). Can it be that one may lessen the amount? Scripture teaches, 'Like this' (ibid. 15:13)." How much can he add? If you say four or six [*lugim*, then that is obvious], how is it different? Three is used for a lamb, and four and six are also used for a ram and a bull. No, rather, five. We thus conclude that there is no fixed amount for libations. It is concluded.

[Antithesis] Rav Ashi said: But have we not learned in the Mishnah, "One may not donate one, two, or five *lugim*"? It teaches five in comparison to two; just as two are not fit at all so too five are not fit at all.

[Solution] Is this an argument? This is as it is and that is as it is.

[Additional Question] Abaye said: If you want to say that there is no fixed amount for libations then there is no fixed amount. If you want to say that there is a fixed amount, then until ten it is simple [to divide]. For eleven, however, I ask what one does. Does a person intend it to be for two bulls and it is not offered until he completes it? Or perhaps, a person intends it for two rams and a lamb. Do we say that [he intends to donate for] two of one species and one of another species or not?

The question stands (*tequ*).

Abaye first attempts to prove that libations must be donated in a fixed amount that can be offered since there was no storage container in the Temple to hold surplus funds for libations. However, the Stam

147 M. Sheqalim 6:5; Y. Sheqalim 6:4, 50b; and B. Menaḥot 107b–108a.

148 "Rava said" is lacking in MS Paris 1o4b but is found in all other MSS.

rejects this since such surpluses could immediately be combined and offered. Rava then offers a proof for the opposite position that any donated amount can be split since an extraneous word in the verse teaches that one may donate more than the fixed amounts. In the next line, Rav Ashi challenges Rava's proof, but the Stam responds and upholds it. This sugya can be accurately appreciated as an example of a rabbinic controversia that follows the structure of law, theoretical case, and arguments.[149]

One difference between the progymasmata and the Talmud is that the former is presented by a single speaker and the latter accumulates the statements of various sages over generations. Furthermore, each Greek controversia forms a unified, sustained and lengthy argument, while a typical sugya includes only short amoraic statements and arguments that oscillate between one side of the debate and the other. If we are correct in our arguments in the previous chapters that rabbinic education included the presentation of public orations and lengthy lectures to and by students in declamatory style, then the difference between the controversiae and the Talmud may lie in the way orations were recorded for posterity. While rabbinic students may have made private written notes of lectures they heard from their teachers, they did not officially record these orations.[150] Instead, students committed to memory only short snippets of their sages' rulings, interpretations, and arguments. The Talmudic redactors – especially in the Bavli – compiled these traditions into sometimes elaborate sugyot by combining and inserting questions, answers, interpretations, and conversations.[151]

Here too, however, we can gain a fascinating insight from the way controversiae themselves were recorded. As mentioned earlier, controversiae have come to us in three different forms: (1) full orations, (2) Quintilian's lecture notes, and (3) Seneca's epitomes. In the first category of full orations, each controversia contains just the law and theoretical case at the beginning and then the oration that was usually several pages long. Quintilian, in his lecture notes, did not preserve his full declamations but rather only short summaries of the main points of

[149] This sugya presents an example of a simpler, mostly amoraic form of the *ta shema* form that develops into the more elaborate, more common, and more heavily Stammaitic, *ta shema* sugyot like that in B. Baba Qama 27b–28a, analyzed on p. 145. Both, however, follow similar formats.

[150] On the oral publication and transmission of rabbinic works, see Lieberman, *Hellenism in Jewish Palestine*, 83–99; Elman, "Orality," 52–99; Strack and Stemberger, *Introduction*, 31–44.

[151] See previous note and Halivni, *Formation*, 117–54.

each oration. He also preceded each declamation summary with an informal discussion of the strategies he intended to use, called *sermo, dialexis*, or *praelocutio*. This section derives from the short informal introduction that orators would give while seated that sketched the outlines of the case and the arguments that he considered the most effective.[152]

During his old age, Seneca acceded to the request of his sons and wrote down what he remembered from the declaimers that he heard in his youth. He did not remember complete orations but rather only snippets of the basic arguments that various declaimers on each side said about a given case. These snippets, ranging from a single sentence to a paragraph, focus on epigrams, or *sententiae*, that epitomize the main idea of the original orations. Seneca then adds a section of divisions, in which he analyzes the various lines of argumentation used. Seneca concludes with *coloures* – a summary of how the speakers interpreted the facts to their advantage.[153]

Seneca's approach of summarizing orations that he heard when he was young by citing a short paraphrase of each side together with an analysis of their arguments bears a striking similarity to the style of many Yerushalmi and Bavli sugyot in which the Stam collects short amoraic statements and adds its own analysis. There is no reason to presume that the redactors of either the Yerushalmi or Bavli ever read Seneca or anything like these summaries of controversiae. Nevertheless, we can still compare the two analogically in that they both strive to preserve and analyze orations of the past about theoretical legal cases from memory, and both sets of literature are composed by teachers to train a next generation. The two genres obviously bear many differences in subject matter, style, and form of transmission; but at their root, these two sets of literature reflect two branches that grow from a common and shared educational model of rhetorical argumentation.[154]

152 See Penella, *Rhetorical Exercises*, 26–8; Bonner, *Roman Declamation*, 51–2; Quintilian, *The Minor Declamations Ascribed to Quintilian* (Edited by Michael Winterbottom. Berlin: Walter De Gruyter, 1984), XI; and see p. 81 n. 25.

153 Seneca, *Declamations*, 1.xii–xix.

154 An additional point of comparison is that controversiae are written in the voice of one of the plaintiffs, while the Talmud is most often written in a third-party narrator's voice. In this aspect, the Talmud is more similar to the progymnasmatic introduction of a law, which takes the perspective of someone presenting a law rather than discussing a specific case. The method of declamations that involves speaking from the perspective of a historical person or a plaintiff is already found in the progymnasmatic *êthopoiia*; see Gibson, *Libanius's Progymnasmata*, 355–425. The

Returning to B. Menaḥot 104a, if we peel back the chronological layers of the sugya, we find that its earliest layer dates back to the fourth-generation Amoraim and includes only the proof by Abaye for one position, the proof by Rava for its opposite, and Abaye's concluding question. Abaye and Rava were participating in a rhetorical exercise by devising arguments for and against a proposed legal question. I assume that this is more of a thought exercise rather than a practical legal dispute between these two sages given that we lack any record that this was a particular matter of controversy between these sages.

Furthermore, Abaye's concluding question considers a case that is not directly addressed by the Mishnah and which Abaye evaluates both according to the position he supported as well as according to the view he challenged! Abaye promoted one side for the purpose of the first exercise but was open to considering the other side as well. Compare this with Seneca's controversia above in which the same orators, Cestius Pius and Fulvius Sparsus, are quoted on both sides of the debate. It is further noteworthy that although Rava's proof ends with a definitive, "It is concluded,"[155] Abaye nevertheless treats the issues as still open for debate. Therefore, it seems that Abaye and Rava took on the task of proving each side not out of any personal previous conviction but more as an exercise to see how various sources and lines of reasoning could be squared with each interpretation.

The final redacted sugya includes a secondary layer of arguments in which Abaye's statement is successfully challenged by the Stam while Rava's statement is challenged by Rav Ashi, only to be defended by the Stam. These added challenges on each side make the sugya doubly dialogical in a form similar to that of the progymnasmatic exercise cited above.[156] In both, an argument is presented on either side of a question and the proofs for each argument are themselves questioned. If indeed Abaye and Rava originally offered longer orations of which we have only a short epitome, then we can compare the activity of the Stam with that of Quintilian and Seneca in their controversiae. All that remained in the

Talmud, however, does occasionally speak in the plaintiff's voice, such as at B. Baba Qama 8b with the phrase, "למימר דמצי."

155 It is not clear whether, "We thus conclude ... It is concluded," is part of Rava's statement or an addition of the Stam. In either case, Abaye's statement and the final form of the sugya which concludes with it certainly consider the debate still open, regardless of the Stam's rejection of Abaye's proof and deflection of Rav Ashi's challenge. See also Tosafot to B. Menaḥot 104a s.v. *amar Abaye* who (anachronistically) think that Abaye accepted the challenge of Rav Ashi.

156 Pp. 142–8.

memory of the sages long after the original performances were epitomes of their main points. The Stam gathers these short named traditions and arranges them together and then adds its own commentary and discussion, which is exactly what Seneca does.[157]

There remains a difference in that Seneca initially simply lists the opinions on one side, then the opinions on the other, and only afterwards adds his own comments. Quintilian includes all of his discussion before the summary. The Talmudic redactors are more heavy handed in combining many tannaitic or amoraic epitomes, placing them in a strategic order, and adding comments and dialogue between citations of amoraic traditions. However, if we view the Bavli as a heavily redacted text – as modern scholars do – then we can consider the final form of the Bavli as itself the work of a single authorial voice, even if it does draw from prior sources.[158] While Abaye and Rava may originally have composed two separate arguments on each side, the redacted sugya links them into one dialogue by rejecting Abaye, thereby allowing Rava to continue the dialogue with his alternative view. The Stam here takes soundbites and comments of previous orations and molds them into a single new complex but continuous declamation.

Overall, more significant than any differences between the two sets of literature is the similarity that both the progymnasmata and the *ta shema* sugyot are exercises in argumentation on either side of an issue, and both employ dialectical monologues that quote an opposing interlocutor towards the goal of proposing or defeating a law. Whether by attempting to prove or to refute both sides, this genre of exercise trained students with skills that would assist them in making persuasive arguments for or against actual legal positions. The controversiae provide even closer parallels to *ta shema* and other similarly structured sugyot that cite a law and then focus on a hypothetical case that can often be strange or outlandish. These sugyot particularly resemble the summaries and lecture notes of Seneca and Quintilian in preserving just the main point of an ancient oration, citing statements by a series of orators,

[157] There may be an additional similarity between the work of the redactors of both Quintilian's *Minor Declamations* and the Talmud. Michael Winterbottom argues that the *Minor Declamations* includes many doublets and misplaced passages because they were prepared for publication by an editor rather than the author himself; see Quintilian, *The Minor Declamations Ascribed to Quintilian*, XII. Doublets and passages that seem out of place in the Talmud can also be explained as the work of the redactors.

[158] See Moulie Vidas, *Tradition and the Formation of the Talmud* (Princeton: Princeton University Press, 2014) and scholarship cited there.

and adding their own explanations and commentary. These sugyot can therefore be best categorized as rabbinic variations of Roman controversiae epitomai.

RABBINIC PAIDEIA

The Talmuds do not generally provide details about the educational methods and settings that eventually gave rise the *sugyot* as they appear in the redacted Talmud. However, as Alexander notes, the Yerushalmi preserves a precious example of just such a study session.[159] Ḥaifa, a fourth generation Pumbeditan Amora, decides to test his brother Avimai's knowledge of the laws of oaths. Ḥaifa first presents a case of one who swears not to eat any one of the five loafs of bread before him. Then he swears not to eat any two of them and so on until he swears not to eat all of them. If this person then eats one of them, on how many counts is he liable? Abimai responds that he is liable for five counts for each of the oaths that he violated. Ḥaifa corrects him that only the first oath applies since the subsequent oaths add no new restriction and an oath upon something already prohibited is void.

After Ḥaifa shows up his brother with his own more sophisticated analysis, he presents a second challenge. The oath taker again has five loaves but now he swears first that he will not eat all five, then takes another vow not to eat any four, and so on until he swears not to eat any one loaf. Abimai, not appreciating how this case might differ from the previous, responds that he is liable on only one count if he eats all five loaves. Ḥaifa, however, corrects him that in the second case, each successive vow adds a stringency to the previous one such that all five are valid and the oath taker is liable on five counts. I would bet that Ḥaifa would have disagreed with his brother no matter what Abimai had responded. Interestingly, R. Yose then comments that he agrees with Abimai in the first case and Ḥaifa in the second case, revealing how later generations of sages continued to enjoy opening ever-new possible lines of thinking. This story retells a live rabbinic setting for the presentation of outlandish hypothetical cases and each case is argued for in two opposite ways. This example thus combines the various aspects of declamation analyzed in this chapter: use of theoretical cases, arguments on both sides of an issue, and a paideic setting. In her analysis of this case, Alexander comes to this conclusion:

159 Y. Shebu`ot 3:7, 34d, cited at Alexander, *Transmitting Mishnah*, 180–1.

> Throughout the talmudic period, sages recreated the structure of the borderline case as a means of exploring legal ambiguities. Talmudic sages formulated problem cases like that of Abimai in order to promote sophisticated analytic thinking. As with *teyku* problems, one measure of a case's ambiguity came to be the existence of two equally plausible resolutions. Proposing two different resolutions was a common strategy for exploring legal ambiguities. Even when the different resolutions were not equally appealing, both were argued for vigorously as a means of instilling intellectual versatility. Since the presence of a dispute was a mark of ambiguity, disputes were analyzed in great detail.[160]

I agree wholeheartedly and would add that this pedagogic style is not uniquely rabbinic but rather the standard curriculum throughout Hellenistic civilization. The connection between Hellenistic rhetorical and rabbinic teaching methodologies has already been pointed out by Nathan Morris:

> The method of the Jewish high school, the Talmudic method of disputation...owed a great deal to Hellenistic influence. Thus we read, for example, of a famous scholar of the second century C.E., who could effectively argue on both sides of a case, proving "the unclean (ritually) to be clean," and *vice versa*. But this was the method of the Hellenistic rhetorical school, where the students were trained to speak for and against a given proposition. Some of these propositions, suitably translated into Hebrew or Aramaic, would easily pass as of Talmudic origin. It is difficult to avoid the view that this method...was greatly stimulated by the example of the Hellenistic school.[161]

Morris cites explicitly the student who could purify the reptile as an example for the general tendency of Talmudic discussion to analyze both sides of each issue. Propositions that were the subjects of declamations in Hellenistic schools, he adds, parallel similar Talmudic propositions. He does not elaborate on what examples he has in mind but the analysis of this chapter bears out his thesis.

Building on Brodsky's comparison of the dialogic form of the progynmasmata and its counterpart in rabbinic literature, this chapter fills in several more pieces of the puzzle. Progymnasmata are not only dialogical, they are doubly dialogical in the sense that one exercise could

[160] Ibid., 218.
[161] Morris, *Jewish School*, 74.

require students to write a composition for a thesis and another composition against a thesis, while at the same time requiring that each composition cite and resolve challenges from the opposing point of view. Many Talmudic sugyot reflect this double dialogism as well. Teachers and students would present arguments on both sides of an issue and each argument would cite and refute the other side. Furthermore, the two sides would often focus on the very same points to show how one could spin them in opposite directions.

Analyzing the controversiae reveals further parallels with Talmudic educational methods. Both the Greek orators and the rabbis took special pride in developing argumentational skills using outlandish theoretical cases, although the rabbis usually chose somewhat more realistic scenarios. At the same time, both cultures also included voices that criticized these fanciful subjects because they were not practical and verged on making a mockery of legal argumentation. Although we lack any systematic description of educational practices in Talmudic study circles, the hints to such practices that we can glean from sugyot like that of Rava and Abaye regarding wine libations or Ḥaifa and Avimai regarding vows indicate close parallels with the training in rhetorical schools. The activity of the rabbinic study circles thus comfortably took part in the wider culture of paideia in the form of rhetorical training. Furthermore, the transmission of rabbinic legal discussions over time and their compilation into *sugyot* fits into a pattern similar to that of controversiae. Orations on theoretical cases were often not recorded in full but rather epitomized by students who collected various arguments on both sides and added their own comments. The work of the Stam in redacting *ta shema* and similar sugyot emerges as simply a rabbinic variation on a widespread Greco-Roman rhetorical practice.

These similarities, however, also highlight a fundamental contrast. Greek rhetorical training assumes a cynical stance towards truth. Rhetorical instruction does not focus on distinguishing veracity from falsehood or wisdom from foolishness. Rather, it strives to perfect the students' ability to persuade an audience of any position, the more preposterous the better, because truth is unattainable and perception is all that matters. Therefore, the goal of any given exercise oration is to prove one side and disprove the other. Talmudic *ta shema* sugyot, in contrast, strive to uphold all sides of a halakhic controversy. As we will see later,[162] various midrashim imbue all possible viewpoints with Sinaitic prophetic

[162] Pp. 277–83.

authority. Therefore, disproving any one given viewpoint is considered a failure, and the sophistic skill for arguing all sides helped the rabbis realize their belief in multiple prophetic truths. In these sugyot, the rabbis appropriate and apply widespread Hellenistic rhetorical techniques in the service of maintaining and transmitting their own particularistic religious traditions. We have thus seen how rhetorical training lies at the heart of various genres of rabbinic legal dialogic literature; the next chapter will explore how it penetrated deeply into rabbinic hermeneutics as well.

5 Talmudic Topoi: Rhetoric and the Hermeneutical Methods of Midrash

CUSTOMER:	I came here for a good argument.
PROFESSIONAL ARGUER:	No you didn't, you came here for an argument.
CUSTOMER:	Well, an argument's not the same as contradiction.
ARGUER:	It can be.
CUSTOMER:	An argument is a connected series of statements intended to establish a proposition.
ARGUER:	No it isn't.
CUSTOMER:	Yes it is. It's not just contradiction.
ARGUER:	Look, if I argue with you, I must take up a contrary position.
CUSTOMER:	But that's not just saying, "No it isn't."
ARGUER:	Yes it is.
CUSTOMER:	No it isn't. An argument is an intellectual process. Contradiction is just the automatic gainsaying of any statement the other person makes.
ARGUER:	No it isn't.
CUSTOMER:	Yes it is.
ARGUER:	Not at all.[1]

Scholars have long noted an affinity between midrashic hermeneutics and Greco-Roman rhetoric, affirming that the rabbis participated in their surrounding intellectual culture. Although the rabbis employed

[1] "Argument Clinic," *Monty Python's Flying Circus*, first broadcast November 2, 1972 by BBC, directed by Ian MacNaughton and written by John Cleese and Graham Chapman. For no apparent reason, the script names the professional arguer as Mr. Vibrating, which I have changed for clarity.

these exegetical rules extensively, they also expressed a deep skepticism about their use, given their potential to threaten the authority of traditional teachings. This chapter will first review the parallels between midrashic methods of exegesis and Greco-Roman commonplace argumentative forms called *topoi*.[2] It will then discuss the historical context for the adoption of these forms of reasoning into the rabbinic legal system as well as the rabbis' apprehension about their application. We will illustrate the multifaceted and nuanced approach of the rabbis towards these forms of rhetorical reasoning with further analysis of the *qal va-ḥomer* and the *gezerah shavah*. This study will provide us with yet another window into the rabbinic encounter with the Greco-Roman rhetorical tradition.

MIDRASHIC HERMENEUTICS AS RHETORICAL TOPOI

The midrashic hermeneutical rules[3] are introduced in T. Sanhedrin 7:11:[4]

> Hillel the Elder expounded seven methods before the elders of Betera:[5]
>
> [1] *a minori ad maius* (*qal va-ḥomer*[6]),

2 Singular, *topos*. See Sara Rubinelli, *Ars Topica: The Classical Technique of Constructing Arguments from Aristotle to Cicero* (Dordrecht: Springer, 2009).

3 These rules are called *midot*, i.e. characteristic styles of the Torah. Establishing that the Torah's language follows certain conventions allows the reader to properly interpret and derive laws from it. See Wilhelm Bacher, *'Erkhe midrash* (Jerusalem: Carmiel, 1969), 1.70; and Yadin, *Scripture as Logos*, 120–1.

4 Translation follows MS Vienna, unless otherwise noted. See parallels at Sifra, Baraita d'R. Ishmael, *perek* 1, 7, and Avot d'Rabbi Natan A 37.

5 On the identity of the elders of Betera, see Gedaliah Alon, *Jews, Judaism and the Classical World: Studies in Jewish History in the Times of the Second Temple and Talmud* (Jerusalem: Magnes Press, 1977), 328–34; and Louis Finkelstein, *Ha-Perushim ve-'anshe keneset ha-gedolah* (New York: Jewish Theological Seminary of America, 1950), 1–16. This group is sometimes identified as elders of Petera or sons of Betera; I have used "elders of Betera" in my translations throughout this chapter for consistency.

6 Literally, "lightness and heaviness." Some MSS read *qol va-ḥomer*. *Qol* is found more often in older manuscripts and *qal* is more prevalent in Babylonian manuscripts. The pronunciation *qal* is grammatically problematic since *qal* (light) is an adjective and does not match *ḥomer* (heaviness), which is a noun. However, Moshe Bar-Asher, "On Corrections and Marginal Versions in Codex Parma B (De Rossi 497) of the Mishna," [Hebrew] in *Segulla to Ariella*, ed. Moshe Bar-Asher et al. (Jerusalem: Hoṣa'at Hamishpaḥa, 1990): 129, argues that *qal* can also be a nominal form and is therefore equally correct. We have chosen to use *qal* in this book in deference to popular pronunciation. See further in Yochanan Breuer, *The Hebrew in the Babylonian Talmud according to the Manuscripts of Tractate Pesahim* (Jerusalem: The Hebrew

[2] comparison of equals (*gezerah shavah*),
[3] a principle (*binyan av*) derived from one passage,
[4] a principle derived from two passages,
[5] a general category followed by a specific instance,[7]
[6] something similar in another place,
[7] and something derived from its context.

These are the seven rules that Hillel the Elder expounded before the elders of Betera.[8]

Already medieval writers linked these hermeneutical methods to Greek rhetoric and interpretation.[9] David Daube and Saul Lieberman have similarly confirmed that many of the rules are directly related to parallels found in the Greco-Roman rhetorical tradition.[10] This is most obvious for the first two, which relate to what Greek writers call comparison of lesser, greater, and equal. Beginning with Aristotle, we find among his list of *topoi*,

> From the more and the less (*ek tou mallon kai hētton*); for example, "If not even the gods know everything, human beings can hardly do

University Magnes Press, 2002), 278–9; E. Weisenberg, "Observations on Method in Talmudic Studies," *Journal of Semitic Studies* 11, no. 1 (1966): 18–19; and Bacher, *`Erkhe midrash*, 1:118.

7 The Tosefta in both MSS Vienna and Erfurt reads "*kelal u-frat u-frat u-kelal*." The parallel in the Sifra, however, includes only "*kelal u-frat*" in all manuscripts except for Vatican 31 which has only "*u-frat u-kelal*." Menahem Kahana, "Kavvim le-toldot hitpatḥutah shel midat kelal u-frat bi-tkufat ha-Tannaim," in *Meḥqarim ba-Talmud uva-Midrash: sefer zikaron le-Tirza Lifshitz*, ed. Moshe Bar-Asher, Joshua Levinson, and Berachyahu Lifshitz (Jerusalem: Mossad Bialik, 2005): 210, suggests that the version in the Tosefta, which includes both, was influenced by R. Ishmael's thirteen *midot*. I have therefore translated only "*kelal u-frat*" in accordance with the Sifra.

8 For a clear explanation of each rule see, W. Sibley Towner, "Hermeneutical Systems of Hillel and the Tannaim: A Fresh Look," *Hebrew Union College Annual* 53 (1983): 101–35.

9 See the citation of Judah Haddasi at Lieberman, *Hellenism in Jewish Palestine*, 55, and further on p. 178 n. 17.

10 Ibid., 47–82; David Daube, "Rabbinic Methods of Interpretation and Hellenistic Rhetoric," *Hebrew Union College Annual* 22 (1949): 239–64; and see also Alexander, "Quid Athenis," 116–17; and Yonatan Moss, "Noblest Obelus: Rabbinic Appropriations of Late Ancient Literary Criticism," in *Homer and the Bible in the Eyes of Ancient Interpreters*, ed. Maren Niehoff (Leiden: Brill, 2012): 245–9. See also Fischel, "Story and History," 459, comparing Hillel's seven rules to other similar lists. On the related topic of Jewish exegesis in the context of Alexandrian textual analysis of Homer, see Maren Niehoff, *Jewish Exegesis and Homeric Scholarship in Alexandria* (Cambridge: Cambridge University Press, 2011); and Yakir Paz, "From Scribes to Scholars: Rabbinic Biblical Exegesis in Light of the Homeric Commentaries" (PhD diss., 2014).

> so"; for this is equivalent [to saying,] "If something is not the fact where it would be more [expected], it is clear that it is not a fact where it would be less."[11]

The next *topos* in Aristotle is "from analogy or precedent":

> Further, [there is a related form of argument] if [something is] neither more nor less. This is the source of the statement ... that if Theseus did no wrong [in abducting Helen], neither did Alexander [i.e., Paris, who abducted her later].[12]

This schema is copied by Cicero:

> From comparison all arguments are valid which are devised in this way: What holds in a wider sphere, should hold in a more restricted one (*quod in re maiore valet valeat in minore*), e.g., if boundaries are not regulated in the city, neither should water be excluded in the city.[13]
>
> Again, conversely: What holds in the more restricted sphere, should hold in the wider one. Here one can use the same example in reverse.
>
> Again: what holds in the equivalent sphere, should hold as well in this case, which is equivalent; e.g. Because use and warranty of a piece of land run for two years, it should also be two years for a house. Yet in the law a house is not mentioned, and it is (evidently) treated as belonging with the category 'all other things' for which use is one year. Let equity prevail which requires equal rights for equal cases.[14]

Cicero derives the law of usucapion of houses from the law regarding land versus all other things using an analogy.[15] In his progymnasmata,

[11] Aristotle, *On Rhetoric*, II.23.4.

[12] Ibid., II.23.5. Aristotle then continues with yet another topic similar to the more and less. Aristotle elaborates on these categories in his *Topics*, 3.6, 119b, 17–35.

[13] Actions regarding boundaries of fields and the right to exclude or deny a water channel to pass through one's territory were generally limited to the country. The regulation of water flow is less applicable in the city than the regulation of boundaries. See further at Cicero, *Topics*, 43; *Justinian's Digest*, 10.1.4.19 and 39.3.1.17; and Tobias Reinhardt, *Cicero's Topica* (Oxford: Oxford University Press, 2003), 249–50.

[14] Translation from ibid., 4.23 (p. 125). See also paragraph 22.84 (p. 161). See further elaboration at 18.68–71 (p. 150–3). These categories of comparison are also discussed in Quintilian, *Institutes of Oratory*, 5.10.86–88 and 8.4.9–11. For more on legal analogies see also Cicero, *On Invention*, II.50.148–53.

[15] Although it seems quite clear from the Twelve Tablets that immovable property, including houses, would require two years, Cicero reinterprets the law by analogizing houses with all other things besides land. For a comparison with Talmudic law, where

Aelius Theon combines these three forms of comparison into the title *synkrisis*:

> Then from comparison (συγκρισεωσ), and this is threefold; for we compare what is charged to something greater (μείζονι ἑαυτοῦ συγκρίνομεν) or lesser (ἐλάττονι) or equal (ἴσῳ) ... When we make a comparison to the lesser we shall speak as follows: "If the thief is punished for taking men's money, how much the more will this man be punished for looting the possessions of the gods?"[16]

The link between the *qal va-ḥomer* and the Greek comparison of lesser to greater was made explicit in the early nineteenth century by Rabbi Isaac Samuel Reggio (1784–1855):

> It is evident that our holy rabbis, authors of the Mishnah and Talmud, were fluent in [philosophical] knowledge for it is well known that the 13 rules of R. Ishmael and the 32 rules of R. Eliezer the son of R. Yose the Galilean, which are the key to understanding all of the oral law, behold most of them are founded on the principles of logic. For example, the first rule called *qal va-ḥomer* is regularly referred to by the logicians in the name *argomentatio a minori ad majus*.[17]

Saul Lieberman explains that the strange term *gezerah shavah* derives its etymology from *synkrisis*, which means both comparison and

three years is required for all property, see Boaz Cohen, *Jewish and Roman Law: A Comparative Study* (New York: The Jewish Theological Seminary of America, 1966), 1.19. Sifra, Behar, parasha 6, 4, similarly derives the use of *ḥazaka* for slaves from its use for land, although *ḥazaka* there means usus (T. Kiddushin 1:5), not usucapion (as in M. Baba Batra 3:1). Cf. Y. Kiddushin 1:3 and B. Kiddushin 22b where this is called *heqesh*. See further at ibid. 1.290–1.

16 Translation from Kennedy, *Progymnasmata*, §108, 44. See also the progymnasmata of Hermogenes, ibid. §13, p. 80, and §18–20, pp. 83–4, those of Aphthonius, ibid., §34, p. 107, and those of Libanius in Gibson, *Libanius's Progymnasmata*, 149–53. One of the standard exercises in the progymnasmata is "*synkrisis*," wherein the student is to compare two people or things to show that what is usually considered the lesser is actually the greater. This comparison is typically epideictic whereas judicial comparisons form part of the earlier stage of progymnasmata called "*topos*." For a good example of epideictic *synkrisis* in rabbinic literature see the comparison of sacrifices and righteousness at Deut Rabbah 5:3.

17 Isaac Samuel Reggio, *Ha-Torah ve-ha-filosofia: ḥoverot 'isha 'el 'aḥota* (Vienna, 1827), 30. See also Aviram Ravitsky, "Aristotelian Logic and Talmudic Methodology: The Commentaries on the 13 Hermeneutic Principles and their Application of Logic," in *Judaic Logic*, ed. Andrew Schumann (Piscataway: Gorgias Press, 2010), 131; and Daube, "Rabbinic Methods," 251.

decision.[18] While *gezerah* does not itself mean comparison, it could have been the translation of *synkrisis* in the sense of legal decision[19] and would have then been applied as a term for analogy since the Greek comparison uses the same word.[20] Lieberman concludes: "Hence we unhesitatingly translate the term גזירה שוה σύγκρισις πρός ἴσον."[21] The first two rules in Hillel's list thus correspond to the three types of analogy (*synkrisis*): from greater, from lesser, and from equal. Lieberman summarizes: "The Greek rhetors counted them as three rules, while the Rabbis considered them two norms."[22]

One could argue that deriving laws using analogies is a part of natural reasoning and not something the rabbis learned from the Greeks. Indeed, Lieberman only claims to explain the terminology of Hillel's rule, not the origin of the method itself.[23] David Daube, however, goes further and argues that the rabbis' very modes of reasoning and the explicit awareness of their hermeneutics also derive from Greek

[18] See Henry George Liddell and Robert Scott, *A Greek-English Lexicon* (Oxford: Clarendon Press, 1940), s.v. σύγκρισις II and III.2.

[19] *Synkrisis* translates Hebrew *mishpat* whenever the Targum translates it as דחזי (rather than the more common דינא, which the Septuagint renders as κρίσις), as in Num 9:3, 29:6, 11, 18, 21, 24, 27, 30, 33, 37. In these cases, it carries the sense of "proper interpretation." *Synkrisis* also translates *mishpat* in Jud 18:7 where the sense is "decision" or "law." *Synkrisis* is also the standard word in the Septuagint for dream interpretation, as in Gen 40:12, 18, Jud 7:15 and many times in Daniel.

[20] Solomon Zeitlin, "Hillel and the Hermeneutic Rules," *The Jewish Quarterly Review* 54, no. 2 (1963): 166–7, rejects Lieberman's hypothesis because גזירה only means decree or law, not comparison. Zeitlin prefers the standard explanation of גזירה שוה as "equal laws," i.e. cases that are analogous and therefore require the same decision. This is also how Bacher, *`Erkhe midrash*, 1.10, explains the term. Lieberman counters that this idea would better be expressed in rabbinic Hebrew by גזירה אחת, as in Tanḥuma, Va'ethanan, 1.

Feldman, *Jew and Gentile*, 35, objects that the phrase σύγκρισις πρός ἴσον occurs for the first time in Hermogenes in the second century CE while Hillel used the Hebrew in the first century BCE. However, much Greek literature has been lost and the phrase could easily have been used by earlier writers; each work of progymnasmata mostly copied from those before it with very little innovation. In any case, it is very possible that the גזירה שוה was termed only in the second century CE and then put into Hillel's mouth; see Zeitlin, "Hillel and the Hermeneutic Rules," 161–73. Feldman objects further that the Greek analogy is generally conceptual while the rabbinic גזירה שוה is a verbal comparison. However, there is sufficient evidence showing that the *gezerah shavah* was first used as a basic conceptual analogy and only later came to be applied exclusively to verbal analogies; see further at p. 207 n. 125.

[21] Lieberman, *Hellenism in Jewish Palestine*, 59.

[22] Ibid., 60. Notably, Aristotle counts them as two parts of one *topos* in *On Rhetoric*, 2.23, topic 4.

[23] Visotzky, "Midrash," 122–4, suggests various reasons for Lieberman's "excess of caution" on this issue.

thought.[24] First, analogies in rabbinic literature do not follow the type of reasoning one might find in everyday conversation but can be rather technical. Second, the project of naming, listing, and systematizing one's modes of exegesis goes beyond natural popular reason and most likely derives from the classical rhetorical tradition. As further support for a genetic connection between Hillel's principles and Greco-Roman thought, Daube cites parallels to the next three rules as well.

The third and fourth rules are "a principle derived from one passage" and "a principle derived from two passages." With the former, the midrash applies a detail of one law to others like it. For example, Sifra, Aḥare Mot, *parasha* 4, 4, states:

> Aaron shall lay both of his hands upon the head of the live goat (Lev 16:21): This teaches that laying of hands is with both hands. This is an archetype (*binyan av*) for all the layings that they must be with both hands.

Since Lev 16:21 specifies explicitly that both hands must be laid upon a sacrifice before slaughter, the midrash derives that all laying of hands for all sacrifices must use both hands, even when the verse uses "hand" in the singular, as in Lev 1:4.[25] The "principle derived from two passages" works the same way except that one uses the common denominator between two passages as an archetype from which to derive a general principle.[26]

Daube points to an example of similar reasoning in Roman Law.[27] The first chapter of the *Lex Aquilia* establishes that one who kills the cattle of another must pay the highest valuation of the animals during

[24] To be sure, Daube does make a statement along the same lines as that of Lieberman in his earlier essay: David Daube, "The Civil Law of the Mishnah: The Arrangement of the Three Gates," in *The Collected Works of David Daube*, ed. Calum Carmichael (Berkley: University of California, 1992): 269. However, his later essays emphasize the Hellenistic influence on both the terminology and the content of the midrashic hermeneutical rules. See n. 36.

[25] See also B. Menaḥot 93b and Ibn Ezra to Lev 1:4.

[26] See, for example, Mekhilta d'R. Ishmael, Nezikin, 9; and further at *Encyclopedia Talmudit*, s.v. "*binyan av*." On the similarity between this form of induction and J. S. Mill's "method of agreement," see Louis Jacobs, *Studies in Talmudic Logic and Methodology* (London: Vallentine, Mitchell, and Co., 1961), 9–15.

[27] David Daube, "On the Third Chapter of the Lex Aquilia," *Law Quarterly Review* 52 (1936): 265. See also Jacob Milgrom, "The Qumran Cult: Its Exegetical Principles," in *Temple Scroll Studies*, ed. George Brooke (Sheffield: Sheffield Academic Press, 1989): 165–80, who traces *binyan av* back to the Temple Scroll's hermeneutic of homogenization.

that year.[28] The third chapter of the *Lex Aquilia* legislates compensation for non-lethal damage to cattle as well as to all other animals and property including, "not only burning and breaking, but also cutting, bruising, spilling, and all kinds of damage, destruction, or spoiling."[29] Here, however, the requirement to pay the "highest value" does not appear. While some jurists say that it is up to the judge to decide whether the litigant must pay its greatest value or an inferior value, "Sabinus held that we must interpret as if here too the word *plurimi* had been inserted, the legislator having thought it sufficient to have used the word in the first chapter."[30]

The Mekhilta deals with almost the exact same problem. Exodus 22:4 requires that someone whose livestock grazes in another person's land must make restitution with the best of his land. However, this requirement to pay with the best land is neither mentioned in the next verse where a person starts a fire that spreads and destroys another's field, nor in other laws of damages. Mekhilta d'R. Shimon bar Yoḥai, 22:4, teaches:

> "The best of his field and the best of his vineyard he shall pay" (Exod 22:4). This teaches that we assess him only from the best land. I know only this case; what is the source for anyone who pays a fine that we assess it only from the best land? Therefore, the verse comes to teach, "the best of his field and the best of his vineyard he shall pay." This is an archetype (*binyan av*) for anyone who pays a fine that we assess it only from the best land.[31]

The fifth rule governs passages that list both a general category and specific examples of items to which a law applies.[32] For example:

[28] Cited in *Institutes of Gaius*, 3.210, and *Justinian's Digest* 9.2.2.

[29] *Institutes of Gaius*, 3.217. Translations are from Francis De Zulueta, *The Institutes of Gaius* (Oxford: Clarendon Press, 1946), 225. See also *Justinian's Digest* 9.2.27.5.

[30] *Institutes of Gaius*, 3.218. See similarly Cicero, *On Invention*, II.50.151: "Many provisions have been omitted in many laws, but nobody thinks that they have been omitted, because they can be inferred from the other cases about which rules have been laid down."

[31] See also M. Baba Qama 1:1.

[32] While Hillel's list of seven rules includes only "*kelal u-frat*" (see n. 7), it seems clear that this includes all combinations of general categories following or preceding specific instances. Kahana, "Kavvim," suggests that originally all such cases would be interpreted to include items that are in some essential respect similar to the specific instance. By the time of the scholion to the Baraita d'R. Ishmael in the Sifra, however, this interpretation was limited only to *kelal u-frat u-kelal*. See also Michael Chernick, *Le-ḥeqer ha-midot "kelal u-ferat u-khelal" ve-"ribui u-mi'ut" ba-midrashim uva-*

> When a man gives to another an ass, an ox, a sheep" (Exod 22:9) – these are specific instances; "or any other animal to guard" (ibid.) – this is a general category. When a specific instance is followed by a general category then the general category adds to the specific instance.[33]

The verse introduces the law about an animal that dies or is injured while in the care of a second party. Although the verse specifies three types of animal, the midrash explains that the law in fact applies to any animal, in accordance with the general category that follows. Similarly, in the citation from *Lex Aquilia* above, a list of various types of damage is followed by the more general category, "destroying." Celcus comments on this that "burning" and "breaking" are also included in the category of "destroy," and, "it is not unusual for a statute first to enumerate a few cases specially and then to add a comprehensive term by which to embrace any special cases."[34]

These parallels between the midrashic rules and Roman legal interpretation can certainly be mere coincidence and a natural result of trying to interpret and apply any legal code. However, Daube argues for a genetic connection considering the very naming and listing of these rules. The project of distilling general rules of reasoning from specific instances and the awareness that any given interpretation results from an application of these rules are features not found among any previous group of Jews,[35] but rather have a distinctly Greek flavor.[36] Having established this connection, we still need to explain why the rabbis incorporated these rules. What were the historical circumstances that led to their use and formulation? What was the attitude of the rabbis towards this form of reasoning and its relationship with legal traditions?

talmudim (Lod: Habermann Institute for Literary Research, 1984); and Benjamin De Vries, *Meḥqarim be-sifrut ha-Talmud* (Jerusalem: Mossad Harav Kook, 1968), 161–4.

33 Sifra, Baraita d'R. Ishmael. See also Mekhilta d'R. Ishmael, Nezikin 16, cited on p. 211.

34 *Justinian's Digest* 9.2.27.16. Translation from Daube, "Rabbinic Methods," 253.

35 See Moshe Bernstein and Shlomo Koyfman, "The Interpretation of Biblical Law in the Dead Sea Scrolls: Forms and Methods," in *Biblical Interpretation at Qumran*, ed. Matthias Henze (Grand Rapids, MI: Eerdmans, 2005): 61–87.

36 Daube, "Rabbinic Methods," 254. For further analysis of foreign influence on rabbinic modes of exegesis, see Daube, "Alexandrian Methods of Interpretation and the Rabbis," in *Essays in Greco-Roman and Related Talmudic Literature*, ed. Henry Fischel (New York: Ktav, 1977): 239–64; and Stephen Lieberman, "A Mesopotamian Background for the So-Called Aggadic 'Measures' of Biblical Hermeneutics," *Hebrew Union College Annual* 58 (1987): 157–225.

MIDRASHIC HERMENEUTICS AS ANTI-SECTARIAN POLEMICS

Tosefta Pesaḥim 4:13–14 provides greater detail regarding the circumstances in which Hillel introduced these exegetical methods:

> Once the fourteenth [day of Nisan] fell on the Sabbath. They asked Hillel the Elder, "Does the Passover [sacrifice] supersede the Sabbath?"
>
> He said to them, "Do we have but one Passover [sacrifice] during the year that supersedes the Sabbath? We have more than three hundred Passovers during the year, and they supersede the Sabbath."
>
> The whole courtyard [of the temple] joined up against him.
>
> He said to them, "The regular sacrifice [offered each morning and twilight] is a communal sacrifice, and the Passover is a communal sacrifice. Just as the regular sacrifice is a communal sacrifice that supersedes the Sabbath, so the Passover is a communal sacrifice that supersedes the Sabbath.
>
> "Another proof: It [Scripture] says in connection with the regular sacrifice, *[Present to me] at its appointed time* (Num 28:2), and it says in connection with the Passover, *[Keep the Passover] at its appointed time* (Num 9:2). Just as the regular sacrifice, of which it says, *At its appointed time,* supersedes the Sabbath, so the Passover, of which it says, *At its appointed time,* supersedes the Sabbath.[37]
>
> "Moreover, [it can be deduced from a] *qal va-ḥomer*. If the regular sacrifice, for which one is not subject to [the punishment of] excision, supersedes the Sabbath, is it not logical that the Passover, for which one is subject to [the punishment of] excision, supersedes the Sabbath?
>
> "In addition, I have received [a tradition] from my masters that the Passover supersedes the Sabbath. Not only the First Passover but even the Second Passover, and not only the communal Passover but even the individual Passover."

[37] See parallels at Mekhilta d'R. Ishmael, Pisḥa, 5; and Sifre Num 65 and 142. This exegesis is there stated not in the name of Hillel but in the name of R. Yoshiah. See analysis at Alexander Guttmann, "Foundations of Rabbinic Judaism," *Hebrew Union College Annual* 23 (1950–1951): 462–3.

On that very day they appointed Hillel patriarch [*nasi*], and he taught them the laws of the Passover.[38]

This *chreia* tells of a time when Passover fell out on Saturday night so that the sacrifices would have to be prepared on the Sabbath. However, the leaders of the time, the elders of Betera,[39] did not know whether they were permitted to violate the Sabbath in order to prepare the Passover sacrifices.[40] They turned to Hillel who, sure enough, used three different analogies to the daily burnt offering in order to prove that one is permitted to offer the Passover sacrifice on the Sabbath.[41] Hillel, however, did not stop there, but rather continued to adduce an oral tradition from his teachers, Shemaya and Avtalion, confirming and even generalizing the same outcome as the analogical derivations. In fact, ancient halakha

[38] Translation from Jeffrey Rubenstein, *Rabbinic Stories* (New York: Paulist Press, 2002), 72–3. On the relationship between this text and T. Sanhedrin 7:11, see Louis Finkelstein, *Sifra on Leviticus*, 5 vols. (Jerusalem: The Jewish Theological Seminary of America, 1983–1992): 5:120–2.

[39] See p. 175 n. 5. They are not identified in the Tosefta but do appear in parallel sources.

[40] Many have wondered how the Temple leaders could have forgotten such a law; surely Passover would have fallen out on the Sabbath every few years under an empirical lunar calendar. Rubenstein, *Rabbinic Stories*, 71, writes that "the story creates a fictional scenario to teach the audience about how one derives law in general, not to provide information about this particular law." However, Isaac Sassoon, *Destination Torah* (Hoboken, NJ: Ktav, 2001), 186–92, suggests that the Second Temple followed a fixed calendar for most of its history until it was changed to an empirical calendar during later Hasmonean times – perhaps as a renunciation of Greek influence. Under the fixed calendar, the eve of Passover could have been preset never to fall on the Sabbath in order to avoid this very problem, just as it was preset in amoraic times when they reverted back to a fixed calendar in order that the shofar and the ritual of the willow branches did not fall on the Sabbath (Y. Sukkah 4:1, 54a). It is therefore possible that during Hillel's time, Passover fell out on Sunday for the first time since the fixed calendar was replaced with an empirical calendar. See also Sacha Stern, *Calendar and Community: A History of the Jewish Calendar, Second Century BCE – Tenth Century CE* (Oxford: Oxford University Press, 2001), 113, who argues that a lunar empirical calendar was in use during Hasmonean times, though evidence for this is only "sporadic." Some Jewish groups followed a solar calendar during this period. However, there is no evidence as to whether those groups following a lunar calendar in the pre-Hasmonean period used a fixed or empirical system. While the months of the Babylonian lunar calendar were decided empirically, by the Hellenistic period, astronomers already had tables that could predict the first visibility of the new moon. See George Sarton, *Hellenistic Science and Culture in the Last Three Centuries B.C.* (Cambridge: Harvard University Press, 1959), 337.

[41] Although the Tosefta only names the *qal va-ḥomer*, the Yerushalmi plausibly matches up the other two with the rules of *heqesh* and *gezerah shavah*. The main point here is not that Hillel used the named rules but that he turned to exegesis at all rather than tradition.

would most likely have prohibited preparing the Passover on the Sabbath,[42] which explains why the people present ganged up on Hillel.[43]

While historians cast doubt on various details of this story,[44] we can at the very least accept that towards the end of the Second Temple period, these exegetical methods began to circulate among the Pharisees and early rabbis. It is furthermore plausible that Hillel, an important religious leader of the Pharisaic movement, played a central role in advancing the authority of the Pharisaic oral law and the project of legal biblical exegesis.[45] Note that Hillel is depicted in many Talmudic sources as someone well-educated in the science and philosophy of his day. In particular, many of his sayings parallel those of Seneca the Younger, the great Roman Stoic.[46] Hillel is also storied to exemplify the Stoic virtues of remaining calm and never becoming angry even in the face of great provocation.[47] It is therefore noteworthy that of all of the various philosophical schools in the Hellenistic world, only the Stoics supported rhetoric and considered it an art.[48] This lends support

[42] See Damascus Document 11:17–18: "A man may not offer anything on the altar on the Sabbath except for the burnt offering of the Sabbath for so it is written, 'except for your Sabbaths' (Lev 23:38, MT reads Sabbaths of the Lord)." See further at Joseph Angel, "Damascus Document," in *Outside the Bible: Ancient Jewish Writings Related to Scripture*, ed. Louis Feldman, James Kugel, and Lawrence Schiffman (Philadelphia: Jewish Publication Society, 2013): 3021; Lawrence Schiffman, *The Halakhah at Qumran* (Leiden: Brill, 1975), 128–31; Harold Weiss, "The Sabbath among the Samaritans," *Journal for the Study of Judaism in the Persian, Hellenistic and Roman Period* 25, no. 2 (1994): 264; and Bernard Revel, *The Karaite Halakah and Its Relation to Sadducean, Samaritan and Philonian Halakah* (Philadelphia: Ktav, 1913), 41.

[43] Compare this with the parallel story where Beth Shammai gangs up against Hillel also in the Temple courtyard at T. Ḥagigah 2:11 = Y. Ḥagigah 2:3, 78a = B. Beṣah 20a. See analysis at Hidary, *Dispute*, 183–6. On the usage of חבר על to mean to join against, see also Job 16:4.

[44] See n. 40; Armand Kaminka, "Hillel's Life and Work," *The Jewish Quarterly Review* 30, no. 2 (1939): 78–9; Fischel, "Story and History," 452–3; and Jacob Neusner, *From Politics to Piety: The Emergence of Pharisaic Judaism* (New York: Ktav, 1979), 23–35.

[45] On the image of Hillel in other aggadic sources as a central figure in reconstructing oral law, see Menachem Katz, "Stories of Hillel's Appointment as Nasi in the Talmudic Literature: A Foundation Legend of the Jewish Scholar's World," [Hebrew] *Sidra* 26 (2011): 111–14. See also Faur, *Golden Doves*, 124.

[46] Kaminka, "Hillel's Life and Work," 115–22.

[47] B. Berakhot 60a.

[48] See Yosef Liebersohn, *The Dispute Concerning Rhetoric in Hellenistic Thought* (Göttingen: Vandenhoeck & Ruprecht, 2010), 32–5. Unlike other schools of philosophy, Stoicism became popular among the general Roman population and its teachers would teach and deliver lectures in public spaces, thus explaining their support of rhetoric. See further at Christopher Gill, "The School in the Roman Imperial Period," in *The Cambridge Companion to the Stoics*, ed. Brad Inwood (Cambridge: Cambridge University Press, 2003): 37; and Dirk Baltzly, "Stoicism," *The Stanford Encyclopedia of*

to the possibility that the historical Hillel took steps to institute midrashic hermeneutics in some form.

Regardless of whether the historical Hillel played a role in the development of legal midrash, norms of interpretation surely existed in some form before him, and their systematization continued long after him.[49] There is no way to confirm that Hillel formulated the particular seven rules listed in T. Sanhedrin 7:11, nor the historicity of any of the details of T. Pesaḥim 4:13–14. We must therefore analyze these sources less for what they teach about the historical Hillel and more for the light they shed on the rabbis who authored and transmitted them as the founding narratives of their own exegetical project. In that spirit, we ask, what was the purpose in introducing these exegetical rules? Why does Hillel figure so prominently in this connection? Why does Hillel in the Passover story put so much effort into deriving the law exegetically when he had an authoritative tradition on the matter all along? What was the significance of these details in the minds of the story's narrators?

Recall that the last two centuries of the Second Temple period were a time of great sectarian strife. While the sects disputed some philosophical points, their primary focus of contention related to Jewish law.[50] Fundamental to their legal disputes was the reliance of the Pharisees on the unwritten traditions of their fathers.[51] Because these oral traditions were not bound to Scripture, they became the subject of intense attack by the Sadducees and Qumran sectarians as being unfounded.[52] The Pharisees must have felt pressure to respond and convince their adherents and the masses at large of their own authenticity. Heinrich Graetz argues that Hillel accepted the Sadducean challenge and introduced the hermeneutical rules in order to ground the Pharisaic oral law within Scripture. Hillel took the mass of traditions he learned from his teachers and "he traced them back to their first principles, and raised them out of the narrow circle of tradition and mere custom to the height of reason ... After this demonstration by Hillel, no dispute amongst the schools

Philosophy (2014). The nature of Stoicism as a popular philosophy also prompts Josephus, *Life*, 12, to compare them to the Pharisees. See Steve Mason, *Flavius Josephus on the Pharisees* (Leiden: Brill, 1991), 354.

49 See Zeitlin, "Hillel and the Hermeneutic Rules," 161–73.

50 See Yaakov Sussman, "The History of Halakha and the Dead Sea Scrolls: Preliminary Observations on *Miqsat Ma'ase Ha-Torah* (4QMMT)," [Hebrew] *Tarbiz* 59 (1990): 36; and Hidary, *Dispute*, 33.

51 Joseph Baumgarten, "The Unwritten Law in the Pre-Rabbinic Period," *Journal for the Study of Judaism in the Persian, Hellenistic and Roman Period* 3 (1972): 7–29.

52 Azzan Yadin, *Scripture and Tradition: Rabbi Akiva and the Triumph of Midrash* (Philadelphia: University of Pennsylvania, 2015), 183–6.

could arise as to the binding power of traditional law. By the introduction of seven methods, the oral law could be imbued with the same weight and authority as that actually contained in the Scriptures."[53] Along the same lines, Daube writes:

> The greatest Pharisaic scholar of all times, Hillel, not without some difficulty, convinced his party that the main Sadducean point had to be conceded: in principle there could be no binding law independent of Scripture. But the way he convinced them was by showing that nothing would be lost; and that by energetic and systematic interpretation, the entire mass of traditional observances, sanctioned over the centuries by the religious leaders and sages, could be derived from the Pentateuch.[54]

This is the reason why Hillel first proved from Scripture in various ways that the Passover trumps the Sabbath and only afterwards relayed the tradition he inherited from his teachers. He wanted to show that midrashic exegesis was a reliable method for deriving halakha and for supporting Pharisaic oral law.[55] Hillel utilized rhetorical modes of reasoning common in Roman culture and jurisprudence in order to persuade his audience as to the legitimacy of the oral law. No longer could the Sadducees claim that only their laws had biblical basis. Perhaps it is

[53] Heinrich Graetz, *History of the Jews*, 6 vols. (Philadelphia: The Jewish Publication Society of America, 1891–98), 2.98. See also Jay Harris, *How Do We Know This?: Midrash and the Fragmentation of Modern Judaism* (Albany: State University of New York Press, 1995), 175–90; Zeitlin, "Hillel and the Hermeneutic Rules," 172; Guttmann, "Foundations of Rabbinic Judaism," 453–73; Daube, "Texts and Interpretations," 188–99; and Epstein, *Mevo'ot le-sifrut ha-Tannaim*, 521. Graetz's position here relates to a larger scholarly debate as to whether the oral law of the Pharisees was transmitted apodictically, similar to the form of the Mishnah, or as commentary to the Pentateuch, like midrash. See the literature cited at Harris, ibid.; Strack and Stemberger, *Introduction*, 126–9; and David Weiss Halivni, *Midrash, Mishnah, and Gemara: The Jewish Predilection for Justified Law* (Cambridge: Harvard University Press, 1986), 18–19. Evidence for either side is scant, and even those who claim that midrash came first should agree that the end of the Second Temple period saw a great increase in exegetical material and its systematization, as does, for example, Jacob Lauterbach, *Rabbinic Essays* (Cincinnati: Hebrew Union College Press, 1951), 210.

[54] Daube, "Texts and Interpretations," 189. Kaminka, "Hillel's Life and Work," 114–15, points to M. Avot 1:12 as another attack by Hillel against the Sadducean priests. See further p. 200–2 on the centrality of the *qal va-ḥomer* in debates between Pharisees and Sadducees.

[55] See Guttmann, "Foundations of Rabbinic Judaism," 465–6. The same goal drives a number of traditions about rabbis successfully deriving halakha through exegesis even after the halakhic tradition had been forgotten or corrupted. See Sifre Num 75; T. Zebaḥim 1:8; and B. Temurah 16a.

for this reason that Resh Laqish says: "When [Torah] was forgotten, Hillel the Babylonian went up [to Israel] and reestablished it."[56] As a case in point, let us analyze a more elaborate version of Resh Laqish's statement at Y. Pesaḥim 6:1, 33a:[57]

> Over three matters did Hillel come up from Babylonia.
>
> [1] "It is pure" (Lev 13:37). Can it be that he can take leave and walk away [after the skin has healed]? [Scripture] teaches, saying: "the priest shall purify him" (ibid.). Since [the verse states] "the priest shall purify him," can it be that if the priest declares the impure to be pure then it will be pure? [Scripture] teaches, saying: "it is pure" (ibid.) and "the priest shall purify it" (ibid.). For this did Hillel come up from Babylonia.[58]
>
> [2] One verse states, "You shall slaughter the Passover sacrifice for the Lord your God, from the flock and the herd" (Deut 16:2). But another verse states, "You may take it from the sheep or from the goats" (Exod 12:5). How can this be? Flock is for the Passover sacrifice. Flock and herd are for the festival sacrifice.
>
> [3] One verse states, "You shall eat unleavened bread for six days" (Deut 16:8). But another verse states, "You shall eat unleavened bread for seven days" (Exod 12:15). How can this be? Six [days you shall eat] from the new grain and seven [days you shall eat] from the old grain.[59]
>
> He expounded, he accorded [his interpretation with the tradition], he went up [to Palestine] and received the tradition.

Hillel noticed three places where Scripture contains a contradiction and resolved each of them through midrashic reasoning. He went up to Palestine in order to test his theories and found that they accorded with the established traditional halakha as taught there. This text again illustrates how derivations through biblical exegesis can successfully arrive at traditional Pharisaic halakha.

[56] B. Sukkah 20a. See also Frank Moore Cross, *From Epic to Canon* (Baltimore: The Johns Hopkins University Press, 1998), 217.

[57] Translation follows MS Leiden.

[58] See parallel at T. Nega'im 1:16. This text may relate to the question of the necessity for a priest to rule on skin afflictions even when others are more learned, on which see Steven Fraade, "Shifting from Priestly to Non-Priestly Legal Authority: A Comparison of the Damascus Document and the Midrash Sifra," *Dead Sea Discoveries* 6, no. 2 (1999): 109–25.

[59] See parallels at Mekhilta d'R. Yishmael, Pisḥa 8 and 17; Sifra, Emor, *perek* 17, 5; Sifre Deut 134; and B. Menaḥot 66a.

The third case in this Yerushalmi is especially significant because it is the subject of one of the most important sectarian controversies. The Sadducees and other sectarians understood Leviticus 23:11 to prescribe the offering of the barley grain on the Sunday after Passover. The Pharisees, in contrast, interpreted "after the Sabbath" to refer to the day after the first day of Passover. This controversy became especially heated when the first day of Passover fell on a Friday, whereupon the Pharisees proceeded to cut the grain offering on the eve of Sabbath and thus needlessly violated the Sabbath in the eyes of the Sadducees. M. Menaḥot 10:3 recounts in detail how the Pharisees made a public display of the cutting of the barley offering with great pomp, precisely in order to polemicize against the Sadducees. The Pharisees would presumably have been challenged by the Sadducees and perhaps by their own adherents to ground their interpretation in Scripture. Hillel ingeniously derived the Pharisaic position through his resolution of Exodus 12:15 and Deuteronomy 16:8. Since the new harvest may be eaten only after the barley offering, the command to eat seven days must refer to unleavened bread made from old grain, which is permitted on all seven days of Passover. The command to eat only six days must therefore refer to the last six days of Passover on which one may eat of the new grain, proving that the barley offering must be performed on the second day of Passover. From that point on, the Pharisees were able to uphold their oral traditions while also being assured that they were in accord with Scripture.

Alexander Guttman makes a further point that Hillel's method would have been effective not only in defending Pharisaic traditions, but more importantly, in developing those laws to meet the challenges of new historical realities: "The principal way of molding Judaism, of harmonizing changing conditions of life with hallowed ideas and practices was that of interpretation ... The endorsement of a practice or the introduction of a new practice could be made effective, usually, by pointing to a basis in the Torah."[60] While the views of Shammai generally reflect an older layer of halakhic development, the view of Hillel is often creative, representing a newly evolved stratum.[61] Accordingly, the methods of midrashic interpretation played a key role in the ability of Hillel and his successors to direct halakha along a path that

[60] Guttmann, "Foundations of Rabbinic Judaism," 455–6.

[61] See Hillel's enactments at M. Shevi`it 10:3 and M. `Arakhin 9:4 (= Sifra, Behar, *parasha* 4, 8) and the scholarly literature cited at Vered Noam, "Beth Shammai veha-halakha ha-kitatit," *Mada`e ha-Yahadut* 41 (2002): 48–49.

could withstand the vicissitudes of the coming wars and the Temple's destruction.[62] In their efforts to persuade their coreligionists to accept their halakhic traditions, the rabbis turned to the most effective and widespread persuasive tools available, those of the classical rhetorical tradition that pervaded their cultural environment.

THE SKEPTICAL PUSHBACK

The rabbis' use of rhetoric turned out to be very effective in promoting their halakhic views and advancing their movement ahead of that of the sectarians.[63] The success of the hermeneutical rules, however, became a problem in itself. Once one allows reasoned exegesis into the system as an authoritative way to derive laws, then one must accept whatever outcome such exegesis may generate. The same force and flexibility of the hermeneutical rules that empowered them to establish the basis of oral tradition also threatened to undermine that very tradition. Just as one can apply a *qal va-ḥomer* or *gezera shava* to prove a transmitted law, so can one use them to disprove the very same laws. How did the rabbis respond to this paradoxical challenge?

As we will see below, the Tannaim and Amoraim were aware of the dangers to tradition inherent in relying on unbridled reason and were also conscious of the way rhetoric could be used to arrive at mutually opposite conclusions. Accordingly, they introduced a measure of skepticism about the rules, though not enough to nullify their use altogether. They applied the hermeneutical rules throughout their literature, but they also formulated limits to their application. These limits become foregrounded in the Yerushalmi's retelling of the story about Hillel and the Passover sacrifice. As above, we read these stories not as historical reports about Hillel but rather for what they reveal about the origin and reception of the hermeneutical methods. Here is the Yerushalmi version:

> **[Narration]**
> This law [of M. Pesaḥim 6:1] was concealed from the elders of Betera. Once the fourteenth [day of Nisan] fell on the Sabbath, and they did not know whether the Passover supersedes the Sabbath or not. They said, "There is here a certain Babylonian named Hillel, who served Shemaya and Avtalion. He knows whether the Passover supersedes the Sabbath or not. Perhaps something good will come from him."

[62] See Hidary, "The Rhetoric of Rabbinic Authority."

[63] For other factors contributing to the decline of the sects, see Hidary, *Dispute*, 31–6.

He said to them, "Do we have but one Passover alone throughout the whole year that supersedes the Sabbath? Do not many Passovers throughout the year supersede the Sabbath?"

... They said, "Thus we thought that something good would come from you."

[Partition]

He started to expound [the law] for them based on [1] a *heqesh*, [2] a *qal va-ḥomer* and [3] a *gezera shava*.

[Proof]

[1] From a *heqesh*: Since the regular sacrifice is a communal sacrifice that supersedes the Sabbath, so too the Passover is a communal sacrifice that supersedes the Sabbath.

[2] From a *qal va-ḥomer*: If the regular sacrifice, for which one is not subject [to the punishment of] excision, supersedes the Sabbath, then the Passover, for which one is [subject to the punishment] of excision, – is it not logical that it supersedes the Sabbath?

[3] From a *gezerah shavah*: Just as the daily sacrifice, in connection with which it says *At its appointed time* (Num 28:2), supersedes the Sabbath, so too the Passover, in connection with which it says *At its appointed time* (Num 9:3), supersedes the Sabbath.

[Refutation]

They said to him, "Did we think that something good would come from a Babylonian?

[1] "The *heqesh* that you stated can be refuted: What you say of the regular sacrifice, which has a limit [of two per day], you cannot say of the Passover, which has no limit [in the number that may be offered.]

[2] "The *qal va-ḥomer* that you stated can be refuted: What you say of the regular sacrifice, which is of the Most Holy [class of] sacrifices, you cannot say of the Passover, which is of the Lesser Holy sacrifices.

[3] "The *gezerah shavah* that you stated – one may not infer a *gezerah shavah* on his own [but only if he received it as a tradition from his masters]."

R. Yose b. R. Bon said in the name of R. Abba b. Memel: "If one should come and reason based on a *gezerah shavah* on his own, he can make the reptile cause tent impurity and a corpse cause impurity with the size of a lentil, for he can interpret 'clothing ... skin' (Lev 11:32) 'clothing ... skin' (Num 31:20) as a *gezerah shavah* ... "

R. Yose b. R. Bon said in the name of R. Abba b. Memel: "One may infer a *gezerah shavah* in order to uphold his teaching [as received from tradition] but one may not infer a *gezerah shavah* to nullify his teaching."

R. Yose b. R. Bon said in the name of R. Abba b. Memel: "One may infer a *qal va-ḥomer* on his own but one may not infer a *gezerah shavah* on his own. Therefore, we do refute based on a *qal va-ḥomer* but we do not refute based on a *gezerah shavah*."

[Peroration]

Even though he [Hillel] was sitting and expounding for them the whole day, they did not accept it [the ruling] from him until he said to them, "May [harm] befall me if I did not learn thus from Shemaya and Avtalion."

As soon as they heard that from him, they rose and appointed him patriarch over them.

As soon as they appointed him patriarch over them he began to rebuke them with words saying, "What caused your need for this Babylonian [=me]? Is it not that you did not serve the two great men of the world, Shemaya and Avtalion, who were dwelling with you?"

As soon as he rebuked them with words the law was concealed from him. They said to him, "What will we do for the people – they did not bring their knives?"

He said to them, "This law I heard and forgot. But leave Israel be; if they are not prophets, they are the sons of prophets."

Immediately, he whose Passover was a lamb stuck it [the knife] in its hair. He whose Passover was a kid tied it between its horns. It turned out that their Passovers brought their knives with them.

As soon as he saw the event, he remembered the law. He said, "Thus I learned from Shemaya and Avtalion."[64]

The Yerushalmi version of the story expands upon and modifies the Tosefta version.[65] The Yerushalmi is more dramatic and includes many

[64] Y. Pesaḥim 6:1, 33a. Translation from Rubenstein, *Rabbinic Stories*, 77–9, with modifications.

[65] I here follow Katz, "Stories," 81–115, and others who show that the Tosefta contains the more original version of this story while the Yerushalmi inserts several amoraic expansions. While Katz also opines that the Bavli version is later than the Yerushalmi, Jeffrey Rubenstein, *Stories of the Babylonian Talmud* (Baltimore: Johns Hopkins University Press, 2010), 217–28, argues that this is a rare instance of Yerushalmi postdating the Bavli version of this story. Both scholars agree, however, that the Bavli shares many points with the Tosefta that are not in the Yerushalmi.

satiric statements.[66] For example, the elders of Betera repeatedly denigrate Hillel as a Babylonian, only to have the roles reversed at the end when Hillel comes to power and he rebukes them in return. The most significant difference for our purposes is that T. Pesaḥim 4:13–14 has Hillel present his midrashic proofs alongside his received tradition all at once, and the elders of Betera immediately accept his teaching. The Yerushalmi, however, introduces resistance and limitations to Hillel's exegesis. The elders of Betera rudely reject the former and proceed to list detailed rebuttals of each of Hillel's hermeneutical methodologies. This stands in stark contrast to their enthusiastic embrace of Hillel's apodictic tradition. This Yerushalmi, at least in its portrayal of the elders of Betera, maintains a skeptical stance towards the hermeneutical rules by showing how easily they can be refuted, limiting their applicability, and promoting received tradition.[67]

Although the elders of Betera in the Yerushalmi reject rhetorical reasoning, the sugya as a whole ironically follows the arrangement of rhetorical oratory, as discussed in previous chapters. After narrating the circumstances of the case, the storyteller introduces the three different proofs that Hillel will use.[68] The sugya then presents the details of each proof and continues with the elders' rejection of each proof in turn. In a typical monological declamation, the refutation section serves to preempt or respond to any objections from the opposition.[69] This sugya veers from the typical rhetorical structure by having the opposing party itself express its objections, which are never refuted.[70] Finally, the peroration closes the narrative with the story of Hillel's inauguration as patriarch.

[66] David Lifshitz, "ʿAliyato shel Hillel la-nesi'ut be-askpaqlariah satirit," *Moreshet Yisrael* 5 (2008): 18–30.

[67] One can trace how the Yerushalmi may have developed from the Tosefta. After all, the Tosefta also says that Hillel's audience harassed him after he first introduced his view (see p. 185 n. 43), though that resistance seems to have been directed at the sarcastic style of Hillel's opening remark rather than focused on the use of exegetical rules. The Yerushalmi storyteller may have further wondered why there was a need in the Tosefta for an argument from tradition following the exegetical proofs. A logical solution is that Hillel's audience must have remained unconvinced by the latter, thus requiring the former. All the Yerushalmi does is move the listeners' objections after all of Hillel's exegetical proofs.

[68] I am analyzing the entire sugya as a single unit that might have been presented by a later teacher to an audience. One can also, however, pick out Hillel's own words and perform a rhetorical analysis on his speech. He, in fact, begins with a provocative exordium that grabs everyone's attention, "Do we have but one Passover alone… " The narrative is the case at hand, which he has no need to repeat. Hillel then continues with the partition, proof, and finally the peroration where he testifies to the tradition received from Shemaya and Avtalion.

[69] Aristotle, *On Rhetoric*, III.17.14–15.

[70] See similarly on p. 127 n. 82.

Since the sugya approvingly cites a series of statements by R. Yose b. R. Bon limiting the application of *gezerah shavah,* it would not be accurate to say that the redactors ascribe the hesitation at the hermeneutical rules to the elders of Betera. Rather, the rejection of Hillel's hermeneutics in the Yerushalmi, not found in the Tosefta, reflects the rabbinic redactor's own anxieties about the application of the rules.

The Bavli version of the story[71] consists of two parts: first, it cites a version of the story similar to that of the Tosefta, then it follows up with an addendum that echoes the Yerushalmi's insertions.[72] The first part of the Bavli has Hillel simply present two midrashic proofs from a *qal va-ḥomer* and a *gezerah shavah,* which are immediately accepted. It records no objection to Hillel's reasoning and requires no recourse to a received tradition specifically about this law. According to David Rosental, this contrast between the Yerushalmi and Bavli versions of this story exemplifies a more general difference between the Talmuds about the relative value of tradition versus reason.[73] Elaborating on this point, Rubenstein demonstrates that the Yerushalmi generally praises memorization of traditions as the highest value, while the Bavli denigrates these skills as trivial. Instead, the Bavli celebrates dialectics, argumentation, and exegetical dexterity.[74]

This contrast between the Talmuds certainly has strong basis in other sources, but must not be exaggerated for this text. The Bavli, after all, retains the description of Hillel as a student of Shemaya and Avtalion, which suggests that he in fact did have a tradition from his teachers.[75] Furthermore, the second part of the Bavli contains rejections

[71] B. Pesaḥim 66a, the second part of the Bavli is quoted below. See translation of the entire story at Rubenstein, *Rabbinic Stories,* 74–6.

[72] The Bavli, understandably, does not include the satiric denigration of Hillel as a Babylonian, as found in the Yerushalmi.

[73] David Rosental, "Mesorot Ereṣ-Yisraeliyot ve-darkan le-Bavel," *Cathedra* 92 (1999): 34–6; and see similarly at Binyamin Lau, *The Sages: Character, Context and Creativity* (Jerusalem: Koren, 2010), 189–90. See also Yadin, *Scripture and Tradition,* 196.

[74] Rubenstein, *Culture,* 39–53. See also Israel Ben-Shalom, "'And I Took Unto Me Two Staves: The One I Called Beauty and the Other I Called Bands' (Zakh. 11:7)," [Hebrew] in *Dor-Le-Dor: From the End of Biblical Times up to the Redaction of the Talmud. Studies in Honor of Joshua Efron,* ed. A. Oppenheimer and A. Kasher (Jerusalem: Bialik, 1995): 215–34; and Hidary, *Dispute,* 17–27.

[75] See Lieberman, *Tosefta ki-fshutah,* Pesaḥim, 566–7. That Hillel did have a tradition permitting the slaughter of the Passover sacrifice on the Sabbath becomes obvious in the second half of the story where Hillel recalls a tradition about how to bring the slaughtering knives to the Temple; see Katz, "Stories," 104–5.

of Hillel's proofs, except that they are recorded after the story rather than in the middle.[76] The Bavli cites and analyzes Hillel's proofs:[77]

> [A] The master said: "Also, it can be deduced from a *qal va-ḥomer*. If the regular sacrifice, for which one is not punished with excision, supersedes the Sabbath, then the Passover, for which one is punished with excision – is it not logical that it supersedes the Sabbath?"
>
> One can refute it: the regular sacrifice is brought more often and is completely burnt.[78]
>
> They say, he [Hillel] first told them the *qal va-ḥomer* and they refuted it and then he told them the *gezerah shavah*.
>
> [B] But since he learned the *gezerah shavah* [from tradition], why did he need to tell them the *qal va-ḥomer*?
>
> Rather, he spoke to them in their terms: it is well regarding the *gezerah shavah* since you have not learned it and[79] one does not infer a *gezerah shavah* on his own. However, they should have learned from a *qal va-ḥomer* on their own.
>
> They told him, "The *qal va-ḥomer* is also refuted since the regular sacrifice is brought more often and is completely burnt."

As Halivni points out, parts [A] and [B] oppose each other in their text and interpretation of the *baraita*.[80] According to [A], Hillel presented the *qal va-ḥomer*, which Bnei Betera rejected, followed by the *gezerah shavah*, which they accepted. According to [B], Hillel first presented the *gezerah shavah*, which Bnei Betera could only accept because Hillel had a tradition behind it, followed by the *qal va-ḥomer*, which Hillel hoped they would accept based on reason alone. This entire gloss, especially the rejection of the *qal va-ḥomer* by Bnei Betera, closely aligns with the Yerushalmi version of the story.[81] Read with this gloss, the Bavli, like the Yerushalmi, also pictures this group of Temple functionaries valuing tradition over hermeneutical rules, towards which they show great

76 This is noted by Guttmann, "Foundations of Rabbinic Judaism," 466.

77 B. Pesaḥim 66a. Translation follows MS Columbia.

78 This shows that in some respects, the regular offering is actually weightier than the Passover sacrifice and therefore one cannot deduce from the regular offering that the Passover supersedes the Sabbath.

79 Printed editions read, "for." Translation follows MSS Munich 6, JTS, and Columbia. MS Vatican 109 and 134 omit from here to the end of the sentence and MS Vatican 125 adds it as a gloss.

80 Halivni, *Meqorot u-mesorot*, Pesaḥim, 468–9.

81 See p. 192 n. 65.

skepticism. Here too, this resistance to the rules probably reflects the Bavli redactors' own anxieties about exegetical derivations, which they express through the dialogue they ascribe to Bnei Betera.

To summarize, the Tosefta reflects an older Tannaitic version of the story that may retain some historical kernels about Hillel's involvement in promoting hermeneutics to ground tradition. According to this source, whether it dates back to Hillel or to a later point during the Tannaitic period, the exegetical methods were deemed a useful tool to combat Sadducean attacks. The Talmudic elaborations, however, include a skeptical viewpoint to the exegetical methods based on reason, which can be more dangerous and unwieldy than helpful. While the viewpoint of the rabbis and redactors remains ambiguous in these stories, the next section will elaborate on the skeptical stance expressed by the rabbis and redactors of these stories and will further trace the presence of this viewpoint already in some Tannaitic sources. We will accomplish this by examining the two most frequently used rules, the *qal va-ḥomer* and the *gezerah shavah*, in more detail.

QAL VA-ḤOMER

Adolf Schwarz argued over a century ago that the *qal va-ḥomer* was a type of Aristotelian syllogism.[82] Louis Jacobs, however, demonstrates that these two forms of reasoning fundamentally differ from each

[82] Adolf Schwarz, *Der Hermeneutische Syllogismus in der Talmudischen Litteratur, Ein Beitrag Zur Geschichte Der Logik Im Morgenlande* (Karlsruhe, 1901). Schwarz recognized that the *qal va-ḥomer* does not have the form of a complete syllogism. He therefore posits that it is an enthymeme (ibid., 159–60 and 172), which Aristotle defines as a rhetorical syllogism wherein not all of the premises are stated explicitly (*On Rhetoric*, I.2.13 and II.22.3). However, there is little difference between the enthymeme according to this definition and the full syllogism; one need only provide the missing premise. Therefore, the criticism of Schwarz noted below still applies since the typical *qal va-ḥomer* cannot be faithfully translated into a formal syllogism. Since Schwarz's time, scholars such as Myles Burnyeat have rejected the traditional strict understanding of an enthymeme as a deductive syllogism with one premise implied and argue that Aristotle meant to include within the term enthymeme various types of arguments that are plausible even if defeasible. This would include the *topos* of the more and the less (*On Rhetoric*, I.2.21), even when based on probabilities (*Prior Analytics* 2.27). Since the *qal va-ḥomer* falls within this description it could be called an enthymeme according to its more inclusive definition, but that is not how Schwarz meant it. See further at Myles Burnyeat, "Enthymeme: Aristotle on the Logic of Persuasion," in *Aristotle's Rhetoric: Philosophical Essays*, ed. David Furley and Alexander Nehemas (Princeton: Princeton University Press, 1994): 3–55; and Douglas Walton and Fabrizio Macagno, "Enthymemes, Argumentation Schemes and Topics," *Logique and Analyse* 205 (2009): 39–56. See also Arthur Prior, "Argument A Fortiori,"

other.[83] The Aristotelian categorical syllogism relates a genus and a species: if the species falls within the category of the genus then it will have the same properties that are common to all members of that genus. This is different from the *qal va-ḥomer* where two different categories are compared as long as they have an essential commonality that relates the two.[84] For example, Mishnah Ḥulin 12:5 teaches: "If regarding a light commandment (the prohibition against sending away the mother bird in Deut 22:6–7) which is like an *issar*,[85] the Torah says, 'in order that you may fare well and have a long life' (Deut 22:7), then *qal va-ḥomer* regarding weighty commandments of the Torah." This is clearly not a syllogism since weighty commandments are not a species of light commandments; they are comparable simply because they are both commandments.

Rather, as discussed above, the *qal va-ḥomer* is a rhetorical form of reasoning that Aristotle and Cicero list as a type of analogy. Quintilian also provides an example of analogy from lesser to greater in a legal context: "If it is lawful to kill a thief in the night [when one is not sure if he threatens violence], how much more is it lawful to kill an armed robber [who definitely threatens violence]?"[86] The midrash includes a similar a fortiori argument, except it deals with a thief who does not threaten violence who may not be killed and teaches the contrapositive: "If when a person definitely comes to steal [without threatening violence] and he [the homeowner] kills him [the thief], he [the homeowner] is liable, all the more so [*qal va-ḥomer*] one about whom there is a doubt whether he comes to steal or whether he does not come to steal [that his killer would be liable]."[87]

Analysis 9, no. 3 (1949): 49–50, for an attempt to express a fortiori arguments as syllogisms.

83 Jacobs, *Studies*, 3–8. See also Dolgopolski, *What is Talmud*, 285 n. 58.

84 See Arnold Kunst, "An Overlooked Type of Inference," *Bulletin of the School of Oriental and African Studies* 10, no. 4 (1942): 986–8; Towner, "Hermeneutical Systems," 115; Handelman, *Slayers of Moses*, 52–7; and Avi Sion, *Judaic Logic: A Formal Analysis of Biblical, Talmudic and Rabbinic Logic* (Geneva: Editions Slatkine, 1997), 60.

85 This prohibition would not require an expenditure of more than an *issar*, a very small amount of money, if one did not send the bird away and instead had to buy new one.

86 *Institutes of Oratory*, 5.10.88. For more examples of a fortiori reasoning in classical writings, see Lysias, "On the Murder of Eratosthenes," 1.31–32; Lysias, "On the Olive Stump," 7.26; Isocrates, "Against Lochites," 20.2–3; Dinarchus, "Against Demosthenes," 1.45; Gaius, Institutes, 2.73; and further at Georgiana Palmer, "The Topoi of Aristotle's 'Rhetoric' as Exemplified in the Orators" (PhD diss., University of Chicago, 1932), 15–19.

87 Mekhilta d'R. Ishmael, Nezikin 13. See also Jeffrey Rubenstein, "Nominalism and Realism Again," *Diné Israel* 30 (2015), 88–97, who has similarly rejected the categorization of *qal va-ḥomer* as "natural or logical."

Having established the close affinity between the rhetorical comparison of lesser and greater, and the rabbinic *qal va-ḥomer*, we can now analyze the rabbis' use of and attitude towards the *qal va-ḥomer* as a window into their view of reason and rhetoric in general. We find, on the one hand, that rabbinic literature includes well over one thousand *qallin va-ḥamurin*.[88] This ubiquitous use shows that the rabbis are entrenched within the rhetorical tradition, or at least their version of it. On the other hand, as we will demonstrate below, the rabbis also show a deep ambivalence and skepticism about the application of *qal va-ḥomer* reasoning in many cases. They are apprehensive about *qal va-ḥomer* arguments that contradict tradition and recognize that *qal va-ḥomer* reasoning can be used in mutually opposing directions, thus casting doubt on its very reliability.

For example, R. Yoḥanan, cited in the epigraph to this book, demands that a judge who opens the deliberation in a capital case must be able to argue that a reptile is pure and impure in one hundred ways.[89] The Talmud continues with an illustration:

> R. Yannai said: If a snake, which kills [and causes impurity], is itself pure, then all the more so a mouse, which does not kill, should be pure. Or the inverse: if a mouse, which does not kill, is impure, then all the more so a snake, which does kill, should be impure. R. Pineḥas objected, "Behold a scorpion kills, yet it is pure." A tradition was found stating, "[The same reasoning applies to] both a snake and a scorpion."[90]

By assuming that an animal which causes impurity by killing must be more impure than a non-lethal animal, R. Yannai is able to prove that the carcass of a mouse is pure – a direct contradiction to Leviticus 11:29. Although R. Pineḥas cites a counterexample, the Talmud quickly upholds R. Yannai's *qal va-ḥomer* by subsuming the counterexample within the original argument itself. If one can contradict the Torah using such reasoning, then that does not mean that the Torah is incorrect but rather that the method of reasoning is not always reliable.

The extent to which *qal va-ḥomer* does not represent universal logic but rather subjective reasoning is further evident by the numerous

88 There are over five hundred in Tannaitic midrashim, many hundreds in amoraic midrashim, and more than five hundred others in the Bavli, although many of these are repeating parallels. There are fewer *qallin va-ḥamurin* in the Mishnah, Tosefta and Yerushalmi.

89 See p. 1 n. 3.

90 Y. Sanhedrin 4:1, 22a. See parallels at B. Sanhedrin 17a-b and B. `Eruvin 13b.

examples where controversy erupts over the validity of a *qal va-ḥomer*. M. Makhshirin 6:8, for example, records an extended debate over the validity of a *qal va-ḥomer* presented by R. Akiva and rejected by his colleagues.[91] In the following controversy, Rabbi and his colleagues utilize the same aspect of a law to argue both for the stringency and leniency of that law:

> "He shall bring his wife to the priest" (Num 5:15): The biblical ordinance is that the husband brings his wife [who is suspected of adultery] to the priest, but [the sages] said: Two disciples of the sages are to accompany him on the way lest he have intercourse with her.
>
> Rabbi [Yehudah] says: Her husband is deemed reliable as may be learned by *qal va-ḥomer*. Since in the case of a menstruant the husband is deemed reliable, and that is a transgression whose punishment is *karet* [cutting off], in the case of the suspected adulteress, [intercourse with whom] is not punishable by *karet*, does it not stand to reason that her husband be deemed reliable with regard to her?
>
> They said to him: No, for if that is the case for a menstruant who is permissible after the prohibition, then surely it is thus with the suspected adulteress who is not permissible after her prohibition, and, moreover, since intercourse with the wife is not punishable by *karet*, the husband is not deemed reliable with regard to her.[92]

The very same quality of the menstruant – that relations with her are punishable by *karet* – is considered as a reason to deem the menstruant both more stringent as well as less stringent than the suspected adulteress. If one is able to argue a *qal va-ḥomer* in diametrically opposite directions, then it can hardly be considered a foolproof method for deriving laws from the Torah. It is true that R. Yehudah ben Betera, in excoriating Yoḥanan ben Bagbag, presumes that deducing laws by *qal va-ḥomer* is a simple matter, saying: "I was sure that you are an expert in the depths of the Torah. Are you ignorant of how to reason from a *qal va-ḥomer*?"[93] But numerous cases of *qal va-ḥomer* arguments that contradict the Torah or oral tradition, or whose logical validity is contested, show that *qal va-ḥomer* reasoning is anything but simple and often subject to rebuttal.

[91] See further examples at M. Shevi`it 7:1; M. Nazir 7:4; M. Eduyot 6:2; M. Ḥulin 2:7; and M. Keritot 3:9-10 (= Sifra, Ḥova, 1, 11–13).

[92] Sifre Num 8. Translation from Yadin, *Scripture as Logos*, 84–5. See a similar phenomenon at B. Berakhot 21a.

[93] Sifre Num 117.

Similarly, using a *qal va-ḥomer*, one sage argues the absurd thesis that almost all marriages are prohibited:

> This is a question that R. Yose ben Tadai from Tiberius asked Rabban Gamaliel: If my wife, to whom I am permitted, I am prohibited from her daughter, then a married woman, to whom I am prohibited, all the more so should I not be prohibited to her daughter?" He replied, "Go out and provide for me [an answer regarding] a high priest concerning whom it is stated, 'But he shall marry a virgin from his nation' (Lev 21:14), and I will provide you [with an answer regarding] all the rest of Israel." Another version: [Rabban Gamaliel replied,] "We do not use reason to uproot a matter from the Torah." And Rabban Gamaliel excommunicated him.[94]

R. Yose ben Tadai reasons that since one is prohibited from cohabiting with his step-daughter, even though he is permitted to her mother (his wife), then he should all the more so be prohibited from cohabiting with any other married woman's daughter, considering that he is prohibited from cohabiting with her mother. By focusing on the permissibility of cohabiting with a woman's mother as a factor in one's own permissibility to the woman herself, R. Yose ben Tadai succeeds in prohibiting all women whose parents are married. This is obviously a ridiculous conclusion, but it poses a logical challenge to Rabban Gamaliel. Rabban Gamaliel does not question the reasoning behind the *qal va-ḥomer* but simply points out that this contradicts the Torah and therefore must be invalid. A high priest, after all, may marry a virgin despite being prohibited in all cases from marrying her mother, even if the mother is divorced or widowed. In a second version, Rabban Gamaliel excommunicates R. Yose ben Tadai for using such sophistic reasoning to undermine the Torah.[95]

While in the cases just cited it is a rabbi who proposes a fallacious *qal va-ḥomer*, other texts present the *qal va-ḥomer* as a favorite method of rival sectarians. As Daniel Schwartz shows, of the twenty or so explicit controversies between the Pharisees and the Sadducees/Boethusians mentioned in rabbinic literature, approximately half hinge on a *qal*

[94] Derekh Ereṣ, `Arayot, 6. See parallel at Yalqut Shi`oni, Emor, 631.

[95] On sophistical *qal va-ḥomer* inferences, see M. Mielziner, "The Talmudic Syllogism or the Inference of Kal Vechomer," *Hebrew Review* 1 (1880): 51–3. For more on reflexively uprooting interpretations, see Azzan Yadin, "The Chain Novel and the Problem of Self-Undermining Interpretation," *Diné Israel* 25 (2008): 43–71.

va-ḥomer.[96] In some cases, the rabbis use a *qal va-ḥomer* to show the absurdity of the Sadducean position. In most of the cases, the Sadducees present a *qal va-ḥomer* to disprove the rabbinic view. For example:

> The Sadducees say, "We complain against you Pharisees, for you say that I am liable for my ox or ass that cause damage but I am not liable for my slave or maidservant who cause damage. If my ox and my ass regarding whom I am not responsible to ensure that they observe commandments, yet I am responsible for their damage, all the more so my slave and my maidservant regarding whom I am responsible to ensure that they observe commandments, I should certainly be responsible for their damage." They said to them, "No. If you say [that I am liable] regarding my ox and my ass, which have no intelligence, would you say [that I am liable] regarding my slave and my maidservant who have intelligence? If I make them angry, they will go and burn another's grain pile and I will be liable to pay."[97]

The Sadducees here analogize two types of responsibility: the responsibility of an owner to ensure that his property adheres to the commandments of the Torah and the responsibility of an owner to pay for damage caused by his property. The greater the former, they reason, the greater should be the latter. While an owner must ensure that his slaves fulfill commandments, he need not stop his animal from grazing on its own on the Sabbath. Since an owner is liable to pay for the damages of his animal, though he is not responsible for its fulfillment of commandments, he should all the more so be responsible to pay for the damages of his slave, for whose fulfillment of commandments the owner is responsible.[98] The Pharisees successfully rebut this argument by severing the analogy between the two cases. Considering that, unlike animals, slaves have intelligence, it would be absurd for the owner to be held responsible for his slave's actions.[99]

Schwartz argues that there is likely some degree of historical authenticity behind some of these traditions and that the Sadducees used the *qal va-ḥomer* extensively because it is the most logical form of reasoning, and therefore it fits with their legal realism.[100] However, it

[96] Daniel Schwartz, "Ti`une 'qal va-ḥomer' ke-realism Ṣaddoqi," *Masechet* 5 (2006): 145–56. See also Daube, "Texts and Interpretations," 186–7.

[97] M. Yadaim 4:7.

[98] See further at Schwartz, "Ti`une 'qal va-ḥomer'," 153.

[99] See also Daube, "Texts and Interpretations," 196–8.

[100] Schwartz, "Ti`une 'qal va-ḥomer'," 155–6; and see further on p. 285. Schwartz further proposes that the rabbis refrained from using *qal va-ḥomer* reasoning during their

is doubtful that the Sadducees themselves historically based their laws on *qal va-ḥomer* reasoning, considering that the Dead Sea Scrolls and other Second Temple literature record very few if any examples of a fortiori arguments.[101] Qumran and related sectarians envision a system of law and interpretation that accepts a Platonic-like view of absolute unchanging law that accords with nature; biblical interpretation, in their view, is only valid through direct prophecy.[102] They therefore would have little need or regard for a *topos* like *qal va-ḥomer* that derives from the realm of rhetoric and depends on human reason. It is possible that the Sadducees sometimes cited *qal va-ḥomer* arguments polemically, to use the Pharisees own arguments against them. Most likely, however, the rabbis invented these dialogues to express their anxieties about their own legal derivations.[103] By placing such subversive arguments into the mouths of the Sadducees, the rabbis denounce those, such as R. Yose ben Tadai, who would use this form of reasoning against the rabbinic establishment.[104] These Sadducean debates reflect the rabbis' self-doubts towards such reasoning and their skepticism towards its ability to reach valid conclusions.

polemics with the Sadducees, and only reclaimed its use after the threat of sectarianism was gone and Christianity rose up. However, rabbinic literature shows continuous use of the *qal va-ḥomer* throughout the generations of the Tannaim.

101 See Bernstein and Koyfman, "Interpretation," 79; and Richard Hidary, "Hellenism and Hermeneutics: Did the Qumranites and Sadducees Use Qal Va-ḥomer Arguments?," (forthcoming). For the case of M. Yadaim 4:7, specifically, see Eyal Regev, *The Sadducees and Their Halakhah: Religion and Society in the Second Temple Period* [Hebrew] (Jerusalem: Yad Ben-Zvi Press, 2005), 107–9 and references at n. 27.

102 Steven Fraade, "Looking for Legal Midrash at Qumran," in *Biblical Perspectives: Early Use and Interpretation of the Bible in Light of the Dead Sea Scrolls*, ed. Michael E. Stone and Esther Chazon (Leiden: Brill, 1998): 77–8. See similarly at Mandel, "Midrashic Exegesis and Its Precedents in the Dead Sea Scrolls," 149–68.

103 For a similar interpretation of rabbinic debates with outsiders, see Christine Hayes, "Displaced Self-Perceptions: The Deployment of 'Mînîm' and Romans in b. Sanhedrin 90b–91a," in *Religious and Ethnic Communities in Later Roman Palestine*, ed. Hayim Lapin (Bathesda: University Press of Maryland, 1998): 271–89. See also N. Janowitz, "Rabbis and Their Opponents: The Construction of the 'Min' in Rabbinic Anecdotes," *Journal of Early Christian Studies* 6, no. 3 (1998): 44–62; Christine Hayes, "The 'Other' in Rabbinic Literature," in *The Cambridge Companion to Talmud and Rabbinic Literature*, ed. Charlotte Elisheva Fonrobert and Martin Jaffee (Cambridge: Cambridge University Press, 2007): 259; and Jenny Labendz, *Socratic Torah: Non-Jews in Rabbinic Intellectual Culture* (Oxford: Oxford University Press, 2013), 9–11.

104 Schwartz, "Ti`une 'qal va-ḥomer'," 154–5. Koraḥ similarly challenges Moses' authority using *qal va-ḥomer* arguments. See Num Rabbah 18:3 and its parallel at Y. Sanhedrin 10:1, 27d–28a.

Considering the unwieldiness and untrustworthiness of the *qal va-ḥomer*, we can understand why rabbinic literature limited its use. Some texts insist that a *qal va-ḥomer* could only be used to uphold a tradition but not to derive a new law. For example, M. Yebamot 8:3 teaches:[105]

> An Amonite and a Moabite are prohibited [in marriage to a Jew] and their prohibition is forever; however, their females are permitted immediately. An Egyptian and an Edomite are prohibited for only three generations [after conversion to Judaism], both males and females. R. Shimon permits [Egyptian and Edomite] females immediately. R. Shimon said, "It is a *qal va-ḥomer*. If in a place where [the Torah] prohibits the males forever, it permits the females immediately, in a place where it prohibits the males for only three generations should we not all the more so permit the females immediately?" They told him, "If it is a tradition we will accept but if it is based only on a deduction [from a *qal va-ḥomer*] then we have a response." He said to them, "No, I am teaching a tradition."

As with the Yerushalmi version of the Hillel story cited above, the minority position is granted legitimacy only because it is based on a received tradition. *Qal va-ḥomer* reasoning alone proves insufficient. If the sage presenting the *qal va-ḥomer* lacks a tradition, then his reasoning may be rejected as in M. Nazir 7:4, where R. Akiva uses a *qal va-ḥomer* to challenge a law taught by R. Eliezer in the name of R. Yehoshua. R. Eliezer responds: "What is this Akiva? We do not reason here from a *qal va-ḥomer*." R. Yehoshua similarly rebuts R. Akiva, saying: "You have spoken well; however, this is how they taught the tradition."

This strict limitation may have been necessary at the height of anti-halakhic polemics. For most times and places, however, the *qal va-ḥomer* was used even to derive new laws.[106] Nevertheless, various rabbinic sources include at least three significant limitations to its application. The first is that one may not deduce a law that is more stringent than the very source of the derivation.[107] For example, Num 12:14 records an early example of a fortiori reasoning: "The Lord said to

[105] See parallel at Sifre Deut 253. For similar cases where an individual challenges the majority opinion using a *qal va-ḥomer*, see M. Baba Batra 9:7, M. Makhshirin 6:8, T. Ketubot 5:1 (= Sifre Num 117), and Sifre Num 8, cited on p. 199.

[106] See Y. Pesaḥim 6:1, 33a, cited above: "One may infer a *qal va-ḥomer* on his own."

[107] Lysias, "On the Murder of Eratosthenes," 1.31, also does not seem to abide by this principle.

Moses, 'If her father spat in her face, would she not bear her shame for seven days? Let her be shut out of camp for seven days.'" Sifre Numbers 106 comments:[108]

> If her father, who is of flesh and blood, [requires her to be punished for] seven days, then He Who Spoke and Created the World [should require her to be punished for] fourteen days. It is enough that what is deduced should be like the source of the deduction (*dayo la-ba min ha-din lihiot ka-nidon*). Just as her father, who is flesh and blood, [requires her to be punished for] seven days, so too He Who Spoke and Created the World [requires her to be punished for] seven days.

Although one might be tempted to apply a more severe punishment to one shamed by God rather than by a human, God declares it sufficient to punish Miriam with the same seven-day banishment.[109] The authority of the *qal va-ḥomer*, comments Azzan Yadin, "does not derive from human reasoning but from its explicit use in the Torah."[110] According to the Sifre, both the use of inference by *qal va-ḥomer* as well as the limitation of *dayo* are exemplified in the Torah by God Himself.

The second limitation confirms this reading. Mishnah Yadaim 3:2 teaches: "One may not derive matters of Torah from matters of the scribes, nor matters of the scribes from the words of the Torah, nor matters of the scribes from matters of the scribes." The reason seems to be that the scribes[111] legislated decrees and enactments according to the needs of the times and were not necessarily consistent in being more stringent in weighty matters.[112] The Bavli similarly rules: "One may not infer using a *qal va-ḥomer* from a legal tradition (halakha)."[113] Rashi comments: "The oral law was not given to be interpreted through the

[108] See also Sifra, Baraita d'R. Yishmael and further analysis at Menahem Kahana, *Sifre on Numbers: An Annotated Edition* (Jerusalem: The Hebrew University Magnes Press, 2011), 1.264–5 and 3.690–92. On the principle of *dayo* generally, see *Encyclopedia Talmudit*, s.v. "*dayo la-ba min ha-din lihiot ka-nidon*"; and Allen Conan Wiseman, "A Contemporary Examination of the A Fortiori Argument Involving Jewish Traditions" (PhD diss., University of Waterloo, 2010).

[109] There is some disagreement on the applicability of this limitation; see B. Baba Qama 25a and B. Baba Meṣi'a 95a.

[110] Yadin, *Scripture as Logos*, 84. See further herein p. 210–1.

[111] The term "scribes" here simply refers to rabbinic sages or their Second Temple predecessors. On the history of this term, see Anthony J. Saldarini, *Pharisees, Scribes and Sadducees in Palestinian Society: A Sociological Approach* (Wilmington: Michael Glazier, 1988), 241–76.

[112] See R. Asher (Rosh) in his commentary to this Mishnah.

[113] B. Nazir 57a and B. Shabbat 132a.

thirteen principles."[114] That is, the applicability of the exegetical principles to the Torah depends not on their rationality but rather on the nature and character (*midah*) of the Torah.[115]

A third limitation is that the rabbis will not impose a punishment on the basis of a *qal va-ḥomer* (*en `onshin min ha-din*).[116] Sifra, Kedoshim, *perek* 10, 10, derives this rule from the Torah itself:

> "If a man marries his sister, the daughter of his father or the daughter of his mother" (Lev 20:17). I only know [he is prohibited to marry] the daughter of his father who is not the daughter of his mother and the daughter of his mother who is not the daughter of his father. How do I know [he is prohibited from his sister] from his father and from his mother? Scripture teaches, "his sister" – in any way. Even without Scripture teaching this, I can derive it by *qal va-ḥomer*: If he is liable for his sister from his father and not from his mother or [for his sister] from his mother and not from his father, all the more so [he should be liable for his sister] from his father and from his mother. However, if you say so, you have punished based on a *qal va-ḥomer*. Therefore, it is stated, "his sister," to teach you that they do not punish based on a *qal va-ḥomer*.

By adding the words "his sister," the verse clarifies that one is liable for marrying his full sister and not only his half-sister. Although one could logically derive the liability for one's full sister from the liability for one's half-sister, the verse nevertheless lists that case explicitly with the words "his sister" in order to teach that logic alone would be an insufficient basis for meting out punishment.[117] The continuation of the Sifra teaches further that one may also not derive a warning from a

[114] Rashi to B. Shabbat 132a, s.v. "*Aqiva.*" See further on this principle at Faur, *Golden Doves*, 14, and 100–8.

[115] See further at Yadin, *Scripture as Logos*, 120–1. Also related to this is the Ishmaelian rule that one may not make an inference from the result of another inference, on which see Epstein, *Mevo'ot le-sifrut ha-Tannaim*, 524–5.

[116] On this principle, see Yadin, *Scripture as Logos*, 83–6. This limitation was not universally accepted; see Epstein, *Mevo'ot le-sifrut ha-Tannaim*, 525–7; and Elyakim Friedman, "'En `onshin min ha-din," *Mi-perot Ereṣ Ha-ṣevi* (2009): 11–12. Greek writers regularly apply a fortiori arguments to punishments, as, for example, Isocrates, "Against Lochites," 20.3.

[117] See similarly, Mekhilta d'R. Ishmael, Nezikin 11, and analysis at Yadin, *Scripture as Logos*, 85–6. Even where a *qal va-ḥomer* does not involve a punishment, the Bavli states, "Matters that can be derived by *qal va-ḥomer*, Scripture nevertheless takes the trouble to write" (B. Pesaḥim 18b, et al.). The *qal va-ḥomer* inference is not considered significant enough to make redundant an explicit verse teaching the same thing. This rule, however, is not agreed upon by all (B. Pesaḥim 77b).

qal va-ḥomer.[118] Significantly, the Bavli cites this limitation as a reason not to accept a Sadducean legal interpretation based on a *qal va-ḥomer.*[119]

The reason for this limitation seems to be that, as Samuel ha-Nagid explains, "Sometimes one is mistaken in his reasoning and the *qal va-ḥomer* is invalid even though we do not realize it."[120] The court cannot physically punish someone on the basis of uncertain, even if convincing, reasoning. Susan Handelman similarly concludes from these restrictions that the *qal va-ḥomer* "is not a universal principle or an apodictic premise" but rather can provide us with only "a relative conclusion based on a hypothesis and subject to continual testing and scrutiny."[121]

Howard Eilberg-Schwartz invokes the rabbinic *qal va-ḥomer* as an example of a form of reasoning that a Western mind cannot make sense of and therefore as proof that all rationality is relative. The *qal va-ḥomer,* he writes, made sense for the rabbis because it functioned within a given set of myths regarding the perfection of the Torah, just as modern science makes sense for moderns within its given set of myths.[122] What he misses is that the rabbis themselves recognized the problematic nature of *qal va-ḥomer* arguments and were the first to criticize irrational arguments presented by their colleagues. They never made the claim that a *qal va-ḥomer* furnished syllogistic proof; instead, they worked within the realm of rhetoric: "The tasks the rabbis faced were not tasks that could be solved with mathematics, but instead tasks of finding the most persuasive analogy in a world of infinite analogies."[123] The tenuousness and arbitrariness that we often sense in *qal va-ḥomer* arguments, and that the ancient rabbis sensed as well, is inherent to the realm of rhetoric. Thus, while the rabbis made extensive use of *qal va-ḥomer* reasoning, they were also aware of its pitfalls and knew to proceed with caution.

[118] Sifra, Kedoshim, *perek* 10, 12.

[119] See B. Makkot 5b.

[120] See his introduction printed in the Vilna edition of the Bavli at the end of tractate Berakhot. See further in Friedman, "'En `onshin min ha-din."

[121] Handelman, *Slayers of Moses*, 56–7.

[122] Howard Eilberg-Schwartz, "Myth, Inference and the Relativity of Reason: An Argument from the History of Judaism," in *Myth and Philosophy*, ed. F. Reynolds and D. Tracy (Albany: SUNY, 1990): 247–86.

[123] Naomi Janowits and Andrew Lazarus, "Rabbinic Methods of Inference and the Rationality Debate," *The Journal of Religion* 72, no. 4 (1992): 495. I do not dispute that reason is, to some extent, relative; that is, after all, an axiom of the rhetorical tradition. Rather, I agree with Janowits and Lazarus that Eilberg-Shwarz is mistaken in his assessment of the *qal va-ḥomer* as logic and therefore as a proof for strong relativity. Rather, it is, like the Hellenistic a fortiori, a persuasive analogy whose validity cannot be proven but must be argued.

GEZERAH SHAVAH

The *gezerah shavah* in rabbinic literature generally refers to an analogy between two laws in the Bible that share a common word. We saw a good example of a *gezerah shavah* above in Hillel's argument that since the word "at its appointed time" occurs in the context of the daily burnt offering as well as the Passover offering, we can analogize that just as the daily burnt offering supersedes the Sabbath so does the Passover offering.[124]

In Greek sources, the comparison of equals refers not to verbal analogies but to conceptual analogies, such as Cicero's comparison of houses to land regarding the law of usucapion. The original rabbinic *gezerah shavah* also seems to have been a conceptual analogy, as we find in M. Beṣah 1:6.[125] Even when *gezerot shavot* include verbal analogies, there is usually a conceptual analogy as well. However, whereas in Greek and early rabbinic analogies, the conceptual element was the focus, by the middle of the Tannaitic period, the weight of the argument shifted to the verbal. One can witness this shift in the formula found numerous times in Akivan midrashim, "let us see to which it is similar." Here is one example:

> [After a period of] seven years [you shall practice remission of debts] (Deut 15:1). Can this mean seven years for each and every individual? Behold you can reason: There is a requirement of seven years

[124] See further analysis of this exegesis at Yitzhak D. Gilat, *Studies in the Development of the Halakha* (Jerusalem: Bar-Ilan University Press, 1992), 368–9.

[125] See Lieberman, *Hellenism in Jewish Palestine*, 60. Zeitlin, "Hillel and the Hermeneutic Rules," 168–70, argues that the words "*gezerah shavah*" are later insertions into the Mishnah considering their absence from B. Beṣah 21b. However, "*gezerah shavah*" does appear in T. Beṣah 1:12–13, as Zeitlin admits. For an analysis of these sources, see Moshe Weiss, "Ha-'otentiut shel ha-shaqla ve-ṭaria be-maḥloqot bet Shamai u-vet Hillel," *Sidra* 4 (1988): 3–64.

Lieberman, *Tosefta ki-fshutah*, Yom Tov, 5.931, also cites Sifre Zuta to Num 9:2 where R. Eliezer uses the term *gezerah shavah* to refer to conceptual analogies. In fact, R. Eliezer's statement is an explanation of his earlier *qal va-ḥomer*, confirming what was stated above that *qal va-ḥomer* and *gezerah shavah* are simply two types of analogies. See also Albeck, *Mishnah*, Kodashim, 403–4; Gilat, *Studies*, 369–71; Yitzhak D. Gilat, *The Teachings of R. Eliezer Ben Hyrcanos and Their Position in the History of the Halakha* (Tel Aviv: Dvir, 1968), 55–62; and Yerahmiel Bergman, "Gezerah shavah mahi?," *Sinai* 71 (1972): 132–79. In addition to Lieberman's two examples, we should also consider texts that use the term "*shavah*" alone in the context of a conceptual analogy unrelated to Scripture. See M. Keretot 1:6 = Sifra, Tazria, *perek* 3, 1; B. Niddah 72a; and further analysis at Moshe Weiss, "Ha-gezerah shavah veha-qal va-ḥomer ba-shaqla ve-taria shel bet Shammai u-vet Hillel," *Sidra* 6 (1990): 47–50.

regarding land Sabbatical and there is a requirement of seven years regarding a debt. Just as seven years mentioned regarding land Sabbatical is for the whole world, so too seven years mentioned by a debt is for the whole world.

Or go in this direction (או כלך לדרך זו[126]): There is a requirement of seven years regarding a Hebrew slave and there is a requirement for seven years regarding debts. Just as seven years mentioned regarding a Hebrew slave means seven years for each and every individual so too seven years mentioned regarding a debt means seven years for each and every individual.

Let us see to which it is similar (נראה למי דומה)? We derive something (debts) that is not dependent on the Jubilee from something (land Sabbatical) that is not dependent on the Jubilee and let not the Hebrew slave, who is dependent on the Jubilee, serve as proof.

Or go in this direction (או כלך לדרך זו): We derive something (debts) that applies both in the Land [of Israel] and outside the Land from something (Hebrew slave) that applies both in the Land and outside the Land and let not land Sabbatical, which applies only in the Land, serve as proof.

Therefore, Scripture teaches "seven years," "seven years," for a *gezerah shavah*. Just as "seven years" (Deut 31:10) mentioned regarding land Sabbatical means seven years for the whole world, so too "seven years" (Deut 15:1) mentioned regarding a debt means seven years for the whole world.[127]

The Pentateuch includes three different laws that involve seven-year periods: debts must be remitted after seven years (Deut 15:1), the land must lie fallow in the seventh Sabbatical year (Lev 25:4), and a Hebrew slave goes free in the seventh year (Exod 21:2, Deut 15:12). The seven years for the Hebrew slave are counted individually for each slave starting from the time he or she becomes a slave. The seven years for land Sabbatical, on the other hand, follow a collective

[126] On this term, see Yaakov Elman, "The Order of Arguments in כלך-Baraitot in Relation to the Conclusion," *Jewish Quarterly Review* 79 (1989): 295–304; Shamma Friedman, "Ha-munaḥ 'o kelakh le-derekh zo' ve-shimusho be-midreshe ha-tannaim," *Sidra* 9 (1993): 61–74; Menachem Katz, "Ṣurato shel midrash halakha "o kelakh le-derekh zo'," *Mishlav* 29 (1996). That this term consistently marks out a four-part dialectical pattern is yet another indication of the rabbis' conscious effort to create and conform to preset argumentational forms.

[127] Sifre Deut 111. Translation follows text printed in Louis Finkelstein, *Sifre on Deuteronomy* (New York: The Jewish Theological Seminary of America, 1969), 171–2.

count such that the entire country leaves the land fallow during the same year. The midrash inquires whether the remission of debts should be counted individually from the start of each loan, or collectively like the land Sabbatical. The midrash then attempts to make a conceptual analogy. On the one hand, the remission of debt resembles land Sabbatical in that both apply even when the Jubilee is not in effect, unlike the law of Hebrew slaves, which does not. On the other hand, the remission of debt is akin to the freeing of Hebrew slaves in that both laws apply even outside the Land of Israel, unlike land Sabbatical, which does not. Since these conceptual analogies are inconclusive, the midrash resorts to a *gezerah shavah* using the phrase *"miqeṣ sheva` shanim,"* which occurs only in the contexts of debt remission and land Sabbatical.[128]

In this midrash, as in others of this form, the rabbis attempt to apply a conceptual analogy, only to find that one can form analogies between almost any given pair of laws by focusing on one or another aspect that they share. Conceptual analogies are thus ambiguous and inconclusive. The only reliable analogy is one that is not based on human reasoning alone but that is sanctioned by the Torah itself. If the Torah uses a phrase in only two places, then we can be sure that the Torah itself is directing us to compare the two verses.[129]

In Akivan midrashim, *gezera shavah* was generally limited to comparing words or expressions that occur only twice in the Pentateuch, as seen in the example above.[130] Ishmaelian midrashim, in contrast, allow for *gezerot shavot* to use words that occur more than twice in the Pentateuch, so long as the words are extraneous (*mufneh*) in their own contexts and therefore free to be used for the *gezerah shavah*. For example, consider the version of the

[128] Although the midrash only cites the words "seven years," I am assuming here that it implicitly refers to the entire three-word phrase, *"miqeṣ sheva shanim."* I make this assumption based on the general methodology of Akivan midrashim, as discussed in the next paragraph, to cite unique phrases, whereas just the two words "seven years" occur many times in the Torah. Alternatively, it may be that the two words "seven years" cited in the Sifre are sufficient to exclude the Exod 21 pericope; these two words may appear many times in the Torah but they are unique among the various laws involved here, appearing only in regards to debt remission and land Sabbatical.

[129] See similarly at Ouaknin, *Burnt Book*, 91–2.

[130] See Daube, "Rabbinic Methods," 241 n. 7; and Michael Chernick, *Midat "gezerah shavah": ṣuroteha ba-Midrashim uva-Talmudim* (Lod: Habermann Institute, 1994), 12–35. Even in these cases, there is nearly always also a conceptual similarity between the two contexts. Chernick, ibid., 15–16, shows that Akivan midrashim occasionally perform a *gezerah shavah* using two phrases that occur many times in the Pentateuch but only twice in a given pericope.

gezerah shavah regarding preparing the Passover on the Sabbath as it appears in Ishmaelian midrashim:

> R. Yoshiah said to him [R. Yonatan]:[131] Since it says, "Command the Israelite people and say to them: My offering [you must sacrifice to Me at its appointed time (*bemo`ado*)]" (Num 28:2). If this comes to teach that the daily burnt offering supersedes the Sabbath, this is not necessary, for it is already stated, "On the Sabbath day: two yearling lambs" (Num 28:9). What does "at its appointed time (*bemo`ado*)" come to teach?
>
> Rather, it is free (*mufneh*) to be used to draw an analogy and form a *gezerah shavah*. It is stated here "at its appointed time (*bemo`ado*)" (Num 9:2) and it is stated below "at its appointed time (*bemo`ado*)" (Num 28:1). Just as "at its appointed time (*bemo`ado*)" stated below supersedes the Sabbath, so too "at its appointed time (*bemo`ado*)" stated here supersedes the Sabbath.[132]

The very same *gezerah shavah* found in the Tosefta and Amoraic sources cited above without the feature of *mufneh* is here presented with this Ishmaelian requirement.[133] In nearly all Tannatic *gezerot shavot*, the two laws under discussion bear a conceptual linkage.[134] However, the conceptual analogy alone is insufficient to derive a law; rather, the analogy must be validated by a verbal parallel.

Taking this point even further, Yadin shows that Ishmaelian midrashim consistently limit the role of the reader as interpreter and instead present Scripture as a self-interpreting text. Yadin locates this self-interpreting activity in the term "*ha-katuv*," which serves in these midrashim as the personified Scripture that actively teaches and explains the words of the Torah. R. Ishmael advocates for a submissive reader who does not impose his will or explanation onto the text but rather waits passively until Scripture itself, *ha-katuv*, makes the meaning clear. Yadin therefore proposes that by requiring that one of the verses used in a *gezerah shavah* must be *mufneh*, R. Ishmael "shifts the agency of the analogy from the reader to Scripture. … The reader cannot roam the biblical text in search of paired terms to interpret, but must carefully attend to the language of Scripture, seeking out

[131] These two sages were both students of R. Ishmael; see B. Menaḥot 57b.

[132] Sifre Num 65. See parallels at Sifre Num 142 and Mekhilta d'R. Ishmael, Pisḥa, 5.

[133] On the relationship between this version of the midrash and that of Hillel, cited above, see Kahana, *Sifre on Numbers*, 3.439. It should be noted that Akivan midrashim also occasionally utilize *mufneh*, as in Sifra Kedoshim *perek* 9, 12; and Sifre Deut 249. See further at Chernick, *Midat "gezerah shavah,"* 44–51.

[134] See Gilat, *Studies*, 369–71; and Chernick, *Midat "gezerah shavah,"* 43–4.

redundancies that free up words for a *gezerah shavah*. No independent interpreter, the reader carries out the exegetic instructions already inscribed in the text."[135]

Accordingly, the list of thirteen *midot* in the Baraita d'R. Ishmael – which has been curiously transmitted as an introduction to the Akivan Sifra – should be read independently from the Ishmaelian midrashim, Mekhilta d'R. Ishmael and Sifre Numbers. These midrashim employ only six of the thirteen methods and refer to only two of them as *midot*.[136] The few occurrences in these midrashim of *midah* in a hermeneutic sense, do not refer to logical methods of deriving new laws but rather to a generalization about the characteristics of Scripture, which serves to limit the interpretive possibilities of various elements of biblical style.[137] Yadin argues further that even these principles are derived not from human reason but from Scripture itself. For example, Mekhilta d'R. Ishmael, Nezikin 16, teaches:

> "When a man gives to another an ass, an ox, a sheep [or all animals to guard]... " (Exod 22:9): I thus know only about an ass, an ox, and a sheep. How about any other beast? [Scripture] teaches, saying: "Or all animals to guard." I read, then, "All animals to guard." What does it teach by saying, "an ass, an ox, a sheep"? Because if it had read only "all animals" I might have understood that the keeper is liable only if all beasts have been put in his care. Therefore, it says, "an ass, an ox, a sheep," to declare him liable for each one by itself. And what does [Scripture] teach by saying, "all animals"? *Ha-katuv* comes to teach you that a general statement that is added to a specific statement includes everything.[138]

Exodus 22:9 contains a list of particulars followed by a general class, a potential source of confusion as to what exact cases the law covers. The midrash explains that the law covers all members of the class and that the particulars are also listed in order to teach that one is liable for every single member of the class and not only the collective. This midrash, however, goes further and derives from this example a general rule that any time Scripture expresses itself in such a format, it should be interpreted thus. This principle comprises the fifth of Hillel's rules and the sixth rule in the Baraita d'R. Ishmael. As discussed above, this rule can be easily explained based on parallels in Roman law. However, for this

135 Yadin, *Scripture as Logos*, 83.
136 Ibid., 99–106.
137 Ibid., 109.
138 Translation from ibid., 126.

midrash, this rule is not derived from human reason or external influence but rather from within the Torah as a self-interpreting text. The *mufneh* requirement that one verse in a *gezerah shavah* be extraneous similarly functions as a Scriptural warrant for performing an analogy between two Scriptural laws.

Moving past the Tannaitic era, we find a great expansion in the use of *gezerah shavah* arguments in both the Yerushalmi and the Bavli as the definitions of and requirements for valid *gezerot shavot* become looser. The distinctions between the schools of R. Akiva and R. Ishmael faded, and verbal analogies that would have previously been considered illegitimate by either school now came to be recognized as bona fide *gezerot shavot*.[139] With this increase in use and decrease in limitations, the *gezerah shavah* had the potential to become unwieldy in its ability to pair any two words in the Torah and thereby derive laws in almost infinite possibilities.[140] The early Amoraim therefore established the principle: "One may not infer a *gezera shava* on his own"[141] but rather can only repeat one that he has received from tradition. Similarly, "One may infer a *gezerah shavah* in order to uphold his teaching [as received from tradition] but one may not infer a *gezerah shavah* to nullify his teaching."[142] In effect, this principle does away with the entire method of *gezerah shavah* since it is entirely subsumed under and dependent upon the authority of received tradition.[143] Ironically, the expansion of the application of *gezerah shavah* led to its extinction.[144]

CONCLUSION

To summarize, many of the exegetical methods of the rabbis parallel similar *topoi* and hermeneutics of Greco-Roman rhetoric and law. This

139 Chernick, *Midat "gezerah shavah,"* 117–53.

140 See the comment of Nahmanides to Maimonides, *Sefer ha-Misvot, shoresh* 2.

141 Y. Pesaḥim 6:1, 33a, cited above. Although this principle is cited within a *baraita*, it is absent from the parallel at T. Pesaḥim 4:14. See analysis at Chernick, *Midat "gezerah shavah,"* 136–42; and Gilat, *Studies*, 372. This principle is also cited at B. Pesaḥim 66a; and B. Niddah 19b.

142 Y. Pesaḥim 6:1, 33a.

143 See further on this principle at Gilat, *Studies*, 365–8.

144 Tension over the legitimacy of the *gezerah shavah* argument is further evidenced in the statement: "Let not a *gezerah shavah* ever be light in your eyes" (B. Keretot 5a). Also relevant is B. Sanhedrin 99a cited on p. 22 n. 113. For a similar phenomenon, see Aaron Panken, *The Rhetoric of Innovation: Self-conscious Legal Change in Rabbinic Literature* (Lanham: University Press of America, 2005), who shows that the increase in rabbinic enactments by Babylonian Amoraim actually reflects greater conservatism rather than greater innovation.

is especially evident in the identification, naming and codifying of these methods in the lists attributed to Hillel and R. Ishmael, activities unparalleled anywhere in Second Temple literature. These similarities likely derived from the shared cultural and legal milieu of the early sages in Palestine (and perhaps Babylonia as well) who may have learned of such lists in their dealings with lawyers, traveling sophists, or innumerable people who studied in the nearby schools of rhetoric.

Perhaps more significant than the integration of these rhetorical methods into their program of Scriptural exegesis is how the rabbis adapted, limited, and in some cases, ultimately rejected these very methods. The reason for their apprehensiveness is made explicit by R. Yannai and R. Yose b. R. Bon who demonstrate how the *qal va-ḥomer* and *gezerah shavah* can be used to derive obviously incorrect laws concerning reptile impurity. Human reason can lead to contradictions and conclusions that oppose tradition and is simply too subjective and open-ended to serve as a method through with to explicate Divine law. Precisely because the *qal va-ḥomer* is not a genus to species syllogism but rather an analogy between different categories, there is no clear criterion for deciding the validity of the comparison. *Gezerah shavah* is also an analogy between equals, often buttressed by verbal links, but otherwise dependent on the subtleties of human reason.

Having accepted that some analogies are valid and necessary for interpreting the Bible, the rabbis pushed the possibilities of this analogical reasoning to their fullest, sometimes ad absurdum, to test its limits. This was useful for grounding previous oral tradition, authorizing new legislation, and proving the perfection of the Torah. However, it also became a double-edged sword wielded by sectarians and dissidents alike, threatening to undermine the Torah through its powerful sweep. The rabbis therefore had to limit its applicability and give highest priority to tradition. This analysis reveals that the rabbis were entrenched in the rhetorical realm, actively engaged in developing persuasive arguments and reasoning through analogies; but at the same time, they also remained skeptical of the subjectivity and volatility of human reason.

Concerning Ishmaelian midrashim, Yadin writes: "The refusal to accept a midrashic conclusion as the basis for analogy is motivated by the ineluctable contingency of human interpretation, a matter raised time and again by the midrashim themselves."[145] Instead, Ishmaelian midrashim tend to limit the role of the reader and view Scripture as

[145] Yadin, *Scripture as Logos*, 93.

self-interpreting. Therefore, Yadin argues, even if modern scholars are correct in finding parallels to techniques of Greco-Roman rhetoric, the internal view of the midrash itself traces the origin of the rules as coming from within Scripture. These midrashim do not repudiate the use of rhetorical methods; far from it, they apply them throughout the Torah. Rather, they subsume the rhetorical methodology into their overall system by integrating human reason into the scripturally led exegetical process. Neusner similarly writes that the purpose of the authorship of Sifre Numbers is to make the point that "Reason unaided by Scripture produces uncertain propositions. Reason operating within the limits of Scripture produces truth."[146]

Regarding Akivan midrashim, Neusner makes the same claim above for Sifra.[147] Yadin also shows that the early strata of the Akivan midrashim share an approach to Scriptural interpretation that is very close to that of R. Yishmael.[148] However, Yadin concludes that the later anonymous voice of the Sifra "engages in a hermeneutic of camouflage, producing a veneer of midrashic rhetoric"[149] in order to pass off halakhic oral traditions as grounded in Scripture. In this reading, these midrashim represent rather extreme sophistry.[150] Obviously, not all of rabbinic literature shares the same approach and different voices within each midrash vary in their balance between tradition, interpretation, reason, and rhetoric.

When it comes to the Talmud, Brodsky shows that the Bavli's approach to midrash takes on yet a new turn by requiring that every verse correspond exactly to one law. No two verses can teach the same law and no verse or phrase can yield multiple laws.[151] Brodsky suggests that the ban on multiple verses for one law is already in Tannaitic sources and is consistent with the progymnasmata of Theon who

[146] Jacob Neusner, *Sifre to Numbers: An American Translation and Explanation* (Atlanta: Scholars Press, 1986), 1.38.

[147] Jacob Neusner, *Uniting the Dual Torah: Sifra and Problem of the Mishnah* (Cambridge: Cambridge University Press, 1990).

[148] Yadin, *Scripture and Tradition*, 124–40.

[149] Ibid., 100.

[150] One could also argue that the sages of the midrash were genuinely trying their best to create a systematic objective reading of Scripture, even if it does not seem that way to a modern ear. In that case, the Sifra's sometimes vacuous and plodding interpretations may actually be more in line with the Bavli's approach described next. This subject, however, requires more extensive analysis.

[151] This rule does not contradict the general pluralistic approach to opinions and interpretations assumed in most of rabbinic literature and especially in the Bavli. A verse can legitimately be interpreted in two different ways by two sages as long as each sage can account for how every other law matches up with a corresponding verse.

teaches that law should be free from redundancy.[152] However, the requirement of a precise one-to-one correspondence between verses and laws is original to the Bavli. This development may derive from a desire to limit the ambiguity of language towards a more objective system of interpretation. By way of analogy, in the seventeenth century, Bishop John Wilkins proposed a new universal language that would allow for neither superfluities nor equivocals so that every word perfectly corresponds to its referent and all subjectivity is removed.[153] Wilkins thereby attempted to recover the original Divine language given to Adam just as the Bavli strives to access the Divine word.[154] The similarity between the hermeneutics of the Bavli and Wilkins suggests that both systems strive to move away from sophistical interpretation towards a perfectly objective language.

A full analysis of the variety of approaches to interpretation throughout rabbinic literature is beyond the scope of this chapter. However, I hope to have at least offered an outline of the rabbis' struggle over these issues and the complexity of their views. While they shared fundamental assumptions and methodologies with classical rhetoric, they also navigated their own unique set of approaches towards truth and subjectivity. The Dead Sea Scrolls, by way of contrast, contain almost no legal exegesis because they believed that the Teacher of Righteousness had the power of prophetic interpretation and thereby taught the one true law.[155] The rabbis rejected the role of prophecy in legal exegesis and instead made room for human reason that inevitably resulted in multiple interpretations and many valid legal positions. As we will see in the Conclusion, this polysemy does not repudiate the existence of truth as the sophists would have it; rather, the multivocality of the Torah is precisely what characterizes its prophetic richness. The next two chapters will continue to explore the unique and complex rabbinic attitude towards rhetoric in general by investigating one area of its primary application – the realm of the courthouse.

[152] Brodsky, "From Disagreement to Talmudic Discourse," 208–9.

[153] John Wilkins, *An Essay towards a Real Character, and a Philosophical Language* (London, 1668), part 1 chapter 4.

[154] Ibid., part 1 chapter 1; and see Fish, *Doing What Comes Naturally*, 477. The connection between Wilkins and Jewish biblical interpretation is also drawn by Jorge Luis Borges, "The Analytical Language of John Wilkins," in *Selected Non-fiction*, ed. Eliot Weinberger (New York: Viking, 1999): 230: "The words of John Wilkins' analytical language are not dumb and arbitrary symbols; every letter is meaningful, as those of the Holy Scriptures were for the Kabbalists."

[155] See Fraade, "Looking for Legal Midrash," 57–79; Bernstein and Koyfman, "Interpretation"; and Hidary, "Hellenism and Hermeneutics."

6 The Role of Lawyers in Roman and Rabbinic Courts

> I ask you, judges – just because *he* is eloquent, must *I* be convicted?[1]

> "Your lips have spoken lies" (Isa 59:3): this refers to lawyers.[2]

> Juror #8: I'm not trying to change your mind. It's just that … we're talking about somebody's life here. We can't decide it in five minutes. Supposing we're wrong?
> Juror #7: Supposing we're wrong! Supposing this whole building should fall down on my head. You can suppose anything!
> Juror #8: That's right.[3]

Rhetorical training prepared a young Roman not only for a life in politics, entertainment, or education, but also for a career as a lawyer.[4] The tension between the search for truth and the persuasive power of rhetoric becomes especially pointed in courts of law where a person's life and liberty can depend on a subtle matter of factual or textual interpretation and where a juror's verdict can be swayed by a talented orator.[5] Legal systems navigate these tensions through rules governing evidence and court procedure. These rules encode fundamental assumptions about truth and interpretation held by the creators and adherents of that legal system. The rabbis of the Talmud did not write any systematic philosophical essays; we can, however, analyze Talmudic court procedures in order to uncover some of the epistemological assumptions of the rabbis. By doing so, we will be able to put the rabbis in conversation with their Roman contemporaries, and discover within rabbinic thought a

1 Seneca, *Declamations*, II.95, controversiae 7.4.6, p. 95.
2 B. Shabbat 139a.
3 Reginald Rose, *12 Angry Men*, directed by Sidney Lumet (MGM Studios, 1957), film.
4 Marrou, *History of Education*, 288–9.
5 See Robert Cover, "Violence and the Word," in *Narrative, Violence, and the Law: The Essays of Robert Cover*, ed. Martha Minow, Michael Ryan, and Austin Sarat (Ann Arbor: The University of Michigan Press, 1995): 223.

complex and subtle approach to issues of truth, rhetoric, and legal interpretation.[6]

ADVERSARIAL AND INQUISITORIAL COURTS

As we saw in the Introduction, Plato and the philosophers insisted that there exists in the world of ideas a single objective truth that humans can attain through intellectual perfection and logical proofs. The sophists, on the other hand, contended that our understanding of reality is in constant flux and that the most convincing argument that society accepts at any given moment is what establishes truth and justice. These two worldviews parallel two systems of court procedure: adversarial and inquisitorial. In the adversarial model, the system dominant in England and the United States, it is the responsibility of the parties and their lawyers to collect the evidence, cross-examine witnesses and present legal arguments. The judge acts as an umpire while the jury members passively listen to the adversarial advocates each present its side and then deliberate amongst themselves over which they find more convincing. The adversarial system can also involve bench trials in which the judges take on the fact-finding role of the jury, but the trial remains a contest between two active parties.

In the inquisitorial system, on the other hand, it is the duty of the judge to collect the evidence, interrogate the witnesses, and work through the legal arguments themselves while the advocates – if there are any – occupy a minor role.[7] In practice, working legal systems are never purely adversarial or inquisitorial but rather combine elements of both.[8] These ideal models nevertheless offer a useful typology since legal systems can be generally categorized as predominantly one or the other.

6 On the role of interpretation in law, see James Boyd White, *Heracles' Bow: Essays on the Rhetoric and Poetics of the Law* (Madison, WI: University of Wisconsin, 1985); Dworkin, *Law's Empire*; and Fish, *Doing What Comes Naturally*, 97–140.

7 For descriptions of each system, see Peter van Koppen and Steven Penrod, "Adversarial or Inquisitorial: Comparing Systems," in *Adversarial Versus Inquisitorial Justice*, ed. Peter van Koppen and Steven Penrod (New York: Plenum Publishers, 2003): 1–19, as well as other essays in that book; Michael Louis Corrado, "The Future of Adversarial Systems: An Introduction to the Papers from the First Conference," *North Carolina Journal of International Law and Commercial Regulation* 35 (2010): 285–96, as well as other articles in that volume; James Diehm, "The Introduction of Jury Trials and Adversarial Elements into the Former Soviet Union and Other Inquisitorial Countries," *Journal of Transnational Law and Policy* 11, no. 1 (2001): 1–15; and Patrick Robardet, "Should We Abandon the Adversarial Model in Favour of the Inquisitorial Model in Commissions of Inquiry?," *Dalhousie Law Journal* 12, no. 3 (1989–90): 111–14.

8 See Mirjan Damaška, *The Faces of Justice and State Authority: A Comparative Approach to the Legal Process* (New Haven: Yale University Press, 1986), 3–6; Joseph Grano, "The Adversarial-Accusatorial Label: A Constraint on the Search for Truth,"

The benefits and deficiencies of each system can be illustrated through the contrasting trials of Job and Susanna. The shortcomings of the adversarial system become apparent in the heavenly Adversary's successful suit against a blameless Job. In fact, it is precisely Job's righteousness that Satan attacks as superficial: "Lay Your hand upon all that he has and he will surely blaspheme You" (Job 1:11). Job, Satan charges, is loyal to God only because God showers him with prosperity. Even after Job passes his first trial and God complains to Satan, "you have incited Me against him to destroy him for no good reason" (Job 2:3), Satan manages to convince God to punish Job further. An innocent Job is made to suffer not because of his guilt, but because of the persuasive power of a strong prosecutor arguing before a seemingly weak and fickle Judge. In the next forty chapters, Job has to represent himself. In the adversarial system, uneven representation is a common occurrence and leads to unfair results. Passive judges and juries are likely to follow the most persuasive orator, which is not the same as the best evidence.[9]

If the adversarial system fails to ensure equality of representation, the inquisitorial system places too great a burden on the judge to champion both sides. The book of Susanna exemplifies the problems of the inquisitorial system. Two elders accuse the innocent Susanna of committing adultery and they testify against her. The assembled court trusts the testimony of the "distinguished" elders and condemns the woman to death. At the last moment, Daniel speaks out in defense of Susanna. He cross-examines the witnesses, exposes their lie, and reverses the penalty. It takes a good defense lawyer to reveal the truth and achieve justice. The assembled court in this case was not corrupt but simply

Harvard Journal of Law and Public Policy 20 (1996–7): 513–18; Felicity Nagorcka, Michael Stanton, and Michael Wilson, "Stranded between Partisanship and the Truth? A Comparative Analysis of Legal Ethics in the Adversarial and Inquisitorial Systems of Justice," *Melbourne University Law Review* 29 (2005): 448–77; and William Pizzi, "Sentencing in the US: An Inquisitorial Soul in an Adversarial Body?," in *Crime, Procedure and Evidence in a Comparative and International Context: Essays in Honour of Professor Mirjan Damaška*, ed. John Jackson, Maximo Langer, and Peter Tillers (Oxford: Hart Publishing, 2008): 65–79, and other essays in that volume.

9 See further problems with the adversarial system discussed by Kent Roach, "Wrongful Convictions: Adversarial and Inquisitorial Themes," *North Carolina Journal of International Law and Commercial Regulation* 35 (2010): 387–446; Theodore Kubicek, *Adversarial Justice: America's Court System on Trial* (New York: Algora Publishing, 2006); Amalia Kessler, "Our Inquisitorial Tradition: Equity Procedure, Due Process, and the Search for an Alternative to the Adversarial," *Cornell Law Review* 90 (2005): 1181–275; and Carrie Menkel-Meadow, "The Trouble with the Adversary System in a Postmodern, Multicultural World," *William and Mary Law Review* 38, no. 1 (1996): 5–44.

easily swayed and quick to judge. In the inquisitorial system generally, judges simply do not have the same motivation or time as a hired advocate to think of all possible legal arguments, to seek out every witness and piece of evidence, or to comprehensively refute the opposing arguments.[10]

The debate over these two systems dates back to and correlates with the disputes between the sophists and the philosophers. The legal system in fifth-century BCE Athens was an adversarial system "taken to the extremes."[11] The role of judge and jury were combined in the *dikastai* who were ordinary citizens selected by lot and who were responsible for determining both factual as well as legal questions. The number of *dikastai* judging a case was typically 500 (as in the trial of Socrates) but could reach several thousand in some cases.[12] As the litigants presented their arguments, these judges watched passively as if they were at a sporting event or at the theater.[13] There was no chance for the judges to examine witnesses or ask questions of the litigants; nor was there even any officially allotted time for them to deliberate.[14] There were officially no lawyers; Athenians, with their populist mentality, expected citizens to be able to represent themselves in court and looked down upon those incapable of doing so. In practice, however, litigants would usually hire speech-writers (*logographoi*) to compose an oration which the litigant would memorize and perform for the court. In other cases, a *synegoros* was allowed to join the litigant in court and assist him. *Synegoroi*, however, were not permitted to be paid but rather needed to claim to be a friend or relative of the litigant.[15] Thus, vicarious advocacy for hire and friendly support in court more than made up for the absence of professional lawyers.[16] In the Athenian court system, sophists and their art thrived.

[10] See Gerald Walpin, "America's Adversarial and Jury Systems: More Likely to Do Justice," *Harvard Journal of Law and Public Policy* 26 (2003): 175–86.

[11] S. C. Todd, *The Shape of Athenian Law* (Oxford: Clarendon Press, 1993), 68, and see also pp. 126–7, 145 and 160–3.

[12] Ibid., 83; and Douglas MacDowell, *The Law in Classical Athens* (Ithaca: Cornell University Press, 1978), 35–6. Homicide cases would be judged by the Areopagos consisting of 100 to 200 judges, or by the 51 members of the ephetai; see ibid., 116–17.

[13] Adi Parush, "The Courtroom as Theater and the Theater as Courtroom in Ancient Athens," *Israel Law Review* 35 (2001): 118–37.

[14] Todd, *The Shape of Athenian Law*, 132.

[15] See Demosthenes 46.26.

[16] Jonathan Powell and Jeremy Paterson, *Cicero the Advocate* (Oxford: Oxford University Press, 2004), 10–12; Lene Rubinstein, *Litigation and Co-Operation: Supporting Speakers in the Courts of Classical Athens* (Stuttgart: Franza Steiner Verlag Stuttgart,

Plato, not surprisingly, criticizes sophists generally and their function as court advocates in particular. In the *Laws*, he envisions a utopian city called Magnesia where the court system is inquisitorial[17] and where lawyers deserve the death penalty. In the voice of the Athenian stranger, Plato writes:

> None would deny that justice between men is a fair thing, and that it has civilized all human affairs. And if justice be fair, how can we deny that pleading (συνδικεῖν) is also a fair thing? But these fair things are in disrepute owing to a kind of foul art, which, cloaking itself under a fair name, claims, first, that there exists a device for dealing with lawsuits, and further, that it is the one which is able, by pleading and helping another to plead, to win the victory, whether the pleas concerned be just or unjust; and it also asserts that both this art itself and the arguments which proceed from it are a gift offered to any man who gives money in exchange. This art – whether it be really an art or merely an artless trick got by habit and practice – must never, if possible, arise in our State.[18]

The "foul art" to which Plato refers is rhetoric.[19] For Plato, legal advocates might seem like they practice a noble art but they are actually responsible for corrupting justice. These advocates argue any case for pay – whether just or not – and thereby pervert the judicial system and obscure the search for truth. The adversarial system is anathema to Plato, who instead prefers an inquisitorial system where impartial judges examine the evidence and arrive at the one objective truth in each case. The two systems of court procedure thus relate directly to the two epistemological worldviews discussed. The adversarial system fits hand-in-glove with the epistemology of the sophists; rhetorical debate by partial advocates before a passive jury and judge is, according to them, the best and only path towards arriving at the most probable and just verdict. In the inquisitorial system, on the other hand, the judge operates

2000); J. A. Crook, *Legal Advocacy in the Roman World* (Ithaca: Cornell University Press, 1995), 30–7; and Todd, *The Shape of Athenian Law*, 94–6.

[17] *Laws* 766d, 855d–856a, and see further at Trevor Saunders, "Plato's Later Political Thought," in *The Cambridge Companion to Plato*, ed. R. Kraut (Cambridge: Cambridge University Press, 1992): 336.

[18] *Laws* 937e–938c. Translation from Plato, *Laws*, trans. R. G. Bury (Cambridge: Harvard University Press, 1926). See discussion at Glenn Morrow, *Plato's Cretan City: A Historical Interpretation of the Laws* (Princeton: Princeton University Press, 1960), 280–3; and Trevor Saunders, *Plato's Penal Code: Tradition, Controversy, and Reform in Greek Penology* (Oxford: Clarendon Press, 1991), 332–3.

[19] *Gorgias* 462b–466a.

like a philosopher, perceiving evidence objectively, without the hindrance of rhetorical tricks and illusions, and is thus best able to arrive at Justice.[20]

THE ROMAN COURT SYSTEM

The preceding introduction serves as a theoretical model by which to evaluate the legal procedure of the rabbis. First, however, we need to recall the historical background of legal procedure in Roman courts in order to contrast it with the rabbinic system. Roman court procedure in large part continued the adversarial Greek system, except that it gradually introduced professional lawyers directly and not only through logographers or *synagoroi*.[21]

Roman civil procedure went through three overlapping phases: the *legis actio* procedure during most of the Republic, the formulary system from the second century BCE until the third century CE, and the *cognitio extraordinaria* during the post-classical period of the Empire.[22] The formulary system, which was in effect during the tannaitic and early

[20] See Thomas Weingend, "Should We Search for the Truth, and Who Should Do It?," *North Carolina Journal of International Law and Commercial Regulation* 36 (2011): 389–415, who associates the inquisitorial system with the correspondence theory of truth, which accords with the Platonic view that something is true if it corresponds with objective reality. The adversarial system, in turn, is generally associated with consensus theory, which is similar to the rhetorical tradition that defines truth as the communal consensus resulting from a procedure evaluating both sides. This is not to say that every participant in an inquisitorial system believes in correspondence theory or vice versa; in real life, judicial systems are complex hybrids that do not consistently follow any single epistemological model. However, in concept and in an ideal world, such as the utopian world of Plato, the inquisitorial model will tend to attract adherents of correspondence theory and vice versa. See also Joseph Fernandez, "An Exploration of the Meaning of Truth in Philosophy and Law," *University of Notre Dame Australia Law Review* 11 (2009): 53–83; and Matthew King, "Security, Scale, Form, and Function: The Search for Truth and the Exclusion of Evidence in Adversarial and Inquisitorial Justice Systems," *International Legal Perspectives* 12 (2002): 185–236.

[21] Advocacy evolved from the patron–client system in the archaic period where the *patronus* would speak on behalf of his client of lower status in court. By the late Republic, *patroni* would make their services available to anyone who asked, although in 204 BCE, the *lex Cincia* prohibited advocates from taking fees for their services. This law, however, was later relaxed and advocacy took on a more professional character. See Crook, *Legal Advocacy*, 37–46; Powell and Paterson, *Cicero the Advocate*, 12–18; and Catherine Steel, *Roman Oratory* (Cambridge: Cambridge University Press, 2006), 29–30, 55–6.

[22] See George Mousourakis, *A Legal History of Rome* (London: Routledge, 2007), 32. The formulary system was officially abolished in 342 CE but had effectively already become obsolete beforehand. See Andrew Borkowski and Paul du Plessis, *Textbook on Roman Law* (Oxford: Oxford University Press, 2005), 79.

amoraic periods, was highly adversarial.[23] George Mousourakis describes it as follows:

> During the trial, the accuser and the defendant dominated the scene, with their advocates and witnesses engaged in cross-examinations that were often rancorous. The jurors listened in silence, while the presiding magistrate was mainly responsible for the orderly progress of the proceedings. Both oral and documentary evidence was admissible. Witnesses testified under oath and were examined by their own side and cross-examined by the other. After all the evidence was presented and the closing speeches delivered, the magistrate convened the jury and placed the question of the defendant's guilt or innocence to the vote.[24]

Of course, court procedure varied greatly depending on the place, time, court, and type of case. Under the *cognitio extraordinaria* court procedure became more inquisitorial, with the judge interrogating the witnesses.[25] However, even in this period, legal advocacy remained an important part of trials.[26] Lawyers played a prominent role in courts not only in the west of the Empire, where evidence abounds, but even in the east. Dozens of papyri from Egypt preserve court documents that feature advocates, thus indicating that their presence was "ubiquitous," even if not universal.[27]

THE RABBINIC COURT SYSTEM

Many sources indicate that the rabbis were familiar with the Roman legal system.[28] In some cases, there are clear parallels between the two systems. For example, court procedure for selecting a judge in both

[23] See Andrew Riggsby, *Roman Law and the Legal World of the Romans* (Cambridge: Cambridge University Press, 2010), 115. See also Kathryn Tempest, *Cicero: Politics and Persuasion in Ancient Rome* (New York: Continuum, 2011), 61, for examples of Cicero cross-examining witnesses. Crook, *Legal Advocacy*, 66, on the other hand, finds that the magistrate questions witnesses in some Egyptian papyri.

[24] Mousourakis, *A Legal History*, 80–1. Juries in Roman law were smaller than those in Athens and were sometimes dispensed with altogether. See ibid., 130.

[25] Ibid., 174.

[26] See Olga Tellegen-Couperus, "Roman Law and Rhetoric," *Revue Belge De Philologie Et D'histoire* 84, no. 1 (2006): 63, citing E. P. Parks, *The Roman Rhetorical Schools as a Preparation for the Courts under the Early Empire* (Baltimore: John Hopkins University, 1945), chapter 2.

[27] Crook, *Legal Advocacy*, 123.

[28] Saul Lieberman, "Roman Legal Institutions in Early Rabbinics and in the Acta Martyrum," *Jewish Quarterly Review* 35, no. 1 (1944): 1–57.

Roman and Talmudic law involved the two parties taking turns at rejecting names from a list of men qualified to serve as judges.[29] Given this overlap, it is instructive to compare the adversarial system of Roman law and the role of advocates therein with the court system envisioned in rabbinic sources. Was the rabbinic legal system adversarial or inquisitorial, and what was the place of lawyers in rabbinic courts? Furthermore, what can Talmudic sources reveal about the epistemological viewpoints of the rabbis? This study assumes that the rabbinic sources about court procedure are not necessarily describing a functioning court system but are more likely a theoretical construct. However, the extent to which the sources are theoretical makes them all the more significant for discovering the underlying philosophical assumptions of their authors in describing their utopian system.[30]

Let us begin with a tannaitic prohibition relating to advocates that appears in Mekhilta d'Rabbi Yishmael, Kaspa, 20:

> "Keep far from a false matter" (Exod 23:7)... This is a warning to the judge ... that he should not place advocates (*sanegorin*)[31] beside him, for the verse states, "the claims of both parties shall come unto God" (Exod 22:8).[32]

This midrash forbids a judge to appoint defense advocates because doing so would bias his judgment.[33] He must objectively hear both sides directly, not through partial intermediaries. Exod 22:8 dictates this by stating that all claims are to reach God, who is represented by the

[29] See Riggsby, *Roman Law*, 114, and M. Sanhedrin 3:1; see Tzvi Novick, "The *Borer* Court: New Interpretations of mSan 3," *Zutot* 5, no. 1 (2008): 1–8.

[30] On this methodology, see Berkowitz, *Execution and Invention*, 17–19, 64–70, 92–4, 152, and 177–9. For an attempt to describe actual court procedure in various periods of Jewish history, see Jonah Ostrow, "Tannaitic and Roman Procedure in Homicide," *Jewish Quarterly Review* 52, no. 2 (1961): 164. He writes that "Tannaitic procedure was decidedly accusatory" (p. 165) but does not sufficiently analyze the relevant sources or explain his conclusion.

[31] *Synegoros* (סניגורין, συνήγορος) is a term that dates back to Athenian courts where it referred to a friend or relative of the litigant who advocated in his defense in court. Lawyers were not permitted to be paid but relatives were allowed to offer free counsel. See Demosthenes 46.26. *Synegoros* continued to be the term used for advocates in the Roman East, when a professional class of paid lawyers arose.

[32] Translation follows MS Oxford-Bodleian 151.

[33] I disagree here with the commentary *Zet Ra`anan* cited approvingly by Yuval Sinai, *The Judge and the Judicial Process in Jewish Law* (Jerusalem: Hebrew University, 2010), 475, who says that the object of this statement is the litigant. The context makes clear that the warning is to the judge. The parallel at B. Shevu'ot 30b also addresses the judge explicitly. In this sense, this midrash is similar to M. Avot 1:8 discussed below.

human judge. This source does not explicitly prohibit the litigants from benefiting from the services of advocates but only proscribes the judge from appointing one.

A parallel midrash in Mekhilta d'R. Shimon bar Yoḥai, Mishpatim, 23:1 legislates a broader prohibition:

> "Do not carry false rumors" (Exod 23:1): [This teaches] that advocates (*sanegorin*) should not speak before them [the judges].

This midrash seems to ban advocates from the courtroom altogether. It is too terse, however, to provide a definite conclusion without further evidence.[34] Fortunately, support for both of the prohibitions in these midrashim is found in the Mishnah. The first five chapters of Mishnah Sanhedrin discuss the various aspects of rabbinic court procedure from the number of judges required for various types of cases to the procedure for tallying the final vote. The first thing we notice is the absence of any mention of advocates, even where we might expect them most. Consider M. Sanhedrin 3:6, which describes the procedure for examining witnesses:[35]

> How do they [the judges] examine the witnesses? They bring them[36] in and admonish them and remove them[37] outside [the courtroom] and leave the older of them [the witnesses]. They say to him, "Tell, how do you know that this one is liable to that one?" ... Then they bring in the second [witness] and they examine him. If their words are found to line up, they [the judges] deliberate on the matter.

Examining the witnesses is probably the most central aspect of the rabbinic trial and the place where a good lawyer would have the most effect. (Remember how Daniel reversed the verdict in Susanna's trial.) Yet, this Mishnah explicitly assigns the role of examining the witnesses to the judges. So far, these tannaitic sources describe an inquisitorial

[34] This is true especially because this midrash derives from Midrash haGadol and not from the Cairo Geniza, so its status as an authentic tannaitic tradition is questionable; see Sinai, ibid.

[35] Translation follows MS Kaufman. Major variants are noted below.

[36] MS Kaufman reads אותו "him" here, which I have emended to אותן based on all other textual witnesses. From the context as well, it is evident that all witnesses would need to enter the courtroom to hear the intimidation since all witnesses but one are later removed.

[37] Printed editions of the Mishnah and ed. Venice of the Bavli read "את כל האדם – everyone." However, ed. Soncino of the Bavli and all manuscripts of the Mishnah, Yerushalmi, and Bavli as well as T. Sanhedrin 6:3 read "אותן – them." The former is a corruption based on M. Sanhedrin 7:5. See Tosafot Yom Tov and Dikduke Soferim.

system. In fact, the only mention of advocates in the entire Mishnah appears in M. Avot 1:8, and it is a negative one:[38]

> Yehudah ben Ṭabai says, "Do not make yourself as advocates (כְּעֶרְכֵי הַדַּיָּנִים),[39] and when the litigants stand before you they should be guilty in your eyes and when they leave from before you they should be innocent[40] in your eyes for they have accepted[41] upon themselves the judgment."
>
> Shimon ben Shaṭaḥ says, "Examine the witnesses greatly and be careful with your words lest [the witnesses] learn to lie from them."

Yehudah ben Ṭabai advises judges on how to deal with litigants while Shimon ben Shaṭaḥ instructs them on how to examine witnesses. The latter statement backs up M. Sanhedrin 3:6 in assuming that the judges have the role of interrogating the witnesses. Yehudah ben Tabai's statement, however, is more ambiguous. While the modern Hebrew word for lawyers is עורכי דין "arrangers of law," the Mishnah's ערכי דיינים "arrangers of judges" is difficult to explain.[42] For this reason, Yechezkel Kutscher argues that the original reading follows the minority of manuscripts that read ארכי הדיינים to mean "do not act as a chief justice."[43] Yuval Sinai,

[38] Translation follows MS Kaufman. Major variants are notes below; for a full list of variants see Shimon Sharvit, *Masechet Avot le-doroteha: mahadura mada`it, mevo'ot ve-nispaḥim* (Jerusalem: Mosad Bialik, 2004), 70–2.

[39] Lit. arrangers of the judges; see discussion below. MSS London, Rome, and ten extant Geniza fragments read ערכי, כערכי or כעורכי with an *`ayin*. MS Parma and four Geniza fragments read ארכי or כארכי with an *'alef*. MS Kaufman originally read ארכי but was then changed to כערכי.

[40] MSS Kaufman, Parma, London, and most Geniza fragments read כצדיקים. MS Rome, some Geniza fragments, and printed editions read כזכאין.

[41] Some MSS and the printed ed. read כשקבלו "when they accept."

[42] Maimonides, in his Mishnah commentary, explains as follows: "These are the people who learn how to plead so that they can advocate for people in their litigations. They propose questions: if the judge will say this, the response is this and if the litigant should claim this then the response will be this, as if they arrange the judges and the litigants before them. For that reason, they are called 'arrangers of judges,' as if they arranged the judges before them." See Yosef Kafiḥ, *Mishnah with the Commentary of Rabbenu Moses ben Maimon* (Jerusalem: Mossad Harav Kook, 1963–7), *Nezikin*, 270; and Albeck, *Mishnah, Nezikin*, 494.

[43] Yechezkel Kutscher, *Milim ve-toldotehen* (Jerusalem: Kiryat Sefer, 1965), 89–91. Kutscher explains that ארכי is a transliteration of the Greek prefix ἀρχι. In fact, Kutscher traces the same shift from Greek to Hebrew in the manuscript tradition of Gen Rabbah 50. MS London includes the original Greek word ארכיקריטיס (ἀρχικρίτης), which is changed in MS Vatican to ארכי דיינים, and then appears in Midrash Sekhel Tob as ערכי הדיינין. Similarly, ארכי יודיקי (archiiudex) in MS London is changed to עורכי דין in MS Oxford 2335. See all manuscript variants at Albeck and Theodor, *Bereshit Rabba*, 519, and cf. p. 625. Avot d'Rabbi Natan A, 10, assumes the reading of ארכי in m. Avot 1:8 in

however, counters that ארכי is more likely to be a misspelling of the original ערכי and that the term in all manuscripts should be understood to refer to someone who provides legal advice to the litigant.[44] Even if Kutscher is correct, the change to ערכי דיינים happened very early on in the Mishnah's transmission so that even the early Amoraim understood it to refer to advocates.[45] The reading with an *`ayin* has the advantage that both parts of Yehudah ben Tabai's statement emphasize the same point that the judge should not side with or help either litigant but should rather distrust both of them.[46] Furthermore, it is reminiscent of the Mekhilta d'R. Yishmael cited above, and so we should not be surprised to find the same idea in another tannaitic source.

To be sure, the Mishnah does not ban advocates altogether but only prohibits the judge from acting as an advocate by providing legal advice to one party.[47] However, the Talmuds greatly expand the application of this Mishnah by prohibiting not only judges from acting like advocates – as the context of the statement suggests – but by forbidding anyone from being a lawyer. Y. Baba Batra 9:4, 17a, states:[48]

> It was taught: Rabban Shimon ben Gamaliel says, "Any ailment that has a fixed cost is healed [using the funds of] her *ketubah*. If it does not have a fixed cost, it is healed from the property [of the husband's estate].
>
> As the case of a relative of Rabbi Shimon bar Va who suffered pain in her eye. She came to R. Yoḥanan. He told her, "Does your physician charge a fixed fee? If he does charge a fixed fee then [it will be deducted] from your *ketubah*. If he does not charge a fixed fee then your husband will give it to you.

its gloss: "How so? This teaches that if you came to the House of Study and heard a matter or a halakha, do not hurry in your mind to respond. Rather sit and ask what is the reason they said this, what is the context of this law or halakha that they asked me about." See also Albeck, *Mishnah*, ibid.; and Zvi Aryeh Steinfeld, "`Asinu `aṣmenu ke-`orkhe ha-dayanin," *Te`udah* 7 (1991): 112 n. 5.

44 Sinai, *Judge*, 46–7.

45 See Y. Baba Batra 9:4, 17a, and B. Ketubot 52b, cited below.

46 Regarding the difficulty of parsing the phrase עורכי הדיינים, Sinai, ibid., 43–4 and 473–6, cites scholars who claim that the term refers to the magistrates of the court who would prepare the case, gather the evidence, assess that there is a legitimate plea, and reveal to the plaintiff the punishment for which he should sue.

47 The mention of advocates here also suggests that the rabbis were familiar with the role that advocates played in Roman courts. See Yuval Sinai, "'Do Not Make Yourself as Advocates': On the Place of a Rule in Court Procedure," [Hebrew] in *Studies in Jewish Law: Judge and Judging*, ed. Ya`akov Habba and Amihai Radzyner (Ramat-Gan: Bar-Ilan University, 2007): 99–100.

48 Translation is based on MS Leiden. For textual issues see Steinfeld, "`Asinu," 117–19. This sugya has a partial parallel at Y. Ketubot 4:11, 29a.

> But did they not teach us: Do not make yourself as advocates? And R. Ḥagai said in the name of R. Yehoshua ben Levi: It is prohibited to reveal to an individual his judgment.
>
> Say that R. Yoḥanan knew that that woman was upright and for that reason he revealed it to her.
>
> If her husband wants it to be a fixed amount and she does not want it to be a fixed amount, to whom do we listen, not to her husband?
>
> R. Matnaya said, this is only said for someone whose law is not with him but for someone whose law is with him he may tell him something.

A widow is generally sustained by the estate of her husband, which is inherited by his children. This sustenance includes not only food but also medical care. Rabban Shimon ben Gamaliel qualifies that the estate is required to pay only ongoing medical care, whereas a one-time ailment with a fixed cost must be paid by the widow herself, i.e. it is deducted from the amount owed to her in her *ketubah*. Controversially, R. Yoḥanan once gave legal advice to a widow based on this ruling. The Talmud challenges the permissibility of doing so considering the prohibition in M. Avot 1:8 and the comment of R. Yehoshua ben Levi, even though R. Yoḥanan here does not seem to be the judge, considering that only the woman comes to him and not the other litigant.[49] The Talmud thus assumes a general prohibition against anyone providing legal advice that may help someone use a technicality in the law to their advantage in court. The Talmud responds that R. Yoḥanan was permitted to offer advice because he knew the woman to be upright and would not unjustly manipulate her plea based on his advice. In any case, adds the Talmud, the structure of doctor payments would have to be approved by the husband and is not up to her.[50] R. Matnaya's statement generalizes the caveat already proposed: one may provide legal advice to someone who is in the right and whose plea will already be successful because that advice will not change either the plea or the outcome.[51]

A parallel to this sugya appears in the Bavli where R. Yoḥanan challenges his own previous action:[52]

49 See Steinfeld, ibid.

50 For other interpretations of this line see ibid., 119–20. I do not read this line as a new question (as does R. Eliyahu Fulda) nor as part of the response of the previous line (as does Pnei Moshe) but rather as a separate second response to the original question.

51 For a different interpretation of R. Matnaya's statement see Steinfeld, ibid., 120–5.

52 B. Ketubot 52b. Translation based on Geniza fragment Cambridge T-S NS 329.237. For variants, see Abraham Liss, *The Babylonian Talmud with Variant Readings*

A relative[53] of R. Yoḥanan had a step-mother who needed medical care every day. They[54] came before R. Yoḥanan. He told them,[55] go and set a price for her medical care. R. Yoḥanan said, "We have made ourselves as advocates!" What did he think at first and what did he think in the end? At first, he thought, "Do not ignore your own kin" (Isa 58:7). At the end he thought, it is different for an important person.

Both the Yerushalmi and the Bavli interpret Mishnah Avot as prohibiting even non-judges from acting as advocates.[56] Nonetheless, both Talmuds also allow for exceptions: the Yerushalmi permits one to give advice if it will not change the plea and the Bavli allows a layperson to help his or her relative. Other sources allow even the judges to help the plea of one side in exceptional cases.[57] But the general principle that runs throughout these sources demands that advocates may not be active in the rabbinic court itself.

To be sure, court advocates make some appearances in exceptional cases. For example, a trustee (אפוטרופוס – ἐπίτροπος) may act as an advocate for the estate of young orphans who cannot represent themselves. B. Ketubot 109b relates that one such trustee successfully regained ownership of a contested field using far-fetched but legally valid pleas. Abaye, who was the judge, then commented: "Any person who appoints a trustee should appoint one like this who knows how to turn [the verdict]

(Jerusalem: Yad Harav Herzog, 1983), Ketubot, 1.386–87, and see the parallel sugya at B. Ketubot 85b.

53 All MSS read קריביה, indicating a single relative. Some MSS, however, use a plural pronoun later in this sentence (untranslated here), that may indicate many relatives.

54 One MS reads "he." If only one person came before R. Yoḥanan, then he certainly was not acting as a judge. However, even according to most manuscripts that read a plural here, it still seems that only one party consisting of many people came to him and he was not acting as judge. First, R. Yoḥanan would not be able to give his advice if both parties were present. Second, another case at B. Ketubot 54b uses a plural pronoun even though it is clear that R. Yoḥanan was not acting as a judge there. See Steinfeld, "ʿAsinu," 113–15; and Sinai, *Judge*, 50.

55 Two MSS have a singular pronoun here.

56 It is difficult to date when this interpretation first appears. According to the Bavli it is R. Yoḥanan himself and in the Yerushalmi it is R. Yehoshua ben Levi, at least according to the Talmud's application of his statement. However, Steinfeld, ibid., argues for a later date. According to his timeline, the later anonymous layer that prohibits lawyers coincides with the *cognitio extraordinaria*, which similarly moved away from the adversarial method. However, based on the Mekhilta d'R. Shimon bar Yoḥai and M. Sanhedrin 3:6 discussed above, it seems more likely that the Tannaim already opposed the adversarial system and its use of lawyers.

57 See B. Sanhedrin 29a; B. Giṭṭin 58b; and B. Baba Batra 23a.

in favor of the orphans." While this source demonstrates how a skilled advocate can make a big difference, it also allows for such advocacy only in exceptional cases of young orphans.

In order to explain why the rabbinic court system rejects the use of advocates, it is tempting to look to Y. Sanhedrin 2:1, 19d: "Let him appoint a representative (אנטלר[58])? Think about if he was required to swear – could a representative swear!" This line entertains the possibility of having someone represent the high priest in a suit since it is undignified for the high priest to be tried in person. The Yerushalmi rejects the possibility of using representation when the litigant is absent because only the litigant can swear about his own affairs. However, this cannot be the reason for the general antipathy of the Talmud towards lawyers because the problem of the lawyer not being able to swear only arises if the litigant is absent. In a general case of a lawyer who joins the litigant in the courtroom, this reason would not apply.

Rather, the rabbis seem to hold the adversarial system suspect because it does not lead to justice or promote honesty. The Talmud views the Roman court system as corrupt and capricious to the point that it can say: "Anyone who goes up to the *gradus* (גרדום)[59] to be judged, if he has great advocates (פרקליטין) he is saved but if not he is not saved."[60] Once the trial goes into the hands of hired lawyers, it becomes simply a debating contest in which the most persuasive orator wins, regardless of truth or justice. It is therefore understandable why the rabbis, counter to their surrounding culture, disallowed lawyers from their own courts. As Eliezer Segal puts it:

> The Traditional Jewish court does not permit the use of lawyers at all ... The Talmudic sources, which were familiar with the Roman court system and its susceptibility to persuasion by mellifluous rhetoric, warned the rabbis, "Do not act like the professional pleaders." It was the judge's job to get at the truth without its being packaged by a professional.[61]

[58] On this word, see Lieberman, *Greek in Jewish Palestine*, 12–14; and Cohen, *Jewish and Roman Law*, 54.

[59] This refers to a movable step on which the defendant sat in Roman trials. See Lieberman, "Roman Legal Institutions," 13–15; and David Potter, "Performance, Power, and Justice in the High Empire," in *Roman Theater and Society: E. Togo Salmon Conference Papers I*, ed. William Slater (Ann Arbor: University of Michigan Press, 1996): 147.

[60] B. Shabbat 32a. See similarly B. Berakhot 60a stating that an innocent person who cannot find an advocate is at risk of being put to death by the courts.

[61] Eliezer Segal, *Holidays, History, and Halakhah* (Northvale, NJ: Jason Aronson, 2001), 16. See also Segal, "Jewish Perspectives on Restorative Justice," in *The Spiritual Roots*

Does this mean that the rabbis imagined a purely inquisitorial court along the lines of Plato? Did they reject the rhetorical tradition entrenched in Greco-Roman culture as thoroughly as did Plato? The continuation of Mishnah Sanhedrin that details procedures for the deliberation of the judges suggests a more complex picture. M. Sanhedrin 4:1–3 reads:[62]

> Both monetary cases and capital cases require interrogation and investigation as it is said, "You shall have one standard" (Lev 24:22).[63]
>
> What is the difference between monetary cases and capital cases?
>
> [1] Monetary cases require three [judges] while capital cases require twenty-three.
>
> [2] In monetary cases they investigate[64] [the testimony] either for guilt or acquittal while in capital cases they investigate [the testimony] for acquittal but they do not investigate for guilt.
>
> [3] In monetary cases they incline based on one [vote] whether for acquittal or for guilt while in capital cases they incline based on one [vote] for acquittal but based on two [votes] for guilt.

of Restorative Justice, ed. Michael Hadley (Albany: State University of New York Press, 2001): 183–4.

62 Translation follows MS Kaufman.

63 This refers to the previous verse which mentions both monetary and capital punishments.

64 For this translation of Hebrew, "פותחין," see Mandel, "ʿAl 'pataḥ,'" 49–82. Post-Talmudic commentators have explained פותחין here to mean "begin" and assumed on that basis that the deliberation of the judges must begin with arguments for acquittal. However, as Mandel, ibid., 78–9, points out, this raises a number of difficulties. What is the benefit to the accused of starting the deliberation with acquittal? If anything, it is the final argument that would be the most influential; see ibid., 78 n. 109 citing Cicero, *De Oratore*, trans. E. W. Sutton (Cambridge: Harvard University Press, 1942), II.xxvii.314, and Quintilian, *Institutes of Oratory*, 5.12.14. Furthermore, M. Sanhedrin 4:2 legislates that deliberation begins from the least experienced judge on the side, who certainly has the freedom to argue for guilt and cannot be forced to argue for acquittal. Rather, Mandel argues that line [2] must refer to a stage of investigation of the testimony after the *ḥaqirot* and *bediqot* (see n. 67) ensure the alignment of the testimonies of the two witnesses (M. Sanhedrin 5:1–3) but before the judges excuse the witnesses to deliberate in private (M. Sanhedrin 3:7). During this middle stage, the witnesses are present, as is evident in M. Sanhedrin 5:4, and the judges challenge the witnesses so that they can find reason to acquit. Line [2] teaches that the judges will challenge the witnesses for both guilt and innocence in monetary cases but in capital cases they look only for acquittal. The chief judge would lead this investigation (T. Sanhedrin 9:1) and it is this stage that requires a judge who can purify the reptile, on which see further below.

[4] In monetary cases, they overturn [the verdict] whether for acquittal or for guilt while in capital cases they overturn for acquittal and do not overturn for guilt.[65]

[5] In monetary cases everyone can offer [arguments] for acquittal or for guilt while in capital cases everyone can offer [arguments] for acquittal but not everyone can offer [arguments] for guilt.[66]

[6] In monetary cases, he who argues for guilt may argue for innocence and he who argues for innocence may argue for guilt while in capital cases he who argues for guilt may argue for innocence but he who argues for innocence may not change and argue for guilt.

[7] In monetary cases, they judge during the day and may finish at night while in capital cases they judge during the day and must finish during the day.

[8] In monetary cases they may finish on the same day whether for acquittal or for guilt while in capital cases they may finish on the same day for acquittal or on the next day for guilt. Therefore, they do not judge on the eve of the Sabbath or the eve of a holiday.

[9] In monetary cases and purity and impurity cases they begin from the greatest [judge] while in capital cases they begin from the side.

[10] Everyone is fit to judge monetary cases but not everyone is fit to judge capital cases except priests, Levites, and Israelites who are marriageable to the priesthood.

The Sanhedrin was like half of a round granary so that [the judges] would be able to see each other. Two court scribes stood before them, one on the right and one on the left, who would write the words of those who convict and the words of those who acquit. R. Yehudah says, there were three [court scribes]; one writes the words of those who convict, one writes the words of those who acquit, and the third writes the words of those who convict and the words of those who acquit.

The deliberation of the judges is not simply an open discussion but rather adheres to a detailed protocol. In monetary cases, the protocol follows an inquisitorial procedure: the judges can either support or

[65] This refers to a case when new testimony becomes available after sentencing but before the punishment is given.

[66] This refers to students, witnesses, or other spectators who want to submit an argument to the court that the judges may have missed. This law is expanded at M. Sanhedrin 5:4.

challenge the testimony [2]; the chief judge begins the deliberation [9]; the rest of the judges then argue for one of the two sides and may change their stances either way during the deliberation [6]; if one of the witnesses or students has an argument to add, he may do so [5]; the verdict is decided by a simple majority [3] even on the same day [8] or at night [7]; and a mistaken verdict is overturned in either direction [4].

The protocol for capital cases, in contrast, is much more complex and interesting. The procedure begins by examining the witnesses separately and questioning them regarding the basic facts of the incident, as well as many additional details that can help corroborate the testimony.[67] Once the judges gather this information and verify that the two testimonies match, they proceed to investigate the testimony itself [2].[68] For example they might ask the witnesses, "Do you really think that this person murdered that person?"[69] or "Who says that the matter is as you say?"[70] While in monetary cases, the judges can both support and challenge the testimony, in capital cases, the judges may only challenge the truth of the testimony but may not offer arguments to support it. In monetary cases, the judges must be completely impartial since favoring one side of the lawsuit will inevitably harm the other party. Where the litigant's life is at stake, however, the rabbis prefer to acquit a murderer or a Sabbath violator rather than kill an innocent person. Therefore, the Mishnah takes every measure to ensure that the judges do not overlook any possible argument for innocence. In order to accomplish this without a paid defense lawyer, the judges themselves must fulfill that role. The rabbis are familiar enough with the world of rhetoric to know that there is always a way to argue for either side of an issue and it is precisely for this reason that they choose to stack the arguments in favor of the accused. If the judges focus their efforts exclusively on trying to poke holes in the testimony and still are not able to find a way to dismiss witnesses, only then can they proceed to consider capital punishment. Paul Mandel comments on this requirement:

> This law is essential in the inquisitorial system that characterizes Jewish law in that it corrects one of the most dangerous perversions

[67] This process itself has two parts: *ḥaqirot*, which establish the setting and basic facts of the crime, and *bediqot*, which question minor details of the crime scene that have no bearing on the case itself except to verify the honesty of the witnesses by making sure their testimonies corroborate (M. Sanhedrin 5:1–4).

[68] M. Sanhedrin 5:4. See n. 64.

[69] Y. Sanhedrin 4:1, 22a. The context shows that this question is directed towards the witnesses.

[70] B. Sanhedrin 32b.

> that challenge proper procedure in this system – transforming the trial into an actual "inquisition," into an investigation that is completely directed towards proving the charges against the accused and in which the judges put great efforts in bolstering the proofs of the witnesses.[71]

This consideration explains a further law found in both Talmuds regarding the qualifications for the judges that take part in this investigation:

> Said R. Yoḥanan: One who does not know how to derive that a reptile is pure and impure in one hundred ways, may not investigate [testimony] in merit [of the defendant].[72]
>
> Said Rav Yehudah in the name of Rav: One only seats in the Sanhedrin one who knows how to purify the reptile based on Scripture.[73]

In order to best challenge the testimony of the witnesses even – nay, especially – when that testimony clearly points to guilt, the judge must possess the ability to prove a thesis as preposterous as the purity of a reptile. Leviticus 11:29–30 lists eight impure reptiles and so any argument for the purity of these reptiles would contradict an explicit verse and would be patently false. Only a judge who can disprove the truth of a straightforward Torah law will have the necessary training to discover potential arguments against a given testimony. Whoever takes on the task of challenging the testimony must be as skilled as a highly paid sophist and is required to apply this skill as if he were playing the role of the defendant's lawyer. As Saul Lieberman comments: "The judge must thus be a rhetor who can *disputare in utramque partem* and prove at one and the same time the two opposite points of view."[74] In quoting this one Latin phrase, Lieberman associates the rabbinic court system with the basic foundation of the rhetorical enterprise – arguing both sides of any issue. Quintilian connects the ability to argue both sides of a question to success in the courtroom:

> The Academy will be the most useful school on the ground that its habit of disputing on both sides of a question approaches most nearly to the actual practice of the courts.[75]

71 Mandel, "'Al 'pataḥ,'" 79 n. 114 (my translation).

72 Y. Sanhedrin 4:1, 22a. See also discussion at Hidary, "Classical," 33–64.

73 B. Sanhedrin 17a.

74 Lieberman, *Hellenism in Jewish Palestine*, 63.

75 Quintilian, *Institutes of Oratory*, 12.2.25, and cf. 10.1.22–3. See further at Adelino Cattani, "Subjectivist and Objectivist Interpretations of Controversy-Based Thought," in *Controversies and Subjectivity*, ed. Pierluigi Barrotta and Marcelo Dascak (Amsterdam: John Benjamins Publishing Co., 2005): 185–7.

The rhetorical skill of the lawyers makes all the difference in a Roman adversarial courtroom where each side must make the most persuasive argument for its case based on the same evidence and set of laws. The lawyer must therefore be able to interpret the very same set of sources in opposite directions. These quotes similarly tie into the statement of Cicero and the parallel midrash cited in the opening of this book[76] that education of the young should include the skill of forming multiple conflicting arguments.[77] We see that both Roman and rabbinic legal professionals shared much of the same educational training and emphasis on rhetorical ability.

An important distinction, however, must be made between how the two legal systems apply this talent. Whereas for the Greeks and Romans, rhetorical skill was necessary for the orators who presented their cases before courts and deliberative assemblies, the Talmud makes sophistic reasoning a requirement not of the lawyers but of the judges themselves.[78] As Lieberman notes, for the rabbis, the goal of argumentative skill is not "twisting the law according to the required aim and purpose,"[79] so that one can win a case regardless of the circumstances.[80]

[76] See p. 1.

[77] Cicero, *De Oratore*, I.xxiv.158, similarly writes: "We must argue every question on both sides, and bring out on every topic whatever points can be deemed plausible." See also B. Eruvin 13b and other related rabbinic statements cited by Natalie Dohrmann, "Reading as Rhetoric in Halakhic Texts," in *Of Scribes and Sages: Early Jewish Interpretation and Transmission of Scripture*, ed. Craig Evans (London: T&T Clark International, 2004): 91 n. 3.

[78] Cohen, "Letter and Spirit," 161, writes: "Books on Greek rhetoric were in part handbooks on pleadings for advocates, whereas in Talmudic times, a legal representative empowered to *plead* in behalf of another was unknown . . . ; hence the science of rhetoric typical of the Greeks, with its emphasis upon devices and stratagems to help the client win his case, was not developed by the rabbis." I would argue that the rabbis did develop a system of rhetoric of their own but towards a different goal. Many of the stratagems used by the Greeks may not have been as fully developed by the rabbis, but at least some of them were adopted and adapted by the rabbis who put them to use not for lawyers but for judges.

[79] Lieberman, *Hellenism in Jewish Palestine*, 63.

[80] This was the goal of Roman orators. For example, Aulus Gellius, *Noctes Atticae*, trans. J. C. Rolfe, Loeb Classical Library (Cambridge: Harvard University Press, 1927), 1.6.4, citing Titus Castricius, writes: "It is the orator's privilege to make statements that are untrue, daring, crafty, deceptive and sophistical, provided they have some semblance of truth and can by any artifice be made to insinuate themselves into the minds of the persons who are to be influenced. Furthermore, he said, it is disgraceful for an advocate, even though his case be a bad one, to leave anything unnoticed or undefended." Fritz Schulz, *Principles of Roman Law*, trans. Marguerite Wolff (Oxford: Clarendon Press, 1936), 130 n. 3, summarizes: "The Rhetor does not strive after truth and justice, but is concerned with the victory of his client, even when the latter has a bad case . . . ; he may even lie, provided he is successful."

Rather, the Talmud recognizes that a judge cannot reach the best verdict without the ability to identify ambiguities and think through various possibilities.[81] The Talmud is not interested in developing students who can make the best case regardless of truth, but rather in developing that ability in order to see through false testimony and better arrive at the truth.[82] This methodology is encapsulated by the Spanish Talmudic exegete Rabbi Yiṣḥak Canpanton, who teaches: "The truth cannot be known, except through its opposite."[83] Abraham Shalom, a fifteenth-century Spanish Jewish philosopher, similarly writes, "A man is not called a hero of wisdom, until he can demonstrate a proposition two ways, once positively and once negatively, for a matter is only known through its opposite."[84]

The literary contexts of R. Yoḥanan's and Rav's statements that one cannot judge capital cases unless he can purify the reptile provide further direction for how judges should seek truth. The Yerushalmi passage, for example, details how thoroughly witnesses are to be interrogated depending on the case:

> Ze`ir bar Ḥinena in the name of R. Ḥanina and Rav Yehudah [said]: One [verse] states, "You shall investigate and inquire and

[81] The idea that by recognizing rhetorical language one can better see through it and arrive at a more objective standpoint goes back to Aristotle; see p. 33. Stanley Fish, "Rhetoric," in *Rhetoric in an Antifoundational World: Language, Culture, and Pedagogy*, ed. Michael Bernard-Donals and Richard Glejzer (New Haven: Yale University Press, 1998): 56–8, summarizes this approach, which argues that "the discovery (or rediscovery) that all discourse and therefore all knowledge is rhetorical leads or should lead to the adoption of a *method* by which the dangers of rhetoric can be at least mitigated and perhaps extirpated ... The reasoning is that by repeatedly uncovering the historical and ideological basis of established structures (both political and cognitive), one becomes sensitized to the effects of ideology and begins to clear a space in which those effects can be combated." In this view, the "realization of rhetoric's pervasiveness" (ibid., 56) paradoxically opens up the possibility for a more objective use of language and argumentation.

[82] See this sentiment expressed in the epigraphs to the Conclusion, on p. 264.

[83] Isaac ben Jacob Canpanton and Shemuel al-Valensi, *Darkhe ha-Talmud* (Jerusalem: Isaak Lange, 1980), 34, also cited at Daniel Boyarin, *Ha-`iyun ha-Sefaradi: lefarshanut ha-Talmud shel megureshe Sefarad* (Jerusalem: Yad Izhak Ben Zvi and Hebrew University, 1989), 63; and Boyarin, "Moslem," 11. This aphorism is repeated by other masters of this Spanish school, as for instance by R. Immanuel Sefaradi cited in Abraham ben Don Shelomoh `Aqrah, ed. *Me-harere nemerim* (Venice: Bet Dani'el Zaneṭi, 1599), 3b.

[84] Abraham Shalom, *Haqdamat ha-ma`atiq ha-she'elot veha-teshubot `al mabo ma'amarot u-meliṣah lehe-ḥakham Marsiliyyo* (Vienna: Friedrich Förster, 1859), translation from Boyarin, "Moslem," 11.

> interrogate thoroughly" (Deut 13:15), and another [verse] states, "Justice, justice shall you chase (*tirdof*)" (Deut 16:20). How is this? If you [as judge] see the law is emerging truthfully, then inquire, but if not, then make it just.[85]

The first verse requires a thorough investigation whereas the second verse commands one to rush to the just verdict (implied by the word "chase"). Ze`ir explains that one should follow the normal course of thorough investigation only if the judge sees that it will lead to the truth. If, however, he deems that the procedure is impeding justice, then he should intervene. In a monetary case, for example, if the thorough corroboration of the testimony of the witnesses were to nullify them and lead to one party losing a just suit, then the judge should abbreviate the testing stage and jump to the deliberation. This and other statements within this sugya emphasize that the judge must not let procedure get in the way of justice.[86] R. Yoḥanan's statement similarly seeks to ensure that judges possess the skills needed to see through false argumentation to better access the truth and avoid at all costs sentencing an innocent person to death; this is the same skillset as the ability to purify a reptile.

Just before Rav's statement about purifying the reptile, the Bavli reports: "Rav Kahana said, if the members of a Sanhedrin unanimously see fit to find guilt, then they acquit him immediately. Why? For we have learned [the requirement] to postpone the judgement until the next day in order to produce merit for him, but since these [judges] did not find merit for him from the beginning, they will not find merit for him ever."[87] If all of the judges supported conviction during the deliberation and not even one judge could present an argument for acquittal, then they clearly did not try hard enough to find the accused innocent and so the defendant goes free. The requirement to wait until the next day to convict [9] presumes that sleeping on it may produce a new argument for innocence, which is why making such an effort is an essential part of the court procedure. A court that fails to conceive of even one argument for

[85] Y. Sanhedrin 4:1, 22a. See parallel at B. Sanhedrin 32b.

[86] See also Hayes, "Legal Truth," 73–121; and Halberstam, *Law and Truth*.

[87] B. Sanhedrin 17a following MS Yad Harav Herzog 1. Significantly, Maimonides, Meiri, and Rashbash Duran read "investigate, *pat̤hu*" instead of "see fit, *ra'u*." See Mandel, "`Al 'pataḥ,'" 80 n. 115, who points out that according to this reading, Rav Kahana does not refer to a unanimous verdict but rather to a lack of any attempts to acquit during the investigation by the judges.

innocence would not likely produce any positive lines of reasoning the next day either; the inability to do so violates proper court procedure. Taking its cue from the realm of rhetoric, the Talmud recognizes that it is always possible to argue both sides of every case. Therefore, if nobody offers an argument for acquittal, it is not because no such argument exists; rather it signals the court's incompetence and the judges' descent into groupthink. It is in this context that Rav requires the judges to be able to purify the reptile so that they should have the skills to find all possible arguments in favor of a defendant and therefore prevent an unjust punishment.

This law regarding the investigation of testimony is one in a series of procedures designed to mitigate the negative aspects of the inquisitorial system. After questioning the witnesses, "if the judges find reason to acquit [the defendant], then they dismiss him. If not, then they adjourn the trial until the next day. They would join up in pairs, eat little food and abstain from wine the whole day, deliberate the whole night, and the next day they would get up and come to the court."[88] They would then restate their positions to see if any had changed their minds towards acquittal, but nobody could change their minds and start arguing for conviction [6]. An official secretary records the judges' opinions in order to keep track of the two sides. It is significant that the judges deliberate not only as a group but also in pairs – a setup that encourages each person to take different sides. The lesser judges begin the deliberation [9] because if the chief judge opens to convict, the lesser judges will feel apprehensive about disagreeing with him. Significantly, the Roman Senate began deliberation with the most senior members and junior senators rarely got a chance to speak.[89] Beginning with the lesser judges encourages the most diversity of opinion. All of these laws increase the chances that a significant group of judges will commit to arguing solely on behalf of the defendant.

For this same reason, the rabbis would not convict on the basis of a simple majority [3]; the judgment of one deciding judge who might be swayed to acquit with a few more minutes of deliberation is too thin a margin to take someone's life. It is too easy, even for a group of 23 judges to fall into groupthink and not be creative enough to think of all possible lines of argumentation. The Mishnah [5] thus allows for bystanders to chime in and offer further reasons to acquit, but not to convict. It is best

[88] M. Sanhedrin 5:5.

[89] A. W. Lintott, *The Constitution of the Roman Republic* (Oxford: Oxford University Press, 1999), 77–8; and Steel, *Roman Oratory*, 12–13, 20.

to err on the side of innocence, even to the point of disallowing potential arguments for conviction by bystanders and by judges who have already committed to acquittal. If a student offers a reason to acquit, he is invited to join the court;[90] furthermore, if the defendant ends up being acquitted due to the student's contribution, then the student becomes a permanent member of the court.[91] This system greatly encouraged and incentivized every effort on the part of many people to discover all possible arguments for exoneration.

Throughout the deliberation, the Mishnah sways the process towards acquittal because it is better to let a guilty person go free than to kill an innocent person. I do not believe that the primary purpose of this set of protocols is to ban capital punishment per se.[92] Rather, the rabbis wish their court procedure to reflect mercy and leniency – perhaps as a contrast to the harsh Roman legal system. This push to leniency goes hand in hand with the rabbis' appreciation for the power of rhetoric. In order to acquit as often as possible, the rabbis rely on rhetoric to sway the legal procedure away from conviction.[93] Recognizing that human reason is frail and fickle requires the judges to use their rhetorical abilities to argue for any possibility of innocence.[94]

CONCLUSION

What emerges from the Talmud's courtroom protocol is that the rabbis are not Platonists who believe in one truth that an objective inquisitorial judge can access. Rather, they remain within the realm of rhetoric,

90 M. Sanhedrin 5:4.

91 T. Sanhedrin 9:3.

92 See Berkowitz, *Execution and Invention*, 19–20, and the history of scholarship on this at pp. 25–64. Even if one thinks that the rabbis were against the death penalty, it is still worthwhile asking why they chose this particular method to effectively ban it. See the same methodology used by Devora Steinmetz, *Punishment and Freedom: The Rabbinic Construction of Criminal Law* (Philadelphia: University of Pennsylvania, 2008), 16. In other words, the rabbis could have used various means of doing away with the death penalty. That they focus on the power of argumentation and rhetoric in order to limit capital punishment teaches us as much about their view of truth and argumentation as it does about the death penalty itself.

93 See Sifre Deut 144. An exception is made only for the inciter to idolatry (Deut 13:7–12) to whom none of the procedures at M. Sanhedrin 4:1–3 apply (T. Sanhedrin 10:11 and 7:2; B. Sanhedrin 29a, 33b, and 36b). Because of the gravity of his sin, we judge him without bias towards innocence like a monetary case. The rabbis apparently felt it was worth risking a small chance of killing an innocent person in order to avoid the great danger that an inciter poses to the community.

94 See pp. 205–6 on the principle that the rabbis will not impose a punishment on the basis of a *qal va-ḥomer*.

recognizing the power of persuasion and the near impossibility for humans to arrive at anything like objective truth. Nonetheless, it is precisely for that reason that the power of rhetorical argumentation cannot be trusted in the hands of hired and biased advocates but rather must be delivered into the care of the judges.[95] Is the rabbinic court inquisitorial or adversarial? It is a complex combination of both. The overall structure of the court procedure, including the hearing of pleas and the examination of witnesses, follows the inquisitorial system. However, a substantial adversarial element is introduced during the stage of deliberation – not involving lawyers but the judges themselves. In capital cases, the judges bring all their skill to bear in challenging the testimony of the witnesses and the entire procedure is set up to protect the defendant. In monetary cases, the judges are prohibited from acting like lawyers during the first half of the trial: they may not suggest pleas or direct witness testimony. During the deliberation of all cases, the courtroom is transformed into a mock adversarial trial with the judges lining up on two sides as prosecutors and defendants, and with court stenographers recording the words of both sides.[96]

The rabbis shared with the sophists the epistemological rejection of objective truth; however, unlike the sophists who also repudiate the possibility of achieving justice, the rabbis still strive towards that elusive but essential goal. Consequently, whereas the sophists translated their epistemology into a completely adversarial system, the rabbis legislated that the adversarial element must be limited and better controlled. The surest path towards justice requires two opposing parties arguing for each side. But if those parties are lawyers, then they will introduce deception and trickery, and will obfuscate rather than discover the truth. The best chance for justice entails adversarial argumentation in the hands of competent and honest judges. This complex set of court procedures reveals a highly sophisticated and nuanced epistemology that harnesses but also controls the power of persuasion by synthesizing rhetoric with an honest search for justice and mercy.

[95] See also Sinai, *Judge*, 389–413, for cases that allow for even more involvement by the judge.

[96] These scribes are also mentioned at Lev Rabbah 30:11.

7 Why Are There Lawyers in Heaven?

> A lawyer dies and goes to Heaven, where he is brought before God. "A lawyer, eh?" says God. "We've never had a lawyer in Heaven before. Argue a point of the law for my edification."
>
> The lawyer goes into panic and says, "Oh, God, I cannot think of an argument worthy of Your notice. But I'll tell you what, you argue a point of the law and I'll refute You."[1]

Humorists have long quipped that no lawyers can get into heaven. The rabbis, however, describe the heavenly court as being suffused with lawyers. M. Avot 4:11 describes a huge number of heavenly advocates and prosecutors:[2]

> R. Eliezer ben Yaakov says, One who performs one commandment acquires for himself one advocate (*paraklet*)[3] but one who violates one transgression acquires for himself one prosecutor (*kategor*).[4]

[1] Slightly modified from Marc Galanter, *Lowering the Bar: Lawyer Jokes and Legal Culture* (Madison, WI: University of Wisconsin Press, 2005), 49.

[2] Follows MS Kaufman.

[3] Paraclete (פְּרַקְלִיט, παράκλητος) means a supporter or sponsor and, when used in legal contexts, refers to a defense advocate. The term is found in Greek documents from classical Athens through the first centuries CE. See Kenneth Grayston, "The Meaning of Parakletos," *Journal for the Study of the New Testament* 13 (1981): 67–82.

[4] *Kategoros* (קָטֵיגוֹר, κατήγορος) refers to the prosecutor in ancient Athenian courts and continued to be used in the Roman East. *Kategoros* is also used in the sense of a prosecutor in Josephus (*Antiquities*, 7.6) and in an inscription from Laconia dated to 42 CE; see Kaja Harter-Uibopuu, "The Trust Fund of Phaenia Aromation (IG V.1 1208) and Imperial Gytheion," *Studia Humaniora Tartuensia* 5 (2004): 1–17. See also Sperber, *Dictionary of Greek and Latin Terms*, 126–30. Both *synegoros* and *kategoros* are used regularly by writers such as Lucian and Plutarch. See also Meira Kensky, *Trying Man, Trying God: The Divine Courtroom in Early Jewish and Christian Literature* (Tübingen: Mohr Siebeck, 2010), 306.

Later midrashim explore the role of lawyers in heaven in great detail.[5] Exodus Rabbah 18:5, for example, teaches:

> R. Yose said, To what are Michael and Samael similar? To a defense advocate (*sanegor*)[6] and a prosecutor standing in a judgment. This one speaks and that one speaks. Once this one finishes his oration and that one his, the defense advocate knows that he has won and begins to praise the judge that he should issue a verdict. The prosecutor tries to add something. The defense advocate says, "Be quiet that we may hear the judge." So do Michael and Samael stand before the Shekhina. Satan prosecutes and Michael pleads innocence for Israel. Satan tries to speak but Michael shuts him up . . .

The theme of advocates in heaven, found often throughout rabbinic literature, raises a number of questions. We would expect that an omniscient and omnipotent God should be able to judge perfectly well on his own. In fact, M. Avot 4:22 presents God in precisely these terms as a sole Judge:

> He is God, He is the Maker, He is the Creator, He is Omniscient, He is the Judge, He is the Witness, He is the Plaintiff, and He will judge in the future for there is before Him no perversion, no forgetting, no showing favoritism, no taking of bribes, for all is His, and know that all will be accounted for.[7]

The question of why so many aggadot portray a heavenly court full of lawyers is only compounded when we compare the role of lawyers in earthly courts. As we saw in the previous chapter, the rabbis prohibited the activity of lawyers in their own courts. Instead, they placed the responsibility of advocacy in the hands of the judges, thus creating a system in opposition to the corruption they saw in the Roman legal system. Recall that the Talmud holds the adversarial system suspect because it does not promote honesty or lead to justice. The prominence of advocates in the heavenly court of rabbinic aggadah, therefore, requires explanation.

I propose that the answer is partly historical and partly philosophical. That is, the rabbis incorporated a tradition that already began in the

5 See also Y. Rosh Hashanah 1:3, 57b, and the midrashim discussed below.

6 See p. 223 n. 31. This term is used interchangeably with paraclete in rabbinic literature.

7 MS Kaufman. Cf. Y. Sanhedrin 6:10, 24a. See further sources and discussion at Shoval Shafat, "The Interface of Divine and Human Punishment in Rabbinic Thought" (PhD diss., Ben-Gurion University, 2011), 187–90.

Bible and continued in Second Temple literature. However, they also expanded on that tradition in a way that reveals an important philosophical and theological stance about truth, law, and the nature of God. This analysis will reveal that the rabbis appreciated the power of rhetorical persuasion and adversarial advocacy and – although wary of them in human courts – found an important role for them in engendering God's mercy. These findings will confirm the complex and nuanced approach of Talmudic sources towards truth and rhetoric that we have developed in previous chapters. Let us begin with an overview of heavenly advocates in pre-rabbinic literature, both prosecutors and defenders.

HEAVENLY ADVOCATES IN THE BIBLE AND SECOND TEMPLE LITERATURE

Already the Bible places a prosecuting advocate in the heavenly court.[8] Most famously, the Prosecutor (*satan*) who is a member of the Divine council impugns Job's piety as being superficial (Job 1:6–2:7). The Prosecutor also accuses Joshua the high priest but is in turn rebuked by God (Zechariah 3:1–2).[9] Second Temple literature fleshes out the character of the Prosecutor. Jubilees, for example develops the role of Satan in Job as the angel named Mastema,[10] the chief of the fallen angels (10:8–9) who incites the offspring of Noah to sin (11:5). Mastema also accuses Abraham of lacking faith and convinces God to test Abraham's faith by commanding him to sacrifice Isaac (ibid. 17:16). In addition, he is the agent who nearly kills Moses on his journey (ibid. 48:2). Incidentally, rabbinic aggadah similarly has Satan threaten Moses[11] as well as accuse Abraham before God.[12]

8 A heavenly court is mentioned in 1 Kings 22:19 and Dan 7:26, and is also hinted at in Gen 1:26, 3:22, and 11:7.

9 *Satan* also appears without the definite article in 1 Chron 21:1 where it does not accuse but rather incites David to sin. Other instances of *satan* in the Bible as a noun and verb also do not relate to a heavenly court. See further at Victor Hamilton, "Satan," in *The Anchor Bible Dictionary*, ed. David Noel Freedman (1992): 985–9.

10 See Esther Eshel, "Mastema's Attempt on Moses' Life in the 'Pseudo-Jubilees' Text from Masada," *Dead Sea Discoveries* 10, no. 3 (2003): 359–64; and Devorah Dimant, "Between Qumran Sectarian and Non-Sectarian Texts: The Case of Belial and Mastema," in *The Dead Sea Scrolls and Contemporary Culture*, ed. Adolfo Roitman and Lawrence Schiffman (Leiden: Brill, 2011): 235–56.

11 B. Nedarim 32a. Y. Nedarim 3:9, 38b, does not say Satan but rather just angel and Exod Rabbah 5:8, identifies it as an angel of mercy.

12 B. Sanhedrin 89b. In Gen Rabbah 55:4, instead of Satan it is God and the angels who accuse Abraham. Some MSS variants have the nations of the world accusing Abraham; see Albeck and Theodor, *Bereshit Rabba*, 587. Cf. Gen Rabbah 56:7–8 where Samael tries to stop Abraham and Isaac from going through with the sacrifice.

Scholars have traced the origin of Satan back to Ancient Near Eastern mythology as well as the spy agency of the Persian Empire.[13] However, Satan also fulfills an important need to explain the existence of evil in a monotheistic belief system featuring an omnipotent and benevolent God. Hints to primordial forces of evil already make appearances in Genesis, Isaiah and Psalms.[14] Therefore, it is easy to see how belief in an opposing, even if subordinate, power who seeks to prosecute humanity and bring chaos to the world would have caught on.

Unlike the prosecuting heavenly powers, angelic defenders are more difficult to find in the Bible. The origins and development of defense advocates in the heavenly court, which is the primary focus of this chapter, thus requires a more extensive explanation. Job calls upon the earth and the heavens to speak out for him, to testify on his behalf and be his advocates (מליצי).[15] Elihu similarly says regarding someone disciplined by God and on the verge of death: "If he has a representative (מלאך), one advocate (מליץ)[16] against a thousand to declare the man's uprightness, then He has mercy on him" (Job 33:23–4). However, no such representative ever materializes. Daniel mentions the angel Michael as being the prince of Israel, possibly representing and defending the people in heaven; but, again, there is no mention of a trial involving him.[17] Besides the Jobian speeches, the Bible mentions no other angelic defenders.

Rather, it is humans – and specifically prophets – who arise to fulfill that role: Abraham (Gen 18:17–33), Moses (Exod 32-33; Num 14:13–19), Joshua (Josh 7:6–7), Amos (Amos 7:2, 5), Jeremiah (Jer 14:7–9, 13), and Ezekiel (Ez 11:13), among others. The prophet's primary role is to bring God's message, usually of rebuke, to the people. As the prophet submits before God's majesty he becomes "the instrument of divine severity, the attribute of divine justice."[18] However, as Yochanan Muffs points out:

[13] Marvin Pope, *Job*, The Anchor Bible (Garden City: Doubleday, 1965), 10–11; and Naphtali Tur-Sinai, *The Book of Job: A New Commentary* (Jerusalem: Kiryat Sefer, 1957), 38–45.

[14] Jon Levenson, *Creation and the Persistence of Evil: The Jewish Drama of Divine Omnipotence* (San Francisco: Harper and Row, 1988).

[15] Job 16:18–20. V. 20 calls upon God to arbitrate (ויוכח) between Job and God Himself making God play a dual role of prosecutor and judge. In Job 9:33, Job laments: "There is no arbiter (מוכיח) between us," which ascribes to God only the role of prosecutor since God is not acting as a fair judge. Job 19:25 has Job call for a vindicator (גאלי), perhaps God Himself, to either defend Job or, as judge, declare his innocence.

[16] LXX translates paraclete and the Targum translates the phrase: מלאכא חדא פרקליטא מן בני אלף קטיגוריא.

[17] See Dan 10:13, 21 and 12:1.

[18] Yochanan Muffs, *Love and Joy: Law, Language and Religion in Ancient Israel* (New York: The Jewish Theological Seminary of America, 1992), 9.

> The prophet has another function: He is also an independent advocate to the heavenly court who attempts to rescind the evil decree by means of the only instruments at his disposal, prayer and intercession. He is first the messenger of the divine court to the defendant, but his mission boomerangs back to the sender. Now, he is no longer the messenger of the court; he becomes the agent of the defendant, attempting to mitigate the severity of the decree.[19]

Once the prophet attains an intimate relation with the Divine as a messenger, he is able to turn back and challenge the very messages he was sent to deliver. When God becomes angry at humanity's wickedness, He sends a prophet to warn them of an impending punishment. Hopefully, the sinners will repent and keep God's wrath at bay. Even in the absence of behavioral change, however, the right words from a righteous intercessor can pacify God's rage and convince Him to forgo his threat and forgive the sin. In fact, God sometimes even invites these advocates to help Him relieve His temper before He does something He will regret. This explains why God informs Abraham of His plans for Sodom and why He commands Moses, "Leave Me alone."[20]

Suzanne Last Stone elaborates on the prophet's role as an advocate: "Prophetic intercession takes the form not simply of demanding prayer but of argument and the lodging of a legal complaint or appeal from a decree." In that sense, the prophet is "the ideal lawyer/advocate."[21] Also expanding on Muffs, Yair Lorberbaum encourages us to take the anthropomorphism, and especially the anthropopathism, of the Bible seriously, even literally.[22] God feels the full palette of emotions found in a human personality: jealousy, anger, regret, shame, mercy, love and joy. If man is created in God's image, then God must be at least as emotionally complex as a human being. Precisely because God, unlike the mythological divinities of the Ancient Near East, is invested in human beings and loves them, he becomes jealous and enraged at their infidelity and wickedness. In order that God not destroy the world in these moments of anger, He puts in place mechanisms of self-control, such as the

19 Ibid.

20 Exod 32:10; Deut 9:14. See Moshe Shamah, *Recalling the Covenant: A Contemporary Commentary on the Five Books of the Torah* (Jersey City: Ktav, 2011), 82–4; and Muffs, *Love and Joy*, 28.

21 Suzanne Last Stone, "Rabbinic Legal Magic: A New Look at Honi's Circle as the Construction of Legal Space," *Yale Journal of Law and the Humanities* 17 (2005): 109.

22 Yair Lorberbaum, "The Rainbow in the Cloud: An Anger-Management Device," *The Journal of Religion* 89, no. 4 (2009): 498–540.

rainbow, finding a scapegoat to receive the punishment vicariously, or allowing an advocate to talk Him out of His wrath.

This understanding of God and the role of the advocate is amplified in Second Temple and rabbinic literature. In the Book of Enoch, after Enoch announces to the fallen angels their impending punishment, they request that Enoch petition God for forgiveness on their behalf (1 Enoch 13:4). God, however, tells Enoch to rebuke them: "Go, say to the Watchers of heaven, who have sent you to intercede for them: 'You should intercede for men, and not men for you'" (1 Enoch 15:2). Enoch thus acts here as both a messenger and an intercessor. Furthermore, we see that God had in mind that the angels should act as defense advocates on behalf of humans.[23]

Similarly, the Rule of the Community of the Dead Sea Sect includes a curse of those fated to Belial:

> You shall not have someone who speaks kindly on your behalf among all the intercessors.[24]

Muffs explains that the term for intercessors – אוחזי אבות (i.e. "one who assumes a fatherly attitude on behalf of someone") – is borrowed from a similar term and concept in the Babylonian world. Reflected in these texts is a shift from the human advocates in the Bible to a belief in angelic intercessors as well.[25]

This development is seen more clearly in Philo who lists various defense advocates on behalf of humans in the heavenly court.[26] He writes that those repentant Jews who return from exile can obtain reconciliation with God through three intercessions (*parakletois*): (1) God's mercy and compassion; (2) the prayers of the patriarchs; and (3) the improvement of the repentant.[27] Similarly, one who harms another and repents, and then comes to the Temple with a sacrifice, also brings "with him an irreproachable mediator (*parakleton*), namely, that conviction of the soul which has delivered him from incurable

[23] 1 Enoch 9:1 also identifies Michael, Uriel, Raphael, and Gabriel, as well as "the souls of those who have died" (9:10) as prosecutors before the gates of heaven.

[24] 1QS 2:9. Translation from Muffs, *Love and Joy*, 38.

[25] See also Joseph Baumgarten, "The Heavenly Tribunal and the Personification of Ṣedeq in Jewish Apocalyptic," in *Aufstieg und Niedergang der römischen Welt, Vol 19.1* (Berlin: De Gruyter, 1979): 219–39, who discusses the role of Melchizedek and the hypostatized Ṣedek in the heavenly court.

[26] Grayston, "The Meaning of Parakletos," 73–4.

[27] Philo, *On Rewards and Punishments*, 9:165–7. See further at Harry A. Wolfson, *Philo* (Cambridge: Harvard University Press, 1948), II, 412–13.

calamity, curing him of the disease which would cause death, and wholly changing and bringing him to good health."[28] So far, these references to paracletes can be read metaphorically: God's mercy and man's prayers and repentance help man just like advocates would.

However, Philo goes further in his explanation of the high priest's clothing as a symbol for the Logos:[29] "For it was indispensable that the man who was consecrated to the Father of the world, should have as a paraclete, his son, the being most perfect in all virtue, to procure forgiveness of sins, and a supply of unlimited blessings."[30] God's son here refers to the Logos[31] which acts as a paraclete to intercede and defend Israel's sins before God. Philo elaborates with striking beauty on the intercessory role of the Logos:

> And the Father who created the universe has given to his archangelic and most ancient Word a pre-eminent gift, to stand on the confines of both, and separated that which had been created from the Creator. And this same Word is continually a suppliant to the immortal God on behalf of the moral race, which is exposed to affliction and misery; and is also the ambassador, sent by the Ruler of all, to the subject race. And the Word rejoices in the gift, and, exulting in it, announces it and boasts of it, saying, "And I stood in the midst, between the Lord and you"[32] neither being uncreated as God, nor yet created as you, but being in the midst between these two extremities, like a hostage, as it were, to both parties: a hostage to the Creator, as a pledge and security that the whole race would never fly off and revolt entirely, choosing disorder rather than order;

[28] Philo, Special Laws I. 237. Translations from Philo, *The Works of Philo: Complete and Unabridged*, trans. C. D. Yonge (Hendrickson, 2008).

[29] Philo speaks specifically of the logeum as "an emblem of that reason which holds together and regulates the universe" (*On the Life of Moses II*, 133), a clear reference to the Logos (Wolfson, *Philo*, I, 339). He describes the high priest's other garments as symbols of the physical world. However, although Philo generally describes the Logos as the mind whose object of thought is the intelligible world, since, as with Aristotle, the mind is identical with its intelligible object, the Logos can refer also to the world itself. See Wolfson, *Philo*, I, 246, citing *On the Creation*, 6, 24. In other places, Philo describes the high priest himself as an allegorical reference to the Logos; see Wolfson, *Philo*, I, 259–60, and Ronald Williamson, *Jews in the Hellenistic World: Philo* (Cambridge: Cambridge University Press, 1989), 136–43.

[30] Philo, *On the Life of Moses* II. 134.

[31] For the Logos as God's first-born son, see Philo, *On Husbandry*, 51. See also Wolfson, *Philo*, I, 234.

[32] Yonge gives the citation as Num 16:48 LXX (17:13 MT), but Deut 5:5 is a better fit.

and to the creature, to lead it to entertain a confident hope that the merciful God would not overlook his own work.[33]

The dual role of the Logos here as messenger and advocate parallels the dual role of the prophet discussed above. This dual description continues in the Johannine writings where the paraclete refers to the Logos, the Holy Spirit and Jesus.[34] The Gospel of John (14:16, 26; 15:26; 16:7) refers to the Holy Spirit as a paraclete in the sense of a teacher or prophetic communication with humans, though not as an advocate on behalf of humans.[35] 1 John, in turn, uses the term paraclete to refer to Jesus acting as an advocate for humanity: "If anyone does sin, we have an advocate (*parakleton*) with the Father, Jesus Christ the righteous; and he is the atoning sacrifice for our sins" (1 John 2:1–2, NSRV).[36]

The replacement of the role of the prophet with the heavenly Logos and angelic beings may result from the cessation of advocate-prophets in the late Second Temple period. Although there were some advocate-sages, such as Ḥoni the Circle-drawer,[37] the need for heavenly mercy was apparently greater than the intercession that these figures could supply; therefore, the role of advocacy was transferred to the angelic realm.

HEAVENLY ADVOCATES IN RABBINIC LITERATURE

The few hints of advocates in the Bible, meager as they are, grow in Second Temple literature, but sprout forth a full-fledged heavenly court bureaucracy in rabbinic texts, especially in amoraic midrashim.[38]

33 Philo, *Who is the Heir of Divine Things*, 205–6.

34 See Harold Attridge, "Philo and John: Two Riffs on One Logos," *Studia Philonica Annual* 17 (2005): 103–17; and Margaret Barker, "The Paraclete," in *The Temple in Text and Tradition: A Festschrift in Honour of Robert Hayward*, ed. R. T. McLay (London: Bloomsbury T&T Clark, 2015): 98–112.

35 See further at D. A. Carson, "The Function of the Paraclete in John 16:7–11," *Journal of Biblical Literature* 98, no. 4 (1979): 547–66, on the paraclete as prosecutor but still not defender.

36 See Hans Weder, "*Deus Incarnatus*: On the Hermeneutics of Christology in the Johannine Writings," in *Exploring the Gospel of John: In Honor of D. Moody Smith*, ed. R. A. Culpepper and C. C. Black (Louisville, KY: Westminster John Knox Press, 1996): 339; and George Johnston, *The Spirit-Paraclete in the Gospel of John* (Cambridge: Cambridge University Press, 1970), 53.

37 See M. Ta`anit 3:8, and analysis at Suzanne Last Stone, "On the Interplay of Rules, 'Cases,' and Concepts in Rabbinic Legal Literature: Another Look at the Aggadot on Honi the Circle-Drawer," *Diné Israel* 24 (2007): 125–55; and herein p. 256–7.

38 See Kaufman Kohler, "Paraclete," *Jewish Encyclopedia* (1906). While tannaitic texts mention paracletes as merits before the heavenly court, amoraic texts include paracletes as confrontational defenders; see further on p. 260 n. 87.

As cited above, M. Avot 4:11 teaches that one acquires paracletes and prosecutors (*kategor*) by fulfilling commandments and sinning, respectively. T. Pe'ah 4:21 lists charity and kind deeds as being great advocates (*peraqlet gadol*) between Israel and their Father in heaven.[39] Similarly, in T. Pe'ah 1:1, a sin-offering is likened to "an advocate (*peraqlet*) that enters to plead."[40] Y. Ta`anit 2:4, 65b, has Abraham requesting of God to find a defense (*sanegoria*) for the nation when calamity befalls them. Y. Ta`anit 1:1, 63c, meanwhile, teaches that the four species, which grow on water, act as advocates (*peraqlitin*) on behalf of water.[41]

While Philo and John transferred the roles of messenger and advocate from the prophet to the Logos, the rabbis shifted them again to Torah. Leviticus Rabbah 6:1 teaches:[42]

> "Do not be a false witness" (Prov 24:28): this refers to Israel, "You are My witnesses, declares the Lord, and I am God" (Isa 43:28). "Against your fellow" (Prov 24:28): this refers to the Holy One, blessed be He, "Do not desert your Friend and your father's Friend" (Prov 27:10). "And seduce with your speech" (Prov 24:28): as you seduced me at Sinai and said, "All that the Lord has spoken we will do and obey" (Exod 24:7), but after forty days you said to the calf, "These are your gods, O Israel" (Exod 32:4).
>
> R. Aḥa said, this holy spirit[43] is a mouth of defense (*sanegoria*). It argues merit for this side and for that side. It says to Israel, "Do not be a false witness against your Fellow." And it says to the Holy One, blessed be He, "Do not say, 'What he did to Me, I will do to him" (Prov 24:28).

The holy spirit here is the prophetic voice of Scripture which turns against its Author and becomes an independent intermediary. In this daring midrash, the rabbis use a verse not only to rebuke Israel for its unfaithfulness but also to warn God not to take revenge and deny His

39 See parallel at B. Baba Batra 10a. B. Shabbat 32a similarly lists repentance and good deeds as a person's paracletes. See further at Baruch Bokser, "Rabbinic Responses to Catastrophe: From Continuity to Discontinuity," *Proceedings of the American Academy for Jewish Research* 50 (1983): 44–5.

40 See parallel at Sifra, Meṣora`, perek 3, 14. Y. Berakhot 4:1, 7b, similarly refers to the two daily burnt offerings as paracletes.

41 Similarly, Eccl Rabbah 7 speaks of the holiday of Shemini Aseret as a paraclete for rain.

42 Translation follows MS London. See parallel at Midrash haGadol to Deut 9:16 and Deut Rabbah 3:11.

43 MS Munich reads, "the Holy One, blessed be He," instead of holy spirit, but all other MSS read as above.

covenant with Israel in return. Like Philo's Logos, the midrash's Scripture as holy spirit acts as a heavenly advocate for (and against) both Israel and God. Though scholars have pointed out that the cosmological role of Philo's Logos finds a parallel in the Torah as architect in Genesis Rabbah 1:1,[44] Daniel Boyarin notes that "the difference in the role between the Logos and the Torah is of central importance: the Logos is an actual personified agent, while for the rabbis, Wisdom has been captured in a Book, and there is only one agent."[45] Although Boyarin's caution is appropriate for Genesis Rabbah, this midrash from Leviticus Rabbah surely does personify Scripture as an independent agent.[46]

The Torah also advocates in defense of Israel in Song of Songs Rabbah:

> [1] R. Azariah and R. Aḥa said in the name of R. Yoḥanan: At the moment when Israel at Sinai heard "I," (Deut 5:6) their souls flew out, as is written: "If we continue hearing [the voice of the Lord our God any longer, we shall die]" (Deut 5:22), and as it is written, "My soul left upon His speaking" (Song 5:6). The Word (*dibur*) returned (*ḥazar*) to the Holy One, blessed be He, and said: "Master of the Universe, You are alive and enduring and your Torah is alive and enduring but you have sent me dead people, they are all dead." Thereupon, the Holy One, blessed be He, retracted (*ḥazar*) and sweetened the Word for them, as is written, "The voice of the Lord [in strength, the voice of the Lord in splendor]" (Ps 29:4).
>
> R. Ḥama bar R. Ḥanina said, "The voice of the Lord in strength," for the young people; "the voice of the Lord in splendor," for the old people.
>
> [2] R. Shimon bar Yoḥai taught: The Torah that the Holy One, blessed He, gave to Israel returned their souls to them, as it is written, "The Torah of the Lord is perfect, restoring souls" (Ps 19:8).
>
> [3] Another interpretation: "His mouth is sweet." This is like [a parable of] a king who spoke against his son and he [the son] became frightened and his soul left him. Once the king saw that his soul left him, he began to hug and kiss him and to persuade him

[44] Wolfson, *Philo*, I, 243; Urbach, *The Sages: Their Concepts and Beliefs*, 198–200 and references there; David Winston, *Logos and Mystical Theology in Philo of Alexandria* (Cincinnati: Hebrew Union College Press, 1985), 25; and Stern, *Midrash and Theory*, 27–8. Note, however, the differences between Philo and the midrash discussed by Wolfson, Urbach and Stern.

[45] Daniel Boyarin, "The Gospel of the Memra: Jewish Binitarianism and the Prologue to John," *Harvard Theological Review* 94, no. 3 (2001): 261 n. 66.

[46] On the personified Scripture as Logos, see also Yadin, *Scripture as Logos*, 168–75.

and say to him, "What is with you? Are you not my only son? Am I not your father?" So too, when the Holy One, blessed be He, said, "I am the Lord your God," their souls immediately flew away. Once they died, the angels began hugging and kissing them and saying to them, "What is with you? Do not fear. You are children of the Lord your God." And the Holy One, blessed be He, sweetened the Word in their mouths and said to them, "Are you not My sons? I am the Lord your God. You are My nation. You are beloved unto Me." And He began to persuade them until their souls returned and they began to entreat Him. This is, "His mouth is sweet."

[4] The Torah began requesting mercy for Israel from the Holy One, blessed be He. It said before Him, "Master of the universe! Is there a king who marries off his daughter but kills the members of his household? All of the world is happy for me but your sons are dead." Immediately, their souls returned, as it is written, "The Torah of the Lord is perfect, restoring souls."[47]

As in the previous midrash, God's prophetic word hypostatizes and takes upon itself the role of an advocate before God on behalf of Israel. Here, however, the terminology used is not holy spirit but *dibbur*, which can be translated as Word or Logos. In the continuation of the midrash ([2] and [4]), *dibbur* is substituted with Torah and it is the Torah that acts as Israel's advocate to request mercy before God.[48] The parable in section [3] explains how God sweetens the Word such that, like the biblical prophets, the Word does double duty, both persuading God to help Israel and assuaging Israel's mortal fear of God.[49]

As is evident, the rabbis not only inherited and transmitted the rich heritage of Second Temple interpretations that conceived of advocates in the heavenly court but also expanded upon it. Some of these midrashim include curious and sometimes radical innovations. The rabbis, for instance, introduced the terms *sanegor* and *kategor*, and imported other aspects of Roman courts such as the clepsydra (see below).[50] As Meira Kensky notes, the rabbis not only adopted technical terms from their surrounding Greco-Roman legal culture; their aggadic

[47] Song of Songs Rabbah *parasha* 6, *pasuk* 16, *piska* 3–5. Translation follows MS Vatican 76. See synopsis of variants at www.schechter.ac.il/schechter/ShirHashirim/9.pdf.

[48] A hypostatized Torah is also found in Lam Rabbah, *petiḥta* 24, where God calls upon the Torah and each letter of the alphabet to testify against Israel, but Abraham convinces each of them to withhold their testimonies.

[49] See further at Winston, *Logos*, 16.

[50] Lieberman, "Roman Legal Institutions," 27.

divine courts also feature the sense of trial as *agon* where advocates unscrupulously battle to produce any winning argument they can, regardless of truth or falsehood.[51] The modeling of the divine court on the Hellenistic-Roman court system mirrors the rabbis' tendency to portray God as a Roman Emperor in their king parables.[52] However, this modeling only underscores the question: if the rabbis rejected the adversarial nature of the Roman legal system and the presence of lawyers in their own earthly courts, why would they not only transmit these nearly heretical themes of Second Temple literature but also expand upon them and freely include parallels to Roman courts?

I propose that the rabbis envisioned the heavenly court in terms of Roman courts, not in spite of the corruption of the latter but precisely because of it. They feared that a heavenly court that followed strict justice and judged human actions according to the truth would issue impossibly harsh, even if justifiable, verdicts. Consider the following text where Abraham acts as defense lawyer on behalf of Sodom:

> "What if the fifty innocents should lack five?" (Gen 18:28). R. Ḥiyya bar Abba said: Abraham wished to descend from fifty to five. The Holy One, blessed be He, said to him, "Turn backwards."
> R. Levi said: A clepsydra full of water, as long as it is full the advocate (*sanegor*) defends. Sometimes the judge wishes for the advocate to defend [further] and he says, "Add more water to it."[53]

In ancient Athenian courts and again in Roman courts after Pompey, the speeches by each advocate were timed using a clepsydra (literally, a water-thief). The clepsydra consisted of an open bowl with a hole near the bottom that emptied into a similar bowl below it. At the outset of the trial, the presiding magistrate would determine the amount of water and time allotted to each side.[54] The speaker would be able to tell that

[51] Kensky, *Trying Man, Trying God*, 313–14. Kensky analyzes a wonderful passage from Eccl Rabbah 4:1 in which Elijah helps the children of the condemned vindicate their fathers. Like an Athenian logographer, Elijah composes for them a defense (*sanegoria*) that they should present in the divine court. Kensky insightfully comments: "When Elijah shows up, he does not instruct the children to pray, to appeal to God's compassion, or to concede anything. He teaches them to *win*, to mount an argument" (ibid., 314).

[52] See David Stern, *Parables in Midrash: Narrative and Exegesis in Rabbinic Literature* (Cambridge: Harvard University Press, 1991), 93–7; and Alan Appelbaum, *The Rabbis' King-Parables: Midrash from the Third-Century Roman Empire* (Piscataway, NJ: Gorgias Press, 2010), 48–51.

[53] Gen Rabbah 49:12. Translation follows MS Vatican 30.

[54] William Forsyth, *The History of Lawyers* (Boston: Estes and Lauriat, 1875), 105.

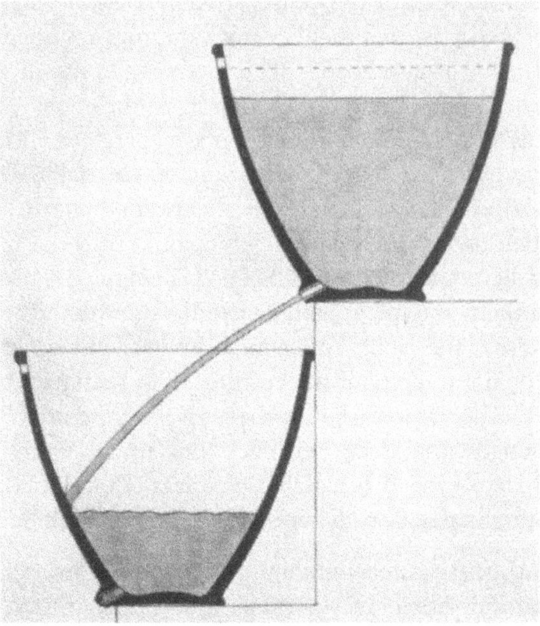

Figure 1. A clepsydra in action. Reproduction courtesy of the American School of Classical Studies at Athens.

his time was running low when the stream weakened and its arc shortened. While the clepsydra was intended to ensure fairness, some advocates apparently attempted to cheat the system by, for example, overfilling the top bowl. One ancient clepsydra found at Athens has an additional hole near the top rim to ensure that the bowl was filled to the same level every time.[55] In Athens, an official was elected by lot each morning to oversee the clepsydra "in order that no mischief be done."[56]

As noted above, God informs Abraham of His plans for Sodom not simply to keep him in the loop but rather to prod Abraham into arguing with Him. A previous midrash provides a parable: "Like a king who had an advisor (סנקתדרין) and he would not do anything without his opinion. One time the king tried to do something without his opinion. The king said, 'Did I not make him an advisor so that I would not do anything without his opinion?' R. Yudan said, so too the Holy One, blessed be He,

[55] Suzanne Young, "An Athenian Clepsydra," *Hesperia: The Journal of the American School of Classical Studies at Athens* 8, no. 3 (1939), 274–84. Figures shown are from ibid., 278 and 282.

[56] Aristotle, *The Athenian Constitution*, 62, 2.

Figure 2. A restored ancient Athenian clepsydra with holes at the top and bottom. Reproduction courtesy of the American School of Classical Studies at Athens.

said, 'Did I not call him my advisor so that I would not do anything without his opinion?'"[57] God does not want to act alone but seeks Abraham's advice. A king who tries to act without asking his advisor must suspect that advisor will disagree. Here too, God knows that Abraham will not approve of His destructive plan but wants Abraham to argue his case anyway.

The midrash of the clepsydra thus extends this theme of God's prompting Abraham to defend Sodom. When Abraham jumps from fifty to five, God senses that Abraham is rushing through his defense and not being sufficiently persistent in his pleas; perhaps he could save the city if given more time. God therefore steps out of His role as an unbiased judge and, violating court protocol and strict justice, allows the defense to take extra time to further argue for acquittal.[58] Rather than rely on His own omniscience and His role as "Judge of all the earth" (Gen 18:22) to act alone as an impartial judge capable of achieving absolute Justice and Truth, God instead invites a defense lawyer into His court and even

[57] Gen Rabbah 49:2. Translation follows MS Vatican 30.

[58] Pliny the Younger, *Letters*, 2.11.14, relates that in his role as prosecutor against Marius Priscus, a corrupt governor of Africa, "I spoke for nearly five hours, for, in addition to the twelve water-clocks – the largest I could get – which had been assigned to me, I obtained four others." This testimony reveals that an orator could receive additional time during a trial (though it is not clear whether this was done so legally or through manipulation) and that it was considered a great benefit towards winning one's case.

gives him extra time on the water-clock. God would prefer to be persuaded towards mercy by a good lawyer, even at the expense of justice.

If in the previous midrash God gives short shrift to justice, in the following midrash, God deceives Justice outright. Genesis Rabbah 8:4 to Genesis 1:26, "And God said, 'Let *us* make man,'" explains that when God conferred with his heavenly council[59] about creating man, "He revealed to the angels that the righteous would issue from Adam, but He did not reveal to them that the wicked would issue forth as well. For if He had revealed to them that the wicked would issue forth from him, the Attribute of Justice (*midat hadin*) would not have allowed him to be created." God here acts to withhold information from the prosecuting Attribute of Justice and instead "joined with the Attribute of Mercy and created man."[60] A fair assessment of man's fate would not have allowed for the creation of human beings. God needed to hide the truth in order to allow human life to begin. We thus see in this midrash two important points. One is the hypostatization of Justice and Mercy, otherwise only aspects of God's personality, but now a separate being.[61] Second is that the art of trickery, often imputed to the sophists, is used here by God to rig the ballot.[62]

The next scene in the midrash pits the angels against each other like prosecutors and defense lawyers in a court room: "Kindness says, [God] should create [man] for he does acts of kindness. Truth says, He should not create [man] for he is all lies. Righteousness says, He should create [man] for he does acts of righteousness. Peace says, He should not create [man] for he is all quarrel. What did the Holy One, blessed be He, do? He took Truth and threw it to the ground."[63] Humans can only exist if God subjugates Truth and discounts its vote in the heavenly council in favor of Kindness and Righteousness. The council of angels, however, reacts with indignity: "Master of the Universe, how can you so disgrace Your Truth (אלטיכסייה, ἀλήθεια)?"[64] God must admit defense lawyers into His

59 Although this is not technically designated as a courtroom setting, it is a sufficiently similar context upon which to derive insight as to the rabbinic conception of heavenly judgement.

60 Gen Rabbah 8:3. Translation from Stern, *Midrash and Theory*, 88. Stern finds in this midrash another example of logos theology.

61 There are actually two versions of this aggadah cited in Gen Rabbah 8:3. The first, by R. Berechiah has God hide the ways of the wicked from before Himself and join with his own Attribute of Mercy. Only in the second, by R. Ḥanina, do we see hypostatization wherein the Attribute of Justice is a separate angel.

62 See the similar theme of God hiding sins at Y. Sanhedrin 10:1, 27c, and Pesikta Rabbati 45.

63 Ibid., 8:5.

64 Ibid. MS Vatican 60.

heavenly court and give them preference precisely in order to vitiate the threat of Truth. Here, God does not even bother tricking Truth but simply tramples over it. To paraphrase the Quaker slogan, "God speaks power to Truth."

Lamentations Rabbah[65] similarly describes a clash between God and the Attribute of Justice where God is forced to give in. God commands an angel to take two coals and throw them down to earth to burn the Temple. The angel Gabriel is given the two coals but keeps them in his hand for three years in the hope that Israel will repent. After losing patience, Gabriel is about to hurl one down in fury when God stops him saying, "Gabriel! Gabriel! Easy, easy! Some of them perform acts of charity for each other." The midrash then cites a praise of God for extending His anger "in the face of the Principle of Justice."[66] Thereupon, the Attribute of Justice convinces God that it is better that He destroy the Temple rather than allow an evil enemy to do so and so God sends down the fire. God is overruled by His own previous command to destroy and the persuasive power of the Attribute of Justice. We see here God's anguish in punishing Israel by arguing in Israel's defense and attempting to overturn His own prior directive to punish.

While in the midrash just discussed God's eagerness to forgive is so strong that the Attribute of Justice must keep it in check, another section from Lamentations Rabbah (*petiḥta* 24) depicts God being stubbornly unforgiving. This midrash poignantly reveals the need for lawyers to pull God out of his anger. It opens with Abraham walking in the ruins of the Temple, crying and tearing out his hair in mourning, and complaining about the disgrace that has befallen his progeny. Empathizing with and amplifying Abraham's complaints, the angels press God to respond. God replies, "Your children sinned and transgressed the whole Torah and upon all twenty-two letters that are in it." God then summons the Torah and all the letters to testify against Israel, but Abraham convinces the Torah and each letter, one by one, to withhold their testimonies. Abraham, Isaac, Jacob, and Moses subsequently proceed to recount their devotion and the sacrifices they suffered so that God would have mercy on Israel on their account. But God remains unmoved. Finally, Rachel reminds God of how she was not jealous of her sister but rather helped her trick Jacob on their wedding night into believing that Leah was Rachel, in order not to cause Leah

[65] 1:13 in the Buber edition and see variants at 1:41 in the Vilna edition.
[66] Translations from Stern, *Parables*, 238–40.

embarrassment; yet God, Rachel challenges, expresses jealousy of worthless idols and proposes to destroy His nation because of them. The midrash ends, "Immediately, the mercy of the Holy One, blessed be He, welled up and He said, 'For you, Rachel, I will return Israel to their place.'"

God feels genuinely and justifiably angry at Israel for their disloyalty, so much so that even the patriarchs fail to pacify Him. Abraham succeeds in obstructing justice and diverting prosecuting witnesses and thereby prevents God from laying further guilt on Israel; but that by no means allays His anger. Rachel's plea, however, is fundamentally different from those of the patriarchs. While the patriarchs list all of the sacrifices they made for God, Rachel mentions a single sacrifice that she made for her sister.[67] That, combined with the shame she imputes to God for His jealousy of hollow idols, succeeds in pulling on God's heartstrings. Her feminine compassion melts away God's masculine stubborn jealousy, and God learns from Rachel how to be merciful.[68]

Note that all of these orators exclusively utilize *pathos*; there are no reasoned legal arguments here or calls to authority. All of the advocates attempt to shame God into acquiescing and Rachel proves to be the most successful in doing so. The summoning of all of the patriarchs and Rachel here to advocate on Israel's behalf is reminiscent of the practice in Roman courts for a defendant to show up with not one but a whole entourage of advocates and well-wishers to more effectively convince the court.[69]

One of the most forceful and controversial advocates in rabbinic literature is Ḥoni the Circle-drawer, mentioned above.[70] He prayed for rain by first drawing a circle around himself and swearing in God's name

[67] Haim Ovadia, "Four Men and a Woman: On Character and Attitude in Eikha Rabba," unpublished paper.

[68] See analysis of this midrash at Stern, *Midrash and Theory*, 85; and a rhetorical reading at David Metzger and Steven Katz, "The 'Place' of Rhetoric in Aggadic Midrash," *College English* 72, no. 6 (2010): 638–53. Note that רחמים (mercy) derives from the same root as רחם (womb), on which see A. Murtonen, ed. *Hebrew in Its West Semitic Setting, Part I: A Comparative Lexicon* (Leiden: Brill, 1986), 397; Emmanuel Levinas, *Nine Talmudic Readings* (Bloomington: Indiana University Press, 1994), 183; and Claire Elise Katz, *Levinas, Judaism, and the Feminine: The Silent Footsteps of Rebecca* (Bloomington: Indiana University Press, 2003), 132.

[69] Crook, *Legal Advocacy*, 73–4. Crook notes that sometimes there were also multiple prosecutors. This is reflected in B. Shabbat 32a, "Even if one has nine hundred and ninety-nine prosecutors and one defender."

[70] P. 247 at n. 37.

that he would not budge from that spot until God showed mercy upon his children. In many ancient cultures, courts convened in circular enclosures that designated the area as legal space such that those within the space came under the jurisdiction and power of that court. Drawing a circle around someone forced that person into a role of defendant and subject to the authority of the circle-drawer.[71] For example, the Roman general Popilius used a circle-drawing ritual when he pressed Antiochus IV to abandon his campaign against Egypt. As Polybius reports: Popilius "drew a circle around Antiochus and told him he must remain inside the circle until he gave his decision."[72] Because Ḥoni cannot encircle God, he symbolically draws the circle around himself as a substitute. As Stone explains, the circle creates a legal space wherein God becomes not only the judge but also the defendant and is thus compelled to respond to his petition.[73] Other midrashim have Moses and Habakkuk adopting the same technique.[74] These sources apply to the Divine court a bold method of making a legal appeal known from classical sources to be particularly impudent.[75]

Sifre Deuteronomy 343 explicitly makes reference to Roman rhetors as the model for the composition of petitions to God:

> "He said: The Lord came from Sinai, He shone upon them from Se`ir" (Deut 33:2). Scripture teaches that when Moses opened [his oration], he did not open with the needs of Israel first until he opened with praise of God. A parable to a rhetor (לוטייר) who was standing on the platform (במה, βῆμα)[76] and was hired by one side to speak on his behalf. He did not present[77] the needs of his client until he first presented the praise of the king: "Fortunate is the world for its king, fortunate is the world for its judge. The sun shines upon us, the moon shines upon us." Others would also praise together with

[71] Stone, "Rabbinic Legal Magic," 113–16.

[72] Polybius, *The Histories*, trans. W. R. Paton, Loeb Classical Library (Cambridge: Harvard University Press, 1975), 29.27.4–7. See also Judah Goldin, "On Honi the Circle Maker: A Demanding Prayer," in *Studies in Midrash and Related Literature*, ed. Barry Eichler and Jeffrey Tigay (Philadelphia: Jewish Publication Society, 1988): 331–5.

[73] Stone, "Rabbinic Legal Magic," 114–19.

[74] Ibid., 107–8.

[75] The brazenness of Ḥoni's demands prompted criticism from Shimon ben Shataḥ, who nevertheless recognized Ḥoni's exceptional status; see M. Ta`anit 3:8.

[76] See Mogens Herman Hansen, *The Athenian Democracy in the Age of Demosthenes: Structure, Principle, and Ideology* (Norman: University of Oklahoma Press, 1991), 143–7, and 387; and Joseph Gutmann, *The Jewish Sanctuary* (Leiden: Brill, 1983), 15.

[77] Translation is based on the analysis of Mandel, "`Al 'pataḥ'," 58 n. 30.

> him. Only then did he present the needs of his client and then again close with praise of the king.[78]

The midrash continues with examples of orations following this rhetorical format from Moses, David, Solomon, and from the prayer of the Eighteen Blessings.[79] The rabbis witnessed the extensive flattery of Roman judges by professional rhetors[80] and apparently saw this as an appropriate and effective way of advocating before God as well. The quotation of the rhetor here matches the encomia of emperors extant from the same period. A treatise ascribed to Menander of Laodicea on the Lycus (fl. fourth century CE), for instance, includes this example of a "Crown Speech": "The whole world crowns you with the greatest crown ... You continue to fight the greatest fights ... on behalf of the whole world that lies under the sun."[81] Evidently, the rabbis were versed in the style of Greco-Roman encomia and applied this style in their liturgical compositions as well.

Exodus Rabbah 43, expounding on Moses' entreaty at Exod 32:11, presents an extended analysis of Moses as an advocate. The midrash opens:[82]

> "Moses implored the face of the Lord his God" (Exod 32:11). R. Tanḥuma bar Abba expounded as follows: "He would have destroyed them ... " What is: "had not Moses His chosen one stood (`*amad*) before (*lefanav*) Him in the breach [to avert His destructive wrath]" (Ps 106:23)? R. Ḥama bar Ḥanina said: "The good advocate (*sanegor*) stands brazen-faced (*ma`amid panim*)[83] before the judge."

78 Translation follows text of Finkelstein, *Sifre*.

79 See further at Furstenberg, "The 'Agon' with Moses and Homer," 321; and Steven Fraade, *From Tradition to Commentary: Torah and Its Interpretation in the Midrash Sifre to Deuteronomy* (Albany: State University of New York, 1991), 28–30. On the resemblance between petitionary prayer and legal forms, see Heinemann, *Prayer in the Talmud: Forms and Patterns*, 193–217; and Stone, "Rabbinic Legal Magic," 109–10. For another example of rhetorical arrangement in rabbinic liturgy, see above p. 97 n. 90.

80 The oration of Tertullus before Felix in Acts 24:1–9, which begins with extensive praise of the judge, fits into this pattern.

81 Menander, *Menander Rhetor*, trans. D. A. Russel and N. G. Wilson (Oxford: Clarendon Press, 1981), 179.

82 Translation of this and subsequent citations from Exod Rabbah 43 follow MS Jerusalem 24 5977.

83 העמיד פמים means to show resistance to, as in Gen Rabbah 44:15. Printed editions read *masbir panim*. הסברת פנים always refer to a positive countenance. M. Avot 1:15 adds a modifier, "סבר פנים יפות." However, it has the same meaning even without the modifier, as in Y. Yoma 6:1, 43b; Gen Rabbah 49:14 and 73:12; B. Berakhot 63b; B. Ta`anit 8a; and B. Soṭah 40a. In this reading, the midrash begins by noting that the usual activity

> Moses is one of the advocates who stood up (*`amdu*) to argue in defense of Israel and they, as it were, stood brazen-faced (*he`emidu panim*) before the Holy One, blessed be He. Moses and Daniel. Moses, as it is stated: "Had not Moses His chosen stood before Him in the breach." What is the source for Daniel? "I turned my face (*panai*) to the Lord God, devoting myself to prayer and supplication" (Dan 9:3). These are two people who presented brazen faces (*natenu penehem*)[84] before the Attribute of Justice in order to request mercy upon Israel.

R. Ḥama says that a competent defense advocate speaks forcefully to the judge. Moses and Daniel therefore speak brazenly to God by attacking, blaming, and antagonizing the Judge and showing anger towards His Attribute of Justice.

The midrash continues with a series of parables describing the various antics performed by Moses in order to save Israel from a guilty verdict. Moses is likened to an advocate who sees the prosecutor winning and so pushes him out of the way and stands in his place. He is then likened to a king's associate (סנקתדרוס, συγκάθεδρος) who snatches the pen away from the Judge just as he is about to write the guilty verdict. These two parables involve a king judging his son, implying that Moses acted with the implicit will of God in preventing Him from punishing His nation.[85]

The same midrash at 43:3 adds:

> R. Nehemiah says: What does "Moses implored (*vayḥal*)" mean? That he brought to God a kind of present, for this language is none other than the language of a present, as you say, "O Tyrian lass, the wealthiest people will court your favor (*yeḥalu*) with gifts" (Ps 45:13). And similarly, "And now implore (*ḥalu*) the favor of God" (Malachai 1:9).
>
> The Rabbis say: What does "Moses implored (*vayḥal*)" mean? He turned the bitter into sweet.

of defense advocates is to present the law in a positive light that the judge will find favorable to the defendant. This has nearly the opposite meaning as that in MS Jerusalem, according to which advocates normally speak brazenly.

[84] נותן פנים means to show anger towards, as in Mekhilta d'R. Shimon bar Yoḥai 17:3.

[85] God's merciful bias is also evident at B. Berakhot 32b where God uses selective memory to remember Israel's good deeds but forgets about the sin of the Golden Calf.

Moses here gives something like a gift to God. Lieberman points to Roman texts depicting defendants who offered a sacrifice before their cases were heard in order to improve their chances of acquittal; he further shows that the rabbis considered this to be a common practice in Roman courts.[86] The author of M. Avot 4:22 would be particularly offended by the idea that such bribery could persuade God.[87] Yet, this midrash praises Moses for saving Israel, no matter what method he uses. The next opinion explains that Moses sweetened what was bitter and overturned God's harsh decrees through argumentation. This is reminiscent of the way Protagoras could "make the worse case seem the better."[88] A fascinating example of how Moses made the worse argument the better is provided in Exodus Rabbah 43:5 regarding the sin of the golden calf:

> R. Yehoshua ben Levi said in the name of R. Shimon bar Yoḥai: The Holy One, blessed be He, disclosed to [Moses] an opening of a response at Sinai: "I am the Lord thy God" (Exod 20:2). When Israel did that deed, Moses stood up and was appeasing God, but He did not pay attention to him. He [God] said to him, "Can it be that we will not apply to them the attribute of justice for forsaking the commandment?" He said to Him: Master of the universe, You said "I am the Lord thy God (singular, *elohecha*)." You did not say "your God (plural, *elohekhem*)." Did you not tell me "I am the Lord thy God"? Did you say it to them [Israel]? Did I forsake your command?!"

The midrash continues to affirm that from this point on, the Torah always states, "I am the Lord your God," using the plural so that this loophole could not be used again. Certainly not the intention of the original formulation, Moses nevertheless takes advantage of a technicality to argue for Israel's acquittal. Moses here applied a typical method abused by lawyers ancient and modern. As Cicero explains, an orator derives the ability to argue for either side of a case using the same source, "by showing that it contains some ambiguity; then on the basis of that ambiguity he may defend the passage which helps his case."[89] Here too, Moses uses a grammatical ambiguity to turn the very source of God's accusation into a reason for acquittal.

[86] Lieberman, "Roman Legal Institutions," 31–2, citing Exod Rabbah 15:12.

[87] See Dov Weiss, "Lawsuits against God in Rabbinic Literature," in *The Divine Courtroom in Comparative Perspective*, ed. Ari Mermelstein and Shalom Holtz (Leiden: Brill, 2014): 277–8, on other tannaitic texts that prohibit criticizing God's actions.

[88] Aristotle, *On Rhetoric*, II.24.9.

[89] Cicero, *On Invention*, II.142.

A good example of Moses presenting a brazen face towards God follows in the next paragraph of the midrash, 43:6:

> R. Nehemiah said: "Why, O Lord, do you let Your anger blaze forth against Your people?" (Exod 32:11). How so? When Israel did that deed [worshipped the golden calf], Moses stood up and appeased the Holy One, blessed be He. He said to Him, "Master of the universe, they have made for you a helper and you are angry at them? Let this calf that they made help you. You light up the sun and it will [light up] the moon. You [light up] the stars and it will [light up] the constellations. You bring down the dew and it will make the winds blow. You will bring down the rain and it will cause the plants to grow." The Holy One, blessed be He, said to him, "You are as mistaken as them [Israel] for it has no strength and no substance." He replied, "If it has no substance and it is nothing, then why are You angry at Your children?" This is, "Why, O Lord, do you let Your anger blaze forth against Your people?" (Exod 32:11).

Again, like a talented lawyer, Moses backs God into a corner by making Him admit that the object of His jealousy is not worthy of attention and, therefore, God has no reason to be angry. Rather than defend Israel's actions as the previous paragraph does, Moses now makes a brazen attack on God's jealousy, just as Rachel does in Lamentations Rabbah cited above.[90]

The rabbis not only continue the theme of advocacy found in the Bible and Second Temple literature, they expand upon it and provide their heavenly advocates with more tools to sway God's judgment. By transforming the heavenly advocates into Roman lawyers, they introduce all the sophistic tricks of the trade that one would find in a typical Roman court. The patriarchs, Moses, Rachel, and even God Himself will do almost anything to obstruct the Attribute of Justice: flatter and bribe the judge, conceal evidence, take extra time, convince witnesses to withhold testimony, use grammatical loopholes to twist the law, and more. In their own earthly courts, the rabbis recognized the corruption of the Roman adversarial system and the dishonesty promoted by the rhetoricians. Accordingly, they made a concerted effort to exclude

[90] See further Dov Weiss, "Divine Concessions in the *Tanhuma* Midrashim," *Harvard Theological Review* 108, no. 1 (2015): 93–4, who suggests that the theme of confronting and challenging God that develops more fully in late midrashim links to the notion of *parrhesia*, freedom of speech even before the emperor and, in some fifth century Christian circles, even against God.

lawyers from their own courts as the best way to ensure truth and justice. When it comes to God's court, however, truth and justice become enemies of sinful humans who cannot survive their high standards. The injustices of the adversarial system are therefore introduced into the heavenly court, usually with God's implicit consent, so that Mercy may triumph.

PLATO'S HEAVENLY COURT

In order to better appreciate the rabbinic worldview, it is instructive to compare it to that of Plato. Plato also criticizes the Athenian adversarial system and the sophists who uphold it. As noted in the previous chapter, Plato's *Laws* envisions a utopian city called Magnesia where the court system is inquisitorial and where lawyers are to receive the death penalty.[91] In the *Gorgias*, Plato's Socrates similarly envisions a heavenly court where rhetoric has no place and where the judges can see things as they really are. Plato describes this post-mortem court in his myth of the naked souls. The myth relates that under the reign of Cronus, the final judgment of people occurred just before their deaths and was conducted by living judges. However, because the people were wearing clothes, they could impress the judges by their external appearances, even if they were wicked underneath. In addition, the judges were likewise living and wearing clothes and were therefore also impressionable and unable to see the truth. As a result, the verdicts were often wrong. Zeus then instituted a reform that the dead should judge the dead so that the disembodied soul of the judge could clearly perceive the soul of the judged. Justice would be based on the naked truth, free from the trappings of rhetoric.[92]

Earlier in the *Gorgias*, Plato divides argumentation between rhetoric, which is just a knack for persuading audiences or jurors to agree with any given position whether right or wrong, and philosophy, which uses logic to analyze reality and find the truth. "Philosophy is always true," declares Socrates. Callicles, the sophist, responds that if Socrates were accused of a crime in an Athenian court he would be incapable of defending himself without recourse to rhetoric, thus leaving his "head spinning and mouth gaping" (486b). Socrates in turn charges that

[91] See p. 220.

[92] Gorgias, 523a–e. See analysis of this myth at Ernest Weinreb, "Law as Myth: Reflections on Plato's *Gorgias*," *Iowa Law Review* 74 (1989): 787–806; and Kensky, *Trying Man, Trying God*, 91–6.

Callicles will have no ability to defend himself in his heavenly post-mortem trial where rhetoric has no force and he tells Callicles, "your head will spin and your mouth will gape there in that world as much as mine would here" (527a).

The rabbis likely never read Plato,[93] but if they did, they would have been terrified at his proposed heavenly court. In fact, M. Avot 4:22, which describes a lawyer-free court resembling that of Plato, is meant precisely to instill a sense of trepidation in its audience and deter them from sin. The vast majority of rabbinic literature, however, describes a heavenly court teeming with advocates of all kinds: patriarchs and matriarchs, angels, the Logos, the Torah, the holy spirit, the Attribute of Mercy, and even God Himself. Many of these sources go so far as to model the heavenly court on Roman courts, with all their deceit, flattery, bribery, and corruption. The rabbis agreed with Plato's assessment of lawyers and their rhetoric as a deterrent from achieving Truth. They also agreed with Plato that there is no place in earthly courts for hired lawyers. However, taking inspiration from the great prophetic advocates in the Bible, they appreciated that God, in His mercy, allows and even requests advocates in His court who can persuade Him out of His rage.[94] Indeed, Callicles would do well to have himself sent to the rabbinic heavenly court.

[93] Interestingly, the rabbis did use Antoninus as a mouthpiece for the view that the soul will be judged separately from the body. In B. Sanhedrin 91a, Antoninus challenges Rabbi on the fairness of this system if, after all, the soul could not have sinned without the body, and vice versa. Rabbi responds by rejecting the assumption that the soul could be judged alone; rather, God will combine the body and soul together for the final judgment at the time of resurrection. Thus, although Rabbi did not likely intend to reject Plato or make a statement about rhetoric, he does coincidentally assume a system more similar to that of Cronus.

[94] See further on this theme at Frank, "Arguing with God," 74, who writes: "God is surprised and changed by the experience of argument, underscoring the risk that God and humans undertake when they engage in argumentation. By arguing, rather than simply exercising raw power, God relinquishes control over and vests freedom to humans ... To God's credit, argumentation leads God to reduce the scope of God's claims in argument with Abraham, change mood and the decision to act in response to arguments posed by Moses, and acknowledge defeat in argumentative exchange with Job."

Conclusion: Rabbinic versus Christian Approaches to Rhetoric

> Anyone who studies our Talmud knows that there are no absolute proofs nor conclusive challenges in the controversies of its interpreters, for there are no clear demonstrations in this area of knowledge as there are in geometry and astronomy. Rather, we apply our utmost efforts that will suffice for any controversy to push away one of the views with decisive reasons and we will throw traditions against it. We will advance the correctness of the opposing view based on straightforward laws and suitable pericopes in agreement with proper reason. This is the goal of our efforts and the aim of any wise and God-fearing person in the study of the Gemara.[1]

> "All of them were given by the same shepherd" (Eccl 12:11). He wants to say that most often we understand a matter well only via its opposite, for we cannot understand it in its essence as we can from its opposite. Therefore, the Holy One, blessed be He, wished to give us the differing opinions, so that when we arrived at the truth, we would understand it clearly.[2]

> The Torah would be the text which leads us through truth to the personal *par excellence*, that of God. It involves an element of seduction without deception, a rhetoric which is holy.[3]

What happens when you slam the Bible and Hellenism together in a particle collider? You get a host of sects and movements that combine the two in various ways. Most of these camps disintegrated relatively quickly but two major groups that remained are Christianity and rabbinic Judaism. When the authority of prophetic and priestly religion encounters the logic and skepticism of Greek philosophy and

[1] Moses Naḥmanides, *Introduction to Milḥamot Hashem* (Venice, 1552).

[2] `Aqrah, *Me-harere nemerim*, 19a; translation based on Boyarin, "Moslem," 12.

[3] Levinas, *Beyond the Verse*, 32.

rhetoric, one can keep them separate for only so long. If they coexist within the same culture, then they will necessarily interact in complex and interesting ways. Under Greek and Roman domination, Jewish life and literature were filtered and refracted through the lens of Hellenism, which thoroughly reshaped their character and structure.

This book has surveyed various aspects of the fundamental natures of truth, persuasion, and interpretation as they relate to rabbinic literature and the Greco-Roman tradition. The rabbis flourished within the culture of the Second Sophistic and found within that tradition a mode of reasoning that resonated with aspects of their own organic thinking. In some ways, the goals of the Second Sophistic parallel those of the rabbis: just as the Greek East turned to the rhetorical tradition to protect classical Greek culture against the onslaught of Roman ascendancy, the rabbis turned to Talmudic debate and midrashic exegesis to protect their own traditions against the threats of both Hellenism and Roman domination. The rabbis effectively and brilliantly accomplished this by adopting some of the philosophical underpinnings as well as various technical aspects of classical rhetoric such as arrangement, certain hermeneutical tools, and select progymnasmatic exercises, even while they rejected many of the more relativistic and sophistic aspects of the Greco-Roman tradition.

On a macro-level, therefore, the rabbinic movement parallels that of the Second Sophistic as twin subcultures of the Greek East. If we zoom in, however, we can view the rabbis as a minority subsumed under the dominance of the Second Sophistic. From this perspective, Jews are in a position comparable to that of the Christians and other minority religions and ethnicities who all must struggle to maintain their unique identities amidst the prevailing Hellenistic cultural forces. Since the church fathers, like the rabbis, also struggled with the dichotomy of rhetoric versus philosophy, we can gain unique perspective on the rabbinic outlook by comparing it with that of Christianity, a perspective that will help us bring together the conclusions from the previous chapters. The next section will review the findings of the previous chapters concerning the relationship of the rabbis to classical rhetoric. We will then compare and contrast the rabbinic integration of rhetoric with Christianity, which fundamentally rejected the epistemological assumptions of rhetoric. The final section will explore how the rabbis succeeded in achieving a unique and carefully balanced amalgamation of Hellenistic reason and rhetoric together with prophetic truth.

THE RABBIS AND CLASSICAL RHETORIC

While the attitude of the rabbis towards classical rhetoric varied, depending on time period, geography, and personal inclination, this section will summarize dominant themes that span the breadth of rabbinic literature and therefore represent the view of "the rabbis" as a group. Talmudic literature never cites Aristotle, Cicero, Quintilian, Libanius or any other writers of Greco-Roman rhetorical handbooks and exercises. Aside from a single letter from Libanius to a patriarch,[4] there is no evidence that any rabbis ever received a formal education in rhetoric. Nevertheless, it is evident that many rabbis were well acquainted with the methods and style of persuasive speech. They explicitly make reference to a prototypical "rhetor"[5] and can accurately describe his speaking style. They are intimately aware of the role that rhetors played in courtrooms and were very familiar with their forms of argumentation and logic.

The previous chapters reveal a complex relationship between the rabbis and Greco-Roman rhetoric. On the one hand, the rabbis were themselves orators who structured their own homiletic and legal presentations according to typical rhetorical arrangement as taught in the classical handbooks. We have analyzed examples of extended rhetorical arrangement in the Yerushalmi, Bavli, and midrash. On the other hand, the rabbis preferred prepared lectures that revealed the meaning of Scripture over displays of extemporization that simply glorified the speaker.[6] They delivered their official lectures seated and with a soft voice, thus focusing on content and leaving the public performance aspects of the speech to a human loudspeaker.[7]

The rabbis also taught students in study circles and schools, just as the rhetors did. The subject matter was different: the rabbis taught biblical interpretation and oral law while the rhetors focused on the art of writing and presenting themes from Greek mythology and Roman law. Nevertheless, the rabbinic style of education through exercises that develop the argumentational skill of the students to debate both sides and the use of hypothetical scenarios precisely parallels the progymnasmata and controversiae. The rabbis resisted

4 See p. 7.

5 See p. 257.

6 See p. 59. I would not deny that rabbis as individuals appreciated recognition for their oratorical abilities (see R. Ḥiyya bar Abbat at B. Soṭah 40a). Rather, I argue that the stated goal of rhetoric is to impress while the explicit goal of rabbinic lectures is to educate.

7 See p. 80–1.

theoretical cases that were so outlandish as to mock the halakhic system or undermine it, but their educational methodology otherwise fits the mold of the rhetorical training that was widespread throughout the Roman Empire.

Chapters One to Four show that, in general, the forms of rabbinic sermons, lectures, and lessons, are much more in line with popular rhetorical models than noted by previous scholars. This insight can help explain much of the agonistic character of rabbinic literature, as well as its sometimes creative leaps, tangents, outlandish cases, and flowery style that can seem strange to the modern ear but would have been natural in the milieu of the classical world. Modern Talmud scholarship has turned, with considerable success, to source criticism in order to address the farfetched interpretations and forced answers found throughout the Talmud. However, this book proposes that we add rhetorical criticism to our toolbox, and that we view much of the Talmud and midrashim as a subset within the genre of rhetorical exercises.

Chapters Five to Seven demonstrate that the rabbis recognized the deep flaws in human reasoning and, consequently, the dangerous power of persuasion to make the false seem true and turn the impure into pure. In response, they developed a sophisticated approach to biblical interpretation and their own set of rules of deduction. On the one hand, their system overlaps with many aspects of the lists of commonplace modes of persuasion codified in the rhetorical handbooks. On the other hand, the rabbis also adapted, expanded and questioned these rhetorical modes of reasoning. Because they viewed all of Scripture as omnisignificant and harmonious, they applied methods of comparison and derivation beyond what we might consider common sense today and perhaps even beyond widespread use among sophists. This allowed the rabbis to ground the oral law in written law, resolve contradictions and repetitions in the Bible, and put forward a robust and systematic set of legal and homiletic teachings.

The rabbis also recognized that these methods of reasoning could lead to false conclusions that contradict biblical and rabbinic law and could even challenge the very authority of the rabbis who developed them. At every turn, the Talmud tests the limits of conceptual comparisons and word analogies by pushing their arguments to the extreme. The rabbis recognized the subjectivity of human reason and, therefore, rather than deny the role of interpretation, they carefully controlled its use in order to distinguish the range of valid interpretations and opinions from those that are invalid.

This multifaceted approach to truth and interpretation is especially apparent in the rabbinic approach to courts. The Mishnah envisions an inquisitorial trial without lawyers that concludes with a mock adversarial deliberation by the judges. Here again, the rabbis neither agree with Plato that there is one truth that a perfectly fair judge can attain; nor do they leave it up to lawyers to let the best debater win without concern for fairness and justice. Rather, the judges are to bring to bear all of the power of rhetoric in order to ensure that an innocent defendant will never be put to death.

On the flip side, the aggadic imagination turns precisely to the Roman adversarial model when it portrays God's heavenly court. God may know the absolute truth of mankind's guilt, but His mercy allows for defense lawyers to enter and practice their sophistry to persuade Him out of His anger. God ignores absolute Truth and submits Himself to work within the realm of rhetoric. He recognizes the possibility and need for multiple explanations and justifications for human frailty and, by extension, must also allow for subjectivity in human interpretation of the Torah and for manifold legitimate halakhic viewpoints.

Taken together, these chapters portray the rabbis as knowledgeable participants in the culture of rhetoric. They take on the roles of rhetors both as public orators and as teachers, except that they replace the Hellenistic content of the curriculum with Torah. At the same time, the rabbis are also wary of sophistic excesses and their tendency to obscure truth and justice. The rabbis therefore do not fit easily into either of the extreme positions of Plato or Gorgias but rather, as noted in the Introduction, transcend the limits of the very dichotomy. They do not affirm monistic absolute truth, nor do they take a skeptical view that denies the possibility of truth at all. Rather, they forge a path of multiple truths that derive from authentic human interpretations of divine prophecy. In order to further appreciate the innovative view of the rabbis it will be instructive to first compare it to the response of the church fathers to the same tensions between truth and rhetoric, and then analyze some of the rabbinic statements that explicitly address the nature of prophecy and interpretation.

CHRISTIANITY AND CLASSICAL RHETORIC

Monotheistic religions, George Kennedy points out, emphasize the significance of speech to a much greater extent than does paganism. This is exemplified in the Bible's presentation of creation by God's word, the holiness of the divine text, and the key role of the prophet as orator.[8] The need to publicly explain Scripture naturally leads to the flourishing of synagogue and church preachers. Having analyzed the rabbinic side of preaching and teaching, let us here examine the style and structure of Christian oration and the general attitude of the church fathers towards truth and rhetoric.

The New Testament writers not only chose to write in Greek but often adopted many conventions of Greek rhetoric so that their message would be as persuasive as possible. Paul and Luke, for example, "were familiar with some Greek literature, and used devices of classical rhetoric freely."[9] We analyzed in Chapter 1 one such example of Paul's sermon at Antioch in Acts 13:14–41, which follows classical rhetorical structure of exordium, narration, proposition, proof, and conclusion.[10] Rhetorical criticism of the New Testament is a well-established field that has shown beyond doubt that many of the New Testament writers were familiar with and utilized classical rhetorical methods.[11]

At the same time, the New Testament contains anti-rhetorical statements such as Mark 13:11, where Jesus says: "Whenever you are arrested and brought to trial, do not worry beforehand about what to say. Just say whatever is given you at the time, for it is not you speaking, but the Holy Spirit."[12] Mark proposes a "radical Christian rhetoric" consisting of apodictic authoritative pronouncements.[13] Even more explicitly, in 1 Corinthians 2:1–5, Paul writes:

> [1]And so it was with me, brothers and sisters. When I came to you, I did not come with eloquence or human wisdom as I proclaimed to you the testimony about God. [2] For I resolved to know nothing while

[8] Kennedy, *New History*, 257–8.

[9] Ibid., 258.

[10] See pp. 44–6.

[11] The scholarly literature on the rhetorical analysis of the New Testament is vast and has proven how much can be gained by reading early Christian writings through the lens of Greco-Roman rhetoric. Some notable titles are Kennedy, *New Testament Interpretation*; Kinneavy, *Greek Rhetorical Origins of Christian Faith*; Duane Watson, "The New Testament and Greco-Roman Rhetoric: A Bibliography," *Journal of the Evangelical Theological Society* 31, no. 4 (1988): 465–72; Duane Watson and Alan Hauser, *Rhetorical Criticism of the Bible: A Comprehensive Bibliography with Notes on History and Method* (Leiden: Brill, 1994); Christopher Forbes, "Paul and Rhetorical Comparison," in *Paul in the Greco-Roman World: A Handbook*, ed. J. Paul Sampley (Harrisburg, PA: Trinity Press International, 2003); and Black, *Rhetoric of the Gospel*, just to name a few examples of this immense literature. See also p. 10 n. 41.

[12] NIV translation here and throughout this section.

[13] Kennedy, *New History*, 258.

> I was with you except Jesus Christ and him crucified. [3] I came to you in weakness with great fear and trembling. [4] My message and my preaching were not with wise and persuasive words, but with a demonstration of the Spirit's power, [5] so that your faith might not rest on human wisdom, but on God's power.

Those who rely on human wisdom are the Greeks.[14] Like Plato, Paul denigrates the art of Greek persuasion because it can make the false seem true. Unlike Plato, who finds truth in philosophical ideas, however, Paul turns to the divine spirit for his source of truth. Therefore, his mode of discourse is not dialectical or logical; rather, he allows the holy spirit to arrange his speech. Paul's primary target here is neither Plato nor the ancient sophists, but rather the Pharisees whom he portrays as sophists. This trope is manifest in the trial of Paul before Felix in Acts 24:

> [1] Five days later the high priest Ananias went down to Caesarea with some of the elders and a lawyer named Tertullus, and they brought their charges against Paul before the governor. [2] When Paul was called in, Tertullus presented his case before Felix:
>
> **[Tertullus' Speech]**
>
> **[Exordium]**
> We have enjoyed a long period of peace under you, and your foresight has brought about reforms in this nation. [3] Everywhere and in every way, most excellent Felix, we acknowledge this with profound gratitude. [4] But in order not to weary you further, I would request that you be kind enough to hear us briefly.
>
> **[Narration]**
> [5] We have found this man to be a troublemaker,
>
> **[Confirmation]**
> **[1 - Insurrection]** stirring up riots among the Jews all over the world.
>
> **[2 - Heresy]** He is a ringleader of the Nazarene sect
>
> **[3 - Sacrilege]**[6] and even tried to desecrate the temple; so we seized him.
>
> **[Peroration]**
> [8] By examining him yourself you will be able to learn the truth about all these charges we are bringing against him.

[14] See 1 Corinthians 1:22.

[9] The other Jews joined in the accusation, asserting that these things were true.

[10] When the governor motioned for him to speak, Paul replied:

[Paul's Speech]

[Exordium]
I know that for a number of years you have been a judge over this nation; so I gladly make my defense.

[Narration]
[11]You can easily verify that no more than twelve days ago I went up to Jerusalem to worship. [12] My accusers did not find me arguing with anyone at the temple, or stirring up a crowd in the synagogues or anywhere else in the city. [13] And they cannot prove to you the charges they are now making against me.

[Refutation]
[1- Heresy] [14]However, I admit that I worship the God of our ancestors as a follower of the Way, which they call a sect. I believe everything that is in accordance with the Law and that is written in the Prophets, [15] and I have the same hope in God as these men themselves have, that there will be a resurrection of both the righteous and the wicked. [16] So I strive always to keep my conscience clear before God and man.

[2- Sacrilege] [17] After an absence of several years, I came to Jerusalem to bring my people gifts for the poor and to present offerings. [18] I was ceremonially clean when they found me in the temple courts doing this.

[3- Insurrection] There was no crowd with me, nor was I involved in any disturbance.

[Peroration]
[19] But there are some Jews from the province of Asia, who ought to be here before you and bring charges if they have anything against me. [20] Or these who are here should state what crime they found in me when I stood before the Sanhedrin – [21] unless it was this one thing I shouted as I stood in their presence: "It is concerning the resurrection of the dead that I am on trial before you today."

The text carefully contrasts the Pharisees, who resort to hiring a professional rhetor to defend their case, with Paul, who serves as his own counsel – thus putting into practice the advice he gives in his letter to the Corinthians. At the same time, one can clearly detect classical rhetorical structures in both speeches. Even as Paul explicitly rejects rhetoric, he adopts its techniques in practice.

Evidence of rhetorical training by prominent Christian writers can be found in subsequent centuries as well. In the early second century CE, Tertullian taught rhetoric in Rome before converting to Christianity and becoming one of Christianity's chief apologists.[15] In the third century, Gregory Thaumaturgus received rhetorical training in Pontus, and studied Christianity under Origen at Caesarea. His farewell speech from Origen's school is an epideictic oration in sophistic style. However, he also praises Christian philosophers for giving priority to the holy and divine power of thought over practicing speech and beauty of expression.[16] Origen himself did not include rhetoric in his curriculum and, in fact, criticized it for not contributing to knowledge of God.[17] In the fourth century, Gregory of Nazianzus started his career as a student and then a teacher of rhetoric in Athens. He was then baptized and became the bishop of Constantinople using his rhetorical training to earn fame as a talented preacher against heresy.[18]

Augustine similarly studied rhetoric in his youth with the goal of becoming a lawyer and taught rhetoric in various academies. However, in 387 CE he accepted Christianity, was baptized and became the bishop of Hippo. Augustine's most important statements on rhetoric appear in his *De Doctrina Christiana*. On the one hand, Augustine affirms the importance of eloquence for persuading audiences:

> Now, the art of rhetoric being available for the enforcing either of truth or falsehood, who will dare to say that truth in the person of its defenders is to take its stand unarmed against falsehood? For example, that those who are trying to persuade men of what is false are to know how to introduce their subject, so as to put the hearer into a friendly, or attentive, or teachable frame of mind, while the defenders of the truth shall be ignorant of that art? That the former are to tell their falsehoods briefly, clearly, and plausibly, while the latter shall tell the truth in such a way that it is tedious to listen to, hard to understand, and, in fine, not easy to believe it? That the

[15] Kennedy, *New History*, 260.

[16] Kennedy, *Classical Rhetoric*, 160–1.

[17] Ronald Heine, *Origen: Scholarship in the Service of the Church* (Oxford: Oxford University Press, 2010), 63.

[18] Kennedy, *Greek Rhetoric under Christian Emperors*, 215–39; and Kennedy, *New History*, 261–3.

> former . . . are by the power of their speech to melt, to enliven, and to rouse them, while the latter shall in defence of the truth be sluggish, and frigid, and somnolent? Who is such a fool as to think this wisdom? Since, then, the faculty of eloquence is available for both sides, and is of very great service in the enforcing either of wrong or right, why do not good men study to engage it on the side of truth, when bad men use it to obtain the triumph of wicked and worthless causes, and to further injustice and error?[19]

At the same time, Augustine also warns against the dangers of sophistic reasoning: "The science of reasoning is of very great service in searching into and unravelling all sorts of questions that come up in Scripture, only in the use of it we must guard against the love of wrangling, and the childish vanity of entrapping an adversary. For there are many of what are called sophisms, inferences in reasoning that are false, and yet so close an imitation of the true, as to deceive not only dull people, but clever men too, when they are not on their guard."[20] This statement and the subsequent example Augustine describes remind us of the rabbis' own rejection of sophistic *qal va-ḥomer* arguments.[21] Augustine instead recommends the use of a simple lowly style called *sermo humilis* for Scriptural exegesis and instruction.[22] Whereas Cicero advocates using the lowly style for business and common events,[23] Augustine considers all matters spoken from the pulpit to be sublime and instead differentiates uses of style not based on content but on "context and purpose."[24] In fact, Christian writers argue that the Bible itself is written in this low style because it is thereby able to deliver sublime messages in plain language for every reader to understand.[25]

19 Philip Schaff, ed. *St. Augustin's City of God and Christian Doctrine, Volume 2 of A Select Library of Nicene and Post-Nicene Fathers of the Christian Church* (New York: Charles Scribner's Sons, 1907), 4.2.3.

20 Ibid., 2.31.48.

21 See Chapter 5.

22 Erich Auerbach, *Literary Language and Its Public in Late Latin Antiquity and in the Middle Ages* (Princeton: Princeton University Press), 33.

23 Cicero, *Orator*, xxix.101.

24 Auerbach, *Literary Language*, 35. See also Celica Milovanovic-Barham, "Three Levels of Style in Augustine of Hippo and Gregory of Nazianzus," *Rhetorica: A Journal of the History of Rhetoric* 11, no. 1 (1993): 1–25; and William M. Purcell, *Ars Poetriae: Rhetorical and Grammatical Invention at the Margin of Literacy* (Columbia, SC: University of South Carolina, 1996), 36–9.

25 Auerbach, *Literary Language*, 47–52. See also Stern, *Midrash and Theory*, 70–1, on the theme of intimate language in midrash.

One last example of a Christian writer who resists rhetoric is Zacharias Scholasticus, the bishop of Mytilenes in the late fourth and early fifth centuries. He headed the school of rhetoric in Gaza and is thus rather close in time and place to the Palestinian rabbis.[26] In his dialogue against his pagan teacher of rhetoric Ammonius, he likens both Plato and the sophists to the Homeric Sirens, "who charm the ears of their eager hearers with the sweetness of their chant and punish those who listen to them with death." He contrasts them to Christian speakers:

> Our theologians do not bewitch the ears of their listeners with finely put speeches or refined phrases or the harmonious ordering of Attic vocabulary or elegance of diction . . .
>
> For our savior and his blessed disciples and the prophets of old who were giving oracles about him set forth the truth not with an abundance of words (as if adorned by the art of an embellisher), but naked without any covering, artifice or wordiness. And so its natural beauty shines through and the words are in agreement with actual facts and all your arguments come to naught.[27]

The references here to naked truth remind us of Plato's heavenly court analyzed in the previous chapter where rhetoric is banned and truth is seen directly without any adornment. Zacharias thus continues the Christian polemic against sophists and the rhetorical tradition.

How does the Christian approach to truth and rhetoric compare with that of the rabbis? Both groups had to negotiate the place of divine and biblical truth within the dichotomy between rhetoric and Platonic truths, the latter seeming like an easier fit to base a religious epistemology. Both groups would also find the art of persuasion and oratory to be attractive and useful in gaining and keeping adherents. However, since these considerations do not fit perfectly together, we will not be surprised to find both areas of overlap between the church fathers and the rabbis as well as points of divergence. A significant point of similarity is that both groups utilize the art of oratory in their public speaking. Erich Auerbach writes that: "The authors of Christian sermons drew on the rhetorical tradition that pervaded the ancient world and spoke in the forms to which their audience was accustomed,

[26] On the school of Gaza, see pp. 6–7.

[27] *Aeneas of Gaza: Theophrastus with Zacharias of Mytilene: Ammonius*, trans. Sebastian Bertz, John Dillon, and Donald Russell (London: Bloomsbury Academic, 2012), 106.

for in those days almost everyone judged an oration by the ring of the words."[28] This matches Lieberman's assessment of the rabbinic use of popular rhetorical style in their speeches.[29]

Another point of overlap is the denigration of many aspects of rhetoric, especially the use of lawyers. Acts 24 negatively contrasts the Pharisees who hire an advocate, with Paul who speaks for himself. Similarly, we analyzed the rabbinic distrust of lawyers in Chapter 6. Both groups also recognize the dangers of rhetoric in obfuscating the truth. We should not be surprised that these writers at once make use of rhetoric and denigrate it almost in the same breath. It was typical of orators to begin their orations by proclaiming their ignorance of rhetoric and commitment to speak plainly and sincerely. Plato's dialogues themselves display highly rhetorical techniques even as they reject rhetoric as mere trickery.[30] So far, the Christian and rabbinic approaches to uses of rhetoric are similar to each other and not out of the ordinary in their environments.

However, at a more philosophical level, a significant difference between these groups emerges. The church fathers fundamentally accepted the Platonic philosophical model that there exists absolute truth in the realm of ideas and that words are mere vessels for those ideas.[31] Therefore, words and the realm of rhetoric and interpretation ultimately prove unnecessary once one can perceive truth directly. Handelman connects this acceptance of a Platonic-based model[32] with the Christian preference for the spirit over the letter of the law and its penchant for allegorical interpretation of Scripture, which both reflect a devaluation of the text. Once one deciphers the allegorical lesson, the text and any other possible interpretations it might contain can be discarded. Taking this line of thinking to its theological conclusion, Paul writes that laws "are only a shadow of what is to come; but the

28 Auerbach, *Literary Language*, 31.

29 See p. 43.

30 See Boyarin, *Socrates and the Fat Rabbis*, 103–32. For a comparison of Platonic dialogues with the Talmud, see Jacob Howland, *Plato and the Talmud* (Cambridge: Cambridge University Press, 2010); and Labendz, *Socratic Torah: Non-Jews in Rabbinic Intellectual Culture*.

31 See Richard Marback, *Plato's Dream of Sophistry* (Columbia, SC: University of South Carolina Press, 1999), 17–45.

32 On the significant differences between Christian and Hellenic interpretations of Plato, see Niketas Siniossoglou, *Plato and Theodoret: The Christian Appropriation of Platonic Philosophy and the Hellenic Intellectual Resistance* (Cambridge: Cambridge University Press, 2008). Despite these differences, however, I find that church fathers such as Augustine accept fundamental Platonic assumptions.

substance belongs to Christ." The letter of the law, like the shadows in Plato's cave, is fake while the only reality is in the spirit of the law that ultimately points to Jesus. Handelman explains, "Jesus becomes the true predicate of all statements, the singular and ultimate referent, a referent beyond language entirely, whose appearance nullifies the written text – which is now considered as a long deviation, a detour, an exile."[33] By locating meaning in ontology rather than text, Paul divorces reality from the word, reads the Bible univocally, and rejects the premise of rhetoric. Even Augustine, who recognized four senses of Scripture, did not consider "the text to have a continuous, simultaneous fourfold meaning in every aspect. It was thought, rather, that the nature of a given particular text determined the level at which it should be read."[34] This is why these Christian writers so explicitly and vehemently denigrate rhetorical oratory in favor of unvarnished truth.

The rabbis, by contrast, limit and control the application of rhetoric, but do not reject its fundamental assumptions of multiple truths, the centrality of language, and the power of interpretation. Because they adhere to the letter of the law, the rabbis embrace the text as the location of meaning: "Rabbinic interpretation never dispenses with the particular form in which the idea is enclothed. The text, for the rabbis, is a continuous generator of meaning, which arises from the innate logic of the divine language, the letter itself."[35] Not reading allegorically or replacing the law with its spirit, the rabbis allow the full multiplicity of interpretations to emerge. At a fundamental level, therefore, the rabbis reject the possibility of knowing absolute truth and accept that meaning can only be conveyed and generated through words. Their view thus diverges from that of the Platonists and the church fathers. Concomitantly, the rabbis are also critical of the sophists as they seek to place limits on cynical, antinomian, and anti-halakhic interpretive possibilities.[36] They are sensitive to the dangers of the reckless application of rhetoric to subvert justice in legislation and in judicial proceedings. They do not reduce all truth value to mere subjective opinion; rhetorical might does not make right. Instead, they work within the realm of rhetoric and activate the power of debate to debunk wrong and harmful

[33] Handelman, *Slayers of Moses*, 88.

[34] Ibid., 109. See further at Marback, *Plato's Dream of Sophistry*, 40; and Emmet Flood, "Augustine and the Classical Tradition of Rhetoric," *History of Education* 11, no. 4 (1982): 237–50.

[35] Handelman, *Slayers of Moses*, 88–9.

[36] See pp. 198–206.

ideas so as to ultimately arrive at the best interpretations and practical laws for their communities. Their notion of truth refers not to universal reason or reality but rather to authentic prophecy. Truth in this sense can include elements of human reason and the art of persuasion because it rests upon the multivocalic nature of prophecy as described in the midrashim that we will presently analyze.

FORTY-NINE WAYS: ON TRUTH AND INTERPRETATION

How were the rabbis, like the sophists and unlike the philosophers and Christians, able to celebrate the multiplicity of truth and yet at the same time maintain their allegiance to the prophetic word of the Bible? The rabbis address the tension between revelatory truth and human interpretation in a series of related aggadot such as this midrash:[37]

R. TANḤUM BAR R. ḤANILAI SAID:	Had the Torah been given clear-cut, then an instructor of the law would not have a leg to stand on; [whereas now], if he declares impure there are others who also declare impure, and if he declares pure, there are others who also declare pure.
R. YANNAI SAID:	The Torah that the Holy One, blessed be He, gave to Moses was given with forty-nine interpretations in favor of pure and forty-nine interpretations in favor of impure. Where is the source? "His banner[38] is beloved to me" (Song 2:4). He [Moses] said to him [God]: How shall it be practiced? He responded, if those who declare impure outnumber then it is impure; if those who purify outnumber then it is pure.
R. ABAHU SAID IN THE NAME OF R. YOḤANAN:	R. Akiva had a distinguished student who knew how to interpret the Torah in forty-nine ways in favor of pure [and forty-nine

[37] Pesikta Rabbati 21; translation based on MS Dropsie. For variants, see Rivka Ulmer, ed. *Pesiqta Rabbati: A Synoptic Edition of Pesiqta Rabbati based upon All Extant Manuscripts and the Editio Princeps* (Atlanta: Scholars Press, 1997), 451–3. While this is a later midrash, a Tannaitic precedent for many of its themes is found in T. Soṭah 7:11–12.

[38] His banner, *ve-diglo*, has the numeric value of forty-nine.

	ways in favor of impure][39] with each reason being different.
THEY SAID:	That student was hewn from Mount Sinai.[40]

The opening statement expresses anxiety over the impossibility of objective and uniform interpretation of the Bible. If the Torah were monistic, the rabbis would have no way to be sure that they could reliably access the Torah's single correct view and so a rabbinic legislator would never be able to issue an authoritative ruling. Rather, the Torah must be multivocal and flexible so that whatever the legislator decides, he knows he will have the support of an interpretive tradition that accords with his view.[41] R. Yannai adds that the polysemy of biblical interpretation does not result from a breakdown of transmission or understanding but is instead inherent and original to the giving of the Torah in the first place. In fact, the pristine Torah encodes the full gamut of arguments on both sides and it is only the practical need to observe one normative position that forces the rabbis to vote and choose one view as the law. Consequently, the highest praise goes to a student who masters not just one correct view but rather all possible views on both sides. Since the original giving of the Torah included the full range of possible interpretations, this student is acclaimed as embodying a piece of Mount Sinai itself. This entire midrash affirms the value of argumentation and the rhetorical penchant to argue both sides of every issue.

Y. Sanhedrin 4:1–2, 22a, includes a parallel to this midrash that expands upon this message.

SAID R. YOḤANAN:	One who does not know how to derive that a reptile is pure and impure in one hundred ways,

[39] The phrase, "and forty-nine ways in favor of impure" is lacking in MSS Parma and JTS and printed editions but is present in MSS Dropsie and Casanata as well as in parallels at Midrash Tehillim 12:4 and Soferim 16:5.

[40] MSS Dropsie, Casnata, and Parma read קטע here. MS JTS and the printed edition read קטא, which would translate to, "that student is a chip off of Mount Sinai." See Marcus Jastrow, *A Dictionary of the Targumim, the Talmud Babli and Yerushalmi, and the Midrashic Literature* (New York: The Judaica Press, 1985), 1345, and further below in n. 43.

[41] See further discussion at Richard Hidary, "Right Answers Revisited: Monism and Pluralism in the Talmud," *Diné Israel* 26 (2009): 229–55, in dialogue with Hayes, "Legal Truth," and Christine Hayes, "Theoretical Pluralism in the Talmud: A Response to Richard Hidary," *Diné Israel* 26–7 (2009–10): 257–307.

may not investigate [testimony] in merit [of the defendant].[42]

RABBI SAID: My master had a distinguished student who could purify the reptile or make it impure in one hundred ways.

THEY SAY: That student did not know how to issue rulings.

R. YAAKOV BAR DOSAI SAID: That student was hewn from[43] Mount Sinai.

R. YANNAI SAID: Had the words of Torah been given as clear-cut decisions, it would not have a leg to stand on. What is the source? "God spoke to Moses . . . " (Num 2:1).[44]

HE [MOSES] SAID BEFORE HIM: Master of the universe, inform me what is the halakha?

HE RESPONDED: "Incline after the majority" (Exod 23:2). If those who declare innocent are more numerous, then declare innocent. If those who declare guilty are more numerous, then declare guilty.

So that the Torah can be interpreted in forty-nine ways to declare impure and forty-nine ways to declare pure. From where do we know this? "His flag (*ve-diglo*)" (Song 2:4).

And so the verse says, "The words of the Lord are pure words, silver purged in an earthen crucible, refined sevenfold" (Ps 12:7).[45] And it says, "Straightly do they love you" (Song 1:4).[46]

[42] See analysis on pp. 233–6.

[43] This follows the translation at Michael Sokoloff, *A Dictionary of Jewish Palestinian Aramaic of the Byzantine Period* (Ramat-Gan: Bar Ilan University, 1992), 487–8, and equates the meaning here with the slightly different spelling in printed editions of Pesikta Rabbati cited above. Pne Moshe and Qorban ha-`Edah, however, understand this as a negative statement that the student was cut off from the revelation at Sinai.

[44] On the relevance of this verse and the flow of the next lines, see Hidary, *Dispute*, 28–9.

[45] The midrash interprets the dual form of שבעתים as seven multiplied by itself, which comes to forty-nine.

[46] In contrast to the multivocality of God's word, God's people show their love by practicing one straight path. This verse is used in Sifra, *Shemini, milu'im* 38, and Gen Rabbah 49:17 to describe Abraham's unquestioning devotion in Gen 22.

As discussed in Chapter 6,[47] R. Yoḥanan requires that a judge master the art of sophistry in order to ensure that he will find every possible argument for acquittal. Rabbi then boasts of a fellow student who in fact had this ability. In response, an anonymous voice tempers the praise with the criticism that this student was too smart for his own good; because he thought of every possibility, he was unable to focus on just one to be the final ruling. Despite this limitation, however, the next lines extol the student as hewn from Mount Sinai where all interpretations of the Torah were presented as significant and equal aspects of God's truth. The process of interpretation is likened again here to mining, similar to B. Sanhedrin 34a.[48] The student who studies Torah is like a miner who breaks off a piece of rock. The ore contains many useful metals and minerals, just as the Torah text is pregnant with many meanings. Argumentation for and against each interpretation is likened to the smelting process of heating up the alloy to separate the elements. Once the various elements separate, the metallurgist can isolate the pure silver just as the sage is best able to pick out the single halakha that he deems should be normative. It is precisely the heated arguments of the sages that break apart the various aspects of each law and makes it possible to then isolate one as the view best suited for practice. The celebration of polysemy and multiple truths does not lead to relativism or nihilism because, when it comes to legislating law, those vast possibilities are constrained by the majority consensus of the interpretive community.[49]

Bavli Eruvin 13b presents yet another variation on this theme:[50]

R. AḤA THE SON OF ḤANINA SAID:	It is revealed and known before He-Who-Spoke-and-the-World-Existed, that there is no one in the generation of R. Meir who is like him. And for what reason did they not establish the halakha like him? Because his colleagues did not reach the extent of his mind for he said about what is impure that it is pure, and about what is pure that it is impure and would demonstrate it with reasons.

[47] See pp. 198 and 233–6.
[48] See p. 30.
[49] Boyarin, *Intertextuality*, 55–6.
[50] Translation follows MS Munich 95, unless otherwise noted.

IT WAS STATED:	His name was not R. Meir but rather R. Maisha. And why was he called R. Meir? For he enlightened the faces of the sages in the halakha.
RAV[51] SAID:	The reason I am sharper than my colleagues is because I saw R. Meir from the back. If I would have seen him from the front I would be even sharper, for the verse states, "Let your eyes see your teachers" (Isa 30:20).
R. ABAHU SAID[52] IN THE NAME OF R. YOḤANAN:	R. Meir had a student whose name was Symmachus who said about each and every matter of impurity forty-eight reasons for impurity and for each and every matter of purity forty-eight reasons for purity.[53]
IT WAS TAUGHT:	There was a distinguished student in Yavneh who could purify the reptile with one hundred and fifty reasons.

[51] MSS Munich 95 and Vatican 109 read "Rav." MS Oxford 366 reads, "Rava." MS Vatican 127 reads, "Rabbah." Printed editions read, "Rabbi." See Boyarin, *Socrates and the Fat Rabbis*, 274 n. 57.

[52] "R. Abahu" is omitted in MS Munich 95 but I have supplied on the basis of all other textual witnesses.

[53] This follows MSS Oxford 366, Vatican 127, printed editions, and the original text of MS Munich 95. However, MS Vatican 109 and a gloss between the lines of MS Munich 95 read: "about each and every matter of impurity forty-eight reasons for purity and for each and every matter of purity forty-eight reasons for impurity." Boyarin, *Socrates and the Fat Rabbis*, 274 n. 58, prefers the latter reading because of the context of the student described next, who also argues the opposite of the halakha. However, I find the latter reading difficult to defend because it is original to only one MS and it is easy to see why the glossator of MS Munich 95 would change it to fit the context. Nevertheless, even according the majority of MSS, I think the sense of the statement is in fact that Symmachus could provide arguments opposing the halakha, especially considering the phrase, "each and every matter." We could paraphrase this line as: "Symmachus was able to take any matter that was declared [by himself or by anyone else] impure and provide forty-eight reasons for its impurity and could also take any matter that was declared pure [by anyone, including the matters in the previous category that might be doubtful or in dispute] and provide forty-eight reasons for its purity." In any case, even if we understand that Symmachus could only argue the correct halakha, David Kraemer, *Reading the Rabbis: The Talmud as Literature* (Oxford: Oxford University Press, 1996), 63–4, shows that it is R. Meir's skill that is emphasized throughout the sugya.

The Bavli assigns the greatest praise to R. Meir as the light of his generation on account of his rhetorical ability to argue opposing views. His talent for providing persuasive arguments for incorrect laws confused his colleagues, for which reason they did not declare the halakha according to his views. Nevertheless, his dialectical talent did not diminish his status but made him comparable to Moses whose face shined after he descended Mount Sinai so that nobody could look at him without his veil (Exod 34:29–35). Rav goes further and likens R. Meir to God Himself who is unknowable in His essence. Moses caught a glimpse of God's back but not His front (Exod 33:23) and Rav holds R. Meir up to that same divine status! If R. Meir's students could be likened to both Moses here and the rock of Mount Sinai in the Yerushalmi, then the teacher R. Meir must be parallel to the Lawgiver Himself. The Bavli inflates the significance of rhetoric beyond that in the previous sources, even increasing the number of possible arguments to one hundred and fifty. David Kraemer comments on this sugya:

> Although it can be difficult to ascertain precisely what the Torah means, it should not be difficult to conclude that an opinion that obviously and directly contradicts a law of the Torah ("pig is kosher") is not possibly a part of divine truth. But in an almost perverse way we are told here that even such opinions are worth offering and pursuing. Because truth is so difficult (read: impossible) to ascertain, kernels of truth might reside in strange places. Even views that appear to be patently untrue, therefore, should be explored.[54]

In other words, the sugya admits the impossibility of attaining objective truth and consequently, but paradoxically, promotes the value of exploring falsehoods. Kraemer attempts to explain this sugya on the background of Greek/Hellenistic philosophy, which offers "the most proximate tradition"[55] to the Bavli. After all, Aristotle writes that "we should be grateful, not only to those with whose views we may agree, but also to those who have expressed more superficial views; for these also contribute something, by developing before us the powers of thought."[56] Kraemer suggests that this statement of Aristotle is comparable to the praise at Bavli Eruvin of R. Meir's ability to argue for wrong positions in order to sharpen the minds of his students. However, as Kraemer correctly acknowledges, the Bavli remains fundamentally

[54] Kraemer, *The Mind of the Talmud* (Oxford: Oxford University Press, 1990), 144.

[55] Ibid., 172.

[56] Ibid., 177, citing Aristotle, *Metaphysics* 2.1. See also p. 33.

different from Aristotle in its embrace of multiple opposing opinions and its denial of a single truth. Unlike the Bavli, both Plato and Aristotle assume, for the most part, that truth – knowledge of reality – is attainable through reason. Kraemer therefore concludes that the Bavli is sui generis in the ancient world in its limitation of both the power of prophecy and of reason. The Bavli, he proposes, is alone among other religious traditions in its unwillingness "to declare the definitive meaning of revelation."[57] For the rabbis, "Truth is present in scripture, to be sure, but … [b]ecause scripture … reveals its truth only through interpretation, truth, like interpretation, is always insecure."[58]

Although Kraemer makes passing reference to the sophists who "denied the determinability of truth,"[59] he nevertheless marginalizes them as a minority voice that gave way to Aristotle's predominance. In fact, however, the sophists were much more entrenched in the popular culture of the Roman Empire than were the philosophers. Therefore, classical rhetoric, not Greek philosophy, stands out as the best context in which to situate this sugya about R. Meir and the general outlook of the Talmud.[60] I agree with Kraemer's assessment that for the Bavli, unlike for the philosophers, truth and interpretation are subjective. However, the Talmud's praise for arguing both sides of every issue is far from sui generis in the dominant classical culture of rhetoric. Rather, as Boyarin writes: "R. Meir's sophism thus connects his character very explicitly with the movement of thought known as the Second Sophistic."[61] R. Meir is portrayed "as a Sophist and thus as a figure who stands directly against, as it were, the truth claims of the halakha."[62]

Does that leave the rabbis squarely in the sophistic camp? The series of texts analyzed in this section as well as various chapters in this book argue that the rabbis maintained a more nuanced view. To recall, Plato dismissed rhetoric and affirmed a monistic truth found in the world of

57 Ibid., 188.

58 Ibid., 189.

59 Ibid., 178.

60 David Kraemer does utilize Chaim Perelman and L. Olbrechts-Tyteca, *The New Rhetoric: A Treatise on Argumentation* (Notre Dame and London: University of Notre Dame Press, 1969) as a framework for understanding the Talmud's argumentative discourse as a mode of rhetorical persuasion where truth "is ambiguous and alternatives are always available" (Kraemer, *Mind*, 112). However, he does not place the Talmud in the historical context of the classical rhetorical tradition. Kraemer primarily analyzes the Bavli, but agrees that his findings are also relevant to the Yerushalmi (ibid., p. 100).

61 Boyarin, *Socrates and the Fat Rabbis*, 277.

62 Ibid., 273.

forms and ideas. The sophists rejected the possibility of objective understanding and conceded that all human knowledge of truth is nothing more than the most persuasive voices in a given society. The rabbis took the best of both worlds by promoting a belief in multiple truths in heaven that were all included in the pristine giving of the Torah.[63] Therefore, the rhetorical struggle of opposing views emerges simply as a human extension of the multifaceted metaphysical world. Platonic truth that must conform to a universal unchanging rational order of ideas leaves no room for multiplicity. In contrast, the rabbinic view of divine truth can include diversity, growth, and continual dialogue between the prophetic words and their human interpreters. Rhetorical technique, in this view, does not obscure the truth, but rather is a necessary tool in unpacking the infinite multifacetedness of God's words.

This conclusion dovetails with that of Christine Hayes in her comprehensive analysis of ancient conceptions of divine law. She demonstrates that for Greek writers, particularly the Stoics, divine law refers to regulations that accord with nature, are rational, true, conducive to virtue, universal for all people, unchanging and unwritten. Human law, in contrast, can be written in concrete rules that can be arbitrary, do not necessarily correspond to truth, are particular to subjects under its coercive force, are changeable and may not produce virtue. Some Jewish thinkers, like Philo, forced the Torah into the Greek conception of divine law.[64] Paul, by contrast, picked up on the similarity between the Torah and human law and thereby denigrated Jewish law and limited its application.[65] Hayes argues that the Talmudic view denies the Greek dichotomy and accepts that the divine Torah can still display characteristics of what the Stoics consider human law: "[T]he rabbis breached conceptual boundaries by insisting that a law could be divine *and* divorced from truth, divine *and* not inherently rational, divine *and*

[63] See further texts and discussion of this theme at Hidary, *Dispute*, 1–31; Steven Fraade, "Rabbinic Polysemy and Pluralism Revisited: Between Praxis and Thematization," *AJS Review* 31, no. 1 (2007): 1–40; Azzan Yadin-Israel, "Rabbinic Polysemy: A Response to Steven Fraade," *AJS Review* 38 (2014): 129–41; Fraade, "Response to Azzan Yadin-Israel"; and Steven Fraade, "'A Heart of Many Chambers': The Theological Hermeneutics of Legal Multivocality," *Harvard Theological Review* 108 (2015): 113–28. Responding to Faur, Eilberg-Schwartz, "When the Reader Is in the Write," 204, writes, "Thus the rabbis do what contemporary criticism finds so problematic: they hold onto the notion of authorial intention while at the same time recognizing the creative role of the reader." See also Ouaknin, *Burnt Book*, 84, who similarly expresses how controversy encodes truth: "*Mahloket* is a way of saying and of thinking the refusal of synthesis and systems: it is an antidogmatism that, alone, makes a living truth possible."

[64] Hayes, *What's Divine about Divine Law?*, 111–24.

[65] Hayes, ibid., 140–64.

subject to moral critique and modification ... [T]he Torah is divine because it originates in the will of the god of Israel, and the attribution of divinity to the Torah does not confer upon it the qualities of universal rational, truth, and stasis."[66] Since the rabbinic view of divine law shares many aspects of Greek human law, we can understand why rhetorical argumentation, which underlies human law, should be so central to rabbinic legal discourse as well.

The unique contribution of this dominant rabbinic approach becomes highlighted when we contrast it with that of the Dead Sea Sect. Viewed from the outside, the Qumran sect reflects many aspects of Hellenism in their thought and way of life, especially the sect's similarity to various utopian philosophical communities such as the Pythagoreans. In their internal self-conception, however, the sect rejects all outside culture and strives to remain purist and wholly devoted to their view of the single correct interpretation of Scripture. The scrolls never cite Greek thinkers and, in fact, their authors consciously strove to remove all Grecisms from their vocabulary as they took a separatist stance against Romans and other Jews.[67] In the sect's conception, Torah law must conform to a monistic truth that is known to the sect's leader and that accords with a divine cosmic plan.[68] Daniel Schwartz has demonstrated that Qumran law tends to take a stance of legal realism such that the law must accord with nature or objective reality, which leaves little room for debate or tolerance for opposing views.[69] Their legal writings therefore do not include multiple opinions or debate and do not reflect familiarity with rhetorical techniques. They apply no hermeneutical rules of exegesis and leave little room for human interpretation, believing instead that the Teacher of Righteousness has

[66] Hayes, ibid., 376–7, italics in original. Hayes uses the word truth here in the Platonic sense of universal static facts, while the rabbis think of truth value as being of divine origin and yet nevertheless flexible and subject to interpretation; see further at p. 27.

[67] Martin Hengel, "Qumran and Hellenism," in *Religion in the Dead Sea Scrolls*, ed. John Collins and Robert Kugler (Grand Rapids: Eerdmans, 2000): 46–56; and Brent Schmidt, *Utopian Communities of the Ancient World: Idealistic Experiments of Pythagoras, the Essenes, Pachomius, and Proclus* (Lewiston, NY: Edwin Mellen Press, 2010).

[68] Hayes, *What's Divine about Divine Law?*, 101–5, 131–4, and 199–200.

[69] Daniel Schwartz, "Law and Truth: On Qumran-Sadducean and Rabbinic Views of Law," in *Dead Sea Scrolls: Forty Years of Research*, ed. Deborah Dimant and Uriel Rappaport (Leiden: Brill, 1992): 229–40. See further discussion at Jeffrey Rubenstein, "Nominalism and Realism in Qumranic and Rabbinic Law: A Reassessment," *Dead Sea Discoveries* 6, no. 2 (1999): 157–83; Christine Hayes, "Legal Realism and the Fashioning of Sectarians in Jewish Antiquity," in *Sects and Sectarianism in Jewish History*, ed. Sacha Stern (Leiden: Brill, 2011): 119–46; and Jeffrey Rubenstein, "Nominalism and Realism Again," 79–120.

prophetic ability to extract the one true law from the Bible.[70] Thus, the Qumranites envision a system of law and interpretation that accepts a Platonic-like view of absolute unchanging truth and they therefore would have little need for the realm of rhetoric.

The rabbis, in contrast, recognized the inevitability of multiple interpretations and subjectivity of human reason. But rather than give up on the possibility of truth, and rather than relegate truth to heavenly forms and deny a place for persuasive speech, the rabbis take a brilliant third path.[71] They teach that all possible legal outcomes and all of the ways of reasoning towards them are themselves part of the Sinaitic revelation and contain truth. The thematization of polysemic revelation attested to across various works of rabbinic literature proves how fundamental it is to the rabbinic worldview even over centuries of development in two countries.[72] The rabbis do not just pay lip service to prophetic multiplicity but also apply it in practice in their pedagogy

[70] See Fraade, "Looking for Legal Midrash." Bernstein and Koyfman, "Interpretation," find only a few examples of rabbinic-type hermeneutical rules in the Qumran scrolls and I think that even those few cases are not convincing. I also do not agree with Daniel Schwartz that the Sadducees utilized *qal va-ḥomer* arguments. See further on this on pp. 201–2 and at Hidary, "Hellenism and Hermeneutics."

[71] A modern equivalent to this third path finds expression in Chaim Perelman, *The Idea of Justice and the Problem of Argument* (London: Routledge and Kegan Paul, 1963), who seeks to navigate between the absoluteness of Cartesian/divine truth and the arbitrariness of human reason by proposing that we accept arguments that "would hold good for the whole intellectual community" (124). He succeeds in making the "transition from the transcendent to the immanent" by means of the "prophetic contribution, with its absolute pattern of the Just transcending rules and systems" (75). That is, particular formulas of justice may change from one person and time to the next, but they all must depend on "the ideal of absolute justice" (ibid.). David A. Frank, "The New Rhetoric, Judaism, and Post-Enlightenment Thought: The Cultural Origins of Perelmanian Philosophy," *Quarterly Journal of Speech* 83 (1997), summarizes Perelman's thesis in these terms: "With an understanding of a Jewish-influenced New Rhetoric, it becomes apparent that Perelmanian philosophy serves as an alternative to the dangers of Enlightenment thinking. Similarly, the New Rhetoric steers clear of the more extreme expressions of postmodernity. The New Rhetoric stands as a counter-model to contemporary critical theory and as a 'third way' between the certainty of the Enlightenment and the radical skepticism of some post-Enlightenment thought."

[72] See Fraade, "A Heart of Many Chambers," 127, who comments on "the endurance with which their [the rabbis'] shared valorization (and problematization) of legal multivocality has crossed several centuries (and two geographic locations) remarkably intact" and concludes that: "The shared pedagogical solution (a wide-open 'ear' and a discerning 'heart') to the challenge of scholastic legal dissensus is notably consistent, mutatis mutandis, and similarly funded by a theology and hermeneutic of scriptural revelation. Given the orally dynamic and textually fluid culture of both tannaitic and amoraic, Palestinian and Babylonian, rabbinic sages, especially at the level of textual redaction, the endurance of this idea (and its textual praxis), manifest as it is with variants, is all the more profound for its consistently coherent core."

and in their compositions. The rabbis deem the creative ability of the sermonizer to link verses together in the proem form to be an experience akin to Sinaitic revelation.[73] This unique approach expresses itself in their forms of rhetorical exercises, which use the technique of rhetoric to uphold all sides rather than proving one at the expense of the others.[74] The rabbis draft rhetoric in service of their view of prophecy by turning to reason and rhetorical topoi to bring out the multiple meanings of biblical texts.[75] Instead of rejecting rhetoric as an intruder from external culture that comes to challenge the Torah's truths, the rabbis elevate rhetoric to the level of prophecy itself.

[73] See pp. 51 and 77.
[74] See Chapter 4.
[75] See Chapter 5.

Bibliography

`Aqrah, Abraham ben Don Shelomoh, ed. *Me-harere nemerim*. Venice: Bet Dani'el Zaneṭi, 1599.

Aberbach, Moshe. *Ha-ḥinukh ha-Yehudi bi-tqufat ha-Mishnah veha-Talmud*. Jerusalem: Rubin Mass, 1982.

Ad Herennium. Translated by Harry Caplan. Loeb Classical Library. Cambridge: Harvard University Press, 1954.

Aeneas of Gaza: Theophrastus with Zacharias of Mytilene: Ammonius. Translated by Sebastian Bertz, John Dillon, and Donald Russell. London: Bloomsbury Academic, 2012.

Albeck, Hanoch. *Mavo la-Talmudim*. Tel-Aviv: Dvir, 1987.

—*Six Orders of Mishnah* [Hebrew]. 6 vols. Jerusalem: Mossad Bialik, 1959.

Albeck, Hanoch, and Judah Theodor. *Midrash Bereshit Rabbah: Critical Edition with Notes and Commentary*. Jerusalem: Shalem Books, 1996.

Alexander, Elizabeth Shanks. *Transmitting Mishnah: The Shaping Influence of Oral Tradition*. New York, NY: Cambridge University Press, 2006.

Alexander, Philip S. "Hellenism and Hellenization as Problematic Historiographical Categories." In *Paul Beyond the Judaism/Hellenism Divide*, edited by Troels Engberg-Pedersen, 63–80. Louisville, KY: Westminster John Knox Press, 2001.

—"Quid Athenis et Hierosolymis? Rabbinic Midrash and Hermeneutics in the Graeco-Roman World." In *A Tribute to Geza Vermes: Essays on Jewish and Christian Literature and History*, edited by P. R. Davies and R. T. White, 101–24. Sheffield: Sheffield Academic Press, 1990.

Alon, Gedaliah. *The Jews in Their Land in the Talmudic Age (70–640 C.E.)*. Translated by Gershon Levi. Jerusalem: Magnes Press, 1984.

—*Jews, Judaism and the Classical World: Studies in Jewish History in the Times of the Second Temple and Talmud*. Jerusalem: Magnes Press, 1977.

Alter, Robert. *The Art of Biblical Narrative*. New York, NY: Basic Books, 1981.

Anderson, Graham. *The Second Sophistic: A Cultural Phenomenon in the Roman Empire*. New York, NY: Routledge, 1993.

Angel, Joseph. "Damascus Document." In *Outside the Bible: Ancient Jewish Writings Related to Scripture*, edited by Louis Feldman, James Kugel and Lawrence Schiffman, 2975–3035. Philadelphia, PA: Jewish Publication Society, 2013.

Anisfeld, Rachel. *Sustain Me with Raisin-Cakes: Pesikta deRav Kahana and the Popularization of Rabbinic Judaism*. Leiden: Brill, 2009.

Appelbaum, Alan. *The Rabbis' King-parables: Midrash from the Third-century Roman Empire*. Piscataway, NJ: Gorgias Press, 2010.

Aristotle. *On Rhetoric: A Theory of Civil Discourse*. Translated by George A. Kennedy. New York, NY: Oxford University Press, 2007.

Arnoff, Stephen Hazan. "Memory, Rhetoric, and Oral-Performance in Leviticus Rabbah." PhD diss., Jewish Theological Seminary, 2011.

Arthurs, Jeffrey. "The Term Rhetor in Fifth- and Fourth-Century B.C.E. Greek Texts." *Rhetoric Society Quarterly* 23, no. 3/4 (1994): 1–10.

Ashkenazi, Duberush. *Sha`are Yerushalmi*. Warsaw: Drukerni N. Schriftgisser, 1866.

Attridge, Harold. "Philo and John: Two Riffs on One Logos." *Studia Philonica Annual* 17 (2005): 103–17.

Atzmon, Arnon. "'The Same Fate Is in Store for the Righteous and the Wicked:' Form and Content in Midreshei Aggadah." *Journal for the Study of Judaism* 43 (2012): 58–77.

Auerbach, Erich. *Literary Language and Its Public in Late Latin Antiquity and in the Middle Ages*. Princeton, NJ: Princeton University Press.

Aune, David, ed. *The Westminster Dictionary of New Testament and Early Christian Literature and Rhetoric*. Louisville, KY: Westminster John Knox Press, 2003.

Avery-Peck, Alan. "Rhetorical Argumentation in Early Rabbinic Pronouncement Stories." In *The Rhetoric of Pronouncement*, edited by Vernon Robbins, 49–69. Atlanta, GA: Scholars Press, 1994.

Avi-Yonah, Michael, and Shimon Gibson. "Elusa." *Encyclopaedia Judaica* (2007): 6:370–1.

Bacher, Wilhelm. *Agadat Amora'e Ereṣ Yisrael*. Translated by A. Z. Rabinovits. Tel-Aviv: Dvir, 1930.

—*`Erkhe midrash*. Jerusalem: Carmiel, 1969.

Bakhtin, Mikhail. *The Dialogical Imagination: Four Essays*. Translated by Caryl Emerson and Michael Holquist. Austin, TX: University of Texas, 1981.

Ball, Warwick. *Rome in the East: The Transformation of an Empire*. London: Routledge, 2000.

Baltzly, Dirk. "Stoicism." *The Stanford Encyclopedia of Philosophy* (2014).

Bar-Asher, Moshe. "On Corrections and Marginal Versions in Codex Parma B (De Rossi 497) of the Mishna." [Hebrew]. In *Segulla to Ariella*, edited by Moshe Bar-Asher, A. Harel Fish, Moshe Idel, Nahum Sarna and Yosef Tobi, 121–58. Jerusalem: Hoṣa'at Hamishpaḥa, 1990.

Bar-Asher Siegal, Michal. *Early Christian Monastic Literature and the Babylonian Talmud*. Cambridge: Cambridge University Press, 2013.

Barker, Margaret. "The Paraclete." In *The Temple in Text and Tradition: A Festschrift in Honour of Robert Hayward*, edited by R. T. McLay, 98–112. London: Bloomsbury T&T Clark, 2015.

Barney, Rachel. *Names and Nature in Plato's Cratylus*. New York, NY: Routledge, 2001.

Baumgarten, Joseph. "The Heavenly Tribunal and the Personification of Ṣedeq in Jewish Apocalyptic." In *Aufstieg und Niedergang der römischen Welt*, edited by Wolfgang Haase, *Vol. 19.1*, 219–39. Berlin: De Gruyter, 1979.

—"The Unwritten Law in the Pre-Rabbinic Period." *Journal for the Study of Judaism in the Persian, Hellenistic and Roman Period* 3 (1972): 7–29.

Becker, Adam. "The Comparative Study of 'Scholasticism' in Late Antique Mesopotamia: Rabbis and East Syrians." *AJS Review* 34, no. 1 (2010): 91–113.

—*Fear of God and the Beginning of Wisdom: The School of Nisibis and the Development of Scholastic Culture in Late Antique Mesopotamia*. Philadelphia, PA: University of Pennsylvania, 2006.

—"Positing a 'Cultural Relationship' between Plato and the Babylonian Talmud." *Jewish Quarterly Review* 101, no. 2 (2011): 255–69.

Bell, Jeremy. "'Empeiria kai Tribe': Plato on the 'Art' of Flattery in Rhetoric and Sophistry." *Epoche: A Journal for the History of Philosophy* 15, no. 2 (2011): 379–94.

Ben-Menahem, Hanina. *Judicial Deviation in Talmudic Law*. New York, NY: Harwood Academic Publishers, 1991.

Ben-Shalom, Israel. "'And I Took Unto Me Two Staves: The One I Called Beauty and the Other I Called Bands' (Zakh. 11:7)." [Hebrew]. In *Dor-Le-Dor: From the End of Biblical Times up to the Redaction of the Talmud. Studies in Honor of Joshua Efron*, edited by A. Oppenheimer and A. Kasher, 215–34. Jerusalem: Bialik, 1995.

Berger, Shlomo. *Classical Oratory and the Sephardim of Amsterdam: Rabbi Aquilar's "Tratado de la retorica."* Hilversum: Verloren, 1996.

Bergman, Yerahmiel. "Gezerah shavah mahi?" *Sinai* 71 (1972): 1323–39.

Berkowitz, Beth. *Execution and Invention: Death Penalty Discourse in Early Rabbinic and Christian Cultures*. New York, NY: Oxford University Press, 2006.

Bernstein, Moshe, and Shlomo Koyfman. "The Interpretation of Biblical Law in the Dead Sea Scrolls: Forms and Methods." In *Biblical Interpretation at Qumran*, edited by Matthias Henze, 61–87. Grand Rapids, MI: Eerdmans, 2005.

Bickerman, Elias. *The Jews in the Greek Age*. Cambridge: Harvard University Press, 1988.

—"La chaine de la tradition Pharisienne." *Revue Biblique* 59 (1952): 44–54.

Black, Clifton. *The Rhetoric of the Gospel: Theological Artistry in the Gospels and Acts*. Louisville, KY: Westminster John Knox Press, 2013.

—"The Rhetorical Form of the Hellenistic Jewish and Early Christian Sermon: A Response to Lawrence Wills." *Harvard Theological Review* 81, no. 1 (1988): 1–18.

Blidstein, Gerald. "Rabbinic Judaism and General Culture: Normative Discussion and Attitudes." In *Judaism's Encounter with Other Cultures*, edited by Jacob J. Schachter, 4–56. Northvale, NJ: Jason Aronson, 1997.

Blum, Jost G. "Zum Bau von Abschnitten in Memre von Jacob von Sarug." In *III Symposium Syriacum*, edited by R. Lavenant. Rome: Pontificium Institutum Orientalium Studiorum, 1983.

Böhlig, Alexander. "Zur Rhetorik im Liber Graduum." In *IV Symposium Syriacum*, edited by H.J.W. Drijvers et al. Rome: Pontificium Institutum Studiorum Orientalium, 1987.

Bokser, Baruch. *The Origins of the Seder: The Passover Rite and Early Rabbinic Judaism*. Berkeley, CA: University of California Press, 1984.

—"Rabbinic Responses to Catastrophe: From Continuity to Discontinuity." *Proceedings of the American Academy for Jewish Research* 50 (1983): 37–61.

Boman, Thorleif. *Hebrew Thought Compared with Greek*. New York, NY: W. W. Norton, 1960.

Bonner, Stanley F. *Education in Ancient Rome*. Berkley: University of California Press, 1977.
—*Roman Declamation in the Late Republic and Early Empire*. Liverpool: Liverpool University Press, 1969.
Borges, Jorge Luis. "The Analytical Language of John Wilkins." In *Selected Non-fiction*, edited by Eliot Weinberger, 229–32. New York, NY: Viking, 1999.
Borkowski, Andrew, and Paul du Plessis. *Textbook on Roman Law*. Oxford: Oxford University Press, 2005.
Bowker, J. W. "Speeches in Acts: A Study in Proem and Yelammedenu Form." *New Testament Studies* 14 (1967): 96–111.
Boyarin, Daniel. *Border Lines: The Partition of Judaeo-Christianity*. Philadelphia, PA: University of Pennsylvania Press, 2004.
—"The Gospel of the Memra: Jewish Binitarianism and the Prologue to John." *Harvard Theological Review* 94, no. 3 (2001): 243–84.
—*Ha-`iyun ha-Sefaradi: lefarshanut ha-Talmud shel megureshe Sefarad*. Jerusalem: Yad Izhak Ben Zvi and Hebrew University, 1989.
—"Hellenism in Jewish Babylonia." In *The Cambridge Companion to the Talmud and Rabbinic Literature*, edited by Charlotte Fonrobert and Martin Jaffee, 336–63. Cambridge: Cambridge University Press, 2007.
—*Intertextuality and the Reading of Midrash*. Bloomington, IN: Indiana University Press, 1990.
—"Moslem, Christian, and Jewish Cultural Interaction in Sefardic Talmudic Interpretation." *Review of Rabbinic Judaism* 5, no. 1 (2002): 1–33.
—"Shattering the Logos – or, The Talmuds and the Genealogy of Indeterminacy." In *The Talmud Yerushalmi and Graeco-Roman Culture III*, edited by Peter Schäfer, 273–99. Tübingen: Mohr Siebeck, 2002.
—*Socrates and the Fat Rabbis*. Chicago, IL: University of Chicago Press, 2009.
Boyd, William. *The History of Western Education*. London: A. & C. Black, 1921.
Brauw, Michael de. "The Parts of the Speech." In *A Companion to Greek Rhetoric*, edited by Ian Worthington, 187–202. Malden, MA: Blackwell Publishing, 2007.
Bregman, Marc. "The Darshan: Preacher and Teacher of Talmudic Times." *The Melton Journal* 14 (1982).
—"Mesorot u-meqorot qedumim be-sifrut Tanḥuma-yelamdenu." *Tarbiz* 60 (1991): 269–74.
—"Revadei yeṣirah va-`arikha be-midreshei Tanḥuma-yelamdenu." *Proceedings of the Tenth World Congress for Jewish Studies* C.1 (1990): 117–24.
—*The Tanhuma-Yalammedenu Literature: Studies in the Evolution of the Versions*. Piscataway, NJ: Gorgias Press, 2003.
—"Tanhuma Yelamdenu." *Encyclopaedia Judaica* (2007).
—"The Triennial Haftarot and the Perorations of the Midrashic Homilies." *Journal of Jewish Studies* 32 (1981): 74–84.
Breuer, Yochanan. *The Hebrew in the Babylonian Talmud according to the Manuscripts of Tractate Pesahim* [Hebrew]. Jerusalem: The Hebrew University Magnes Press, 2002.
Brock, Sebastian. "From Antagonism to Assimilation: Syriac Attitudes to Greek Learning." In *East of Byzantium: Syria and Armenia in the Formative Period*, edited by Nina Garsoian, Thomas Mathews and Robert Thomson, 17–34. Washington, D.C.: Dumbarton Oaks, Center for Byzantine Studies, 1982.

—"A Guide to Narsai's Homilies." *Journal of Syriac Studies* 12, no. 1 (2009): 21–40.
Brodsky, David. "From Disagreement to Talmudic Discourse: Progymnasmata and the Evolution of a Rabbinic Genre." In *Rabbinic Traditions between Palestine and Babylonia*, edited by Ronit Nikolsky and Tal Ilan, 173–231. Leiden: Brill, 2014.
Brody, Robert. *The Geonim of Babylonia and the Shaping of Medieval Jewish Culture*. New Haven and London: Yale University Press, 1998.
Bruns, Gerald. *Hermeneutics Ancient and Modern*. New Haven, CT: Yale University Press, 1992.
Büchler, Adolf. "Learning and Teaching in the Open Air in Palestina." *Jewish Quarterly Review* 4 (1914): 485–91.
Buelow, G. J. "Rhetoric and Music." *The New Grove Dictionary of Music and Musicians* 15 (1980): 793–808.
Burnyeat, Myles. "Enthymeme: Aristotle on the Logic of Persuasion." In *Aristotle's Rhetoric: Philosophical Essays*, edited by David Furley and Alexander Nehemas, 3–55. Princeton, NJ: Princeton University Press, 1994.
Cabezón, José Ignacio, ed. *Scholasticism: Cross-Cultural and Comparative Perspectives*. Albany, NY: State University of New York Press, 1998.
Calderon, Ruth. *A Bride for One Night: Talmudic Tales*. Philadelphia, PA: Jewish Publication Society, 2014.
Campbell, Brian, and Lawrence Tritle, eds. *The Oxford Handbook of Warfare in the Classical World*. Oxford: Oxford University Press, 2013.
Canpanton, Isaac ben Jacob, and Shemuel al-Valensi. *Darkhe ha-Talmud*. Jerusalem: Isaak Lange, 1980.
Carson, D. A. "The Function of the Paraclete in John 16:7–11." *Journal of Biblical Literature* 98, no. 4 (1979): 547–66.
Cattani, Adelino. "Subjectivist and Objectivist Interpretations of Controversy-based Thought." In *Controversies and Subjectivity*, edited by Pierluigi Barrotta and Marcelo Dascak, 185–200. Amsterdam: John Benjamins Publishing Co., 2005.
Chernick, Michael. *Le-ḥeqer ha-midot "kelal u-ferat u-khelal" ve-"ribui u-mi'ut" ba-midrashim uva-talmudim*. Lod: Habermann Institute for Literary Research, 1984.
—*Midat "gezerah shavah": ṣuroteha ba-Midrashim uva-Talmudim*. Lod: Habermann Institute, 1994.
Chin, Catherine. "Rhetorical Practice in the Chreia Elaboration of Mara bar Serapion." *Hugoye: Journal of Syriac Studies* 9, no. 2 (2006): 145–71.
Church, A. J., and W. J. Brodribb. *The Agricola and Germany of Tacitus and the Dialogue on Oratory*. London: Macmillan, 1911.
Cicero. *De Oratore*. Translated by E. W. Sutton. Cambridge: Harvard University Press, 1942.
—*On Invention*. Translated by H. M. Hubbell. Cambridge: Harvard University Press, 1949.
—*Orator*. Translated by H. M. Hubbell. Cambridge: Harvard University Press, 1952.
—*The Speeches*. Translated by John Henry Freese. Cambridge: Harvard University Press, 1945.
Cohen, Boaz. *Jewish and Roman Law: A Comparative Study*. New York, NY: The Jewish Theological Seminary of America, 1966.

—*Law and Tradition in Judaism*. New York, NY: Jewish Theological Seminary of America, 1959.
—"Letter and Spirit in Jewish and Roman Law." In *Essays in Greco-Roman and Related Talmudic Literature*, edited by Henry Fischel, 138–64. New York, NY: Ktav, 1977.
Cohen, Norman. "Structure and Editing in the Homiletic Midrashim." *AJS Review* 6 (1981): 1–20.
Cohen, Richard. "The Relationship Between Topic, Rhetoric and Logic: Analysis of a Syllogistic Passage in the Yerushalmi." In *Judaic and Christian Interpretation of Texts: Contents and Contexts*, edited by Jacob Neusner, 87–125. Lanham: University Press of America, 1987.
Cohen, Shaye. "Patriarchs and Scholarchs." *Proceedings of the American Academy for Jewish Research* 48 (1981): 57–85.
—"The Rabbis in Second-Century Jewish Society." In *The Cambridge History of Judaism. Vol. 3: The Early Roman Period*, edited by W. Horbury, W. D. Davies and J. Sturdy, 922–90. Cambridge: Cambridge University Press, 1999.
Collins, John. *Jewish Cult and Hellenistic Culture: Essays on the Jewish Encounter with Hellenism*. Leiden: Brill, 2005.
Conley, Thomas. "Philo's Rhetoric: Argumentation and Style." In *Aufstieg und Niedergang der römischen Welt II, 21/1*, edited by H. Temporini and W. Haase, 343–71. Berlin and New York, NY: De Gruyter, 1984.
Consigny, Scott. "Edward Schiappa's Reading of the Sophists." *Rhetoric Review* 14, no. 2 (1996): 253–69.
—"Nietzsche's Reading of the Sophists." *Rhetoric Review* 13, no. 1 (1994): 5–26.
Cooper, John, ed. *Plato: Complete Works*. Indianapolis, IN: Hacket Publishing, 1997.
Corbett, Edward, and Robert Connors. *Classical Rhetoric for the Modern Student*. New York, NY: Oxford University Press, 1999.
Corrado, Michael Louis. "The Future of Adversarial Systems: An Introduction to the Papers from the First Conference." *North Carolina Journal of International Law and Commercial Regulation* 35 (2010): 285–96.
Cover, Robert. "Violence and the Word." In *Narrative, Violence, and the Law: The Essays of Robert Cover*, edited by Martha Minow, Michael Ryan and Austin Sarat, 203–38. Ann Arbor, MI: The University of Michigan Press, 1995.
Cribiore, Raffaella. *Gymnastics of the Mind: Greek Education in Hellenistic and Roman Egypt*. Princeton, NJ: Princeton University Press, 2001.
—*The School of Libanius in Late Antique Antioch*. Princeton, NJ: Princeton University Press, 2007.
Crook, J. A. *Legal Advocacy in the Roman World*. Ithaca, NY: Cornell University Press, 1995.
Cross, Frank Moore. *From Epic to Canon*. Baltimore, MD: The Johns Hopkins University Press, 1998.
Daiches, Yisrael Haim. *Netivot Yerushalaim*. Vilna, 1880.
Damaška, Mirjan. *The Faces of Justice and State Authority: A Comparative Approach to the Legal Process*. New Haven, CT: Yale University Press, 1986.
Daube, David. "Alexandrian Methods of Interpretation and the Rabbis." In *Essays in Greco-Roman and Related Talmudic Literature*, edited by Henry Fischel, 165–82. New York, NY: Ktav, 1977.

—"The Civil Law of the Mishnah: The Arrangement of the Three Gates." In *The Collected Works of David Daube*, edited by Calum Carmichael, 1:257–304. Berkeley, CA: University of California, 1992.

—"On the Third Chapter of the Lex Aquila." *Law Quarterly Review* 52 (1936): 253–68.

—"Rabbinic Methods of Interpretation and Hellenistic Rhetoric." *Hebrew Union College Annual* 22 (1949): 239–64.

—"Texts and Interpretaions in Roman and Jewish Law." In *The Collected Works of David Daube*, edited by Calum Carmichael, 1:173–204. Berkeley, CA: University of California, 1992.

De Vries, Benjamin. *Meḥqarim be-sifrut ha-Talmud* [Hebrew]. Jerusalem: Mossad Harav Kook, 1968.

De Zulueta, Francis. *The Institutes of Gaius*. Oxford: Clarendon Press, 1946.

Deissmann, Adolf. *Light from the Ancient East: The New Testament Illustrated by Recently Discovered Texts of the Graeco-Roman World*. Translated by Lionel R. M. Strachan. New York, NY: Harper & Brothers, 1927.

Derrida, Jacques. *Of Grammatology*. Translated by Gayatri Chakravorty Spivak. Baltimore, MD: Johns Hopkins University Press, 1997.

Diehm, James. "The Introduction of Jury Trials and Adversarial Elements into the Former Soviet Union and Other Inquisitorial Countries." *Journal of Transnational Law and Policy* 11, no. 1 (2001): 1–38.

Dilts, Mervin R., and George A. Kennedy. *Two Greek Rhetorical Treatises from the Roman Empire: Introduction, Text and Translation of the Arts of Rhetoric Attributed to Anonymous Segeurianus and to Apsines of Gadara*. Leiden: Brill, 1997.

Dimant, Devorah. "Between Qumran Sectarian and Non-sectarian Texts: The Case of Belial and Mastema." In *The Dead Sea Scrolls and Contemporary Culture*, edited by Adolfo Roitman and Lawrence Schiffman, 235–56. Leiden: Brill, 2011.

Dohrmann, Natalie. "Reading as Rhetoric in Halakhic Texts." In *Of Scribes and Sages: Early Jewish Interpretation and Transmission of Scripture*, edited by Craig Evans, 90–114. London: T&T Clark International, 2004.

Dohrmann, Natalie, and Annette Yoshiko Reed. "Rethinking Romanness, Provincializing Christendom." In *Jews, Christians, and the Roman Empire: The Poetics of Power in Late Antiquity*, edited by Natalie Dohrmann and Annette Yoshiko Reed, 1–21. Philadelphia, PA: University of Pennsylvania Press, 2013.

Dolgopolski, Sergey. *What is Talmud?: The Art of Disagreement*. New York, NY: Fordham University Press, 2009.

Dutsch, Dorota. "Towards a Roman Theory of Theatrical Gesture." In *Performance in Greek and Roman Theatre*, edited by Georgy Harrison and Vayos Liaps, 409–32. Leiden: Brill, 2013.

Dworkin, Ronald. *Law's Empire*. Cambridge: Belknap Press, 1986.

Eilberg-Schwartz, Howard. "Myth, Inference and the Relativity of Reason: An Argument from the History of Judaism." In *Myth and Philosophy*, edited by F. Reynolds and D. Tracy, 247–86. Albany, NY: State University of New York Press, 1990.

—"When the Reader Is in the Write." *Prooftexts* 7 (1987): 194–205.

Elman, Yaakov. "The Babylonian Talmud in Its Historical Context." In *Printing the Talmud: From Bomberg to Schottenstein*, edited by Sharon Lieberman Mintz and Gabriel Goldstein, 19–28. New York, NY: Yeshiva University Museum, 2005.

—"Orality and the Redaction of the Babylonian Talmud." *Oral Tradition* 14, no. 1 (1999): 52–99.

—"The Order of Arguments in כלך-Baraitot in Relation to the Conclusion." *Jewish Quarterly Review* 79 (1989): 295–304.

—"Toward an Intellectual History of Sasanian Law: An Intergenerational Dispute in 'Herbedestan' 9 and Its Rabbinic and Roman Parallels." In *The Talmud in Its Iranian Context*, edited by C. Bakhos and M. R. Shayegan, 21–57. Tübingen: Mohr Siebeck, 2010.

Encyclopedia Talmudit. Edited by M. Berlin and S. J. Zevin. Jerusalem: Talmudic Encylopedia Institute, 1946–2012.

Epstein, Abraham. *Miqadmoniot ha-Yehudim*. Jerusalem: Mosad Harav Kook, 1964.

Epstein, Y. N. *Mevo'ot le-sifrut ha-Tannaim, Mishnah, Tosefta, u-midreshe halakha*. Edited by E. Z. Melamed. Jerusalem: Magnes Press, 1947.

Eshel, Esther. "Mastema's Attempt on Moses' Life in the 'Pseudo-Jubilees' Text from Masada." *Dead Sea Discoveries* 10, no. 3 (2003): 359–64.

Fantham, Elaine. "The Contexts and Occasions of Roman Public Rhetoric." In *Roman Eloquence: Rhetoric in Society and Literature*, edited by William Dominik, 91–105. New York, NY: Routledge, 1997.

Faur, José. *Golden Doves with Silver Dots: Semiotics and Textuality in Rabbinic Tradition*. Bloomington, IN: Indiana University Press, 1986.

—*The Horizontal Society: Understanding the Covenant and Alphabetic Judaism*. Boston, MA: Academic Studies Press, 2008.

—"Retorica y Hemeneutica: Vico y la Tradicion Rabinica." Translated by David Ramirez. In *Pensar para el nuevo siglo: Giambattista Vico y la cultura Europea*, edited by E. Hidalto-Serna, 917–38. Napoli: La Città del Sole, 2001.

—"The Splitting of the Logos: Some Remarks on Vico and the Rabbinic Tradition." *Poiesis: New Vico Studies* 3 (1985): 85–103.

Feldman, Louis. *Jew and Gentile in the Ancient World: Attitudes and Interactions from Alexander to Justinian*. Princeton, NJ: Princeton University Press, 1993.

—*Judaism and Hellenism Reconsidered*. Leiden: Brill, 2006.

Fernandez, Joseph. "An Exploration of the Meaning of Truth in Philosophy and Law." *University of Notre Dame Australia Law Review* 11 (2009): 53–83.

Fine, Steven. *Art and Judaism in the Greco-Roman World: Toward a New Jewish Archaeology*. Cambridge: Cambridge University Press, 2010.

Finkelstein, Louis. *Ha-Perushim ve-'anshe keneset ha-gedolah*. New York, NY: Jewish Theological Seminary of America, 1950.

—"The Oldest Midrash: Pre-Rabbinic Ideals and Teachings in the Passover Haggadah." *Harvard Theological Review* 31, no. 4 (1938): 291–317.

—*Sifra on Leviticus* [Hebrew]. 5 vols. Jerusalem: The Jewish Theological Seminary of America, 1983–92.

—*Sifre on Deuteronomy* [Hebrew]. New York, NY: The Jewish Theological Seminary of America, 1969.

Fischel, Henry, ed. *Essays in Greco-Roman and Related Talmudic Literature*. New York, NY: Ktav, 1977.
—"Greek and Latin Languages, Rabbinical Knowledge of." *Encyclopaedia Judaica* (2007): 8:57–9.
—*Rabbinic Literature and Greco-Roman Philosophy*. Leiden: Brill, 1973.
—"Story and History: Observations on Greco-Roman Rhetoric and Pharisaism." In *Essays in Greco-Roman and Related Talmudic Literature*, edited by Henry Fiscel, 443–72. New York, NY: Ktav, 1977.
—"Studies in Cynicism and the Ancient Near East: The Transformation of a 'Chria'." In *Religions in Antiquity: Essays in Memory of Edwin Ramsdell Goodenough*, edited by Jacob Neusner, 372–411. Leiden: Brill, 1968.
—"The Transformation of Wisdom in the World of Midrash." In *Aspects of Wisdom in Judaism and Early Christianity*, edited by Robert Wilken, 67–101. Notre Dame: University of Notre Dame Press, 1975.
Fish, Stanley. *Doing What Comes Naturally: Change, Rhetoric, and the Practice of Theory in Literary and Legal Studies*. Durham: Duke University, 1989.
—"Rhetoric." In *Rhetoric in an Antifoundational World: Language, Culture, and Pedagogy*, edited by Michael Bernard-Donals and Richard Glejzer, 33–64. New Haven, CT: Yale University Press, 1998.
Flood, Emmet. "Augustine and the Classical Tradition of Rhetoric." *History of Education* 11, no. 4 (1982): 237–50.
Fonrobert, Charlotte Elisheva. "Plato in Rabbi Shimon bar Yohai's Cave (B. Shabbat 33b–34a): The Talmudic Inversion of Plato's Politics of Philosophy." *AJS Review* 31, no. 2 (2007): 277–96.
Fonrobert, Charlotte, and Martin Jaffee, eds. *The Cambridge Companion to the Talmud and Rabbinic Literature*. Cambridge: Cambridge University Press, 2007.
Forbes, Christopher. "Paul and Rhetorical Comparison." In *Paul in the Greco-Roman World: A Handbook*, edited by J. Paul Sampley, 134–71. Harrisburg, PA: Trinity Press International, 2003.
Forsyth, William. *The History of Lawyers*. Boston, MA: Estes and Lauriat, 1875.
Foucault, Michel. *The Archaeology of Knowledge and the Discourse on Language*. Translated by A.M. Sheridan Smith. New York, NY: Pantheon Books, 1972.
Fox, Robin Lane. *The Classical World: An Epic History from Homer to Hadrian*. New York, NY: Basic Books, 2006.
Fraade, Steven. *From Tradition to Commentary: Torah and Its Interpretation in the Midrash Sifre to Deuteronomy*. Albany, NY: State University of New York, 1991.
—"'A Heart of Many Chambers': The Theological Hermeneutics of Legal Multivocality." *Harvard Theological Review* 108 (2015): 113–28.
—"Looking for Legal Midrash at Qumran." In *Biblical Perspectives: Early Use and Interpretation of the Bible in Light of the Dead Sea Scrolls*, edited by Michael E. Stone and Esther Chazon, 59–79. Leiden: Brill, 1998.
—"Rabbinic Polysemy and Pluralism Revisited: Between Praxis and Thematization." *AJS Review* 31, no. 1 (2007): 1–40.
—"Response to Azzan Yadin-Israel on Rabbinic Polysemy: Do They 'Preach' What They Practice?" *AJS Review* 38 (2014): 339–61.

—"Shifting from Priestly to Non-Priestly Legal Authority: A Comparison of the Damascus Document and the Midrash Sifra." *Dead Sea Discoveries* 6, no. 2 (1999): 109–25.

Frank, David A. "Arguing with God, Talmudic Discourse, and the Jewish Countermodel: Implications for the Study of Argumentation." *Argumentation and Advocacy* 41 (2004): 71–86.

—"The Jewish Countermodel: Talmudic Argumentation, the New Rhetoric Project, and the Classical Tradition of Rhetoric." *Journal of Communication and Religion* 26 (2003): 163–94.

—"The New Rhetoric, Judaism, and Post-Enlightenment Thought: The Cultural Origins of Perelmanian Philosophy." *Quarterly Journal of Speech* 83 (1997): 311–31.

Frankel, Zechariah. *Mavo ha-Yerushalmi*. Breslau: Schletter, 1870.

Friedman, Elyakim. "'En `onshin min ha-din." *Mi-perot Ereṣ Ha-ṣevi* (2009): 11–17.

Friedman, Hershey. "Talmudic Humor and the Establishment of Legal Principles: Strange Questions, Impossible Scenarios, and Legalistic Brainteasers." *Thalia: Studies in Literary Humor* 21, no. 1 (2004): 14–28.

Friedman, Mordechai A. *Jewish Marriage in Palestine: A Cairo Genizah Study*. Tel-Aviv: Tel-Aviv University, 1980.

Friedman, Shamma. "Ha-munaḥ 'o kelakh le-derekh zo' ve-shimusho be-midreshe ha-tannaim." *Sidra* 9 (1993): 61–74.

—"Pereq ha-isha rabbah ba-Bavli, be-ṣeruf mavo kelali `al derekh ḥeker ha-sugya." In *Mehkarim u-mekorot*, edited by H. Z. Dimitrovsky. New York, NY: Jewish Theological Seminary, 1977.

—"Some Structural Patterns of Talmudic Sugyot." [Hebrew] *Proceedings of the Sixth World Congress of Jewish Studies* 3 (1977): 389–402.

Furstenberg, Yair. "The 'Agon' with Moses and Homer: Rabbinic Midrash and the Second Sophistic." In *Homer and the Bible in the Eyes of Ancient Interpreters*, edited by Maren Niehoff, 299–328. Leiden: Brill, 2012.

Gadamer, Hans-Georg. *Truth and Method*. London: Continuum, 2004.

Gafni, Isaiah. "`Al derashot be-ṣibur be-Bavel ha-talmudit: ha-pirqa." In *Kneset Ezra: sifrut ve-ḥayim be-bet ha-keneset*, edited by Shulamit Elitzur et al., 121–9. Jerusalem: Yad Yitzḥak ben Zvi, 1994.

—"Nestorian Literature as a Source for the History of the Babylonian *Yeshivot*." [Hebrew] *Tarbiz* 51 (1982): 567–76.

Galanter, Marc. *Lowering the Bar: Lawyer Jokes and Legal Culture*. Madison, WI: University of Wisconsin Press, 2005.

Geiger, Yosef. "No'amim Yevanim be-Ereṣ Yisrael." *Cathedra* 66 (1992): 47–56.

Gellius, Aulus. *Noctes Atticae*. Translated by J. C. Rolfe. Loeb Classical Library. Cambridge: Harvard University Press, 1927.

Gewirtsmann, M. "Ha-munaḥ 'yatib' u-mashma`uto." *Sinai* 65 (1969): 9–20.

Gibson, Craig. *Libanius's Progymnasmata: Model Exercises in Greek Prose Composition and Rhetoric*. Atlanta, GA: Society of Biblical Literature, 2008.

Gilat, Yitzhak D. *Studies in the Development of the Halakha* [Hebrew]. Jerusalem: Bar-Ilan University Press, 1992.

—*The Teachings of R. Eliezer Ben Hyrcanos and Their Position in the History of the Halakha* [Hebrew]. Tel Aviv: Dvir, 1968.

Gill, Christopher. "The School in the Roman Imperial Period." In *The Cambridge Companion to the Stoics*, edited by Brad Inwood, 33–58. Cambridge: Cambridge University Press, 2003.

Ginzberg, Louis. *A Commentary on the Palestinian Talmud*. 4 vols. New York, NY: Jewish Theological Seminary of America, 1941.

—*Yerushalmi Fragments from the Genizah: Vol. I, Text with Various Readings from the Editio Princeps*. Jerusalem: Jewish Theological Seminary of America, 1909.

Goldberg, Arnold. "Form-Analysis of Midrashic Literature as a Method of Description." *Journal of Jewish Studies* 36 (1985): 159–74.

Goldin, Judah. "On Honi the Circle Maker: A Demanding Prayer." In *Studies in Midrash and Related Literature*, edited by Barry Eichler and Jeffrey Tigay, 331–5. Philadelphia, PA: Jewish Publication Society, 1988.

—*Studies in Midrash and Related Literature*. Philadelphia, PA: Jewish Publication Society, 1988.

Goldschmidt, E. D. *Haggadah shel Pesaḥ: meqoroteha ve-toldoteha*. Jerusalem: Mosad Bialik, 1969.

Goodblatt, David. "The End of Sectarianism and the Patriarchs." In *For Uriel: Studies in the History of Israel in Antiquity Presented to Professor Uriel Rappaport*, edited by M. Mor, J. Pastor, Y. Ashkenazi and I. Ronnen. Jerusalem: Zalman Shazar Center for Jewish History, 2005.

—*The Monarchic Principle: Studies in Jewish Self-Government in Antiquity*. Tübingen: Mohr Siebeck, 1994.

—*Rabbinic Instruction in Sasanian Babylonia*. Leiden: Brill, 1975.

Goodman, Martin, ed. *Jews in a Graeco-Roman World*. Oxford: Clarendon Press, 1998.

—"The Roman State and the Jewish Patriarch in the Third Century." In *The Galilee in Late Antiquity*, edited by Lee Levine, 107–19. New York, NY: The Jewish Theological Seminary of America, 1994.

—*State and Society in Roman Galilee, A.D. 132–212*. Totowa, NJ: Rowman & Allanheld, 1983.

Goren, Shlomo. *Torat ha-Shabbat veha-mo`ed*. Jerusalem: Ha-histadrut ha-Zionit ha-`Olamit, 1982.

Graetz, Heinrich. *History of the Jews*. 6 vols. Philadelphia, PA: The Jewish Publication Society of America, 1891–98.

Graf, Fritz. "Gestures and Conventions: The Gestures of Roman Actors and Orators." In *A Cultural History of Gesture*, edited by J. Bremmer and H. Roodenburg, 36–58. Ithaca, NY: Cornell University Press, 1986.

Grano, Joseph. "The Adversarial-Accusatorial Label: A Constraint on the Search for Truth." *Harvard Journal of Law and Public Policy* 20 (1996–7): 513–18.

Grayston, Kenneth. "The Meaning of Parakletos." *Journal for the Study of the New Testament* 13 (1981): 67–82.

Green, William Scott. "Romancing the Tome: Rabbinic Hermeneutics and the Theory of Literature." *Semia* 40 (1987): 147–68.

Grimaldi, William. "How Do We Get from Corax-Tisias to Plato-Aristotle in Greek Rhetorical Theory?." In *Theory, Text, Context: Issues in Greek Rhetoric and Oratory*, edited by Christopher Johnstone, 19–44. Albany, NY: State University of New York Press, 1996.

Grinhut, Eleazar ha-Levi. *Sefer ha-liqutim: qoveṣ midrashim yeshanim u-ma'a-marim shonim*. Jerusalem, 1967.

Gunzberg, Aryeh Leib. *Sha'agat 'aryeh*. New York, NY: Israel Wolf, 1958.

Gutmann, Joseph. *The Jewish Sanctuary*. Leiden: Brill, 1983.

Guttmann, Alexander. "Foundations of Rabbinic Judaism." *Hebrew Union College Annual* 23 (1950–1951): 453–73.

Guttmann, Yechiel. "She'elot 'akademiot ba-Talmud." *Devir* 1 and 2 (1923): 38–87 and 101–63.

Halberstam, Chaya. *Law and Truth in Biblical and Rabbinic Literature*. Bloomington, IN: Indiana University Press, 2010.

Halbertal, Moshe. *Interpretive Revolutions in the Making: Values as Interpretive Considerations in Midrashei Halakhah* [Hebrew]. Jerusalem: Magnes Press, 1999.

—*People of the Book: Canon, Meaning, and Authority*. Cambridge: Harvard University Press, 1997.

Halivni, David Weiss. *The Formation of the Babylonian Talmud*. Translated by Jeffrey Rubenstein. Oxford: Oxford University Press, 2013.

—*Meqorot u-mesorot*. 6 vols. Tel Aviv: Dvir, and Jerusalem: Jewish Theological Seminary of America and Magnes, 1968–2003.

—*Midrash, Mishnah, and Gemara: The Jewish Predilection for Justified Law*. Cambridge: Harvard University Press, 1986.

Hall, Edith. "Pantomime: Visualising Myth in the Roman Empire." In *Performance in Greek and Roman Theatre*, edited by George Harrison and Vayos Liaps, 451–73. Leiden: Brill, 2013.

Hall, Jon. "Cicero and Quintilian on the Oratorical Use of Hand Gestures." *The Classical Quarterly* 54, no. 1 (2004): 143–60.

Hall, Linda. *Roman Berytus: Beirut in Late Antiquity*. London: Routledge, 2004.

Hallewy, Elimelekh E. "Concerning the Ban on Greek Wisdom." [Hebrew] *Tarbiz* 41, no. 3 (1972): 269–74.

—*`Erkhe ha-aggadah veha-halakhah le'or meqorot Yevaniim ve-Latiniim*. 4 vols. Tel-Aviv: Dvir, 1979.

—*`Olamah shel ha-aggadah: ha-aggadah le-'or meqorot Yevaniim*. Tel-Aviv: Dvir, 1972.

Hamilton, Victor. "Satan." In *The Anchor Bible Dictionary*, edited by David Noel Freedman, 985–9, 1992.

Handelman, Susan. "Fragments of the Rock: Contemporary Literary Theory and the Study of Rabbinic Texts – A Response to David Stern." *Prooftexts* 5 (1985): 75–95.

—*The Slayers of Moses: The Emergence of Rabbinic Interpretation in Modern Literary Theory*. Albany, NY: State University of New York Press, 1982.

Hansen, Mogens Herman. *The Athenian Democracy in the Age of Demosthenes: Structure, Principle, and Ideology*. Norman, OK: University of Oklahoma Press, 1991.

Harris, Jay. *How Do We Know This?: Midrash and the Fragmentation of Modern Judaism*. Albany, NY: State University of New York Press, 1995.

Harris, Michael. "Consequentialism, Deontologism, and the Case of Sheva ben Bikhri." *The Torah u-Madda Journal* 15 (2008–9): 68–94.

Harter-Uibopuu, Kaja. "The Trust Fund of Phaenia Aromation (IG V.1 1208) and Imperial Gytheion." *Studia Humaniora Tartuensia* 5 (2004): 1–17.

Harvey, Zev Warren. "Rabbinic Attitudes Toward Philosophy." In *"Open Thou Mine Eyes ...": Essays on Aggadah and Judaica Presented to Rabbi William G. Braude on His Eightieth Birthday and Dedicated to His Memory*, edited by H. Blumber, B. Braude, B. Mehlman, J. Gurland and L. Gutterman, 83–101. Hoboken: Ktav, 1992.

Haut, Irwin. "Self-help in Jewish Law: Literary and Legal Analyses." *Diné Israel* 17 (1993–4): 55–101.

Hayes, Christine. "Displaced Self-Perceptions: The Deployment of 'Mînîm' and Romans in b. Sanhedrin 90b–91a." In *Religious and Ethnic Communities in Later Roman Palestine*, edited by Hayim Lapin, 249–89. Bethesda, MD: University Press of Maryland, 1998.

—"Legal Realism and the Fashioning of Sectarians in Jewish Antiquity." In *Sects and Sectarianism in Jewish History*, edited by Sacha Stern, 119–46. Leiden: Brill, 2011.

—"Legal Truth, Right Answers and Best Answers: Dworkin and the Rabbis." *Diné Israel* 25 (2008): 73–121.

—"The 'Other' in Rabbinic Literature." In *The Cambridge Companion to Talmud and Rabbinic Literature*, edited by Charlotte Elisheva Fonrobert and Martin Jaffee, 243–69. Cambridge: Cambridge University Press, 2007.

—"Theoretical Pluralism in the Talmud: A Response to Richard Hidary." *Diné Israel* 26–7 (2009–10): 257–307.

—*What's Divine about Divine Law?* Princeton, NJ: Princeton University Press, 2015.

Hayman, Pinchas. "From Tiberias to Mehoza: Redactional and Editorial Processes in Amoraic Babylonia." *The Jewish Quarterly Review* 93, no. 1–2 (2002): 117–48.

Heath, Malcolm. "Theon and the History of the Progymnasmata." *Greek, Roman and Byzantine Studies* 43, no. 2 (2002/3): 129–60.

Heger, Paul. *The Pluralistic Halakhah: Legal Innovations in the Late Second Commonwealth and Rabbinic Periods*. Berlin: Walter De Gruyter, 2003.

Heidegger, Martin. *Being and Time*. Translated by John Macquarrie and Edward Robinson. New York, NY: Harper & Row, 1962.

Heine, Ronald. *Origen: Scholarship in the Service of the Church*. Oxford: Oxford University Press, 2010.

Heinemann, Isaak. *Darkhe ha-'aggada*. Jerusalem: Magnes, 1970.

Heinemann, Joseph. "The Amoraim of the Land of Israel as Artists of the Sermon." [Hebrew] *Hasifrut* 25 (1977): 69–79.

—*Derashot be-ṣibbur bi-tqufat ha-Talmud*. Jerusalem: Bialik Institute, 1970.

—"Ha-petiḥot be-midreshe aggadah: meqoran ve-tafqidan." *World Congress for Jewish Studies* 4, no. 2 (1969): 43–7.

—"'Omanut ha-kompoziṣia be-midrash Vayikra Rabbah." *Hasifrut* 2, no. 4 (1971): 808–43.

—*Prayer in the Talmud: Forms and Patterns*. Berlin: de Gruyter, 1977.

—"The Proem in the Aggadic Midrashim – A Form Critical Study." In *Scripta Hierosolymitana*, 100–22, 1971.

—"Profile of a Midrash: The Art of Composition in Leviticus Rabba." *Journal of the American Academy of Religion* 31 (1971): 141–50.

Hengel, Martin. *Judaism and Hellenism: Studies in Their Encounter in Palestine During the Early Hellenistic Period*. Minneapolis, MN: Fortress Press, 1991.

—*The Pre-Christian Paul*. London: SCM Press, 1991.

—"Qumran and Hellenism." In *Religion in the Dead Sea Scrolls*, edited by John Collins and Robert Kugler, 46–56. Grand Rapids, MI: Eerdmans, 2000.

Herman, Geoffrey. *A Prince without a Kingdom: The Exilarch in the Sasanian Era*. Tübingen: Mohr Siebeck, 2012.

Herr, Moshe David. "Synagogues and Theaters (Sermons and Satiric Plays)." [Hebrew]. In *Knesset Ezra – Literature and Life in the Synagogue: Studies Presented to Ezra Fleischer*, edited by S. Eliezer et al., 105–19. Jerusalem: Yad Izhak Ben-Zvi, 1994.

Hershler, Moshe, ed. *Tractate Ketubot: The Babylonian Talmud with Variant Readings*. Jerusalem: Mekhon haTalmud haYisre'eli haShalem, 1972.

Hezser, Catherine. "Die Verwendung der hellenistischen Gattung Chrie in frühen Christentum und Judentum." *Journal for the Study of Judaism* 27 (1996): 371–439.

—*Form Function, and Historical Significance of the Rabbinic Story in Yerushalmi Neziqin*. Tübingen: Mohr Siebeck, 1993.

—"Interfaces Between Rabbinic Literature and Graeco-Roman Philosophy." In *The Talmud Yerushalmi and Graeco-Roman Culture II*, edited by Peter Schäfer, 161–87. Tübingen: Mohr Siebeck, 2000.

—*The Social Structure of the Rabbinic Movement in Roman Palestine*. Tübingen: Mohr Siebeck, 1997.

Hidary, Richard. "The Agonistic Bavli: Greco-Roman Rhetoric in Sasanian Persia." In *Shoshannat Yaakov: Jewish and Iranian Studies in Honor of Yaakov Elman*, edited by Shai Secunda and Steven Fine, 137–64. Leiden: Brill, 2012.

—"Classical Rhetorical Arrangement and Reasoning in the Talmud: The Case of Yerushalmi Berakhot 1:1." *AJS Review* 34, no. 1 (2010): 33–64.

—*Dispute for the Sake of Heaven: Legal Pluralism in the Talmud*. Providence: Brown University, 2010.

—"Hellenism and Hermeneutics: Did the Qumranites and Sadducees Use Qal Va-ḥomer Arguments?" (forthcoming).

—"'One May Come to Repair Musical Instruments': Rabbinic Authority and the History of the Shevut Laws." *Jewish Studies, an Internet Journal* 13 (2015): 1–26.

—"The Rhetoric of Rabbinic Authority: Making the Transition from Priest to Sage." In *Jewish Rhetorics: History, Theory, Practice*, edited by Michael Bernard-Donals and Janice Fernheimer, 16–45. Lebanon, NH: Brandeis University Press, 2014.

—"Right Answers Revisited: Monism and Pluralism in the Talmud." *Diné Israel* 26 (2009): 229–55.

Hirshman, Marc. "The Greek Fathers and the Aggada on Ecclesiastes: Formats of Exegesis in Late Antiquity." *Hebrew Union College Annual* 59 (1988): 137–64.

—"The Preacher and His Public in Third-Century Palestine." *Journal of Jewish Studies* 42 (1991): 108–14.

—*Torah for the Entire World* [Hebrew]. Tel Aviv: Hakibbutz Hameuchad, 1999.

Hock, Ronald, and Edward O'Neil. *The Chreia in Ancient Rhetoric: Volume I. The Progymnasmata*. Atlanta, GA: Scholars Press, 1986.

Howland, Jacob. *Plato and the Talmud*. Cambridge: Cambridge University Press, 2010.

Hüttenmeister, Gil. "Bet ha-kneset u-vet ha-midrash veha-ziqah benehem." *Catehdra* 18 (1981): 38–44.

Ilievski, Viktor. "Language and Knowledge in Plato's *Cratylus*." *Filozofija* 35 (2013): 7–25.

Ish Shalom, Meir, ed. *Mekhilta d'R. Ishmael `al sefer Shemot `im tosafot Me'ir `Ayin*. Vienna, 1870.

Jacobs, Louis. *Studies in Talmudic Logic and Methodology*. London: Vallentine, Mitchell, and Co., 1961.

—*Teyku: The Unsolved Problem in the Babylonian Talmud*. London: Cornwall Books, 1981.

Jacobs, Martin. "Theatres and Performances as Reflected in the Talmud Yerushalmi." In *The Talmud Yerushalmi and Graeco-Roman Culture I*, edited by Peter Schäfer, 327–47. Tübingen: Mohr Siebeck, 2002.

Jaffee, Martin. "The 'Midrashic' Proem: Towards the Description of Rabbinic Exegesis." In *Approaches to Ancient Judaism IV. Studies in Liturgy, Exegesis and Talmudic Narrative*, edited by William Scott Green, 95–112. Chico, CA: Scholars Press, 1983.

—"The Oral-Cultural Context of the Talmud Yerushalmi: Greco-Roman Rhetorical Paideia, Discipleship, and the Concept of Oral Torah." In *The Talmud Yerushalmi and Graeco-Roman Culture I*, edited by Peter Schäfer, 27–61. Tübingen: Mohr Siebeck, 1998.

—*Torah in the Mouth: Writing and Oral Tradition in Palestinian Judaism 200 BCE–400 CE*. Oxford: Oxford University Press, 2001.

Janowits, Naomi, and Andrew Lazarus. "Rabbinic Methods of Inference and the Rationality Debate." *The Journal of Religion* 72, no. 4 (1992): 491–511.

Janowitz, N. "Rabbis and Their Opponents: The Construction of the 'Min' in Rabbinic Anecdotes." *Journal of Early Christian Studies* 6, no. 3 (1998): 449–62.

Jarratt, Susan. *Rereading the Sophists: Classical Rhetoric Refigured*. Carbondale, IL: Southern Illinois University Press, 1991.

Jastrow, Marcus. *A Dictionary of the Targumim, the Talmud Babli and Yerushalmi, and the Midrashic Literature*. New York, NY: The Judaica Press, 1985.

Johansson, Mikael. *Libanius' Declamations 9 and 10*. Göteborg: Acta Universitatis Gothoburgensis, 2006.

Johnston, George. *The Spirit-Paraclete in the Gospel of John*. Cambridge: Cambridge University Press, 1970.

Johnstone, Christopher. "Greek Oratorical Settings and the Problem of the Pnyx: Rethinking the Athenian Political Process." In *Theory, Text, Context: Issues in Greek Rhetoric and Oratory*, edited by Christopher Johnstone, 97–127. Albany, NY: State University of New York Press, 1996.

Jones, Christopher. "Multiple Identities in the Age of the Second Sophistic." In *Paideia: The World of the Second Sophistic*, edited by Barbara Borg, 13–21. Berlin: Walter de Gruyter, 2004.

Jospe, Raphael. "Yefet in the Tents of Shem: Attitudes Towards 'The Wisdom of Greeks'." In *Tra Torah e sophia: orizzonti e frontiere della filosofia Ebraica*, 119–66. Genova: Marietti, 2011.

Kafiḥ, Yosef. *Mishnah with the Commentary of Rabbenu Moses ben Maimon* [Hebrew]. Jerusalem: Mossad Harav Kook, 1963–7.

Kahana, Menahem. "Kavvim le-toldot hitpatḥutah shel midat kelal u-frat bi-tkufat ha-Tannaim." In *Meḥqarim ba-Talmud uva-Midrash: sefer zikaron le-Tirza Lifshitz*, edited by Moshe Bar-Asher, Joshua Levinson and Berachyahu Lifshitz, 173–216. Jerusalem: Mossad Bialik, 2005.

—*Sifre on Numbers: An Annotated Edition* [Hebrew]. Jerusalem: The Hebrew University Magnes Press, 2011.

Kalmin, Richard. *Jewish Babylonia between Persia and Roman Palestine*. New York, NY: Oxford University Press, 2006.

—*Migrating Tales: The Talmud's Narratives and Their Historical Context*. Oakland, CA: University of California Press, 2014.

Kaminka, Armand. "Hillel's Life and Work." *The Jewish Quarterly Review* 30, no. 2 (1939): 107–22.

Kanter, Shamai. *Rabban Gamaliel II: The Legal Traditions*. Ann Arbor, MI: Brown University Press, 1980.

Kasher, Menachem. *Haggadah shelemah*. Jerusalem: Makhon Torah Shelemah, 1967.

Katz, Claire Elise. *Levinas, Judaism, and the Feminine: The Silent Footsteps of Rebecca*. Bloomington, IN: Indiana University Press, 2003.

Katz, Menachem. "Stories of Hillel's Appointment as Nasi in the Talmudic Literature: A Foundation Legend of the Jewish Scholar's World." [Hebrew] *Sidra* 26 (2011): 81–115.

—"Ṣurato shel midrash halakha "o kelakh le-derekh zo.'" *Mishlav* 29 (1996): 33–43.

Kennedy, George A. *Classical Rhetoric and Its Christian and Secular Traditions from Ancient to Modern Times*. Chapel Hill, NC: University of North Carolina Press, 1999.

—*Greek Rhetoric under Christian Emperors*. Princeton, NJ: Princeton University Press, 1983.

—*Invention and Method: Two Rhetorical Treatises from the Hermogenic Corpus*. Atlanta, GA: Society of Biblical Literature, 2005.

—*A New History of Classical Rhetoric*. Princeton, NJ: Princeton University Press, 1994.

—*New Testament Interpretation through Rhetorical Criticism*. Chapel Hill, NC: The University of North Carolina Press, 1984.

—*Progymnasmata: Greek Textbooks of Prose Composition and Rhetoric*. Leiden: Brill, 2003.

Kensky, Allan. "New Light on Midrash Yelammedenu." *Shofar* 13, no. 3 (1995): 44–52.

Kensky, Meira. *Trying Man, Trying God: The Divine Courtroom in Early Jewish and Christian Literature*. Tübingen: Mohr Siebeck, 2010.

Kessler, Amalia. "Our Inquisitorial Tradition: Equity Procedure, Due Process, and the Search for an Alternative to the Adversarial." *Cornell Law Review* 90 (2005): 1181–275.

King, Matthew. "Security, Scale, Form, and Function: The Search for Truth and the Exclusion of Evidence in Adversarial and Inquisitorial Justice Systems." *International Legal Perspectives* 12 (2002): 185–236.

Kinneavy, James. *Greek Rhetorical Origins of Christian Faith*. New York, NY: Oxford University Press, 1987.

Klingbeil, Gerald. *Bridging the Gap: Ritual and Ritual Texts in the Bible*. Winona Lake, IN: Eisenbrauns, 2007.

Kohat, Hanah. "Ben 'aristoqratyah le-demoqratyah – Rabban Gamaliel ve-Rabbi Yehoshua." In *Sefer yeshurun*, edited by Michael Shashar, 213–28. Jerusalem: Shashar Publishing, 1999.

Kohler, Kaufman. "Paraclete." *Jewish Encyclopedia* (New York, NY: Funk and Wagnalls, 1906).

Kosovsky, Y.M. "Ha-meturgeman ba-derasha ha-ṣiburit (pirqa) be-bet ha-keneset." *Sinai* 45 (1959): 233–43.

Kraemer, David. "Composition and Meaning in the Bavli." *Prooftexts* 8, no. 3 (1988): 271–91.

—*The Mind of the Talmud*. Oxford: Oxford University Press, 1990.

—*Reading the Rabbis: The Talmud as Literature*. Oxford: Oxford University Press, 1996.

—"Rhetoric of Failed Refutation in the Bavli." *Shofar* 10, no. 2 (1992): 73–85.

Krauss, Samuel. *Griechische und lateinische Lehnwoerter im Talmud, Midrasch und Targum*. Berlin: S. Calvary, 1899.

—"The Jews in the Works of the Church Fathers." *Jewish Quarterly Review* o.s. 6 (1894): 82–99, 225–61.

Kubicek, Theodore. *Adversarial Justice: America's Court System on Trial*. New York, NY: Algora Publishing, 2006.

Kugel, James. *The Bible As It Was*. Cambridge: Harvard University Press, 1997.

—*The Idea of Biblical Poetry: Parallelism and Its History*. New Haven CT: Yale University Press, 1981.

Kunst, Arnold. "An Overlooked Type of Inference." *Bulletin of the School of Oriental and African Studies* 10, no. 4 (1942): 976–91.

Kutscher, Yechezkel. *Milim ve-toldotehen*. Jerusalem: Kiryat Sefer, 1965.

Labendz, Jenny. *Socratic Torah: Non-Jews in Rabbinic Intellectual Culture*. Oxford: Oxford University Press, 2013.

Lapin, Hayim. *Rabbis as Romans: The Rabbinic Movement in Palestine, 100–400 C.E.* New York, NY: Oxford University Press, 2012.

Lau, Binyamin. *The Sages: Character, Context and Creativity*. Jerusalem: Koren, 2010.

Lauterbach, Jacob. *Rabbinic Essays*. Cincinnati, OH: Hebrew Union College Press, 1951.

Lenhard, Doris. *Die Rabbinische Homilie. Ein formanalytischer Index*. Frankfurt: Gesellschaft zur Förderung Judaistischer Studien, 1998.

Leon, Judah Messer. *The Book of the Honeycomb's Flow*. Translated by Isaac Rabinowitz. Ithaca, NY: Cornell University Press, 1983.

Levenson, Jon. *Creation and the Persistence of Evil: The Jewish Drama of Divine Omnipotence*. San Francisco, CA: Harper & Row, 1988.

Levinas, Emmanuel. *Beyond the Verse: Talmudic Readings and Lectures*. Bloomington, IN: Indiana University Press, 1994.

—*Nine Talmudic Readings*. Bloomington, IN: Indiana University Press, 1994.

Levine, Lee. *The Ancient Synagogue: The First Thousand Years*. New Haven, CT: Yale University Press, 2005.

—*Caesarea Under Roman Rule*. Leiden: Brill, 1975.

—*Judaism and Hellenism in Antiquity: Conflict or Confluence?* Peabody, MO: Hendrickson Publishers, 1999.

—*The Rabbinic Class of Roman Palestine in Late Antiquity*. Jerusalem: Yad Izhak Ben-Zvi Press, 1989.

—"The Status of the Patriarch in the Third and Fourth Centuries: Sources and Methodology." *Journal of Jewish Studies* 47, no. 1 (1996): 1–32.

Lewin, Benjamin, ed. *Iggeret Rav Sherira Gaon*. Jerusalem: Makor, 1972.

Liddell, Henry George, and Robert Scott. *A Greek-English Lexicon*. Oxford: Clarendon Press, 1940.

Lieberman, Saul. *Greek in Jewish Palestine*. New York, NY: The Jewish Theological Seminary, 1942.

—*Hellenism in Jewish Palestine*. New York, NY: The Jewish Theological Seminary, 1962.

—"Roman Legal Institutions in Early Rabbinics and in the Acta Martyrum." *Jewish Quarterly Review* 35, no. 1 (1944): 1–57.

—*The Talmud of Caesarea* [Hebrew]. New York, NY: The Jewish Theological Seminary, 1968.

—*Texts and Studies*. New York, NY: Ktav, 1974.

—*Tosefeth rishonim*. New York, NY: The Jewish Theological Seminary of America, 1999.

—*Tosefta ki-fshutah*. New York, NY: The Jewish Theological Seminary of America, 1955–88.

Lieberman, Stephen. "A Mesopotamian Background for the So-called Aggadic 'Measures' of Biblical Hermeneutics." *Hebrew Union College Annual* 58 (1987): 157–225.

Liebersohn, Yosef. *The Dispute Concerning Rhetoric in Hellenistic Thought*. Göttingen: Vandenhoeck & Ruprecht, 2010.

Lifshitz, David. "`Aliyato shel Hillel la-nesi'ut be-aspaqlariah satirit." *Moreshet Yisrael* 5 (2008): 18–30.

Lightstone, Jack N. *Mishnah and the Social Formation of the Early Rabbinic Guild: A Socio-Rhetorical Approach*. Waterloo, Ontario: Wilfrid Laurier University Press, 2002.

—*The Rhetoric of the Babylonian Talmud, Its Social Meaning and Context*. Waterloo: Wilfrid Laurier University Press, 1994.

Lintott, A. W. *The Constitution of the Roman Republic*. Oxford: Oxford University Press, 1999.

Liss, Abraham. *The Babylonian Talmud with Variant Readings* [Hebrew]. Jerusalem: Yad Harav Herzog, 1983.

Litsas, Fotios. "Choricius of Gaza: An Approach to His Work." PhD diss., University of Chicago, 1980.

Lorberbaum, Yair. "The Rainbow in the Cloud: An Anger-Management Device." *The Journal of Religion* 89, no. 4 (2009): 498–540.

Luft, Sandra Rudnick. *Vico's Uncanny Humanism: Reading the New Science Between Modern and Postmodern*. Ithaca, NY: Cornell University Press, 2003.

MacDowell, Douglas. *The Law in Classical Athens*. Ithaca, NY: Cornell University Press, 1978.

Mack, Hananel. *The Aggadic Midrash Literature*. Tel-Aviv: MOD Books, 1989.

Mandel, Paul. "`Al 'pataḥ' ve`al ha-petiḥah: `iyun ḥadash." In *Higayon le-Yonah*, 49–82. Jerusalem: Magnes Press, 2006.

—"Midrashic Exegesis and Its Precedents in the Dead Sea Scrolls." *Dead Sea Discoveries* 8, no. 2 (2001): 149–68.

Mann, Jacob. *The Bible as Read and Preached in the Old Synagogue*. Cincinnati, OH: Mann-Sonne Publication Committee, 1940–1966; New York, NY: Ktav, 1970.

Marback, Richard. *Plato's Dream of Sophistry*. Columbia, SC: University of South Carolina Press, 1999.

Margulius, Mordechai, ed. *Midrash Vayikra Rabbah*. Jerusalem: Bet Midrash Le-Rabbanim Be-Amerika, 1993.

Marrou, H. I. *A History of Education in Antiquity*. Translated by George Lamb. University of Wisconsin Press, 1956.

Martin, F. "Homélie de Narsès sur les trois docteurs Nestoriens." *Journal Asiatique*, ix, 14–15 (1899): 446–92 and 69–525.

Mason, Steve. *Flavius Josephus on the Pharisees*. Leiden: Brill, 1991.

—ed. *Flavius Josephus: Translation and Commentary, Volume 9: Life of Josephus*. Leiden: Brill, 2001.

Mattingly, David. *Imperialism, Power, and Identity: Experiencing the Roman Empire*. Princeton, NJ: Princeton University Press, 2011.

May, James. *Trials of Character: The Eloquence of Ciceronian Ethos*. Chapel Hill, NC: University of North Carolina Press, 1988.

Maybaum, Siegmund. *Die ältesten Phasen in der Entwicklung der jüdischen Predigt*. Berlin, 1901.

McAdon, Brad. "Rhetoric Is a Counterpart of Dialectic." *Philosophy and Rhetoric* 34, no. 2: 113–50.

McComiskey, Bruce. *Gorgias and the New Sophistic Rhetoric*. Carbondale: Southern Illinois University Press, 2002.

—"Neo-Sophistic Rhetorical Theory: Sophistic Precedents for Contemporary Epistemic Rhetoric." *Rhetorical Society Quarterly* 24, no. 3/4 (1994): 16–24.

McVey, Kathleen. "The Mēmrā on the Three Nestorian Doctors as an Example of Forensic Rhetoric." In *III Symposium Syriacum*, edited by R. Lavenant. Rome: Pontificium Institutum Orientalium Studiorum, 1983.

Meeks, Wayne, and Robert Wilken. *Jews and Christians in Antioch in the First Four Centuries of the Common Era*. Missoula, MT: Scholars Press, 1978.

Melamed, Ezra Zion. *Pirqe mavo le-sifrut ha-Talmud*. Jerusalem, 1973.

Menander. *Menander Rhetor*. Translated by D. A. Russel and N. G. Wilson. Oxford: Clarendon Press, 1981.

Menkel-Meadow, Carrie. "The Trouble with the Adversary System in a Post-modern, Multicultural World." *William and Mary Law Review* 38, no. 1 (1996): 5–44.

Metzger, David, and Steven Katz. "The 'Place' of Rhetoric in Aggadic Midrash." *College English* 72, no. 6 (2010): 638–53.

Mielziner, M. "The Talmudic Syllogism or the Inference of Kal Vechomer." *Hebrew Review* 1 (1880): 42–53.

Milgram, Jonathan. *From Mesopotamia to the Mishnah: Tannaitic Inheritance Law in its Legal and Social Contexts*. Tübingen: Mohr Siebeck, 2016.

Milgrom, Jacob. "The Qumran Cult: Its Exegetical Principles." In *Temple Scroll Studies*, edited by George Brooke, 165–80. Sheffield: Sheffield Academic Press, 1989.

Miller, Stuart. *Sages and Commoners in Late Antique Eretz Israel*. Tübingen: Mohr Siebeck, 2006.

Milovanovic-Barham, Celica. "Three Levels of Style in Augustine of Hippo and Gregory of Nazianzus." *Rhetorica: A Journal of the History of Rhetoric* 11, no. 1 (1993): 1–25.

Moore, George Foot. *Judaism in the First Centuries of the Christian Era, the Age of the Tannaim*. 1927. New York, NY: Schocken Books, 1971.

Moore, Mark. "Seeking Knowledge from the 'Container and Thing Contained'." *Rhetoric Society Quarterly* 18, no. 1 (1988): 15–30.

Morgan, Teresa. *Literate Education in the Hellenistic and Roman Worlds*. Cambridge: Cambridge University Press, 1998.

Morris, Nathan. *The Jewish School: An Introduction to the History of Jewish Education*. London: Eyre and Spottiswoode, 1937.

Morrow, Glenn. *Plato's Cretan City: A Historical Interpretation of the Laws*. Princeton, NJ: Princeton University Press, 1960.

Moscovitz, Leib. "The Formation and Character of the Jerusalem Talmud." In *The Cambridge History of Judaism IV*, edited by S. Katz, 663–77. Cambridge: Cambridge University Press, 2006.

—*Talmudic Reasoning: From Casuistics to Conceptualization*. Tübingen: Mohr Siebeck, 2002.

Moss, Yonatan. "Noblest Obelus: Rabbinic Appropriations of Late Ancient Literary Criticism." In *Homer and the Bible in the Eyes of Ancient Interpreters*, edited by Maren Niehoff, 245–67. Leiden: Brill, 2012.

Mousourakis, George. *A Legal History of Rome*. London: Routledge, 2007.

Muffs, Yochanan. *Love and Joy: Law, Language and Religion in Ancient Israel*. New York, NY: The Jewish Theological Seminary of America, 1992.

Murray, Robert. "Some Rhetorical Patterns in Early Syriac Literature." In *A Tribute to Arthur Vööbus: Studies in Early Christian Literature and Its Environment, Primarily in the Syrian East*, edited by Robert Fischer, 109–31. Chicago, IL: The Lutheran School of Theology at Chicago, 1977.

Murtonen, A., ed. *Hebrew in Its West Semitic Setting, Part I: A Comparative Lexicon*. Leiden: Brill, 1986.

Naeh, Shlomo. "On Structures of Memory and the Forms of Text in Rabbinic Literature." [Hebrew] *Meḥqere Talmud* 3, no. 2 (2005): 543–89.

Nagorcka, Felicity, Michael Stanton, and Michael Wilson. "Stranded Between Partisanship and the Truth? A Comparative Analysis of Legal Ethics in the Adversarial and Inquisitorial Systems of Justice." *Melbourne University Law Review* 29 (2005): 448–77.

Naḥmanides, Moses. *Introduction to Milḥamot Hashem* (Venice, 1552).

Nanos, Mark, ed. *The Galatians Debate: Contemporary Issues in Rhetorical and Historical Interpretation*. Peabody, MA: Hendrickson, 2002.

Neusner, Jacob. "From Biography to Theology: Gamaliel and the Patriarchate." *Review of Rabbinic Judaism* 7 (2004): 52–94.

—*From Politics to Piety: The Emergence of Pharisaic Judaism*. New York, NY: Ktav, 1979.

—*Jerusalem and Athens: The Congruity of Talmudic and Classical Philosophy*. Leiden: Brill, 1997.

—*Sifre to Numbers: An American Translation and Explanation*. Atlanta, GA: Scholars Press, 1986.

—*Uniting the Dual Torah: Sifra and Problem of the Mishnah*. Cambridge: Cambridge University Press, 1990.

Newman, Hillel. "Jerome and the Jews." [Hebrew] PhD diss., Hebrew University, 1997.

Niehoff, Maren. *Jewish Exegesis and Homeric Scholarship in Alexandria*. Cambridge: Cambridge University Press, 2011.

Nietzsche, Friedrich. "On Truth and Lying in an Extra-Moral Sense (1873)." In *Friedrich Nietzsche on Rhetoric and Language*, edited by S. L. Gilman, C. Blair and D. J. Parent, 246–57. Oxford: Oxford University Press, 1989.

Noam, Vered. "Beth Shammai veha-halakha ha-kitatit." *Mada`e ha-Yahadut* 41 (2002): 45–67.

Novick, Tzvi. "The *Borer* Court: New Interpretations of mSan 3." *Zutot* 5, no. 1 (2008): 1–8.

—*Rabbinic Poetry: Late Antique Jewish Liturgical Poetry and Rabbinic Midrash* (forthcoming).

—"Scripture as Rhetor: A Study in Early Rabbinic Midrash." *Hebrew Union College Annual* 82–83 (2011–12): 37–59.

Ong, Walter J. "The Agonistic Base of Scientifically Abstract Thought: Issues in Fighting for Life: Contest, Sexuality, and Consciousness." In *An Ong Reader: Challenges for Further Inquiry*, edited by Thomas Farrell and Paul Soukup. Cresskill, NJ: Hampton Press, 1982.

—*Orality and Literacy: The Technologizing of the World*. London: Routledge, 1982.

Ostrow, Jonah. "Tannaitic and Roman Procedure in Homicide." *Jewish Quarterly Review* 52, no. 2 (1961): 160–7.

Ouaknin, Marc-Alain. *The Burnt Book: Reading the Talmud*. Princeton, NJ: Princeton University Press, 1995.

Outram, Dorinda. *The Enlightenment*. Cambridge: Cambridge University Press, 2013.

Palmer, Georgiana. "The Topoi of Aristotle's 'Rhetoric' as Exemplified in the Orators." PhD diss., University of Chicago, 1932.

Panken, Aaron. *The Rhetoric of Innovation: Self-conscious Legal Change in Rabbinic Literature*. Lanham: University Press of America, 2005.

Parks, E. P. *The Roman Rhetorical Schools as a Preparation for the Courts under the Early Empire*. Baltimore, MD: John Hopkins University, 1945.

Parush, Adi. "The Courtroom as Theater and the Theater as Courtroom in Ancient Athens." *Israel Law Review* 35 (2001): 118–37.

Paz, Yakir. "From Scribes to Scholars: Rabbinic Biblical Exegesis in Light of the Homeric Commentaries." PhD diss., 2014.

Penella, Robert, ed. *Rhetorical Exercises from Late Antiquity: A Translation of Choricius of Gaza's Preliminary Talks and Declamations*. Cambridge: Cambridge University Press, 2009.

Perelman, Chaim. *The Idea of Justice and the Problem of Argument*. London: Routledge and Kegan Paul, 1963.

—*The Realm of Rhetoric*. Translated by William Kluback. Notre Dame: Notre Dame Press, 1982.

Perelman, Chaim, and L. Olbrechts-Tyteca. *The New Rhetoric: A Treatise on Argumentation*. Notre Dame and London: University of Notre Dame Press, 1969.

Phenix, Robert. *The Sermons on Joseph of Balai of Qenneshrin: Rhetoric and Interpretation in Fifth Century Syriac Literature*. Tübingen: Mohr Siebeck, 2008.

Phillips, Gerald. "The Place of Rhetoric in the Babylonian Talmud." *Quarterly Journal of Speech* 43, no. 4 (1957): 390–3.

—"The Practice of Rhetoric at the Talmudic Academies." *Speech Monographs* (1959): 37–46.

Philo. *The Works of Philo: Complete and Unabridged*. Translated by C. D. Yonge. Peabody, MA: Hendrickson, 2008.

Pitts, Andrew. "Hellenistic Schools in Jerusalem and Paul's Rhetorical Education." In *Paul's World*, edited by Stanley Porter, 19–50. Leiden: Brill, 2008.

Pizzi, William. "Sentencing in the US: An Inquisitorial Soul in an Adversarial Body?." In *Crime, Procedure and Evidence in a Comparative and International Context: Essays in Honour of Professor Mirjan Damaška*, edited by John Jackson, Maximo Langer and Peter Tillers, 65–79. Oxford: Hart Publishing, 2008.

Plato. *Laws*. Translated by R. G. Bury. Cambridge: Harvard University Press, 1926.

—*Theaetetus and Sophist*. Translated by H. N. Fowler. Loeb Classical Library. Cambridge: Harvard University Press, 1921.

Polybius. *The Histories*. Translated by W. R. Paton. Loeb Classical Library. Cambridge: Harvard University Press, 1975.

Pope, Marvin. *Job*. The Anchor Bible. Garden City, NY: Doubleday, 1965.

Porter, Stanley, ed. *Handbook of Classical Rhetoric in the Hellenistic Period 330 B.C. - A.D. 400*. Leiden: Brill, 1997.

Porton, Gary. "Midrash and the Rabbinic Sermon." In *When Judaism and Christianity Began: Essays in Memory of Anthony J. Saldarini*, edited by Alan Avery-Peck, Daniel Harrington and Jacob Neusner, 2.461–82. Leiden: Brill, 2004.

Potter, David. "Performance, Power, and Justice in the High Empire." In *Roman Theater and Society: E. Togo Salmon Conference Papers I*, edited by William Slater, 129–60. Ann Arbor, MI: University of Michigan Press, 1996.

Powell, Jonathan, and Jeremy Paterson. *Cicero the Advocate*. Oxford: Oxford University Press, 2004.

Prior, Arthur. "Argument A Fortiori." *Analysis* 9, no. 3 (1949): 49–50.

Purcell, William M. *Ars Poetriae: Rhetorical and Grammatical Invention at the Margin of Literacy*. Columbia, SC: University of South Carolina, 1996.

Quine, W. V. O. *Word and Object*. Cambridge: MIT Press, 1960.

Quintilian. *Institutes of Oratory: or, Education of an Orator in Twelve Books*. Translated by John Selby Watson. London: George Bell & Sons, 1892.

—*The Lesser Declamations*. Translated by D. R. Shackleton Bailey. Cambridge: Harvard University Press, 2006.

—*The Major Declamations Ascribed to Quintilian*. Translated by Lewis Sussman. New York, NY: Verlag Peter Lang, 1987.

—*The Minor Declamations Ascribed to Quintilian*. Edited by Michael Winterbottom. Berlin: Walter De Gruyter, 1984.

Rabinovits, Hosea. "Ḥamesh derashotav shel ha-hu Gelila'a." *Hagige Giv`ah* 3 (1995): 53–64.

Raizel, Anat. *Mavo la-midrashim*. Alon Shevut: Tevunot – Mikhlelet Herzog, 2010.

Rappel, Dov. "Ḥokhmat Yevanit – retorica?" [Hebrew] *Meḥqere Yerushalaim bi-Maḥshevet Yisrael* 2, no. 3 (1983): 317–22.

Ravitsky, Aviram. "Aristotelian Logic and Talmudic Methodology: The Commentaries on the 13 Hermeneutic Principles and their Application of Logic." In *Judaic Logic*, edited by Andrew Schumann, 117–43. Piscataway, NJ: Gorgias Press, 2010.

Reader, William. *The Severed Hand and the Upright Corpse: The Declamations of Marcus Antonius Polemo*. Atlanta, GA: Scholars Press, 1996.

Regev, Eyal. *The Sadducees and their Halakhah: Religion and Society in the Second Temple Period* [Hebrew]. Jerusalem: Yad Ben-Zvi Press, 2005.

Reggio, Isaac Samuel. *Ha-Torah ve-ha-filosofia: ḥoverot 'isha 'el 'aḥota*. Vienna, 1827.

Reinhardt, Tobias. *Cicero's Topica*. Oxford: Oxford University Press, 2003.

Revel, Bernard. *The Karaite Halakah and Its Relation to Sadducean, Samaritan and Philonian Halakah*. Philadelphia, PA: Ktav, 1913.

Reynolds, Anthony. "The Linguistic Return: Deconstruction as Textual Messianism." *SubStance* 43, no. 1 (2014): 152–65.

Riad, Eva. *Studies in the Syriac Preface*. Uppsala: Uppsala University, 1988.

Riggsby, Andrew. *Roman Law and the Legal World of the Romans*. Cambridge: Cambridge University Press, 2010.

Roach, Kent. "Wrongful Convictions: Adversarial and Inquisitorial Themes." *North Carolina Journal of International Law and Commercial Regulation* 35 (2010): 387–446.

Robardet, Patrick. "Should We Abandon the Adversarial Model in Favour of the Inquisitorial Model in Commissions of Inquiry?" *Dalhousie Law Journal* 12, no. 3 (1989–1990): 111–32.

Roberts, W. Rhys. "Caecilius of Calacte." *American Journal of Philology* 18, no. 3 (1897): 302–12.

Robinson, Thomas. *Contrasting Arguments: An Edition of the Dissoi Logoi*. Salem, NH: Ayer, 1979.

Rogoff, Jason. "The Compositional Art of the She'iltot of R. Aḥa: Creating a Babylonian Homiletic Midrash." PhD diss., Jewish Theological Seminary of America, 2010.

Rosen-Zvi, Ishay. "Midrash and Hermeneutic Reflectivity: *Kishmu`o* as a Test Case." In *Homer and the Bible in the Eyes of Ancient Interpreters*, edited by Maren Niehoff, 329–44. Leiden: Brill, 2012.

—"The Rise and Fall of Rabbinic Masculinity." *Jewish Studies, an Internet Journal* 12 (2013): 1–22.

Rosental, David. "Mesorot Ereṣ-Yisraeliyot ve-darkan le-Bavel." *Cathedra* 92 (1999): 7–48.

—"The Torah Reading in the Annual Cycle in the Land of Israel." [Hebrew] *Tarbiz* 53, no. 1 (1983): 144–8.

Rosental, Eliezer Shimshon. "Shnei devarim." In *Sefer Yitshak Aryeh Zeligman: ma'amarim ba-Mikra uva-`olam ha-`atiq*, edited by Yair Zakovits and Alexander Rofe, 463–81. Jerusalem: E. Rubenstein, 1983.

Roth, Lea. "Cappadocia." *Encyclopaedia Judaica* (2007): 4:455.

Rothschild, Clare. *Luke-Acts and the Rhetoric of History: An Investigation of Early Christian Historiography*. Tübingen: Mohr Siebeck, 2004.

Rovner, Jay. "An Early Passover Haggadah According to the Palestinian Rite." *Jewish Quarterly Review* 90, no. 3/4 (2000): 337–96.

—"Rhetorical Strategy and Dialectical Necessity in the Babylonian Talmud: The Case of Kiddushin 34a–35a." *Hebrew Union College Annual* 65 (1994): 177–231.

Rubenstein, Jeffrey. *The Culture of the Babylonian Talmud*. Baltimore, MD: Johns Hopkins University Press, 2003.

—"Nominalism and Realism Again." *Diné Israel* 30 (2015): 79–120.

—"Nominalism and Realism in Qumranic and Rabbinic Law: A Reassessment." *Dead Sea Discoveries* 6, no. 2 (1999): 157–83.

—*Rabbinic Stories*. New York, NY: Paulist Press, 2002.

—"The Rise of the Babylonian Rabbinic Academy: A Reexamination of the Talmudic Evidence." *Jewish Studies, an Internet Journal* 1 (2002): 56–68.

—"Social and Institutional Settings of Rabbinic Literature." In *The Cambridge Companion to the Talmud and Rabbinic Literature*, edited by Charlotte Fonrobert and Martin Jaffee, 58–74. Cambridge: Cambridge University Press, 2007.

—"Some Structural Patterns of Yerushalmi Sugyot." In *The Talmud Yerushalmi and Graeco-Roman Culture III*, edited by Peter Schäfer, 303–13. Tübingen: Mohr Siebeck, 2002.

—*Stories of the Babylonian Talmud*. Baltimore, MD: Johns Hopkins University Press, 2010.

—*Talmudic Stories: Narrative Art, Composition, and Culture*. Baltimore, MD: Johns Hopkins University Press, 1999.

Rubinelli, Sara. *Ars Topica: The Classical Technique of Constructing Arguments from Aristotle to Cicero*. Dordrecht: Springer, 2009.

Rubinstein, Lene. *Litigation and Co-operation: Supporting Speakers in the Courts of Classical Athens*. Stuttgart: Franza Steiner Verlag Stuttgart, 2000.

Russel, Donald A. *Greek Declamation*. Cambridge: Cambridge University Press, 1983.

—*Imaginary Speeches: A Selection of Declamations*. London: Gerald Duckworth, 1996.

Saddington, Denis. "A Note on the Rhetoric of Four Speeches in Josephus." *Journal of Jewish Studies* 58, no. 2 (2007): 228–35.

Safrai, Shmuel. "Education and the Study of Torah." In *The Jewish People in the First Century: Historical Geography, Political History, Social, Cultural and Religious Life and Institutions*, edited by S. Safrai and M. Stern, 945–70. Amsterdam: Van Gorcum, 1976.

—ed. *The Literature of the Sages, Part One*. Philadelphia, PA: Fortress Press, 1987.

Safrai, Shmuel, and Ze'ev Safrai. *Hagadat Ḥazal* [Hebrew]. Jerusalem: Karta, 1998.

—*Mishnat Eretz Israel*. Jerusalem: E.M. Liphshitz College Publishing House, 2008.

Saldarini, Anthony J. *Pharisees, Scribes and Sadducees in Palestinian Society: A Sociological Approach*. Wilmington, DE: Michael Glazier, 1988.

Sandmel, Samuel. "Parallelomania." *Journal of Biblical Literature* 81 (1962): 1–14.

Sarason, Richard. "The Petiḥot in Leviticus Rabba: Oral Homilies or Redactional Constructions." *Journal of Jewish Studies* 33 (1982): 557–67.

Sarton, George. *Hellenistic Science and Culture in the Last Three Centuries B.C.* Cambridge: Harvard University Press, 1959.

Sassoon, Isaac. *Destination Torah*. Hoboken, NJ: Ktav, 2001.

Satlow, Michael. "Beyond Influence: Toward a New Historiographic Paradigm." In *Jewish Literatures and Cultures: Context and Intertext*, edited by Anita Norich and Yaron Eliav, 37–53. Providence: Brown Judaic Studies, 2008.

—"Rhetoric and Assumptions: Romans and Rabbis on Sex." In *Jews in a Graeco-Roman World*, edited by Martin Goodman, 135–44. Oxford: Clarendon Press, 1998.

Saunders, Trevor. "Plato's Later Political Thought." In *The Cambridge Companion to Plato*, edited by R. Kraut, 464–92. Cambridge: Cambridge University Press, 1992.

—*Plato's Penal Code: Tradition, Controversy, and Reform in Greek Penology*. Oxford: Clarendon Press, 1991.

Saussure, Ferdinand. *Course in General Linguistics*. Translated by Wade Baskin. New York, NY: The Philosophical Library, 1959.

Schäfer, Peter. "Die Peticha – ein Proömium?" *Kairos* 12 (1970): 216–19.

Schaff, Philip, ed. *St. Augustin's City of God and Christian Doctrine, Volume 2 of A Select Library of Nicene and Post-Nicene Fathers of the Christian Church*. New York, NY: Charles Scribner's Sons, 1907.

Schellenberg, Ryan. *Rethinking Paul's Rhetorical Education: Comparative Rhetoric and 2 Corinthians 10–13*. Atlanta, GA: Society of Biblical Literature, 2013.

Schiappa, Edward. *The Beginnings of Rhetorical Theory in Classical Greece*. New Haven, CT: Yale University Press, 1999.

—"Dissoi Logoi." In *Classical Rhetorics and Rhetoricians: Critical Studies and Sources*, edited by Michelle Ballif and Michael Moran, 146–8. Westport, CT: Praeger Publishers, 2005.

Schiffman, Lawrence. *The Halakhah at Qumran*. Leiden: Brill, 1975.

Schmidt, Brent. *Utopian Communities of the Ancient World: Idealistic Experiments of Pythagoras, the Essenes, Pachomius, and Proclus*. Lewiston, NY: Edwin Mellen Press, 2010.

Schulz, Fritz. *Principles of Roman Law*. Translated by Marguerite Wolff. Oxford: Clarendon Press, 1936.

Schwabe, Moshe. "The Letters of Libanius to the Patriarch of Palestine." [Hebrew] *Tarbiz* 1, no. 2 (1930): 85–110.

Schwartz, Daniel. "Law and Truth: On Qumran-Sadducean and Rabbinic Views of Law." In *Dead Sea Scrolls: Forty Years of Research*, edited by Deborah Dimant and Uriel Rappaport, 229–40. Leiden: Brill, 1992.

—"Ti`une 'qal va-ḥomer' ke-realism Ṣaddoqi." *Masechet* 5 (2006): 145–56.

Schwartz, Seth. "Gamaliel in Aphrodite's Bath: Palestinian Society and Jewish Identity in the High Roman Empire." In *Being Greek under Rome: Cultural Identity, the Second Sophistic and the Development of Empire*, edited by Simon Goldhill, 335–61. Cambridge: Cambridge University Press, 2001.

—*Imperialism and Jewish Society, 200 B.C.E. to 640 C.E.* Princeton, NJ: Princeton University Press, 2001.

—"The Patriarchs and the Diaspora." *Journal of Jewish Studies* 51, no. 2 (2000): 208–318.

Schwarz, Adolf. *Der Hermeneutische Syllogismus in der Talmudischen Litteratur, Ein Beitrag Zur Geschichte Der Logik Im Morgenlande*. Karlsruhe: G. Braun, 1901.

Schwarzbaum, Haim. "Talmudic-Midrashic Affinities of Some Aesopic Fables." In *Essays in Greco-Roman and Related Talmudic Literature*, edited by Henry Fischel, 443–72. New York, NY: Ktav, 1977.

Segal, Eliezer. *Holidays, History, and Halakhah*. Northvale, NJ: Jason Aronson, 2001.

—"Jewish Perspectives on Restorative Justice." In *The Spiritual Roots of Restorative Justice*, edited by Michael Hadley, 181–97. Albany, NY: State University of New York Press, 2001.

Seneca, Marcus Annaeus. *Declamations*. Translated by M. Winterbottom. Cambridge: Harvard University Press, 1974.

Shafat, Shoval. "The Interface of Divine and Human Punishment in Rabbinic Thought." [Hebrew] PhD diss., Ben-Gurion University, 2011.

Shalom, Abraham. *Haqdamat ha-ma`atiq ha-she'elot veha-teshubot `al mabo ma'amarot u-meliṣah lehe-ḥakham Marsiliyyo*. Vienna: Friedrich Förster, 1859.

Shamah, Moshe. *Recalling the Covenant: A Contemporary Commentary on the Five Books of the Torah*. Jersey City: Ktav, 2011.

Shapira, Haim. "Beit ha-Midrash (the House of Study) during the Late Second Temple Period and the Age of the Mishnah: Institutional and Ideological Aspects." [Hebrew] PhD diss., Hebrew University, 2001.

Sharvit, Shimon. *Masechet Avot le-doroteha: mahadura mada`it, mevo'ot ve-nispaḥim*. Jerusalem: Mosad Bialik, 2004.

Siegert, Folker. "The Sermon as an Invention of Hellenistic Judaism." In *Preaching in Judaism and Christianity: Encounters and Developments from Biblical Times to Modernity*, edited by Alexander Deeg, Walter Homolka and Heinz-Gunther Schottler, 25–44. Berlin: Walter de Gruyter, 2008.

Simon-Shoshan, Moshe. "Halakhic Mimesis: Rhetorical and Redactional Strategies in Tannaitic Narrative." *Diné Israel* 24 (2007): 101–23.

—"The Talmud as Novel: A Bakhtinian Approach to the Bavli, or, How I Learned to Stop Worrying and Love the *Stam*." Paper presented at the Association for Jewish Studies Conference, Chicago, 2012.

Sinai, Yuval. "'Do Not Make Yourself as Advocates': On the Place of a Rule in Court Procedure." [Hebrew]. In *Studies in Jewish Law: Judge and Judging*, edited by Ya`akov Habba and Amihai Radzyner, 93–128. Ramat-Gan: Bar-Ilan University, 2007.

—*The Judge and the Judicial Process in Jewish Law* [Hebrew]. Jerusalem: Hebrew University, 2010.

Siniossoglou, Niketas. *Plato and Theodoret: The Christian Appropriation of Platonic Philosophy and the Hellenic Intellectual Resistance*. Cambridge: Cambridge University Press, 2008.

Sion, Avi. *Judaic Logic: A Formal Analysis of Biblical, Talmudic and Rabbinic Logic*. Geneva: Editions Slatkine, 1997.

Sivan, Hagith. *Palestine in Late Antiquity*. Oxford: Oxford University Press, 2008.

Siverstev, Alexei. *Households, Sects, and the Origins of Rabbinic Judaism*. Leiden: Brill, 2005.

Slater, William. "Pantomime Riots." *Classical Antiquity* 13, no. 1 (1994): 120–44.

Sloane, Thomas. *On the Contrary: The Protocol of Traditional Rhetoric*. Washington, D.C.: The Catholic University of America Press, 1997.

Sokoloff, Michael. *A Dictionary of Jewish Palestinian Aramaic of the Byzantine Period*. Ramat-Gan: Bar Ilan University, 1992.

Solmsen, Friedrich. "Cicero's First Speeches: A Rhetorical Analysis." *Transactions and Proceedings of the American Philological Association* 69 (1938): 542–56.

Spengel, Leonard. *ΣΥΝΑΓΩΓΗ ΤΕΧΝΩΝ sive Artium Scriptores ab initiis usque ad editors Aristotelis de Rhetorica libros*. Stuttgart, 1828.

Sperber, Daniel. *A Dictionary of Greek and Latin Terms in Rabbinic Literature*. Ramat-Gan: Bar-Ilan University Press, 1984.

—*Greek in Talmudic Palestine*. Ramat Gan: Bar-Ilan University Press, 2012.

Spiegel, Boaz. "Madua` ni`nea` mal'akh ha-mavet et ha-'ilanot bi-ftirat David ha-melekh." *Shma`tin* 150 (2003): 286–311.

Steel, Catherine. *Roman Oratory*. Cambridge: Cambridge University Press, 2006.

Stein, Edmund. "Die homiletische Peroration im Midrasch." *Hebrew Union College Annual* 8–9 (1931–32): 353–71.

Stein, M. "Le-ḥeqer midreshe yelamdenu." In *Sefer ha-yovel li-khevod Professor Moshe Shor*, 85–112. Warsaw: Ha-ḥevrah le-hafaṣat mada`e ha-Yahadut be-Polania, 1935.

Stein, Siegfried. "The Influence of Symposia Literature on the Literary Form of the Pesaḥ Haggadah." *Journal of Jewish Studies* 8 (1957): 13–44.

Steiner, Richard. "On the Original Structure and Meaning of *Mah Nishtannah* and the History of Its Reinterpretation." *Jewish Studies, an Internet Journal* 7 (2008): 163–204.

Steinfeld, Zvi Aryeh. "`Asinu `aṣmenu ke-`orkhe ha-dayanin." *Te`udah* 7 (1991): 111–32.

Steinmetz, Devora. *Punishment and Freedom: The Rabbinic Construction of Criminal Law*. Philadelphia, PA: University of Pennsylvania, 2008.

Stemberger, Günter. "The Derashah in Rabbinic Times." In *Preaching in Judaism and Christianity: Encounters and Developments from Biblical Times to Modernity*, edited by Alexander Deeg, Walter Homolka and Heinz-Gunther Schottler, 7–21. Berlin: Walter de Gruyter, 2008.

Stern, David. "Literary Criticism or Literary Homilies? Susan Handelman and the Contemporary Study of Midrash." *Prooftexts* 5 (1985): 96–103.

—"Midrash and Hermeneutics: Polysemy vs. Indeterminacy." In *Midrash and Theory: Ancient Jewish Exegesis and Contemporary Literary Studies*, 15–38. Evanston, IL: Northwestern University Press, 1996.

—*Midrash and Theory: Ancient Jewish Exegesis and Contemporary Literary Studies*. Evanston, IL: Northwestern University Press, 1996.

—"Moses-cide: Midrash and Contemporary Literary Criticism." *Prooftexts* 4 (1985): 193–213.

—*Parables in Midrash: Narrative and Exegesis in Rabbinic Literature*. Cambridge: Harvard University Press, 1991.

Stern, Menachem. *Greek and Latin Authors on Jews and Judaism*. Jerusalem: The Israel Academy of Sciences and Humanities, 1980.

Stern, Sacha. *Calendar and Community: A History of the Jewish Calendar, Second Century BCE–Tenth Century CE*. Oxford: Oxford University Press, 2001.

—*Jewish Identity in Early Rabbinic Writings*. Leiden: Brill, 1994.

Stone, Suzanne Last. "On the Interplay of Rules, 'Cases,' and Concepts in Rabbinic Legal Literature: Another Look at the Aggadot on Honi the Circle-Drawer." *Diné Israel* 24 (2007): 125–55.

—"Rabbinic Legal Magic: A New Look at Honi's Circle as the Construction of Legal Space." *Yale Journal of Law and the Humanities* 17 (2005): 97–123.

Strack, H. L., and G. Stemberger. *Introduction to the Talmud and Midrash*. Translated by Marcus Bockmuehl. Minneapolis, MN: Fortress Press, 1992.

Sussmann, Yaakov. "The History of Halakha and the Dead Sea Scrolls: Preliminary Observations on *Miqsat Ma`ase Ha-Torah* (4QMMT)." [Hebrew] *Tarbiz* 59 (1990): 11–76.

—*Thesaurus of Talmudic Manuscripts* [Hebrew]. Jerusalem: Yad Izhak Ben-Zvi, 2012.

Swartz, Michael. "Scholasticism as a Comparative Category and the Study of Judaism." In *Scholasticism: Cross-Cultural and Comparative Perspectives*, edited by José Ignacio Cabezón, 91–114. Albany, NY: State University of New York Press, 1998.

Tabory, Joseph. *JPS Commentary on the Haggadah: Historical Introduction, Translation, and Commentary*. Philadelphia, PA: The Jewish Publication Society, 2008.

Tellegen-Couperus, Olga. "Roman Law and Rhetoric." *Revue Belge De Philologie Et D'histoire* 84, no. 1 (2006): 59–75.

Tempest, Kathryn. *Cicero: Politics and Persuasion in Ancient Rome*. New York, NY: Continuum, 2011.

Theodor, Judah. "Midrash Haggadah." *Jewish Encyclopedia* (1906): 8:553–4.

—"Zur Komposition der agadischen Homilien." *Monatschrift für Geschichte und Wissenschaft des Judenthums* 29 (1881): 500–10.

Thiselton, Anthony C. "Truth." In *The New International Dictionary of New Testament Theology*, edited by Brown Colin, 3:874–902. Exeter: Paternoster Press, 1978.

Todd, S. C. *The Shape of Athenian Law*. Oxford: Clarendon Press, 1993.

Towner, W. Sibley. "Hermeneutical Systems of Hillel and the Tannaim: A Fresh Look." *Hebrew Union College Annual* 53 (1983): 101–35.

Tropper, Amram. *Wisdom, Politics, and Historiography: Tractate Avot in the Context of the Graeco-Roman Near East*. Oxford: Oxford University Press, 2004.

Tur-Sinai, Naphtali. *The Book of Job: A New Commentary*. Jerusalem: Kiryat Sefer, 1957.

Ulmer, Rivka. "The Advancement of Arguments in Exegetical Midrash Compared to that of the Greek 'δῐατρίβε'." *Journal for the Study of Judaism* 28, no. 1 (1997): 48–91.

—ed. *Pesiqta Rabbati: A Synoptic Edition of Pesiqta Rabbati based upon All Extant Manuscripts and the Editio Princeps*. Atlanta, GA: Scholars Press, 1997.

Urbach, Ephraim. *The Sages: Their Concepts and Beliefs*. Cambridge: Harvard University Press, 1975.

van Koppen, Peter, and Steven Penrod. "Adversarial or Inquisitorial: Comparing Systems." In *Adversarial Versus Inquisitorial Justice*, edited by Peter van Koppen and Steven Penrod, 1–19. New York, NY: Plenum Publishers, 2003.

Vico, Giambattista. *The New Science*. Translated by Thomas G. Bergin and Max H. Fisch. Ithaca, NY: Cornell University Press, 1968.

Vidas, Moulie. "Greek Wisdom in Babylonia." In *Envisioning Judaism: Studies in Honor of Peter Schäfer on the Occasion of his Seventieth Birthday*, edited by Ra`anan Boustan et al., 287–305. Tübingen: Mohr Siebeck, 2013.

—*Tradition and the Formation of the Talmud*. Princeton, NJ: Princeton University Press, 2014.

Visotzky, Burton. *Golden Bells and Pomegranates: Studies in Midrash Leviticus Rabbah*. Tübingen: Mohr Siebeck, 2003.

—"Midrash, Christian Exegesis, and Hellenistic Hermeneutics." In *Current Trends in the Study of Midrash*, edited by Carol Bakhos, 111–31. Leiden: Brill, 2006.

—"The Misnomers '*Petihah*' and 'Homiletic Midrash' as Descriptions for Leviticus Rabbah and Pesikta De-Rav Kahana." *Jewish Studies Quarterly* 18 (2011): 19–31.

Wacholder, Ben-Zion. "Sippure Rabban Gamaliel ba-Mishna uba-Tosefta." *World Congress for Jewish Studies* 4, no. 1 (1967): 143–4.

Walker, Joel T. "The Limits of Late Antiquity: Philosophy between Rome and Iran." *Ancient World* 33, no. 1 (2002): 45–69.

Walpin, Gerald. "America's Adversarial and Jury Systems: More Likely to Do Justice." *Harvard Journal of Law and Public Policy* 26 (2003): 175–86.

Walton, Douglas, and Fabrizio Macagno. "Enthymemes, Argumentation Schemes and Topics." *Logique and Analyse* 205 (2009): 39–56.

Walz, C. *Rhetores Graeci I–IX*. Stuttgart, 1832–6.

Wardy, Robert. *The Birth of Rhetoric: Gorgias, Plato and their Successors*. London: Routledge, 2005.

Wasserstein, A. "Greek Language and Philosophy in the Early Rabbinic Academies." In *Jewish Education and Learning*, edited by G. Abramson and T. Parfitt, 221–32. Switzerland: Harwood Academic Publishers, 1994.

Watson, Duane. "The New Testament and Greco-Roman Rhetoric: A Bibliography." *Journal of the Evangelical Theological Society* 31, no. 4 (1988): 465–72.

Watson, Duane, and Alan Hauser. *Rhetorical Criticism of the Bible: A Comprehensive Bibliography with Notes on History and Method*. Leiden: Brill, 1994.

Watt, John. "Eastward and Westward Transmission of Classical Rhetoric." In *Centers of Learning: Learning and Location in Pre-Modern Europe and the Near East*, edited by J. W. Drijvers and A. A. MacDonald, 63–75. Leiden: Brill, 1995.

Weder, Hans. "*Deus Incarnatus*: On the Hermeneutics of Christology in the Johannine Writings." In *Exploring the Gospel of John: In Honor of D. Moody Smith*, edited by R. A. Culpepper and C. C. Black, 327–45. Louisville, KY: Westminster John Knox Press, 1996.

Weingend, Thomas. "Should We Search for the Truth, and Who Should Do It?" *North Carolina Journal of International Law and Commercial Regulation* 36 (2011): 389–415.

Weinreb, Ernest. "Law as Myth: Reflections on Plato's *Gorgias*." *Iowa Law Review* 74 (1989): 787–806.

Weisenberg, E. "Observations on Method in Talmudic Studies." *Journal of Semitic Studies* 11, no. 1 (1966): 16–36.

Weiss, Dov. "Divine Concessions in the *Tanhuma* Midrashim." *Harvard Theological Review* 108, no. 1 (2015): 70–97.

—"Lawsuits against God in Rabbinic Literature." In *The Divine Courtroom in Comparative Perspective*, edited by Ari Mermelstein and Shalom Holtz, 276–88. Leiden: Brill, 2014.

Weiss, Harold. "The Sabbath among the Samaritans." *Journal for the Study of Judaism in the Persian, Hellenistic and Roman Period* 25, no. 2 (1994): 252–73.

Weiss, Moshe. "Ha-'otentiut shel ha-shaqla ve-ṭaria be-maḥloqot bet Shamai u-vet Hillel." *Sidra* 4 (1988): 53–66.

—"Ha-gezerah shavah veha-qal va-ḥomer ba-shaqla ve-taria shel bet Shammai u-vet Hillel." *Sidra* 6 (1990): 41–61.

Weiss, Zeev. "Theaters, Hippodromes, Amphitheatres, and Performances." In *The Oxford Handbook of Jewish Daily Life in Roman Palestine*, edited by Catherine Hezser, 623–40. Oxford: Oxford University Press, 2010.

White, James Boyd. *Heracles' Bow: Essays on the Rhetoric and Poetics of the Law*. Madison, WI: University of Wisconsin, 1985.

Whitmarsh, Timothy. "'Greece is the World': Exile and Identity in the Second Sophistic." In *Being Greek under Rome: Cultural Identity, the Second Sophistic and the Development of Empire*, edited by Simon Goldhill, 269–305. Cambridge: Cambridge University Press, 2001.

—*The Second Sophistic*. Oxford: Oxford University Press, 2005.

Wilkins, John. *An Essay towards a Real Character, and a Philosophical Language*. London: S. Gellibrand, 1668.

Williamson, Ronald. *Jews in the Hellenistic World: Philo.* Cambridge: Cambridge University Press, 1989.
Wills, Lawrence. "The Form of the Sermon in Hellenistic Judaism and Early Christianity." *Harvard Theological Review* 77 (1984): 277–99.
Wilson, N. G. *Scholars of Byzantium.* London: Gerald Duckword and Co., 1983.
Wimpfheimer, Barry. *Narrating the Law: A Poetics of Talmudic Legal Stories.* Philadelphia, PA: University of Pennsylvania, 2011.
Winston, David. *Logos and Mystical Theology in Philo of Alexandria.* Cincinnati, OH: Hebrew Union College Press, 1985.
Winterbottom, Michael. *Roman Declamation.* Bristol: Bristol Classical Press, 1980.
Wiseman, Allen Conan. "A Contemporary Examination of the A Fortiori Argument Involving Jewish Traditions." PhD diss., University of Waterloo, 2010.
Wolfson, Harry A. *Philo.* Cambridge: Harvard University Press, 1948.
Woolf, Greg. "Beyond Romans and Natives." *World Archaeology* 28, no. 3 (1995): 339–50.
Yadin-Israel, Azzan. "Rabbinic Polysemy: A Response to Steven Fraade." *AJS Review* 38 (2014): 129–41.
Yadin, Azzan. "The Chain Novel and the Problem of Self-undermining Interpretation." *Diné Israel* 25 (2008): 43–71.
—"Rabban Gamliel, Aphrodite's Bath, and the Question of Pagan Monotheism." *Jewish Quarterly Review* 96, no. 2 (2006): 149–79.
—*Scripture and Tradition: Rabbi Akiva and the Triumph of Midrash.* Philadelphia, PA: University of Pennsylvania, 2015.
—*Scripture as Logos: Rabbi Ishmael and the Origins of Midrash.* Philadelphia, PA: University of Pennsylvania, 2004.
Yassif, Eli. *The Hebrew Folktale: History, Genre, Meaning.* Translated by Jacqueline Teitelbaum. Bloomington, IN: Indiana University Press, 1999.
Yelin, Hanoch. "Le-shitat ha-niqud shel ha-Mishnah" in Hanoch Albeck, *Six Orders of Mishnah*, 6 vols. Jerusalem: Mossad Bialik, 1959.
Yeo, Khiok-Khng. *Rhetorical Interaction in 1 Corinthians 8 and 10: A Formal Analysis with Preliminary Suggestions for a Chinese, Cross-Cultural Hermeneutic.* Leiden: Brill, 1995.
Young, Suzanne. "An Athenian Clepsydra." *Hesperia: The Journal of the American School of Classical Studies at Athens* 8, no. 3 (1939): 274–84.
Yuval, Israel. "Christianity in Talmud and Midrash: Parallelomania or Parallelophobia." In *Transforming Relations: Essays on Jews and Christians throughout History in Honor of Michael A. Signer*, edited by Franklin Harkins, 50–74. Notre Dame: University of Notre Dame Press, 2010.
—"Easter and Passover as Early Jewish Christian Dialogue." In *Passover and Easter: Origin and History to Modern Times*, edited by Paul F. Bradshaw and Lawrence A. Hoffman, 89–124. Notre Dame: University of Notre Dame Press, 1999.
Zeitlin, Solomon. "Hillel and the Hermeneutic Rules." *The Jewish Quarterly Review* 54, no. 2 (1963): 161–73.

Index of Sources

Hebrew Bible
Genesis 243
1:1 30n143
1:5, 8, 10 30
1:26 242n8, 254
2:19-20 30
3:22 242n8
9:27 11
10:2 11
11:7 242n8
18:17-33 243
18:22 253
18:28 251
Exodus 50, 70
12:1-20 123n73
12:5 188
12:15 188–89
13:7 125–26
13:8 69n144
20:2 260
20:13 137–38
21 209n128
21:2 208
21:3 119n66
21:35-36 140n39
22:4 181
22:8 223
22:9 182, 211
23:1 224
23:2 279
23:7 223
24:7 248
25:3 50
30:11-16 56, 123n73
32-33 243
32:4 248
32:10 244n20
32:11 258, 261
32:13 62
32:32 31
32:35-36 140n39
33:23 282
34:29-35 282
35:27 50
Leviticus 50–51
1:1 50–51
1:4 180
11:29 198
11:29-30 233
11:32 191
13:37 188
16:21 180
19:9 148n76
19:11 137–38
20:17 205
21:14 200
23:11 189
23:38 185n42
24:22 230
25:4 208
Numbers
2:1 279
5:15 199
9:2 183, 207n125, 210
9:3 179n19, 191
9:10-11 73n159
12:14 203
14:13-19 243
15:1-6 36n145
15:13 165
15:31 22n113
16:48 246n32
19:1-22 123n73
19:2 1n1
28:1 210
28:2 183, 191, 210
28:9 210
29 179n19
31:20 191
35:32 147

Hebrew Bible (cont.)
Deuteronomy
5:5 246n32
5:6 249
5:22 249
9:14 244n20
9:16 248n42
13:7-12 238n93
13:15 235–36
15:1 207–8
15:12 208
16:2 188
16:8 188–89
16:20 236
18:3 75
22:6-7 197
25:17-19 123n73
26:5 69
26:5-10 72
31:10 208
33:2 257
Joshua
7:6-7 243
Judges
7:15 179n19
18:7 179n19
2 Samuel
20 155
Kings
22:19 242n8
Isaiah 44, 243
30:20 281
43:28 248
55:3 45
58:7 119n64, 228
59:3 216
Jeremiah
14:7-9, 13 243
23:29 29
Ezekiel
11:13 243
Hosea
5:1 75
Amos
7:2, 5, 243
Zechariah
3:1-2 242
Malachi
1:9 259
Psalms 50, 243
2:7 45
12:7 279
16:10 45
19:8 249
19:11 41n2
29:4 249
33:6 30
39:5 63
45:13 259
84:11 63
86:17 62
88:6 62
106:23 258
113-18 69
115:17 61
Proverbs
20:15 50
24:28 248
27:20 248
Job
1:6-2:7 242
1:11 218
2:3 218
33:23-24 243
The Song of Songs
1:4 279
2:4 277, 279
5:6 249
Lamentations
3:51 13
Ecclesiastes
4:2 61
9:4 61, 66
10:8 89
12:11 264
Daniel 179n19
7:26 242n8
9:3 259
10:1 27n129
10:13, 21 243n17
12:1 243n17
I Chronicles
21:1 242n9
II Chronicles
6:42 63

Second Temple Sources
I Enoch 245
9:1 245n23
13:4 245
15:2 245
Philo
On Creation **15-25** 31n145
On Creation **24** 246n29
Special Laws **I.237** 246n28
II.62 43n19

II.138 69n145
On Rewards and Punishments
9:165-7 245n27
On the Life of Moses **II.133** 246n29
II.134 246n30
On Husbandry **51** 246n31
Questions and Answers on Genesis 58n88
Who is the Heir 205-6 247n33
Rule of the Community (1QS)
2:9 245
Susanna 218

New Testament
Mark
1:21 44n20
13:11 269
Luke 269
4:16-30 44
John
14:16, 26 247
15:26 247
16:7 247
1 John
2:1-2 240, 247
Acts
2 56n78
13:14-41 44, 269
16:13 44n20
24:1-9 258n80
24:1-21 270–71, 275
1 Corinthians 272
1:22 270n14
2:1-5 269–70

Rabbinic Literature
Mishnah
Berakhot
1:1 85n47, 86, 102n101
2:5 85n46
8:1 143
Shevi'it
7:1 199n91
9:1 89n63, 93n75
10:3 189n61
Terumot
8:12 155
Bikurim
2:8-11 158n108
Shabbat
2:5 64n124
Pesaḥim
1:1-2 161n126
2:2 124
5:7 69n145
6:1 190
7:2 89n67
9:3 69n145
10 68
10:4-10 68–69
Sheqalim
3:3 85n47
6:1 85n47
6:5 165n147
Sukkah
2:5 85n46
Beṣah
1:6 207
2:6 85n46
3:2 89n67
Rosh Hashanah
2:8-9 85n48
2:9 97
4:6 97n90
Ta'anit
3:8 247n37, 257n75
Megilah
1:4 122–23
1:6 124n74
1:8 11n45
4:4 80n19
Yebamot
8:3 203
Ketubot
4:6 114
4:11 119n65
Nazir
5:7 158
7:4 199n91, 203
Soṭah
9:14 11n48
Giṭṭin
1:1-2:2 17n82
Baba Qama
1:1 139n36, 181n31
2:4 140n39
3:1 139, 147n68, 164
3:8 140n39, 164
Baba Meṣi`a
2:11 78n1
Baba Batra
2:6 160n123
3:1 178n15
6:7 148n74
9:7 203n105

Rabbinic Literature (cont.)
Sanhedrin
3:1 223n29
3:6 224–25, 228n56
4:1-3 230, 238n93
4:2 230n64
5:1-4 230n64, 232n67
5:4 231n66, 232n68, 238n90
5:5 237n88
7:5 224n37
Eduyot
6:2 199n91
Abodah Zara
3:4 85n47
Avot 5, 134, 228
1:4 79n6
1:8 223n33, 225, 227
1:12 187n54
1:15 258n83
2:6 133–34
4:11 240, 248
4:22 241, 260, 263
5:7 59n97
Menaḥot
10:3 189
12:4 164
Ḥulin
2:7 199n91
12:5 197
'Arakhin
9:4 189n61
Keritot
3:9-10 199n91
6:9 157n105
'Ohalot
2:6 88n59
Makhshirin
6:8 199, 203n105
Yadaim
3:2 204
4:7 201n97, 202n101
Tosefta
Berakhot
4:15 85n46
4:16 58n90, 58n89
5:25 143
Pe'ah
1:1 248
4:21 248
Terumot
7:20 155
Shabbat
1:22 85n46
2:5 80n13
12:12 88n56
Eruvin
3:5-7 64n127
Pesaḥim
1:8 125n76, 126
4:13-14 183, 186, 193, 212n141
Beṣah
1:12-13 207n125
2:12 85n46
Megilah
1:6 122n72
2:18 42n7
3:41 81n23
Ḥagigah
2:11 185n43
Ketubot
4:8 119
5:1 203n105
Soṭah
7:9-11 42n6, 47n30
7:11-12 277n37
13:3 80n13,
15:8 13n59
Kiddushin
1:5 178n15
Baba Qama
3:6 140n37, 146n62
6:1 159n111
10:38 145n58
Sanhedrin
6:3 224n37
7:2 238n93
7:7 59n97
7:8 82n33
7:11 175, 184n38, 186
9:1 230n64
9:3 238n91
10:11 238n93
Eduyot
1:7 88n59
Abodah Zara
1:20 11n49
Zebaḥim
1:8 187n55
'Ohalot
4:2 88n61, 91
Nega'im
1:16 188n58
Yerushalmi 11–12, 78–105
Berakhot
1:1 84, 86–87, 89n66, 104
4:1 12n50, 81n20, 85n48, 248n40

4:2 75n168, 76n173
8:1 144
Pe'ah
1:1 11n49
8:7 42n8
Demai
3:3 89n67
Kilayim
9:3 62n111
Shevi'it
9:1 89n64, 92
Terumot
2:1 42n8, 80n15
8:4 155n101
Bikkurim
3:3 42n7, 81n20, 82n33
Shabbat
1:4 13n60
14:4 42n8
Pesaḥim
2:2 126n78
4:1 89n67
6:1 1n3, 108n14, 188, 192n64, 203n106, 212n141, 212n142
7:2 89n67
10:4 71n150
Sheqalim
6:4 165n147
Yoma
2:2 143n51
6:1 258n83
Sukkah
4:1 184n40
5:1 42n11
Beṣah
1:7 42n8, 47n29
3:2 89n67
Rosh Hashanah
1:3 128n84, 241n5
Ta'anit
1:1 248
1:2 42n7
2:4 248
4:1 85n48
4:6 13n59
Megilah
1:9 11n46, 11n43
4:10 81n20 and 23
Ḥagigah
2:1 47n30, 51n50, 102n102
2:3 185n43
Yebamot
12:6 58n89
12:7 59n96
Ketubot
4:8 121n68 and 70
4:11 226n48
12:3 62n111
Nedarim
3:9 242n11
Soṭah
1:4 42n7, 47n30
9:15 11n44 and 49
Kiddushin
1:3 178n15
Baba Qama
3:1 139, 159, 161, 164
Baba Meṣi'a
2:11 42n9
Baba Batra
9:4 226
Sanhedrin
1:1 27n129
2:1 229
4:1 1n3, 198n90, 232n69, 233n72, 236n85
4:1-2 278
6:10 241n7
10:1 22n113, 202n104, 254n62
10:2 82n34
11:5 27n130
Shebu'ot
3:7 162n137, 170n159
Abodah Zara
3:10 89n67
Horayot
3:4 42n9
Bavli 8, 12–13, 106–30
Berakhot 206n120
4b 129n92
6b 47n32
21a 199n92
27b-28a 85n48
28b 15n72, 47n32, 47n36
30a 47n32
32b 259n85
60a 185n47, 229n60
63b 115n54, 258n83
Shabbat
30a 60, 61n107
30b 41n2, 115n54
31b 59n92
32a 229n60, 248n39, 256n69

Rabbinic Literature (cont.)
33b 5n18
37a 129n88
59b 42n8
63b 115n54
80b 59n92
88a 59n92
109a 7n28
132a 204n113, 205n114
134a 88n56, 90n68,
139a 216n2
145b 7n28
148a 47n36
150a 119n63
Eruvin 282
13b 1n3, 18n91, 198n90, 234n77, 280
36b 47n32
44b 47n32
46b-47b 17n82
53b 12n58
71a 119n63
Pesaḥim
10b 161n127, 164
18b 205n117
28b-29a 124
30a 126n79,
33a 212n141
50a 80n15
51a-b 93
51b 93n76
66a 194n71, 195n77, 212n141
77b 205n117
79a 119n63
86a 119n63
113b 107n7
115b 69n144, 70n147
116a 70n148
116b 71n154
117a 115n54
Yoma
77b 47n33
78a 47n36
78b 47n32, 119n63
81b 119n63
84a 47n32
Sukkah
20a 188n56
23a 119n63
54a 119n63
54b 143n51
Beṣah
12b 129n89
15b 42n10
18a 129n88
20a 185n43
21b 207n125
31a 128n85
Rosh Hashanah
16a 127–29
33a 119n63
Ta'anit
8a 81n27, 258n83
26b 80n15
28a 129
Megilah
4b 124
6b 122–23, 128
7b 119n63
9b 11n45 and 47
11a 48n41
15b 107n6
16b 27n130
23a 129
28b 42n7
Ḥagigah
14b 160n113
15b 160n114
19b 119n63
Yebamot
13a-16a 17n82
64b 119n63
Ketubot
49 123
49a 114
52b 119n64, 226n45, 227n52
53b 119n66
54b 228n54
64b 129n88
85b 228n52
97b 119n63
109b 228
Nedarim
16a 119n63
23b 80n15
32a 242n11
87a 119n63
Nazir
51a 93n75
52a-b 88n61,
52b 91n70
57a 204n113
Soṭah
40a 59n92, 81n24, 258n83, 266n6
49b 12n50, 14n66 and 71, 85n47
Giṭṭin
20b 160n117
29b 107n5

47a 76n171
58b 228n57
71b 119n63
Kiddushin
22b 178n15
31a 157
31b 81n23
32b-33b 82n33
71a 80n15
Baba Qama
8b 168n154
25a 204n109
27b-28a 145, 166n149
33a 119n63
36a 129n88
52a 59n92
55a 160n118
81b 107n5
82b-83a 12n50
86a 129
Baba Meṣi'a
51a 129n88
95a 204n109
111a-b 129n90
Baba Batra
10a 248n39
22a 160n122
23a 228n57
23b 160n123
141a 115n52, 119n64
Sanhedrin
7b 80n19, 81n20 and 24
17a 1n3, 233n73, 236n87
17a-b 198n90
19b 82n34,
24a 107n8
29a 228n57, 238n93
32b 232n70, 236n85
33b 238n93
34a 30n140, 280
36b 238n93
38b 47n34
59b 160n119
67a 119n63
70a 59n92
71a 7n28
75a 119n63
85b 27n130
86a 138n31
87a-88a 17n82
89b 242n12
90b 127n82
91a 263n93
99a 22n113, 212n144
105a 119n63
113a 59n92
Makkot
5b 206n119
10b 48n41
13a 119n63
23a 59n92
Shebu'ot
3a 129n88
30b 223n33
Abodah Zara
2a-3b 61n104
11b 7n28
28a 47n32
Horayot
3a 119n63
7a 119n63
13b 82n33
Menaḥot
37a 161n124
57b 210n131
64b 12n50,
14n69
66a 188n59
69b 160n120
93a 119n63
93b 180n25
99b 11n49, 13n62, 14n71
104a 164, 168
107b-108a 165n147
Ḥulin
15a 42n8, 47n35, 80n15, 81n21
and 27
26a 129n90
27b 59n92
30b 160n115
70a 160n116
139b 160n121
Bekhorot
36a 85n48
Temurah
13a 119n63
16a 187n55
Me`ilah
7b 106n2, 107n5
8a 119n63
19b 119n63
Niddah
19b 212n141
72a 207n125
Minor Tractates
Avot d'Rabbi Natan 134n18
A 4 42n8
A 6 27n130

Rabbinic Literature (cont.)
A 10 225n43
A 34 27n130
A 36 27n130
A 37 175n4
Tannaitic Midrashim
Mekhilta d'R. Ishmael 141, 211
Pisḥa
5 183n37, 210n132
8 188n59
17 188n59
Ba-ḥodesh
8 138n31
Nezikin
5 137–38
9 180n26
11 205n117
13 197n87
16 182n33, 211
Kaspa
20 223, 226
Mekhilta d'R. Shimon bar Yoḥai
17:3 259n84
21:3 119n66
21:33 159n111
22:4 181
23:1 224, 228n56
Sifra,
Baraita d'R. Ishmael 175n4, 176n7, 181n32, 182n33, 204n108, 211
Ḥoba, perek 10, 10 157n105
Ḥova, perek 1, 11–13 199n91
Shemini, milu'im 38 279n46
Tazria, perek 3:1 207n125
Meṣora`, perek 3, 14 248n40
Aḥare Mot, parasha 4, 4 180
Kedoshim, parasha 1, 9 157n105
Kedoshim, perek 9, 12 210n133
Kedoshim, perek 10, 10 205
Kedoshim, perek 10, 12 206n118
Emor, perek 17, 5 188n59
Behar, parasha 4, 8 189n61
Behar, parasha 6, 4 178n15
Sifre Numbers 209, 214
8 199n92, 203n105
65 183n37, 210n132
75 187n55
106 204
117 199n93, 203n105
142 183n37, 210n132
Sifre Deuteronomy
34 82n34
111 208n127
134 188n59
144 238n93
249 210n133
253 203n105
343 22n114, 257–58
Amoraic Midrashim 8, 49n43, 73, 108, 198n88, 247
Genesis Rabbah 8, 49n42, 52n56
1:1 30n143, 249
8:3 254n60–61
8:4 254
10:7 42n8
17 119n64
28:3 42n8
36:8 11n46
44:15 258n83
49:2 253n57
49:12 251n53
49:14 258n83
49:17 279n46
50 225n43
55:4 242n12
56:7-8 242n12
70:17 81n24 and 27
73:12 258n83
80:1 75n170
81:2 58n89, 59n96
96 27n130
98:11 42n11
98:13 80n17,
Exodus Rabbah 8, 57
5:8 242n11
15:12 260n86
18:5 241
40:1 59n96
43 256n82, 258
43:5 260
Leviticus Rabbah 8, 18, 49n42, 52, 55, 56n79, 249–50
1:6 50n47, 53n63
3:6 59n92
6:1 248–49
16.4 51n50
18:1 42n8
26:2 1n2
30:11 239n96
32:7 42n7
34 119n64
35:12 42n7

Numbers Rabbah 8, 57
18:3 202n104
Ecclesiastes Rabbah
4:1 251n51
7 248n41
9:17 81n20
Deuteronomy Rabbah 8, 57
3:11 248n42
5:3 178n16
7:8 42n7
Song of Songs Rabbah
1:15:2 43n15
1:15:3 42n8
1:53 51n50
6:16:3-5 249–50
Lamentations Rabbah 49
Petiḥta
17 75n168
24 250n48, 255, 261
1:13 255n65
Esther Rabbah
4:12 11n43
Pesikta de-Rav Kahana 49, 52n56, 55n70
2 56
4:2 1n2
28:1 75n168
Pesikta Rabbati 97.150
21 1n3, 277n37, 279n43
45 254n62
Hosafa 1:3 62n110
Tanḥuma 8, 49n44, 57–58, 60n99
Gen 1 30n143
Shoftim 9 61n104
Va'ethanan 1 179n20

Greek, Roman and Patristic Literature
Ad Herennium 35, 113
I.4 36n168
I.17 37n172
III.9-10 38n177
III.16-18 36n168
III.18 97n90
Aphthonius
28 143n48
30 143n48
34 178n16
54 135n22, 178n16
Aristotle
Athenian Constitution **62, 2** 252n56
Metaphysics **2.1** 282n56
On Rhetoric 35, 41
I.1.1 33n155
I.1.13 33n157
I.2.13 196n82
I.2.21 196n82
I.3 3n12
II.22.3 196n82
II.23.4 177n11, 179n22
II.24.9 260n88
II.35.5 177n12
III.13.1-2 36n169
III.13-19 36n167, 37n176
III.14.1 54n65
III.16.1 53n61
III.16.11 96n85
III.17.5 99n93
III.17.14-15 193n69
III.19.3-4 98n91
III.19.4 116n58
Prior Analytics **2.27** 196n82
Synagōgē Technōn 41
Augustine
City of God
2.31.48 273n20
4.2.3 273n19
De Doctrina Christiana 272–73
Cicero 35–37, 45, 118, 174–75n15
De Oratore
I.xxiv.158 234n77
II.xxvii.314 230n64
On Invention 35n165
I.7 3n12
I.9 36n166
I.15 96n81, 115n53
I.20 65n129
I.31 96n87, 116n56
I.32-33 37n170
I.98 98n91
II.116 100n98
II.50.148-53 177n14
II.50.151 181n30
II.142 101n99, 128n87, 260n89
Orator
xiv.46 1n1
xv.50 97n90
xxix.101 273n23
Topics 177
The Speeches 36n169
Dissoi Logoi 3, 16
Hermogenes of Tarsus
On Invention 9n37, 35, 36n167, 37, 38n179, 145n54
Progymnasmata 142, 178n16

Greek, Roman and Patristic Literature (cont.)
Homer
Iliad 41n1, 141n42,
Justinian's Digest 177n13, 181n28, 181n29, 182n34
Menander of Laodicea, Rhetor 258
Lex Aquilia 178
Libanius
Declamations 56n78, 137n28, 153–54
Letters 7, 266n4
Progymnasmata 9n37, 135n25, 141–42, 167n154, 178n16
Philostratus 4–5
Plato
Cratylus 25n125, 29n138
Gorgias 24, 25n121, 33n156, 220n19, 262–63
Laws 220, 262
Phaedo 25n123
Phaedrus 24, 25n120, 25n122, 37n175
Protagoras 137n27
Republic 25n123, 41n1
Sophist 33n154
Symposium 68, 137n27
Theaetetus 25n125
Timeaus 31
Polybius
Histories 257
Quintilian 8n37, 113
Institutes of Oratory 35n65
3.8.9 54n67
4.1.1-3 54n65
4.1.14 65n130
4.2.5 65n128
4.3.9-12 72n155
4.5.9-12 37n171
4.5.22 46n25
5.10.86-88 177n14
5.10.88 197n86
5.12.14 230n64
6.2.8-17 70n146
6.3 115n54
8.4.9-11 177n14
9.2.22 117n59
10.1.22-3 233n75
11.3.92 46n23
11.3.158 46n23
12.2.25 1n1
12.5.25 233n75
Lesser Declamations 150n82, 153–54
Major Declamations 150
Minor Declamations 1n1, 150, 167n152, 169n157,
Seneca, Marcus Annaeus
Declamations 4n17, 150–151, 154n94, 155–56, 166–67, 216n1
Synesius, On Dreams 152
Tacitus, Dialogue on Oratory 152
Theon, Aelius 17, 78n2, 143, 178, 214

Index of Names and Subjects

Abaye, 70n147, 119n63
as court advocate, 228–29
on libations, 165–66, 168n155, 168–69, 172
Rava and, 70n147, 168–69
Abraham
as defense lawyer, 243–44, 248, 250–54, 256, 263n94
test of faith for, 237n12, 242, 279n46
Absurd hypotheticals, 159–61
Adar, readings in Second, 122–24
Adversarial courts, *See* Lawyers and legal system
Afrahat, 109
Afrem, 109
Agamemnon, 141
Agon, 18, 106–8, 129–30, 251, 267
Akiva, R., 87–88, 91–92, 94n79, 97, 100, 199, 203, 212, 277. *See also* Hermeneutics
Alexander, Elizabeth Shanks, 158, 170–71
Alexander the Great, 9
Alexandria, 132, 176n10
Ammonius, 274
Anaskeue, 141
Anderson, Graham, 4
Angels, 63, 66, 242–43, 245–47, 250, 254–55, 263. *See also* Gabriel; Heavenly court advocates
Anton of Tigrit, 112
Aphthonius, 9n37, 132, 135–36, 143
Apollo, 141
Aristides, Aelius, 59, 150
Aristotle, ix, 1–3, 9n37, 33, 35–37, 41, 53–54, 96, 98–99, 176–77, 179n22, 196n82, 197, 235n81, 246n29, 266, 282–83
on enthymeme, 196n82
on reason, 282–83
on rhetoric and persuasion, 33, 52n61
topoi by, 176–77, 179n22
on types of speech, 3, 36n169, 37, 96
Arnoff, Stephen Hazan, 18, 50n45, 51n50, 134n18
Arrangement and reasoning of rhetoric, 9n37, 10n41, 35–39, 44–46, 53, 61, 65, 67, 74, 95–105, 108n14, 112–18, 122–31, 193, 265–66
Ashi, Rav, 165–66, 168
Auerbach, Erich, 273–75
Augustine, 40, 272–73, 275n32, 276
Aurelius, Marcus, 59
Avery-Peck, Alan, 17
Avimai, 170, 172
Avtalion, 184, 190, 192, 193n68, 194

Ba'ya, 145, 163
Balai, 113, 130
Becker, Adam, 109n18, 110–11
Beit Midrash, 79
Berkowitz, Beth, 22n114, 74n162, 76–77, 223n30, 238n92
Berytus, 7
Betera, elders of, 175–76, 184, 190, 193–96
Beth Hillel, 80n12, 89–90n67, 103n104, 143–44, 145n53
Beth Shammai, 13n60, 80n12, 89–90n67, 103n104, 143–44, 145n53, 185n43
Biaion, 145n54
Binyan av, 175–76, 180–81
Black, Clifton, 37–38, 46n26, 53n64, 269n11
Blum, Jost, 113
Boethusians, 200
Böhlig, Alexander, 113
Bokser, Barukh, 68, 71n151, 248n39

Boyarin, Daniel, 41n2, 51n50, 137n27, 149, 235n83, 235n84, 264n2, 280n49, 281n51, 281n53
  on influence of Hellenism, 20n100, 26n128, 109, 110n21, 149
  on Logos *vs.* Torah, 28n135, 29n137, 30n140, 249
  on satire in Bavli, 18
  on Second Sophistic, 283
Brodsky, David, 17–18, 134, 136–37, 139n33, 141, 171, 214–15

Cabezón, José Ignacio, 111–12
Caesarea, 6, 60, 270, 272
Calendrical system, 184n40
Callicles, 262–63
Canpanton, Rabbi Yiṣḥak, 235
Capital legal cases, *See* Lawyers and legal system
Children, rights and obligations of, 114–21, 142, 155–57, 227, 251n51
Choricius of Gaza, 6, 81–82, 150, 154–55
Chreia, 16, 132–34, 143, 183–84
Christianity, 51n51, 60n100, 73n157, 111–12, 261n90, 264–65
  history of rise of, 21, 202n100
  summary of classical rhetoric and, 2, 4, 13–14, 18n93, 20, 23, 38, 40, 43, 60, 106, 109–10, 130, 268–77
Chryses, 141–42, 145
Church fathers, 23, 40, 265, 269, 274–76
Cicero
  on gestures, 45
  on lowly style, 273
  length of orations by, 118
  on rhetorical reasoning, 1, 100–1, 128n87, 234, 260
  on rhetorical arrangement, 35–37, 96, 116
  topoi by, 177, 181n30, 197, 207
Clepsydra, 250–51
Cognitio extraordinaria, 221–22, 228n56
Cohen, Boaz, 16, 41n2, 178n15, 229n58, 234n78
Cohen, Norman, 52n57, 56–57
Cohen, Shaye, 82n35, 85n44, 109
Coloures, 150, 156, 167
Controversiae. *See also* Declamations; Progymnasmata
  on adultery, 152–54
  definition of, 130–32, 150
  as hypotheticals, 150–62
  on murder, 154–55
  on obligation to parents, 155–57
  paradoxes, 157–58
  on rape, 151, 155
  ta shema and, 163–70
Courts. *See* Lawyers and legal system
Cronus, 262, 263n93
Ctesiphon, 109–10
Cynics, 16, 133–34

Dabar, 28–29. *See also* Dibbur
Daniel, 179n19, 218, 224, 243, 259
Daube, David, 16, 40, 134, 176, 178–80, 182, 187, 201n96, 201n99, 209n130
David (biblical), 1, 44–45, 61–67, 155n100, 242n9, 258
Dayo, 204
Dead Sea Scrolls, *See* Qumranites
Demosthenes, 37–38
Derasha. *See* Sermon
Dibbur, 250. *See also* Dabar
Dikastai, 219
Dio Chrysostom, 54, 83n36
Dissoi Logoi, 3, 16
Dolgopolski, Sergey, 26n128, 34, 197n83
Dworkin, Ronald, 103n105, 217n6

Eilberg-Schwartz, Howard, 31n147, 206, 284n63
Eleazar ben Azariah, R., 47, 114, 119
Eliezer, R., 15n72, 42, 75n168, 86–87, 157, 178, 203, 207n125
Elihu, 243
Elman, Yaakov, x, 8n33, 107, 208n126
Enthymeme, 17n82, 98–99, 196n82
Epstein, Avraham, 59–60
Ethos, 70

Fathers, obligations of, 114–21, 154–57
Faur, José, 17n84, 26n128, 27–28, 30n140, 31–32, 79n8, 185n45, 205n114, 284n63
Felix (procurator), 258n80, 270
Filicide, 154
Fischel, Henry, 11n42, 16, 19n95, 21n110, 31n145, 82n36, 133–34, 158n109, 176n10, 185n44
Fonrobert, Charlotte Elisheva, 8n33, 109
Furstenberg, Yair, 18, 72n155, 258n79

Gabriel, 245n23, 255. *See also* Angels
Gadamer, Hans-George, 28, 104n105
Gafni, Isaiah, 111
Gamaliel of Yavneh, Rabban, 16, 75n168
  on Passover, 69–70, 72–73
  on nonconformity, 84–105
  response to heretic by, 127n82, 200
Gamaliel V, Rabban, 7
Gaza, 6–7, 9n39, 79, 274
Gezerah shava, 22n113, 134, 178–79, 190–92, 194–96, 207–13. *See also* Hermeneutics
Gradus, 229
Graetz, Heinrich, 186–87
Greek language, 10–16, 21, 43, 48n41, 60, 74, 225n43, 269
Gregory of Nazianzus, 272
Gregory Thaumaturgus, 272
Guttmann, Alexander, 183n37, 187n53, 187n55, 189, 195n76
Gymnasmata, 132

Habakkuk, 257
Ḥaifa, 170, 172
Ha-katuv, 210–11
Halbertal, Moshe, 93n76, 103–4n105
Halivni, David Weiss, 8n33, 8n35, 83n38, 84n41, 119n66, 124, 125n77, 127n81, 166n151, 187n53, 195
Hallel, 69–70, 73
Ḥameṣ, 161–62
Ha-Nagid, Samuel, 206
Handelman, Susan, 24n118, 26, 28n135, 30n140, 31–32, 197n84, 206, 275–76
Hasmoneans, 12–13, 184n40
Havdalah, 143n49, 144
Hayes, Christine, x, 27n129, 202n103, 236n86, 278n41, 284–85
Heavenly court advocates, 240–63. *See also* Ḥoni the Circle-drawer, Lawyers and legal system; Paracletes; Satan
  in Bible and Second Temple literature, 242–47
  Plato's heavenly court, 262–63
  in rabbinic literature, 247–62
Heidegger, Martin, 103n105
Heinemann, Isaak, 29
Heinemann, Joseph, 39n181, 49n43, 49n45, 52n54, 53n61, 55, 58n85, 58n86, 59n91, 60n104, 61n105, 115n54, 118n62, 258n79
Hellenism. *See also* Boyarin, Daniel; Greek language; Lieberman, Saul; Rabbinic rhetoric; *specific rhetors*
  Qumran and, 285
  Sasanians and, 108–14
  summary of rabbinic interaction with, 9–35, 16n75, 33–35, 264–65
Heqesh, 178n15, 184n41, 191
Hermeneutics, 174–215. *See also* Gezerah shava; Hillel the Elder; Lawyers and legal system; Midah/midot; Qal va-ḥomer;
  as anti-sectarian polemics, 183–90
  as rhetorical topoi, 22, 29, 32, 83n36, 99, 101, 103n105, 132, 134, 174–82
  skepticism of, 190–96
  summary of, 175–76, 212–15
Hermogenes of Tarsus, 17, 84–105, 142, 178n16, 179n20
  On Invention, 9n37, 35, 36n167, 37, 38n179, 145n54
Herr, Moshe David, 75
Hidary, Richard, 17n82, 30n140, 32n153, 66n134, 66n135, 80n12, 80n14, 84n43, 87n52, 90n67, 90n68, 91n69, 92n71, 95n80, 103n103, 105n109, 107n8, 114n50, 122n71, 124n75, 128n86, 149n79, 163n141, 185n43, 186n50, 190n62, 190n63, 194n74, 202n101, 215n155, 233n72, 278n41, 279n44, 284n63, 286n70
Hillel the Elder, 133, 175–76, 179–80, 181n32, 183–96, 203, 207, 210n133, 211, 213. *See also* Beth Hillel; Hermeneutics
Ḥisda, Rav, 119n63, 120
Homer, 41n1, 141–42, 274
Ḥoni the Circle-drawer, 247, 256–57
Hypotheticals, 150–62. *See also* Controversiae

Inquisitorial courts, *See* Lawyers and legal system
Isaac, 62, 242, 255
Ishmael, R., 129n90, 137–38, 176n7, 178, 205n115, 209–14. *See also* Hermeneutics
Isocrates, 54, 78, 133n12, 197n86, 205n116
Issar, 197

Jacob, 255
Jacob of Sarug, 113

Jacobs, Louis, 145n55, 160n123, 163, 180n26, 196–97n83
Jaffee, Martin, 17, 49n45, 82n32, 82n35, 134
Jesus
  Handelman on, 276
  rhetoric and, 269–70
  as paraclete, 247
  sermons about, 44–45
  sermons by, 44
Job, 218, 242–43, 263n94
Josephus, 9–10, 13

Kallah, 80
Karet, 125, 199
Kataskeue, 36n167, 141
Kategor, 135, 240, 248, 250
Kefar Ṭabi, 88, 91
Kennedy, George, 3n9, 4n16, 5n19, 6n22, 7n27, 7n31, 9n37, 9n39, 10n41, 35n165, 36n167, 37n173, 37n174, 38n179, 41n3, 46n26, 54n66, 56n76, 56n78, 59n94, 79n11, 82n31, 131n4, 132n8, 132n9, 133n12, 135n22, 135n25, 136n26, 141n41, 142n45, 143n47, 143n48, 145n54, 268, 269n8, 269n11, 269n13, 272n15, 272n16, 272n18
Kensky, Meira, 240n4, 250–51, 262n92
Ketubah, 114, 119, 226–27
Kitos War, 11, 13n60
Kraemer, David, 17n82, 281n53, 282–83
Kutscher, Yechezkel, 225–26

Language, conception of, 24–32
Lawyers and legal system, 216–39. *See also* Heavenly court advocates; Hermeneutics; Kategor; Paraclete; Sanegor
  adversarial and inquisitorial courts, 217–24, 228n56, 229–34, 237–39, 241–42, 251, 261–62, 268
  capital cases, 128, 138, 198, 230–33, 235–36, 238–39
  Greek court system, 219–20, 251, 262–63
  monetary cases, 138, 147, 230–32, 236, 238n93, 239
  patroni, 221n21
  rabbinic court system, 222–39
  Roman court system, 221–22, 226n47, 229, 234, 238, 241, 250–51, 256–58, 260–61, 263
  summary of rhetoric in, 3, 216–17, 238–39
Legis actio, 221
Libanius
  controversiae and, 150, 152–53, 155
  on filicide case, 154
  on Homer, 141–42
  influence of, 7, 9n37, 132, 266
  progymnasmata and, 137n28, 178n16
  prooemia by, 56
Lieberman, Saul, 6n25, 10n42, 13n60, 14n67, 50n45, 88n60, 119n66, 155n101, 166n150, 194n75, 207n125
  on influence of Hellenism, 15–16, 18, 19n95, 32, 40, 42n8, 43, 134, 176, 178–80, 275
  on rabbinic courts, 222n28, 229n58, 233–34, 250n50, 260
Lives of the Sophists (Philostratus), 4–5
Log/lugim, 164–65
Logographoi, 219, 221, 251n51
Logos, 28–29, 33, 70, 246–50, 254n60, 263
Lorberbaum, Yair, 244
Lucian, 52–53, 150, 240n4
Lydda, 80, 88, 91, 155

Mandel, Paul, 48n41, 50n46, 51n51, 54n68, 202n102, 230n64, 232–33, 236n87, 257n77
Mark, 269
Mastema, 242
Matriarchs, 263
Maybaum, Siegmund, 49n45, 55
McVey, Kathleen, 106n1, 113
Meḥoza, 110
Meir, R., 18, 47, 87–88, 90–91, 92n72, 93n76, 94, 97, 100, 114–17, 120–21, 280–83
Meturgeman, 80–81
Midah/midot, 175n3, 176n7, 205, 211. *See also* Hermeneutics
Midat hadin, 254
Midrash Aggadah, 39, 41, 48–49, 52–53, 57, 61n104, 83n37. *See also* Proem; Yelamdenu
Midrash Halakhah, 39, 134, 137, 139
Miṣvah, 114–17, 119–21
Monetary legal cases, *See* Lawyers and legal system
Mordechai, 14
Morris, Nathan, 131n1, 171
Moses, 31, 45, 50–51, 53n63, 62, 66, 202n104, 204, 242–44, 255, 257–61, 263n94, 277, 279, 282

Mousourakis, George, 221n22, 222
Muffs, Yochanan, 243–45
Mufneh, 209–10, 212
Multivocality, 28, 215, 277–78, 279n46, 286n72
Murder controversiae, 154–55
Musaf, 47, 97n90

Naeh, Shlomo, 17
Naḥman, R., 146–48
Narsai, 106n1, 107, 110, 113, 130
Neharde`a, 147
Nesi'ah, Rabbi Yehudah, 75
Neusner, Jacob, 16, 85n47, 185n44, 214
Nietzsche, Friedrich, 26n127
Nisibis, 110
Noah, 242
Novick, Tzvi, 18, 56n80, 223n29

Olympicus (Dio Chrysostom), 54
Ong, Walter, 106–7, 108n13, 130n93
Origen, 272
Oshaia, R., 107

Paideia, 22, 170–73
Pantomime, 14–15, 74, 76
Paraclete, 240, 241n6, 243n16, 246–48. *See also* Heavenly court advocates; Lawyers and legal system
Paradoxes, 24, 133, 150, 152–54, 157–58
Parmenides, 25
Passover
  leaven and, 69, 73, 124–27, 161, 188–89. *See also* Sabbath, Passover rituals on
Passover Haggadah, 67–73
Pathos, 70, 256
Patriarch (under Romans), 7, 9n37, 13–15, 75–76, 80, 84–85, 104, 109, 184, 192–93, 266
Patriarchs (biblical), 46, 245, 256, 261, 263
Patroni, 221n21
Paul
  on laws, 275–76, 284
  rhetorical evidence by, 10n41, 18, 270–72
  sermon at Antioch by, 39, 44–48, 269
Pe'ah, 147n76, 147–48
Penella, Robert, x, 79n11, 81–82, 150n81, 151n86, 152n91, 154n99, 167n152
Perelman, Chaim, 99–100, 283n60, 286n71
Persian Empire. *See* Sasanians
Pharisees, 31, 46, 80n12, 82n36, 185–89, 200–2, 270–71, 275
Phenix, Robert, 113
Philo, 9–10, 31n145, 43, 58n88, 69n145, 242, 245–49, 284. *See also* Logos
Pineḥas, R., 198
Pirqa, 47, 80–81, 111
Plato
  and rabbis, 18, 35, 268
  heavenly court of, 220, 262–63
  on language, 29
  on law, 230
  on truth and rhetoric, 24–26, 33, 37, 41n1, 202, 217, 221n20, 238, 270, 274–75, 283–84, 286
  Protagoras, 137n27
  Symposium, 68, 137n27
  Timeaus, 31
Procopius, 6, 81–82
Proem, 39, 46n26, 48–58, 73, 118n62, 287. *See also* Midrash Aggadah; Sermon
Progymnasmata, 9n37, 17–18, 39, 131–50, 152, 163, 167n154, 168–69, 171, 177, 178n16, 214, 265–66. *See also* Chreia; Controversiae
  introduction of a law, 132, 135, 143, 167n154
  refutation and confirmation, 141–43, 150
Protagoras, 25, 260
Purity, 18, 88n60, 91, 160, 188, 191, 198, 213, 231, 233, 267, 277–81

Qal va-ḥomer, 22n113, 134, 175, 178, 183, 184n41, 190–206, 207n125, 213, 273, 286n70. *See also* Hermeneutics
Qiddush, 143–44
Quine, W. V. O., 103n105
Quintilian, 2, 9n27, 37, 45, 46n25, 54, 65, 117, 150, 153–54, 166, 168–69, 197, 233, 266
Qumranites, 186, 202, 215, 245, 285–86

Rachel, 255–56, 261
Rape controversiae, 151, 155
Rappel, Dov, 14
Rashi, 13–14n66, 107n5, 160n114, 204–5

Rava, 148
  Abaye and, 70n147, 168–69
  on ḥameṣ, 126, 127n80, 161, 164
  judgement by, 121
  on libations, 165–66, 168–69, 172
  rhetorical techniques of, 115n54
Reggio, Rabbi Isaac Samuel, 178
Reptile purity argument, 1, 40, 171, 191, 198, 213, 230n64, 233, 236–37, 278–79, 281
Resh Galuta, 111
Rhetorical handbooks, 8n37, 19, 35, 39, 41, 53n61, 73–74, 112–13, 118, 131, 136n26, 234n78, 266–67. *See also* Progymnasmata; *specific titles*
Rhetorical schools, 2, 6–10, 14, 24, 33, 35, 39, 43, 60, 74, 78–79, 82, 110, 131–32, 152, 171–72, 213, 233, 266, 274
Riad, Eva, 109–10, 112
Roman court system, *See* Lawyers and legal system
Rosental, David, 60n104, 194
Rosental, Eliezer Shimshon, 16, 25n125
Rubenstein, Jeffrey, 78n3, 79n4, 79n6, 79n10, 80n13, 92n74, 97n89, 102n102, 106n2, 107–8, 111n27, 111n28, 111n33, 163n141, 184n40, 192n65, 194, 197n87, 285n69
Russel, Donald, 41n5, 47n29, 56n77, 59n95, 81n25, 150n81, 151, 152n90, 153n93, 154n97

Sabbath, 123n73, 201, 231–32
  blessings of, 143
  death and sickness on, 61–67, 87–88, 90
  Passover rituals on, 183–85, 187, 189–95, 207, 209–10
  sermon of, 43–48, 59n92
Sabbatical, 92, 207–9
Sadducees, 186–87, 189, 196, 200–2, 206, 286n70
Sanegor, 219, 223–24, 241, 248, 250–51, 258
Sasanians, 108–14. *See also* Syriac culture and language
Satan, 218, 241–43. *See also* Heavenly court advocates
Satlow, Michael, 17n82, 20n100, 21, 22n114
Sausauria, 132–33
Schwartz, Daniel, 200–1, 202n104, 285, 286n70
Schwartz, Seth, 42, 48n39, 85n44
Schwarz, Adolf, 196
Second Sophistic, 2–6, 9n37, 22, 74, 77, 265, 283
Segal, Eliezer, 229
Self-help, 140, 147n67, 152–54
Seneca, Lucius Annaeus, 185
Seneca, Marcus Annaeus, 150–51, 155–56, 166–69
Sententiae, 167
Sermo humilis, 273
Sermon, 4, 10, 35, 38–39, 41–67, 73–83, 104, 113, 130, 267, 269, 274, 287. *See also* Proem
Shalom, Abraham, 235
Shaṭaḥ, Shimon ben, 225, 257n75
Shemaya, 184, 190, 192, 193n68, 194
Sherira Gaon, 128
Sheva ben Bikhri, 155
Shimon bar Yoḥai, R.
  in defense of Israel, 249, 260
  on hermeneutics, 203
  on leaven, 125–26
  on nonconformity, 87–89, 91–94, 97–98, 100
  on Sabbath laws, 64n125
Shimon ben Gamaliel, Rabban, 12–13, 122–24, 226–27
Shimon ben Laqish, R., 75, 120, 188
Sinai, 22, 51, 77, 172, 248–49, 257, 260, 277–80, 282, 286–87
Sinai, Yuval, 223n33, 224n34, 225–26, 228n54, 239n95
Sloane, Thomas, 99
Socrates, 24–25, 68, 219, 262
Sodom, 244, 251–53
Solomon, 61–67, 258
Sopatros, 56
Sophists, 3–6, 9n39, 10, 18, 24, 26, 29, 34–35, 40, 42–43, 52, 54, 59–60, 77, 81, 109, 149, 213, 215, 217, 219–20, 233, 239, 254, 262, 267, 270, 274, 276–77, 283–84. *See also* *specific persons*
Stam/Stammaim, 14n66, 83–84, 102n102, 107–8, 110, 112, 119n63, 124n75, 127n81, 128, 130, 137n27, 148–49, 165–69, 172
Stein, Siegfried, 68, 70n145, 71–72
Stern, David, 30n140-1, 31–32, 75n168, 85n48, 249n44, 251n52, 254n60, 256n68, 273n25
Stone, Suzanne Last, 244, 247n37, 257, 258n79
Susanna, 218, 224

Swartz, Michael, 111–12
Syllogism, 17n82, 27, 33, 95, 98–99, 196–97, 206, 213. *See also* Hermeneutics
Symposium, 68–70, 73. *See also* Passover Haggadah
Synagogue, 41–42, 44, 47–49, 75–76, 78–79, 81, 88, 91, 269, 271. *See also* Sermon
Synegoros. *See* Sanegor
Synkrisis, 134, 178–79
Syriac culture and language, 12–14, 106, 109–14, 130, 132. *See also* Sasanians

Ta shema, 137n27, 145, 148–49, 163–69, 172
Ṭabai, Yehudah ben, 225–26
Tacitus, 152
Tadai, R. Yose ben, 200, 202
Tanḥum, R., 50, 61, 64–65, 67, 258, 270
Teacher of Righteousness, 215, 285
Tequ, 145, 162–63, 165
Tertullian, 272
Theodor, Judah, 49n44-45, 52n56, 55
Theon, Aelius, 17, 143, 178, 214
Tisias, 37
Topos/topoi, 174–215. *See also* Hermeneutics; Progymnasmata
Tropper, Amram, 5, 42–43, 134n15, 134n18
Truth (אלטיכסייה, ἀλήθεια), 2, 22, 24–29, 33–35, 40, 99, 149–50, 172–73, 214–18, 220, 221n20, 229, 232–36, 238–39, 242, 251, 253–55, 262–65, 268–70, 272–77, 280, 282–87

Ulmer, Rivka, 16, 134
Usha, 120–21

Vico, Giambattista, 28
Vidas, Moulie, 11n48, 12n54, 13–14, 169n158
Visotzky, Burton, 7n32, 48n41, 49n42, 49n45, 52–53, 55n70, 56n79, 132n6, 133n13, 179n23

Walker, Joel T., 108–9
Watt, John W., 112
Whitmarsh, Timothy, 4–5, 20n103, 59n94, 151n86
Wilkins, John, 215

Yadin, Azzan, 30n140, 85n47, 175n3, 186n52, 194n73, 199n92, 200n95, 204–5, 210–11, 213–14, 249n46
Yannai, R., 42n8, 198, 213, 277–79
Yassif, Eli, 16
Yavneh, 47, 80, 114, 279, 281. *See also* Gamaliel of Yavneh, Rabban
Yehoshua, R., 11, 203
Yehoshua ben Levi, R., 47, 227, 228n56, 260
Yelamdenu, 46n26, 57–67, 70, 73, 80. *See also* Midrash Aggadah
Yeshiva, 80
Yoḥanan, R., 1, 27n129, 42, 62, 106–7, 119n63, 121, 198, 226–28, 233, 235–36, 249, 280
Yoḥanan ben Beroqa, R., 114–21, 119n66
Yose of Ma`on, 75
Yoshiko Reed, Annette, 20

Zacharias Scholasticus, 7n27, 274
Zeno (Emperor), 110, 113
Zeus, 142, 262

Lightning Source UK Ltd.
Milton Keynes UK
UKHW020420070422
401212UK00018B/421

9 781316 628355